GERMANS ON THE KENYAN

GERMANS ON THE KENYAN COAST

Land, Charity, and Romance

Nina Berman

Indiana University Press

Bloomington and Indianapolis

This book is a publication of

Indiana University Press
Office of Scholarly Publishing
Herman B Wells Library 350
1320 East 10th Street
Bloomington, Indiana 47405 USA

iupress.indiana.edu

The paper used in this publication meets the minimum
requirements of the American National Standard for Information
Sciences—Permanence of Paper for Printed Library Materials,
ANSI Z39.48-1992.

Manufactured in the United States of America

Library of Congress Cataloging-in-Publication Data

Names: Berman, Nina (Nina Auguste), author.
Title: Germans on the Kenyan coast : land, charity, and romance /
   Nina Berman.
Description: Bloomington : Indiana University Press, 2017. | Includes
   bibliographical references and index.
Identifiers: LCCN 2016039210 (print) | LCCN 2016039935 (ebook) |
   ISBN 9780253024244 (cloth : alk. paper) | ISBN 9780253024305
   (pbk. : alk. paper) | ISBN 9780253024374 (e-book)
Subjects: LCSH: Germans—Kenya—Diani. | Diani (Kenya)—Ethnic
   relations. | Diani (Kenya)—Social conditions. | Real property—
   Kenya—Foreign ownership.
Classification: LCC DT433.545.G47 B47 2017 (print) | LCC DT433.545.
   G47 (ebook) | DDC 967.6200431—dc23
LC record available at https://lccn.loc.gov/2016039210

1 2 3 4 5   22 21 20 19 18 17

To the Digo of Diani

Contents

Acknowledgments

Every book is the result of inspirations, coincidences, and collaborations across time and space. My engagement with Kenya began in January 1980 when, right after I completed my public school education, I traveled to Mombasa with the late Dr. John Davira Thomas. John was from the island of Dominica in the Caribbean, and after an odyssey that included several years in the United States, service in the Korean War, and a period in Britain, had received his medical training in Germany. His plan had been to open a clinic in Mombasa, but as a black non-Kenyan, he found it difficult to find his feet in that country. It was when he relocated his clinic from Mombasa to Diani that I was first introduced to the setting and matters that are at the center of this study: tourism, humanitarianism, and romantic relations. Much of what I write about in this book is based on experiences that John made possible for me; he was a most generous person, and this book would not exist without him.

I am also grateful to Eileen Willson who, in the summer of 2005, gave me an opportunity to conduct research on efforts under way then to coordinate the myriad of health initiatives that were operating in Kwale County. The networking organization she had devised, the Kwale Health Forum, no longer exists but remains a visionary model for health service coordination and resource sharing. Her husband, James Willson, a historian in his own right, has been an important interlocutor since 1998. Both Eileen and John taught me much about Diani and provided crucial impetus for me to conduct the research for this study.

My research assistants Peter Uria Gitau, Omari Ali Gaito, and Mohamed Ali Hamadi enabled me to dig deeper into the social fabric of Diani; I am deeply indebted to them. Ingeborg Langefeld, Denis Moser, Raymond Matiba, Mr. Harald Kampa, Mrs. Matthiessen-Kampa, Luciana Parazzi, and many others from the Diani community sat down with me for interviews and helped me find my way around; I greatly appreciate their insights and time.

Katey Borland, Leo Coleman, Kendra McSweeney, May Mergenthaler, RaShelle Peck, Peter Redfield, Dan Reff, Patricia Sieber, Jennifer Suchland, Deanne van Tol, Sarah Willen, and Andrew Zimmerman provided much valued feedback on drafts of this book. I am grateful to Patrick O. Abungu, Frederick Aldama, Sai Bhatawadekar, Jacob Bogart, Natalie Eppelsheimer, Dirk Goettsche, David Gramling, Joshua Grace, Kordula Gruhn, Laura Joseph, Tony Kaes, Susanne Kaul, David Kim, Kwaku Korang, Barbara Kosta, Kennedy Mkutu, Klaus Mühlhahn, Perry Myers, Alain Patrice Nganang, Kimani Njogu, Dorry Noyes,

Thomas Lekan, Kris Manjapra, Glenn Penny, Brett Shadle, Ali Skandar, Kennedy Walibora Waliaula, Ali Wasi, Greg Witkowski, and Barbara Wolbert for sharing ideas and insights relevant to this work. Alamin Mazrui, in particular, was a consistent supporter and friend during the writing process.

Versions of the research presented in this book were communicated at meetings of the German Studies Association, the African Studies Association, and other conferences, symposia, and speaking engagements over the years; I am thankful to organizers, co-panelists, and audiences for their interest in my research and for the feedback I received.

Kenyatta University was the official host during my research stays in Kenya. Professor (and longtime friend) Mbugua wa-Mungai, then Chair of the Department of Literature at KU, arranged several opportunities that allowed me to present my research and to learn much from my Kenyan colleagues. In 2013, an event arranged through Professor Catherine Ndungo of the Institute of African Studies provided another chance for me to benefit from the insights of KU colleagues. Mr. Ogweno, Registrar of Marriages in Mombasa, and employees at the Registrar of Marriages in Mombasa and at statistical services in Germany, Switzerland, and Austria kindly and efficiently provided me with access to data that are central to this study.

The Office of International Affairs, the Division of Arts and Humanities, and the College of Arts and Sciences at The Ohio State University supported this project through several travel grants, a research grant, and two research leaves of absence that allowed me to pursue my work in Kenya. The final preparation of the manuscript was aided by a grant from the College of Arts and Sciences at Ohio State and research funds from the Division of Humanities at Arizona State University. I am also deeply grateful to Barry Shank, Chair of the Department of Comparative Studies at Ohio State; his predecessor Gene Holland; and my colleagues in the department for the support and inspiration they have given me over the years.

Detailed comments provided by thoughtful critical readers enabled me to improve the manuscript in substantial ways. I am greatly indebted to Ann Biersteker and an anonymous reader for taking the time to deeply engage with my scholarship.

I was fortunate to benefit from competent and inspired editors and experts: Kendra Hovey and Ruthmarie Mitsch much improved the coherence and flow of my prose at various stages of the writing process; Nora Sylvander and Vicente Nogueira volunteered their skilled knowledge to help me with tables; Shaun Fontanella created original maps based on handwritten notes; Linnea Lowe proved to be a tremendous help in formatting the bibliography; Jessie Dolch was a thoughtful, meticulous, and congenial copy editor (I am especially grateful to her!); and Charlie Clark competently oversaw the copyediting, typesetting, and composition process. My deepest thanks go to Dee Mortensen, the editorial director at Indiana University Press, who saw merit in my project when I first presented it to her and provided crucial guidance and feedback throughout.

And finally, with great affection, I acknowledge friends and family members who are my core support team and a source of comfort and pleasure: Gifty Ako-Adounvo, Zaki Al Maboren, Julian Anderson, Milena Berman, Sara Berman, Hank Berman, Marlies Brunner, Gabi Cloos, Rhonda Crockett, Fred Dott, Erika Ebert, Salome Fouts, Bernhard Goldmann, Curtis Goldstein, Aki Goldstein Mergenthaler, Kordula Gruhn, Barbara Haeger, Susanne Hafner, Eckehard Hartmann, Elfriede Heise, Lilith Heise, Marlon Heise, Tilman Heise, Amy Horowitz, Hillary Hutchinson, Gregory Jusdanis, Deborah Kapchan, Kwaku Korang, Linnea Lowe, Eberhard Maul, May Mergenthaler, Christoph Müller, Iris Müller, Max Müller, Michael Murphy, Kamel Nikazm, the Sameja family, Michael Schultheiß, Amy Shuman, Patricia Sieber, Sari Silwani, Guni Sommer, Carmen Taleghani-Nikazm, Luca Teixeira Nogueira, Hilde Treibenreif, Daniela Urbassek, Iris Urbassek, Ute Wesemann, and Etsuyo Yuasa.

Parts of chapter 1 originally appeared as "From Colonial to Neoliberal Times: German Agents of Tourism Development and Business in Diani, Kenya," special topic, "The Future of the Past," edited by Susanne Baackmann and Nancy P. Nenno, *Transit: A Journal of Travel, Migration, and Multiculturalism in the German-Speaking World*, 10, no. 2 (2016), http://transit.berkeley.edu/2016/berman/.

Parts of chapter 3 originally appeared as "Contemporary German MONGOs in Diani, Kenya: Two Approaches to Humanitarian Aid," in *German Philanthropy in Transatlantic Perspective: Perceptions, Exchanges and Transfers since the Early Twentieth Century*, edited by Gregory R. Witkowski and Arnd Bauerkämper (Berlin: Springer, 2016), 227–243; "Neoliberal Charity: German Contraband Humanitarians in Kenya," in *Imagining Human Rights*, edited by David Kim and Susanne Kaul (Berlin: de Gruyter, 2015), 119–136; and as "Contraband Charity: German Humanitarianism in Contemporary Kenya," in *The History and Practice of Humanitarian Intervention and Aid in Africa*, edited by Bronwen Everill and Josiah Kaplan (Houndmills: Palgrave Macmillan, 2013), 67–92.

All translations, unless otherwise indicated, are mine.

GERMANS ON THE KENYAN COAST

1 Multitudinal Coastal Entanglements

Pwani si Kenya—Pwani ni Kenya—Pwani ni Ujerumani (na Italia na kadhalika)[1]

> mwenyi lake ana lake
> hataki la mwenzi wake,
> na ukimwendea pake
> wala hakupi shauri.
> *(This is a world of personal interest*
> *don't rely on your neighbor.*
> *And if you go to his place*
> *he won't give you any help.)*
>
> —Mwalimu Mbaraka bin Shomari (1860–1897), "Vita na Hassan bin Omari"

Aɴʏ ᴠɪsɪᴛᴏʀ ᴛᴏ ᴜᴋᴜɴᴅᴀ and the larger Diani area, which is located about thirty kilometers south of Mombasa, will notice the cosmopolitan makeup of its population and the transnational nature of its economic space. Diani is a microcosm of Kenya's ethnically and religiously diverse population: local Digo interact with individuals from Masai, Kamba, Luo, Kikuyo, Kisii, and other ethnic communities; Muslims, Hindu, and Christians live near to one another. Added to this multireligious and multicultural Kenyan population is another diverse group of residents: Germans, Italians, British, Swiss, Austrians, Dutch, Danish, Russians, and citizens of other (mostly European) countries. These Europeans are generally not tourists; tourists spend most of their vacation time at hotels and beaches or on organized tours. Rather, these Europeans live and often work in Diani. They own houses, stores, travel agencies, nightclubs, and restaurants; they manage hotels and diving businesses; and some have moved to Diani as retirees. German-language signs can be found in locations across Diani, and German bread and beer are available, as are pizza and gelato. The number of binational couples is eye-catching; as opposed to dominant practices in Europe and North America, mixing and mingling across boundaries of ethnicity, race, religion, and class is common in Diani. Evidence for these entanglements is also visible in the materiality of Diani's economic space: schools, water tanks, wells, and toilets are built and sponsored by (resident and nonresident) Europeans, and various educational and health-related institutions are run by Europeans or co-directed by Europeans and Kenyans.

For centuries the Kenyan, and the larger East African, coast has been an integral part of the Indian Ocean economy and culture, with particularly strong ties to the Persian Gulf and India.[2] International tourism, which was introduced on the Kenyan coast in the 1960s, marks not a break, but a notable shift in the outward orientation of the coast. Tourism brought a host of new actors to the Kenyan coast, many of them Europeans. Germans in particular, and to a lesser degree Swiss and Austrians, played a pivotal role in creating the coastal tourism infrastructure, and their activities have had far-reaching consequences for the local social, political, and economic environment. (For the sake of convenience and because of their significant cultural similarities, henceforth I refer to German-speaking Germans, Swiss, and Austrians collectively as "Germans.") European-driven tourism became a catalyst that led to an influx of settlers from various European countries and the emergence of an active real estate market; it has also generated diverse forms of connections between African Kenyans and (mostly) European tourists and expatriates. Together, these developments— building on processes that began during the colonial period and were continued after Kenyan independence was gained in 1963—caused shifts in landownership, social structures, and cultural and religious practices as well as, in part, an orientation of the area toward Europe. On a broader level, tourism—which in 2013 overall accounted for 10.6 percent of employment in Kenya—provided one vehicle for Kenya's integration into the global neoliberal economic order.[3] It created the infrastructure that made possible a wide range of consequential activities, including humanitarian assistance and retirement migration, which have had a tremendous effect on the area. But the expansion of the tourism industry also led to substantial changes with regard to internal social, economic, and political Kenyan dynamics. Inland labor migration, for instance, caused a significant increase in the coastal population, and the influx of Kenyans from other parts of the country altered the religious and cultural makeup of the coast.

Germans on the Kenyan Coast offers a *longue durée* perspective on the present-day situation on the Kenyan coast by tying developments presently occurring under neoliberal capitalism to processes that began during, and even before, the period of the East Africa Protectorate (1895–1920) and then British colonial rule (1920–1963). The book argues that shifts in landownership since the colonial period have led to a relentless gentrification process that has dispossessed coastal African Kenyans of land they had previously owned or used. This long-term process of gentrification, in combination with the consequences of intra-Kenyan power struggles and the systemic dependence on the global economy, resulted in the pervasive precarity of the African Kenyan population. This precarity is currently addressed through humanitarian activities that are carried out by mostly expatriate humanitarians, in conspicuous ignorance of the complex reasons for the poverty and need they encounter, and that entangle African Kenyans and expatriates in multidimensional economic and social exchanges. Romantic relations between African Kenyans and Europeans have emerged as another social practice that is born of economic and emotional vulnerabilities that affect the involved individuals in distinct ways.

This book traces changes on the Kenyan coast as they have occurred over the past fifty years by focusing on the Diani area, one of the most prominent tourism resort areas of Kenya. The center of the area is densely populated and known as the town of Ukunda. The indigenous people of the area are Digo, one of the nine ethnic communities known as the Mijikenda.[4] Today the area includes Kenyans of various ethnicities who have migrated to Diani, drawn by the promise of a tourism-related economy. Since the 1960s, when inhabitants of the original villages of Diani numbered in the few thousands, the population has swelled to close to seventy-five thousand. Diani thus has become a contact zone between Kenya's various communities and also between Kenyans and a diverse group of expatriates, many of whom have settled in Diani permanently or semipermanently.

When tourism began to develop in earnest during the 1960s, German entrepreneurs, among others, played a crucial role in pioneering the kinds of enterprises—upscale hotels, restaurants, bars, discotheques, safari businesses, and diving schools—that became the hallmark of coastal tourism. Why this German fascination with Kenya? Ever since the initial interest during the colonial period, East Africa has occupied a special place in the German imagination.[5] In the postindependence era, the films, writings, and activities of Bernhard Grzimek (1909–1987) may be credited with having initiated a second phase of German fascination with the region. His 1959 book and film *Serengeti darf nicht sterben: 367,000 Tiere suchen einen Staat* (Serengeti Shall Not Die: 367,000 Animals Are Looking for a State) and his TV show *Ein Platz für Tiere* (A Place for Animals, with 175 episodes between 1956 and 1987) shaped the German image of East Africa in substantial ways and provided an impetus for what quickly became a successful tourism industry.[6] The US show *Daktari*, which was first aired in Germany in 1969 and continues to be shown to this day, played a similar role.[7] Print media coverage in Germany was sparse, however; until the 1990s, editions of the most popular weeklies in Germany, *Der Spiegel* and *Stern*, rarely featured articles about Africa and less so Kenya. Coverage of Africa was largely restricted to the political situation in South Africa, famine in Ethiopia and surrounding areas, and then, increasingly, AIDS. The few articles on Kenya focused primarily on tourism and at times advertised specific resorts and trips.[8] More important, the experiences of the high number of tourists who have traveled to Kenya since the mid-1960s are reflected in a large corpus of autobiographical, biographical, and fictional texts and films that further stoke a fascination with the country.[9] Tourism was only part of Germany's material involvement with Kenya: West Germany was the first country to recognize independent Kenya, and investors and companies quickly established a host of economic collaborations with the newly formed nation.[10]

This involvement of German entrepreneurs in building Kenya's coastal tourism ensured that a significant portion of Kenya's tourists have come from German-speaking countries: by the mid-1990s, German-speaking tourists outnumbered British tourists and were the largest group of visitors, spending on average a longer period in Kenya than their British counterparts. In 1996, for example, tourists from Germany alone numbered 104,800 (18.9 percent of all tourists), while 97,600 (17.6 percent) tourists came from the United Kingdom.[11] In 2009, a total of 940,386 international arrivals were recorded at the two main airports, with 395,828 of them categorized as tourists. Among those tourists were 63,592 Germans, 15,810 Swiss, and 5,302 Austrians, and though the overall share has decreased in comparison to 1996, German-speaking visitors still make up 21 percent of tourists.[12] In 2013, the market share of overnight stays of tourists from Germany alone was at 19.6 percent, while the numbers for tourists from other European regions dropped.[13] Since Germans vacation mostly on the coast, they were and have been the most visible group in the area.[14]

In Diani, Germans became active participants in the development of tourism after Karl Pollman in the early 1960s bought one of several existing small hotels; it soon emerged as one of the most popular hotels for German tourists. New upscale hotels were built during the 1970s, and until the early 1990s, most were owned or co-owned or managed by Germans. The German presence in hotel management waned after the 1990s, and with it the number of tourists, especially after a crisis in tourism brought on by the Kenyan election-related violence of 1997 and from which the south coast never fully recovered. Germans, however, became leading figures in the real estate market that has been booming since the mid-1990s. In addition, Germans remain the largest group of tourists in Diani, and some have also settled in the area. German expatriates, some of them retirees, play a crucial role in Diani's economic space, as business owners, landlords, employers, and consumers. In 2014, more than one thousand Germans rented and owned property in Diani, and hundreds more lived in adjacent areas. Within a population of seventy-five thousand, these numbers may seem insignificant, but the effect of the presence of about three thousand expatriate entrepreneurs and residents of various origins, along with that of tens of thousands of tourists annually, is in fact profound. Although German entrepreneurs, residents, and tourists are an integral part of Diani's economy and sociocultural life, scholarship on the role of Europeans in Kenya has focused primarily on British-Kenyan relations. Studies on the role of Germans and tourists and residents from other

European countries are rare, despite the significant effect these groups have on Kenya's economic, political, and social life. A paradigm shift seems to be in order.

For the local population, tourism and the real estate boom have had substantial repercussions, especially with regard to landownership and various social practices that structure life in Diani today. Tourism brought economic opportunity by creating jobs, but the effects of the real estate economy have been overwhelmingly adverse. The indigenous Digo people have been subjected to a massive process of gentrification, whereby residents of the original villages now control or own only about 20 percent of the land they once used in the area east of the Mombasa–Lunga Lunga Road. Generally, the word "gentrification" is used to describe processes in (mostly) urban environments whereby poorer and less powerful members of a community are forced to give way to profit-based real estate development. Aspects of ethnicity, race, and religion are intricately intertwined with class-based economic factors in each case of gentrification: one or more ethnically, religiously, and/or economically defined groups move out of a certain area, and other groups move in.[15] Rowland Atkinson and Gary Bridge, who tie global processes of gentrification to the rise of the neoliberal state, argue in *Gentrification in a Global Context* that "gentrification is now global."[16] D. Asher Ghertner raises concerns regarding an inflationary use of gentrification and rightfully warns that "if by gentrification we mean nothing more than a rising rent environment and associated forms of market-induced displacement," then "this definition is so broad that it diverts attention away from more fundamental changes in the political economy of land in much of the world."[17] Linking the analysis of gentrification to practices of the neoliberal state, however, allows us to address distinctions regarding landownership and property rights (Ghertner's relevant point of contention) as well as factors of class, ethnicity, race, and religion as they are salient in various areas of the world. I consider the concept an especially useful vehicle for transcending the limitations of African exceptionalism, whereby connections to global economic and political processes are evaded in favor of a more narrow view of events occurring mostly in sub-Saharan Africa. This view is rooted in a focus on the colonial past or on structural aspects that are perceived to be intrinsic to African states, or both. More than any other concept addressing changes in land, housing ownership, or residency patterns, gentrification captures the developments that have been under way in Diani over the past fifty years.

One aspect of these property developments involves the movement of upcountry immigrants into the area. This group includes Kikuyo, Kisii, Kamba, Luo, and many other Kenyan ethnicities and is collectively known as *wabara*, those from upcountry. Some of the immigrants end up on the winning side of the rush for economic opportunity and real estate in Diani, and others end up on the losing side. In that competition over resources, three groups can thus be identified:

the local Digo, upcountry immigrants, and expatriates. Questions of ethnic and (less so) religious belonging play a considerable role in the story that *Germans on the Kenyan Coast* tells. Overall, however, it is the *combination* of ethnic, religious, and economic factors that reveals clear tendencies regarding the privilege that some individuals and groups have and others do not.

In a comparative perspective, Diani emerges as representative of processes presently under way in tourism centers across the global south, in particular with regard to (1) the *longue durée* effects of structures created by colonialism, the effects of neoliberal economic policies and the global rush for real estate; (2) the role of humanitarian assistance; and (3) the scale and scope of transnational romantic relationships and marriage.

Longue Durée Effects of Structures Created by Colonialism; Effects of Neoliberal Economic Policies and the Global Rush for Real Estate

Longue Durée *Effects of Structures Created by Colonialism*

The gentrification of the Diani area, through both tourism and real estate development, would not have been possible without laws that were first drawn up during the era of the Protectorate and then colonial rule, which correspond to the first phase of gentrification. Beginning with the 1901 East African (Lands) Order-in-Council, various ordinances instituted by the British government significantly affected patterns of landownership along the coast.[18] The 1908 Land Titles Ordinance, for example, ignored not only the longstanding customary use of land by groups of villagers for communal activities, such as hunting and farming, but also indigenous practices that regulated individual ownership of land in ways distinct from British conventions.[19] With the 1915 Crown Lands Ordinance, communal tenure claims were no longer permitted; only individuals were allowed to file claims. Indigenous groups were thus deprived of the opportunity to claim the largest areas of land that they used.[20] A 1919 ordinance that introduced a system of registration of titles completed the disinheritance of the indigenous people, as it had the consequence that only a few title claims by locals were approved and registered.[21] While the coast was officially under the sovereignty of the sultan of Zanzibar, some developments that occurred in other areas of Kenya also occurred at the coast. Many Digo were placed in the South Nyika Reserve, and land they had previously used was made available for development by settlers. The most infamous example was the 1908 granting of 260,000 acres (105,218 hectares) of land south of Mombasa to East African Estates Ltd., one of the largest British colonial companies operating in Kenya at the time.[22]

Perhaps the most astounding aspect of postindependence approaches to landownership in Kenya lies in the continuity of colonial policies, especially regarding the lack of land reform, the introduction of new settlement schemes, and continuing cases of land alienation during and after the transition to independence—all of which aggravated the situation of landless peasants and signal the second phase of gentrification.[23] Although the category of "trust land," which goes back to the colonial era, was meant to accommodate communal landownership after independence, communal claims and practices were generally not addressed by the new government. (Per the new constitution of Kenya from 2010, this category of land is now termed "community land.")[24] The notion of private property remained key to landownership; the acquisition of title deeds for plots became central and continues to dominate the discussion on landownership to this day. Without a mechanism for registering communally used land or giving legal status to untitled land used by individual or groups of villagers, the colonial process of robbing villagers of their land continued after independence. West Germany played a crucial role in setting up fateful structures that burdened the newly independent country for decades. For instance, that country figured prominently as one of the lenders of the Million Acre Scheme, an arrangement the British government devised when it became clear that the days of colonial rule were over and by which Kenya was forced (or agreed) to buy back a section of its own (especially fertile) land via loans that were granted by the World Bank, the Colonial Development Corporation (the development finance institution owned by the British government), and West Germany.[25]

Most consequential for Diani were transactions that occurred under President Jomo Kenyatta's rule allowing preferred parties to acquire plots close to or on the beach, appropriating land that villagers had used for centuries.[26] The situation of landless peasants and squatters on the coast remains a volatile issue to this day, and the condition of the indigenous villagers in Diani is no exception. A 1978 report about the situation on the coast states that "the strip now has probably the largest single concentration of landless people, in the whole country."[27] Thirty years later, a 2007 government report confirmed the lack of improvement in the situation, asserting that "the abuse of the Land Titles Act has had a great negative impact on coastal land leading to the area having the largest single concentration of landless indigenous people."[28] Present-day tensions along the coast continue to be tied primarily to questions of landownership. As Catherine Boone's recent study demonstrates, land tenure issues—in defiance of "modernization theory and theories of economic development, which predicted that land politics would decrease in salience over time"—are central to conflicts across Africa, as they define "relationships among individuals, groups, markets, and the state."[29] *Germans on the Kenyan Coast* adds to discussions of landownership in Kenya and beyond by considering the consequences of recent neoliberal transactions in light of colonial and postcolonial policies.

The lack of infrastructure development along the coast is one of the primary grievances coastal peoples have with the central government, which they see as supporting its own, largely upcountry, constituencies. There is no better example to illustrate this grievance than the lack of a bypass around the island of Mombasa. To this day, all travelers who want to move beyond Mombasa from the north and west toward the south coast and Tanzania (or in the reverse directions) have to drive through Mombasa and take the ferries at Likoni to cross the waterway into Mombasa harbor. Passengers are crammed together but usually cross within half an hour, whereas trucks, cars, and tourism-related vehicles are often stuck for two, three, and more hours in the blistering heat on either side of the crossover (unless bribes are passed out). Plans for this bypass go back to the 1960s; forty years later, in 2009, the Dongo Kundu Bypass was approved, but construction began only in 2015.[30] The lack of this bypass is detrimental not only to the economy of the coast (especially the south coast), but to the Kenyan economy more broadly, since it hinders traffic along the coast and between the coast and the hinterland. With significant infrastructure development occurring in other parts of the country, to the coastal peoples, the government's inaction in this regard is symbolic of its overall attitude toward the coast.

Kenyans I interviewed have well-defined idealized expectations of their government: they consider it responsible for ensuring that their basic needs are met and complain about the lack of governmental accountability and care. I was often perplexed by the positive views of European expatriates, who, in the view of African Kenyans in Diani, do a better job of taking care of them than their own government.[31] The image of the state that becomes apparent in the comments of ordinary Kenyans merges notions of the welfare state with ideas that are tied to expectations regarding the responsibilities of elders, as they existed and continue to persist especially in rural Kenya. Discussions of the role of the state in this book take as a starting point the popular view of the state as it emerged in interviews and is also omnipresent in the media; thus, when I talk about the state, I foreground the local ideal of the state as caretaker, despite the obvious discrepancies between the hopes of citizens and the actions of the Kenyan government. When Kenyans are asked publicly for their opinion, they often reply, "Inapaswa kutuma msaada" (the government should send help) and "Serikali yetu iko wapi?" (our government, where is it?). Across the country, people loudly and clearly express their frustration with the lack of correspondence to the popular ideal; and increasingly, as regional protests and violence throughout the country amply illustrate, they see the state as their enemy (once more, after hopes for the opportunities of a multiparty democracy seem to be fading). Public debates in Kenya generally do not entail a critique of capitalism; in fact, the connection between governmental action and the economic system is usually not part of mainstream discussions. Often, what amounts to defining features of the neoliberal model (albeit not expressed in these terms) are seen as solutions to the status quo.

But more than anything, Kenyans see the state as responsible for both economic and political affairs in the country. *Germans on the Kenyan Coast* is less an attempt to bring to light how the state or an oil company sees or tends to matters on the ground; rather, I hope to elucidate the ways in which ordinary people, both Kenyan and expatriate, cope with the fallout of action or inaction at the level of state and international politics and economy.[32] I take the expectations of Kenyans seriously and suggest that their ideals bear within them the potential for future change. By focusing on various kinds of material practices and social modes of entanglements, I aim to deepen our understanding of the nexus of national and transnational political, economic, and social processes on the coast of Kenya.

We can observe similar developments around the world, whereby the concerns of large constituencies are sidelined in favor of the interests of more powerful groups. Struggles over land emerge as a crucial issue in areas that provide opportunity for various economic enterprises, such as tourism, mining, and agriculture. Local residents usually face an alliance of foreign investors and local politicians. In many cases, the affected populations have fought for their rights for centuries—only the nationality of the invaders and the nature of locally created alliances between internal and external wielders of power have changed over time. Anayansi Prado's 2011 documentary *Paraiso for Sale*, for example, shows the alienation of land from indigenous peoples in the archipelago of Bocas del Toro, Panama. While the ancestors of local people were subjected to the physical, political, economic, and cultural violence of Spanish conquistadores five hundred years earlier, their descendants now lose their land (and more) to US developers who are allied with local politicians.[33] Similar stories can be told about other areas in the Caribbean and Central and South America, areas that faced the first onslaught of European colonialism.[34] Countless cases can also be found in Africa and Asia, but the cast of invaders now includes non-Western actors. Indigenous Anuak, Mezenger, Nuer, Opo, and Komo of Ethiopia, for example, are displaced by a collaboration between the Ethiopian government and Karuturi Ltd., an Indian company.[35] Although the Digo of Kenya are not acknowledged as indigenous people, their economic and political struggles clearly date back to the colonial period. *Germans on the Kenyan Coast* recounts the longer history that led to the current situation in Diani and sheds light on the historical roots of a contemporary conflict. The epigraph to this chapter by Mwalimu Mbaraka bin Shomari poignantly expresses the sentiment that self-interest is the new rule of the land; the poem dates to the late nineteenth century and signals a fundamental moment in the *longue durée* of social and economic relations along the coast.

Effects of Neoliberal Economic Policies and the Global Rush for Real Estate

Following transformations that began during the colonial period and continued after independence, the third phase of gentrification in Diani occurred in conjunction with the tourism boom and the subsequent rise of the real estate market. To understand these developments comprehensively, one needs to consider how migration, tourism, and global economic developments are connected. Migration studies scholarship—which has looked at global processes by focusing on migration and global economic development[36] and economic and political migration from the global south to the north,[37] from poorer to richer countries,[38] and from the country to the city[39]—is now increasingly paying attention to lifestyle, retirement, and amenity migration that flows in the opposite direction.[40] Tourism has often been seen as salient to modern identity; Dean MacCannell, for instance, suggests that "'the tourist' is one of the best models available for modern-man-in-general" and John Urry writes that "to be a tourist is one of the characteristics of the 'modern' experience."[41] Tourism has inherited from colonialism a penchant for exotic places and peoples as well as fundamental structures that are most obviously reproduced in the role of the (Western) tourist who is tended to by the native.[42] Scholars of tourism have long highlighted the complex repercussions of tourism on local communities. Various models of interaction between tourists and those communities have developed, some of them amiable in character and others more antagonistic and even outright destructive.[43]

Tourism and various forms of migration emerged in the context of specific economic structures; the relevant economic framework here is the neoliberal model that pushed for deregulation and enabled rich nations to invade markets of recently decolonized and often nationalized economies. The real estate market in Diani surfaced in its current shape during the early 1990s, when the World Bank and the International Monetary Fund (IMF) pressured Kenya to open its market to foreign investors.[44] The negative effect of these policies, especially on poorer populations around the world, has been well documented.[45] In Diani, villagers were often displaced from their land; others sold their land voluntarily, but what seemed to them to be high profits were not invested beneficially: villagers were unaccustomed to an investment-oriented economy and in many cases quickly lost the substantial sums they received from the sale of land. German entrepreneurs, settlers, and tourists became the driving force in Diani's real estate market, with numerous commercial structures, private residences, and massive security fences being visible testaments to the effect of German real estate and commercial activity in the area. As a result of these shifts in landownership, some of the individuals who were previously able to sustain themselves by growing food on their land (for consumption and sometimes for sale) and who owned their own homes now pay rent and work salaried jobs, if they can find any work at all. Within the course of five decades, Diani went from being a group of largely self-sustaining villages to an urbanized area with high rates of poverty, crime, prostitution, and drug-trafficking and with needs in all essential areas, such as health care, education, sanitation, and even food.

These various processes are comparable to developments around the world; a substantial north-to-south migration has occurred over the past twenty years, driven by neoliberal economic opportunities that have diminished the obstacles to global investments via tax laws, residency status, and visa types that are conducive to business transactions. Public and scholarly discussion has focused on areas that are targeted for minerals and other raw materials (in Africa and across the globe), so the global rush for real estate has received less attention.[46] What the villagers of Diani have experienced over the past thirty years is part of a global trend: areas with attractive beachfronts are especially popular, as revealed by developments on the Canary Islands and in Thailand, Morocco, and Ghana. Some of these developments are discussed in the literature as examples of "second home tourism," "residential tourism," and the effect of "time share ownership" and often are considered primarily national phenomena; however, most examples of these types of tourism, even in Europe, have distinct global dimensions.[47] The volume and effect of expatriate and local real estate acquisitions in tourism areas has been discussed critically by Central American and European scholars, but analyses are still rare with regard to Africa and many other areas. Real estate activity, however, is apparent.[48] Global real estate transactions have become easier to accomplish and more frequent over the past twenty years, with many international companies involved in and facilitating the current real estate shifts.[49] Along with online search options that real estate companies provide, newspapers also enable the global buying frenzy.[50] A potential buyer can carry out a "property search" for real estate, for example, on the "Great Homes and Destinations" and the "Real Estate" web pages of the *New York Times*. The German daily *Süddeutsche Zeitung* also features a search option for international real estate. The popular US television show "House Hunters International," aired by HGTV, is a testament to how land grabbing on a global scale inspires the imagination of the general public. Houses and plots in Italy, Barbados, Australia, France, the Caribbean, Nicaragua, and many other places are advertised to consumers in more affluent nations who dream of living a life that they either cannot afford in their home countries or that simply provides a welcome distraction in the form of a second or third home in an attractive location. Dreams about exotic places, fueled in the 1970s and 1980s by TV series such as *The Love Boat* in the United States and its German equivalent, *Das Traumschiff* (The Dream Ship), have transformed from dreams into very real real estate.[51]

"How do you measure the value of land to people?" asks Kenyan sociologist Chris Owalla in a book by Fred Pearce about the global extent of land grabbing. The question goes to the heart of the grief associated with the loss of land for the Digo (and other individuals and groups) and, as Pearce points out, "is not just about money, it is about land and identity and dignity."[52] Whether or not the Digo are classified as indigenous people, the importance of their land for the community's life is addressed in the following statement by Albert Kwokwo Barume about land rights for indigenous peoples: "For indigenous communities, land is not just for use, but also and more importantly land sustains their whole livelihood and culture. Furthermore, the indigenous communities also have a distinctive and profound spiritual and material relationship to their land."[53]

How do African Kenyans in Diani cope with the economic pressures resulting from the loss of land and the development of the tourism industry? *Germans on the Kenyan Coast* identifies and analyzes two social practices that did not exist in their current form before the arrival of tourism: international humanitarianism and transnational romantic relationships. These practices have emerged in Diani over the past three decades and significantly structure interactions between Kenyans and mostly European-born expatriates and tourists. While gentrification pushed African Kenyans off land they once owned or used, humanitarianism and romantic relationships provide opportunities for them to gain or regain control over material resources. These practices entangle African Kenyans with various groups of immigrants and tourists in most intimate ways, and here again, the role of Germans in Diani is distinct. In comparison to other groups of Europeans, interaction between Germans and African Kenyans occurs at a much higher frequency and intensity. Germans and Kenyans engage with one another with different intentions, but the two practices they have developed together address their distinct needs.

Humanitarian Assistance

Many tourists and settlers feel compelled to improve the living conditions of African Kenyans and engage in humanitarian aid activities that take place locally under the rubric of "charity." The extent of charitable activity is so great that in Diani, for example, not a single private or public school exists that is not funded fully or partly by foreign donors. Overall, the dominant model of charity in Diani shifts the responsibility for addressing health care, sanitation, and education-related needs away from Kenyan institutions to foreign humanitarians. Although Kenyans display a significant degree of agency in securing funds from expatriate humanitarians and foreign donors, the structures of charity release the Kenyan government *and* the local community from accountability. Historical forms of solidarity (such as the *utsi* and *mweria* systems of the local Digo people discussed in chapter 2, also in their relation to the top-down Kenyan self-help movement *harambee*) have been replaced by appeals to charitable organizations to meet infrastructure and other community needs, such as building toilets and digging wells. Traditional forms of communal self-help were based on principles of reciprocity and mutuality, but the present-day Kenyan contribution to humanitarian projects in the Diani area is minimal.[54] Perhaps the way in which African Kenyans manage to get expatriates to contribute money and time on their behalf has an element of subversiveness to it, but it is also conditioned on locals having to and being willing to transfer degrees of control over their affairs to outsiders. While calls for the *serikali* (government) to address local need remain unanswered, the eagerness of European humanitarians to take care of matters is more than welcomed by the Diani community, albeit on terms that only rarely consider mutuality and reciprocity.[55]

Humanitarianism has long been integral to global power relations; under different names, it dates back to the beginnings of colonial rule, when Christian missionaries provided moral legitimacy to but also criticized civilizing endeavors of the Spanish and Portuguese empires in the New World.[56] Critics of colonialism identified humanitarianism as an ideological tool integral to colonial rule and have long chastised it. In a short essay titled "Murderous Humanitarianism," the Surrealist Group of France wrote in 1932: "The clergy and professional philanthropists have always collaborated with the army in this bloody exploitation. . . . The white man preaches, doses, vaccinates, assassinates and (from himself) receives absolution. With his psalms, his speeches, his guarantees of liberty, equality and fraternity, he seeks to drown the noise of his machine guns."[57] The kinds of connections established here between colonial rule and humanitarian activities, however, remained insights articulated and embraced by the colonized and their allies. For mainstream European and other Western societies, the ideological appeal of humanitarianism was and continues to be based in its ability to mitigate actual power relations and oppressive practices.

For Germans, the roots of humanitarian impulses can be traced to specific institutional models, such as the Red Cross, and specific individuals, such as Albert Schweitzer, who mobilized humanitarian energies for aid to Africa.[58] German humanitarian impulses, as Glenn Penny argues, are also grounded in a long-standing identification with indigenous peoples (most importantly, American Indians), which sensitized (some) Germans to the plight of indigenous peoples and to the repercussions of colonial conquest.[59] In addition, as Michael Rothberg and others have pointed out, critical discussions of the Shoah in Germany and elsewhere opened a space for the discussion of genocide and thus helped generate the human rights framework that was crucial for the emergence of humanitarian initiatives and new legal norms regarding humanitarian responsibilities.[60]

Humanitarianism has become even more significant to north-south relations during the postcolonial period and, in the past decade or so, has been discussed critically more widely. If we consider humanitarian assistance as a continuation of what previously was described as "development" and "development aid," then the critique of mostly Western-based projects in "developing" countries dates back to the 1970s.[61] Then and now, the question of whether development aid creates dependence and how it may address specific issues in the long term remains at the center of the discussion. Humanitarianism has become one of the keywords through which a range of activities are described, within both rich and poor nations. Today, "humanitarian reason," using the term suggested by Didier Fassin, inspires the actions of governments and nongovernmental organizations (NGOs), as well as the deeds of ordinary citizens.[62] Thus far, critical inquiry has primarily focused on officially organized and institutionalized forms of humanitarian activity. For example, scholarship has debated the success of humanitarian interventions (mostly military in nature) into crisis areas, including those led by the United Nations, NATO, and various world powers.[63] Scholars have also questioned and argued for the success of both governmental and nongovernmental economic and political development programs.[64] However, humanitarianism has cast a much wider net, as it incorporates a vast array of actors from both NGOs and international NGOs (INGOs) and structures north-south relations at the level of everyday life experiences in a range of diverse scenarios. The discussion of representative cases of humanitarian activity in Diani addresses precisely the role that humanitarianism plays at the microlevel. Humanitarians in Diani are mostly self-styled; they have no training in humanitarian work, and although they usually draw on the support of registered donor networks in Europe, many are not associated with registered organizations in Kenya.

The effect of international (and here, specifically German) humanitarianism on communities such as Diani is substantial. Scholars of Africa and Kenya have warned that INGO and NGO activity in the country undermines civil society, feeds corruption, and weakens the state; in fact, Maurice Amutabi refers to these organizations as having created a "philanthrocracy."[65] The notion of "philanthropic colonialism," as Peter Buffett put it in a 2013 *New York Times* op-ed piece titled "The Charitable-Industrial Complex" comes to mind. Humanitarian activities in Africa are indeed deeply structured by colonial forms of "helping Africans," and significantly, unlike human rights debates and activism, humanitarianism does not primarily refer to rights; even when it does, the gesture is mostly rhetorical. On one hand, human rights—in our current historical moment—have no teeth; unless they are legislated locally and made part of the citizenship rights of a nation-state, they are not enforceable in our current global legal landscape.[66] On the other hand, humanitarianism brings into focus the gap between citizenship rights and human rights. Whereas in the Kenyan context, citizenship rights, as defined in the Kenyan constitution and various pieces of legislation (regarding education, health, and the rights of the disabled, among others), are often not guaranteed in ways expected by the population, the legitimacy of expatriate humanitarians in becoming the guardians of Kenyan citizenship rights and, more broadly, human rights is questionable.

In addition, humanitarianism is intrinsically related to global patterns of social inequality yet masks this relation by emphasizing *affect* rather than rights and ideas of social justice. Contemporary humanitarianism, as Fassin has argued, is grounded in "a politics of inequality" and draws on "the mobilization of empathy rather than the recognition of rights."[67] Critics of global capitalism, such as Joseph Stiglitz and Thomas Piketty, have pointed to the negative effect of financial and capital market liberalization and the lack of regulatory frameworks, especially for poorer nations.[68] As the detrimental repercussions of neoliberal deregulation for poor populations have become visible, humanitarian assistance emerges as the Band-Aid offered to address the fallout of neoliberal economic policies. The rise of humanitarianism accompanies the rise of neoliberal capitalism; charity compensates for the inequalities exacerbated by globalization. Yet, those involved in charitable action usually have no knowledge of World Bank and IMF structural adjustment policies; they lack historical knowledge; they are unaware of the connections between, for example, debt politics, currency politics, and privatization; and they do not understand that poverty levels have increased as a result of some of these policies.[69]

In her study of welfare and citizenship in Italy, Andrea Muehlebach traces the disappearance of the twentieth-century welfare state ethos of social contract and the rise, instead, of a new ethos of charity. This charity, she argues, creates "wounds woven into the very fabric of a society that has placed the unrequited gift at its moral center at a moment of intense neoliberalizaton." Muehlebach's study confirms central insights of my analysis of humanitarian activity in Kenya: I agree with her that "morals do pulsate at the heart of the market; that the gospel of laissez-faire is always already accompanied by hypermoralization . . . markets and morals [are] indissolubly linked and . . . the contemporary neoliberal order works to produce more than rational, utilitarian, instrumentalist subjects."[70]

What emerges in the analysis of German activities in present-day Kenya are a number of unintended and poorly understood consequences of humanitarian work. While humanitarians who are active in Diani are quick to talk about sustainability and insist that "Africa must help itself," they tend to *culturalize* the situation they intend to address, identifying culture and premodern lifestyles as the root causes of Kenya's economic and political challenges. In addition, most of them do not see their actions and attitudes as part of a continuum that includes the colonial period; rather, they emulate historical models of charity. Nicholas Stockton, a former executive director of Oxfam, uses the term "moral economy" to describe the aid industry, thus evoking a concept that was first popularized by E. P. Thompson to describe moral expectations of the economy embraced by eighteenth-century English poor, a concept further propagated through James C. Scott's study on South Asian peasants.[71] When the economic objectives are considered from the perspective of the aid industry, however, this contemporary "moral economy" seems greatly designed to serve the needs of the helpers (for instance, it creates jobs and internships that improve résumés, provides tax write-offs, and offers emotional benefits) rather than the needs of the aid recipients; its ethics ought to be deeply questioned in terms of material long-term outcomes. If the World Bank celebrates the lifting of millions of people out of poverty (in terms of gross domestic product values) while simultaneously the same populations lose control over land and resources to mining companies and developers, humanitarian aid turns out merely to be hush money.

At the same time, the economic benefits of humanitarian projects to the community in Diani are indisputable and substantial, and mobilization of humanitarian energies to address areas of need is one strategy of resilience that individuals and groups successfully pursue in the absence of governmental support and community-based solutions. Seen as a moral economy from the perspective of the recipients of aid (such as the villagers of Diani), the similarities to the situations Thompson and Scott describe are compelling: humanitarian aid speaks to expectations of economic fairness and is supposed to right the wrongs without a substantial reform of the system within which it operates. Are government (in)action and the lack of community-based solutions produced or at least coproduced by expatriate humanitarianism? This book intends to shed light on this question.

Romantic Relationships and Marriage

North-south romantic entanglements that address the lack of economic choices of the local population have emerged in Diani and other tourism centers along the Kenyan coast and, in fact, throughout the global south. These romantic relationships, which are considered here in distinction from prostitution, are significantly shaped by the "culture of charity," but they evolve according to a different dynamic. Most media and other cultural discussions do not distinguish between sex tourism and romance tourism. Typically, there is a presumption that tourists intend to engage in sexual activity during a holiday, and the analysis is then focused on what is generally seen as abusive or, at best, highly problematic behavior of tourists, both male and female.[72] And indeed, sex tourism in tourism centers around the world—in Brazil, Thailand, Egypt, Costa Rica, the Dominican Republic, and countless other locations—is a pressing social and human rights issue in our contemporary world.[73] Sex trafficking and child prostitution are rampant in areas that do not control prostitution at significant levels, often involving corrupt police forces and governments that do not make sufficient efforts to protect women and children.[74] Kenya is no exception in this regard: prostitution, trafficking, and child prostitution are acknowledged social problems of substantial dimensions.[75] Scholarship on sex and romance tourism, however, has established that, first, various types of sexual and romantic relationships emerge between tourists and locals, and second, locals display a great deal of agency in structuring the relationships.[76]

My discussion of romantic relations in Diani focuses on long-term relationships and marriages. I first became aware of the increase of marriages between locals and tourists in the 1990s and compiled statistical data on the basis of marriage licenses kept at the Office of the Registrar of Marriages in Mombasa for the years 1994 to 1998. For the present study, I analyzed records of the years 2000 to 2012. Overall, the comparison of annual data shows that German-Kenyan marriages made up between 38 and 64 percent of all Kenyan marriages to foreigners over this twelve-year period. While the total number of transnational marriages registered in Mombasa may not seem high (close to three thousand over the period I studied), it is only a fraction of the total of all transnational romantic relationships. Transnational marriages, along with other long-term transnational romantic relationships, substantially affect the coastal population and beyond. As my discussion of the data shows, in conjunction with insights gained during my fieldwork, the overall effect of such marriages and romantic relations is profound: assuming that, in each case, between ten and twenty Kenyan family members are affected economically by both transnational marriages and long-term romantic relations, I suggest that between one and two million Kenyans have seen some sort of economic effect from these transnational relationships over the past twenty years. Most of that effect is felt among the coastal population; the overall influence that the more than twenty thousand foreigners who are currently registered in Kenya as permanent residents and the hundreds of thousands of tourists, humanitarians, and businesspeople who come to Kenya every year have on Kenyan lives is even greater. If we add to the picture the effect of informal and formal humanitarian aid (as discussed in chapter 3), the degree to which Kenya's coast (and Kenya more generally) is economically subsidized through its connection to Europe is tremendous. The government's figure for *wage* employment in Kenya was, in 2013, 2.27 million individuals, among a population of 44.35 million (estimated for 2013), indicating a low rate of salaried labor. While some sources cite an employment figure of more than 6 million, and both of these figures do not nearly capture economic activity in the country, the economic effect of activities discussed in the following chapters explains much of Kenya's resilience.[77]

My research for this book sheds more light on unions between Kenyans and Germans and their various effects on people and communities. The relationships display varying degrees of stability and duration and are distinguished by distinct kinship structures (often involving multiple German and African families), substantial age differences, conflicting motivations, and economic differentials that have a range of repercussions. Kenyan gains are especially visible with regard to landownership and housing; in fact, by engaging in romantic relationships and mobilizing the "humanitarian reason" of their partners, many African Kenyans have been able to "recuperate" the land that they or others lost in the process of gentrification that occurred over the past one hundred years. Houses built with funds from European partners, in addition to school fees for children, health-care expenditures, and career development measures, mirror the areas of humanitarian activities in the area. Extended walking tours that I took through Diani—*dériving* (or "drifting") in the sense of the concept developed by Guy Debord—exposed the degree to which romantic relationships affect the physical landscape of the area and, most important, the economic situation of African Kenyans. While *dériving* was developed by Debord and other members of the Situationist group as a method of exploring urban areas, I found it useful in acquiring an intimate sense of Diani (as shown especially in chapters 2 and 4).[78]

The extent and effect of the interaction between the local population and German (and other) tourists and settlers, in light of the combined economic effect of romance, marriage, sex tourism, humanitarianism, and remittances, is the basis of my argument that the longstanding outward orientation of the coast toward Indian Ocean communities has experienced a shift toward Europe.[79] The figures and descriptions of processes I bring to the debate are certain to challenge some of the "poor numbers," to use Morten Jerven's phrase, that have defined the development discussion in Kenya and Africa more broadly.[80] Although my data are bound to contain some flaws, I hope to highlight the extent of economic transactions that, to date, have not been factored into the assessment of Kenya's economy.[81]

The structure of this study is essential: changes in economic conditions, including the loss of land, necessitate the development of social practices to address the resulting economic precarity. Humanitarian action is for the most part controlled by expatriates; but in romantic relations, agency lies predominantly with Kenyans, who thereby have the (limited) potential to recuperate a measure of the loss of land—bringing the argument made here full circle. Similar to what AbdouMaliq Simone has been able to show about the vitality of informal "shifting forms of social collaboration" in various African cities, *Germans on the Kenyan Coast* documents the practices ordinary Kenyans devise to address economic precarity.[82] The main aspects brought to light through this study—the *longue durée* effects of structures introduced during the colonial period, the effect of neoliberal economic policies on economically poorer regions, the role of humanitarian assistance, and the scale and scope of transnational romantic relationships and marriage—make the case study of Diani representative of similar developments that are under way around the world, especially in tourism resort areas in the global south, such as Brazil, Thailand, India, the Caribbean, Ghana, and other countries.

Method

Germans on the Kenyan Coast draws substantially on ethnographic fieldwork. I have been visiting the area since 1980 and pursued my first research project in Diani in 1998.[83] Fieldwork for this project was conducted from November 2009 to February 2010, in July and August of 2011 and 2012, in October and November of 2013, and during December 2014. Two brief visits in December 2015 and June 2016 allowed me to gather a sense of recent developments. Traveling to the area over the past three decades and then conducting research over seven years have given me insight into change over time and allowed me to build crucial relationships with individuals who were willing to share their views with me. I conducted more than two hundred formal and informal interviews with close to 150 individuals from different ethnic societies and diverse age, religious, and social groups. I carried out interviews in English, German, and Kiswahili (my knowledge of Arabic also proved useful several times, for example, in conversations with the imam of the Kongo Mosque in Diani and other Muslim leaders of the area), and I followed up with some individuals throughout the duration of the study. I observed and listened, especially to gossip, which turned out to be crucial to the process of corroborating and revising what I had learned during formal interviews. I conducted archival research at the Office of the Registrar of Marriages in Mombasa and in Kwale; gleaned statistical data from interviews and marriage licenses; visited humanitarian initiatives onsite; made use of statistical data provided by the official statistical agencies of Germany, Switzerland, Austria, and Kenya; and applied geographical information system (GIS) tools to create maps of the area. I also gathered data through *dériving*, on extensive walking and driving tours in the area. In fact, an up-close view of the building activity and the act of counting houses in Diani became indispensable in the process of archiving landownership and documenting the presence of Germans who live in the area. I was also able to get aerial views of Diani during several short flights in small passenger planes, which brought to light the extent of building activity in the area.[84] In addition, I have drawn on the insights of historians, cultural anthropologists, social scientists, filmmakers, novelists, and authors of life narratives.

I chose not to do some things, however, and also encountered some obstacles. I decided not to go to the Land Registry in Kwale, as it became obvious that the records kept there are inconsistently accurate; real estate agents and local residents suggested that about one-third of the title deeds are forged, disputed, or both. After walking through and flying over the area, I decided to register building activity rather than assess landownership. While my figures amount to estimated values, they provide insight into building activity and numbers of residents by way of a systematic assessment. With one exception, I encountered no obstacles from Kenyan authorities; a leading German real estate company in Diani and German official institutions, however, were highly resistant to sharing information. The German Embassy in Nairobi (unlike its Austrian and Swiss counterparts) refused to give out figures on the number of registered German residents in Kenya, despite several written and phone attempts on my part. The Organization for International Collaboration (Gesellschaft für Internationale Zusammenarbeit, GIZ), the key development agency of Germany, which I contacted to inquire about a scandal that occurred in the 1990s and also about the murder of a development worker in Kwale in 1998, also blocked my attempts to get access to records about these issues.

Overview of Chapters

The chapters that follow are devoted to the three main dimensions of this book's subtitle: land, charity, and romance. Chapter 2, "Land," first reviews the longer history of landownership in Kenya and Diani based on existing scholarship. It then draws on oral history accounts of a wide range of actors in Diani as well as various supporting sources and describes economic, social, and demographic changes of the past fifty years as they occurred as a result of tourism and real estate development. In addition, the chapter includes original data (derived from walking and driving tours and the evaluation of satellite images) documenting the extent of the shifts in landownership in Diani.

Chapter 3, "Charity," opens with an account of traditional Digo institutions of solidarity and community work and a discussion of the German propensity to support humanitarian aid in Africa. It then presents four cases of German-run or German-supported humanitarian work in the area, each of which is grounded in a distinct approach to the local community and context. A comparative analysis considers how these humanitarian activities affect the state (as understood by African Kenyans I interviewed), the economy, and the local community.

Chapter 4, "Romance," evaluates the frequency and nature of Kenyan-German marriages by presenting data gleaned from an analysis of thirteen years of marriage certificates kept at the Office of the Registrar of Marriages in Mombasa and Kwale and draws upon extensive interviews with individuals who are or were engaged in long-term binational relationships. The discussion assesses the motivations, areas of conflict, questions of kinship, and economic dimensions of these relationships.

An epilogue considers future prospects for the area, in light of broader developments along the coast and across the globe. An appendix contains maps documenting aspects of landownership in Diani and tables summarizing details about landownership and intermarriage and romance.

The Kiswahili subtitle of this chapter reflects the multidirectional alliances of the coast: "Pwani si Kenya," which means "the coast is not Kenya," is the rallying cry of the secessionist movement known as the Mombasa Republican Council and harkens back to precolonial days, when the coast was in fact closely tied to non-African empires, Arab and Portuguese, and was part of the Indian Ocean economy. "Pwani ni Kenya," "the coast is Kenya," acknowledges that today, the coast, comparable to a metropolis, reflects all the various ethnicities of Kenya that have come to the coast to work and look for opportunity. "Pwani ni Ujerumani (na Italia na kadhalika)," "the coast is Germany (and Italy and so on)," speaks to the close ties that the coast has formed with citizens from European countries. The scope and scale of these ties, specifically to Germany, Switzerland, and Austria, are the focus of this book.

The story of Diani is a story of opportunities and oppression, of resilience and exploitation, of *longue durée* and contemporary modes of domination and accommodation. It illustrates effects of neoliberal capitalism and the tendency of Kenyans to rely on paternalistic charity ("humanitarianism") and complicated patterns of "romance" to sustain themselves instead of forcing their own government into accountability. It acknowledges the repercussions of the German presence in contemporary Kenya and the role of resilient individuals in creating economic and sociocultural realities. But it is also a story of global economic, political, and social change, one that is rooted in the deep structures of colonial history and the transformations of the global capitalist system. It highlights the schemes that distinguish the present "Second Scramble for Africa," in which land and natural resources are leased to and left for exploitation by foreign companies, with only minimal profit to the country that owns the resources. The case of Diani also adds a chapter to the history of the global rush for beachfront property. It tells a story that contributes to our understanding of the "big picture," yet also brings to the fore the attempts of ordinary people to make sense of the complex challenges that confront them.

2 Land

The land issue remains what could be termed as the central nervous system of most Kenyans.

    —Njeri Kabeberi, *Ours by Right, Theirs by Might*

"Land crimes" are as much a part of Kenya's past wrongdoings as economic crimes and human rights crimes.

    —Ndungu Report

Da gab es keine Digo!
(There were no Digo! [in Diani])

    —German business owner, Diani, July 2012

Da wohnte keiner.
(Nobody lived there.)

    —German realtor about development on Chale Island, Diani, July 1999

THE PLACE-NAME "Diani" refers to various geographical and sociocultural locations. Diani Beach is located between Tiwi Beach to the north and Galu Beach to the south. The Kongo, or Mwachema, River marks the northern boundary; locals consider an enormous baobab tree that is located close to the beach as a signpost between Diani Beach and Galu Beach to the south (see map 1, appendix). An area farther inland, which was until the early 1990s referred to as "the end of the tarmac road" (*mwisho wa lami*) or "Four Twenty South" (in reference to the latitude of the point), is also often referred to as the southern end of Diani Beach. Officially, Diani is the name of an administrative unit in Kwale County, and its center is referred to as the town of Ukunda.[1] Diani stretches from north to south for about ten kilometers along the beach from the Kongo River to Galu Beach, and inland from the beach west to the Mombasa–Lunga Lunga Road (A14) for about two and a half to three kilometers and another four to five kilometers west of the road inland. According to the 2009 census, Diani covers an area of eighty-one square kilometers and is subdivided into the areas of Ukunda, Gombato, and Bongwe.[2] Gombato is located in the northern parts west and east of the main road, and Ukunda makes up the southern part, starting around the T-junction that connects the Mombasa–Lunga Lunga Road with the beach road, with some areas lying to the west of the road and most to east. Bongwe stretches to the west of the Mombasa–Lunga Lunga Road. Gombato includes the villages of Mwaroni, Mvumoni, Mwakamba, Mwamambi (A and B), and Maweni A. Ukunda consists of Kilolapwa (A and B, identical with areas that locals refer to as Kibundani, Ganzoni, and Jamaica), Magutu (which includes Mandingo and Maskrepu), Mkwakwani, the Diani settlement scheme of Umoja and Kosovo,[3] the Ukunda settlement scheme of Mvindeni, Kona ya Musa, Mwalubemba, and Skimu, and Maweni B. Bongwe, which is not considered in this study, extends west of the main road and borders Kibundani. It begins about three hundred to five hundred meters west of the main road and includes the villages of Mabokoni, Mbuwani, Mwamanga, Bongwe, Shamu, Mlungunipa, Mwanjamba, and Vukani.[4]

The majority of the population lives in Ukunda (38,629) and Gombato (24,024), with a smaller population in Bongwe (10,822).[5] Most areas close to the Mombasa–Lunga Lunga Road and the road from Diani to the beach and along the beach road are very densely populated. The population density in Gombato and Ukunda—2,271 and 1,542 people per square kilometer, respectively—is comparable to the density common for cities with moderate density, such as San Francisco/Oakland (2,350) and Antwerp (1,550).[6] In the Kenyan context, Gombato and Ukunda are among the more densely populated areas, though the average density seen in Mombasa (3,200) and Nairobi (4,509, with some locations within these urban areas showing a density of more than 10,000 people per square kilometer) is still higher. However, the density seen in Diani is much higher than the average population density for Kwale County (79 people per square kilometer).[7]

This relatively high population density is a very recent phenomenon and is mainly a result of the dramatic developments associated with the expansion of the tourism industry in the area. The tourism infrastructure emerged slowly during the 1970s and 1980s along the beach road, but until the early 1980s the several thousand indigenous villagers living there were not affected much by the changes occurring around them. When I walked with a friend in 1986 from his house in the village of Mvumoni to his mother's house in Magutu, we did not come across a single building in more than an hour of walking. At the time, the space between the beach road and the Mombasa–Lunga Lunga Road was almost exclusively inhabited by Digo villagers, the indigenous population of the area. Today, the same area features, among other structures, residential housing, from lavish private villas to small huts; commercial buildings, such as restaurants and supermarkets; a hospital; various schools; and an airstrip. A dramatic increase in building activities and population began in the late 1980s and early 1990s and continues to this day. Today, the original villages are surrounded by large villas that have security fences and walls, and villagers' control over land is restricted to only about 20 percent of the land they once considered theirs.

What are the main factors that have brought these substantial changes to the Diani area? How have the transformations of the past five decades affected local villagers? A review of the longer history of the south coast, with a focus on the Diani area, reveals an astounding continuity. In particular, the trends that have occurred over the past one hundred years, from colonialism to independence and the neoliberal dimensions of globalization, amount to an unremitting story of gentrification. In considering shifts in landownership and residency in Diani as a gentrification process, I draw on a concept that allows for a comparative perspective.[8] Generally, studies of gentrification have focused on urban spaces, but increasingly they are also taking into account rural spaces. The case of Diani describes an area that displays features of both rural and urban settings. Linking gentrification to the rise of the neoliberal state, in particular, offers a conceptual framework that is also applicable to Diani, which transformed during the process of gentrification from a collection of villages to a town and now to emerging urban area. In their study of global processes of gentrification, Rowland Atkinson and Gary Bridge identify "spatial scales of global transformation and forces shaping neighbourhood change." Among the relevant factors they list and that have without a doubt formed the developments in Diani are the "migration of the rich and educated, global governance and trade policy rules, financial markets, communications and travel" on the global level; "policies on inward investment; migration of the poor; welfare infrastructure, property rights and legislation, the relative scale of the middle class" on the national level; aspects related to "city administration" and the "local infrastructure—amenity environment, quality of life" on the city level; and "ghettoization, ghettoized poverty" on the neighborhood level."[9] All of these factors play a role in the gentrification of Diani.

What has occurred in Diani over the past one hundred years is not unique to the East African coast or even to Africa; similar processes have been under way across the planet, especially in areas close to attractive beaches. The past twenty years in particular have witnessed a global rush for beachfront property, facilitated by the movement of capital and people from the global north to the global south. These real estate shifts have profoundly affected local populations and brought into contact individuals and groups from a wide range of cultural and socioeconomic backgrounds. Reviewing Diani's history of gentrification can provide background and insights relevant to comprehending the range of limitations and opportunities that structure the area's sociocultural landscape today. This chapter first recounts the colonial and early postindependence history of landownership in both Kenya and Diani that laid the groundwork for more recent developments. Then it focuses on tourism and real estate developments of the past fifty years. Oral history accounts from a wide range of individuals living in Diani as well as various supporting sources provide details regarding the economic, social, and demographic changes occurring during this period. They also acknowledge in particular the role of Germans in building Diani's tourism infrastructure and in creating the real estate market—and thus in bringing about substantial shifts in landownership.

Gentrification 1: The Colonial Period

The East African coast has been inhabited from Somalia to Mozambique since before the first century of the first millennium, with most settlements situated close to the coastline and on the adjacent islands, such as Lamu, Pemba, and Zanzibar (Unguja).[10] The area flourished through the Indian Ocean trade and other trading networks that encompassed an area stretching "from the Great Lakes of central Africa to the islands of Indonesia and to China, and from Europe to southern Mozambique."[11] This trading system brought a wide range of civilizations, ethnicities, and religions into contact through mercantile activity.[12] One result of this interaction and the main component of the coastal culture past and present is the Swahili society, with its roots in African, Arab, Indian, and other cultures and with a long history of shared linguistic, cultural, religious, legal, and social practices and points of reference.[13] From the ninth century onward, economic ties were especially close with Oman, Aden, Yemen, and Hadhramaut.[14] Early archaeological evidence of settlement in the Diani area is the Kongo Mosque, also known as the Diani Persian or Shirazi Mosque, which is associated with Shirazi settlers who built it in the sixteenth century and which is said to have been in use without interruption since then.[15]

The Portuguese arrived on the coast in 1498 and dominated it—with intermittent challenges from the British and Ottomans throughout—until Omani rulers, in response to a petition by the Town of Mombasa, reestablished "coastal Islamic sovereignty" over the area in the late seventeenth century.[16] The Mazrui Omanis who first came as *liwalis* (governors) in 1698 held power for 139 years.[17] They ruled Mombasa and other areas of the coast independently from Oman until they were ousted in the 1830s by the al-Busaidi dynasty. After the departure of the Mazrui, the al-Busaidis ruled the Kenyan and Tanzanian coast, including Zanzibar, which became the seat of the sultan of Zanzibar after a split between Omani and East African al-Busaidis. As we will see, however, the Mazrui dynasty continued to play a role in the political life along the coast.

In addition to Swahili society, the other major constitutive component of the coastal population are the Mijikenda peoples, who are spread out along the coast between Somalia and Tanzania.[18] According to Mijikenda traditions, some time in the sixteenth and seventeenth centuries several groups of peoples who migrated away from territories in the north moved into the coastal areas of Kenya. Most often the common ancestral place is identified as Singwaya or Shungwaya. These groups are today known as the Mijikenda, a confederation of nine ethnic groups. As Justin Willis has shown, however, this term dates back to the 1930s and is thus a relatively recent invention; the question of their common origin and migration mythology remains contested.[19]

The Digo, who inhabit the south coast (and live in other locations of Kwale County and Tanzania), are, in their current self-representation, one of the nine ethnic groups associated with the Mijikenda. They settled in fortified *kayas* (sacred areas and homesteads) on the south coast during the sixteenth century and founded Kaya Kwale in Shimba Hills.[20] At the time, new arrivals on the south coast had to negotiate coexistence with the Shirazi, whose settlements were part of the Shirazi network along the East African coast.[21] The second kaya was Kaya Kinondo, just south of the Diani area and north of Gazi.[22] By the late sixteenth century, the south coast was tied to one of the *Thelatha Taifa* (Three Tribes, or Nations) of Mombasa, the Kilindini, who "were in the possession of Ukunda, a mainland district considerably to the south of the city."[23] The Kilindini, according to F. J. Berg, "claim to have been part of the exodus of Nyika and other groups from Shungwaya."[24] Tradition identifies them as the first of the Mijikenda groups who settled in Mombasa and, relevant for the history of Diani, the first with a connection to the south coast.[25] During the seventeenth century, the Digo spread out and founded villages in the larger area of Kwale and other south coast locations.[26] The presence of the Portuguese until the late seventeenth century disrupted the coastal trading networks, and the coastal economy declined until the area saw a recovery under Mazrui rule. In response to the stable period under the Mazrui and then the expanse of trade during the nineteenth century, the Digo and other Mijikenda peoples dispersed throughout the area, living in villages of often up to one thousand and more inhabitants.[27] As a result of expanding economic opportunities, the Digo population swelled during the nineteenth century, and some Digo leaders, such as Mwakikonga and Abdallah Mwaketa, became powerful players in trade and politics.[28]

There is much fluidity between Mijikenda and Swahili societies, as the two groups interacted with one another and with the hinterland and various trading communities. At the end of the nineteenth century, British and, to the south, German colonizers came into this situation. The coastal area attained a special status under colonial rule, as the sultan of Zanzibar controlled a strip of sixteen kilometers, called the "ten-mile strip," inland along the coast even after the arrival of the British and Germans, and even after Zanzibar—as a result of the 1890 Heligoland-Zanzibar Treaty between the British and the Germans—became a British protectorate.[29] Five years later, the British also declared Kenya its protectorate, and in a treaty that same year with the sultan of Zanzibar, they leased the administration of the coastal strip.[30] The agreement "enabled the British Government to take over administration and protection of the ten-mile strip from the Imperial British East Africa Company (IBEAC), to whom the Sultan had leased this territory in 1888."[31] The Diani area was part of this coastal strip that was under the nominal sovereignty of the sultan of Zanzibar throughout the British colonial period.

But this arrangement did not go uncontested. As James Brennan points out: "the treaty also represented Britain's ubiquitous reliance upon collaborative authorities. . . . Pre-colonial Zanzibari titles such as *liwali* (governor), *mudir* (lieutenant), and *kadhi* (court judge), which had been fluid appointments along the coast, became formalized administrative offices within the new Protectorate, remaining nominally part of the Sultan's civil service."[32] Segments of the Arab and Swahili elite were thus integrated into the colonial power structure, while other coastal leaders were marginalized. As a result, Brennan states, "realizing the loss of local autonomy, some coastal leaders in 1895 took up political resistance against IBEAC and British encroachment after the latter clumsily intervened in a local office succession dispute."[33] Anger at missionary activities among the Muslim population of the area and British abolitionist activities were also among the factors feeding the rebellion.[34] At its center was Sheikh Mbaruk bin Rashid bin Salim el Mazrui, the son of the last Mazrui governor of Mombasa who had been deposed in 1837 when Zanzibari competitors put an end to Mazrui rule. As T. H. R. Cashmore points out, "the disaster of 1837 was not, however, the end of the Mazrui as a force in the politics of the east coast."[35] In fact, the Mazrui have remained a political reality in Kenya and beyond; these days, they mostly fight with the pen. Alamin Mazrui especially has advocated on behalf of the Swahili and the Mijikenda.[36]

For the better part of the second half of the nineteenth century, Sheikh Mbaruk bin Rashid battled the sultan, other members of the Mazrui clan, various local leaders, and, after several years of cooperation, the British.[37] Mbaruk was first based in Gazi, on the coast south of Mombasa, where some of the Mazrui had located after they had been expelled from Mombasa. The fact that the Gazi Mazrui had "allied themselves with the Digo" is relevant with regard to our understanding of Diani and its place in the *longue durée* of events on the coast.[38] In fact, the Mazruis' struggle against the British and the Omani sultanate was largely supported by the Mijikenda and other groups of the area for economic and political reasons, though with the impending defeat of the rebellion, many changed sides.[39] Even groups of runaway slaves supported what has become known as the Mazrui Rebellion, despite the fact that Mbaruk, like other Mazruis, used slave labor on his plantations and was also said to engage in slave trading.[40]

The Mazrui Rebellion marks but one chapter in the history of attempts to insist on local rule along the coast. Here, we should acknowledge that the coastal region needs to be understood beyond the boundaries of today's nation-states. At the same time that Mbaruk and others revolted in what is Kenya today, coastal leaders to the south, in today's Tanzania, fought against not only the Germans, but also the Omanis and other members of the local elite who had teamed up with the invading colonizer. In fact, as Jonathon Glassman points out for the Tanzanian case, "At the root of the uprising lay not so much resentment of the German Company [the German East Africa Company] but deep internal tensions that had been mounting for decades: the indebtedness of the patricians and their political marginalization at the hands of the Omani Sultanate; conflicts over the status of slaves; the insistent demands of villagers and upcountry folk for more active roles within the urban communities."[41] These factors also played a role in the northern part of the East African coast.

The Kenyan anti-British rebellion of 1895–1896, instigated by an alliance of coastal leaders among whom Mbaruk only gradually emerged as the prominent force, was crushed by units of the newly formed East Africa Rifles. In fact, the Mazrui Rebellion was a factor in the establishment of this military organization, which became part of the King's African Rifles in 1902.[42] Originally recruited by the British from among "Zanzibaris, Sudanese, Indians, and ex-slaves," the East Africa Rifles later also drew upon other coastal Muslims and a wide range of Kenyans, some of whom joined voluntarily; others were coerced into service by their chiefs.[43] As historian H. Moyse-Bartlett writes, "Mbaruk and about 3,000 rebels had crossed into Germany territory. On 20th April 1,100 of them, of whom 600 were armed, surrendered to Major von Wissmann."[44] Mbaruk lived out his days under German protection near Dar es Salaam where he died in 1910. The repercussions of the months of fighting along the entire coast were grave: the British "victory was gained at the cost of wholesale devastation and disorganization."[45]

The coast was thus affected by the overall developments in Kenya, even if—per the administrative agreement with the sultan of Zanzibar—the area remained a "protectorate" and did not become Crown colony territory, as the rest of Kenya became in 1920. In reality, the British had access to most land on the coast through the 1895 agreement; as Willis points out, "there was for several years no system of land registration or survey," a situation that "coincided with a considerable boom in land sales" and led to fraud of all kinds.[46] The desire to control land in the entire protectorate generated a series of land-grabbing ordinances. A first step was to claim land that was "waste and unoccupied" through the East African (Lands) Order-in-Council in 1901, which gave "the Commissioner of the Protectorate power to dispose of all public lands on such terms and conditions as he might think fit."[47] The 1902 Crown Lands Ordinance brought additional detail to the measure by asserting that "the Crown and not the local people had original title to some land, however vaguely defined," which in effect was the precondition for the exploitation of Kenya's resources.[48]

Quickly, European settlers started claiming land the same year "in an ad hoc and irregular manner," as David Anderson has put it. "Farms were pegged out on the ground and occupied by the settlers long before any proper survey could be completed, and before any formal title deed was issued."[49] The 1902 ordinance made it possible to issue freehold titles, which the settlers especially desired, and long-term leases. Only a few years later, the Land Titles Ordinance of 1908 and the Crown Lands Ordinance of 1915 went even farther by eliminating a number of restrictions that protected the rights of the native population and now included land that was occupied by the native population under the umbrella of "Crown Land." The most salient aspect with regard to our discussion of Diani is that the Land Titles Ordinance of 1908 not only privileged individual ownership but also defined individual ownership according to British law. The ordinance ignored both the longstanding customary use of land by groups of villagers for communal activities, such as hunting and farming, but also indigenous practices that regulated individual landownership. The 1915 Crown Lands Ordinance "declared all land in the protectorate Crown Land and therefore subject to the Governor's power of alienation" and "gave settlers not simply leases in place of licences but 999-year leases."[50] H. W. O. Okoth-Ogendo writes that "the effect of the Crown Lands Ordinance, 1915, coupled with the change from protectorate to colony status in 1920, was to render Africans mere tenants at the will of the Crown."[51] A 1919 ordinance introduced a system of title registration, and with this legislation, "the disinheritance of the natives within the framework of colonial law was complete."[52]

The establishment of native reserves, which originated with the Masai treaty of August 1904, was another step in dispossessing the indigenous population of its land.[53] Seemingly designed "to protect African rights to land," it allowed the colonial state to move the native population from areas that settlers desired to less desirable areas and to control the space on which the native population lived.[54] In 1921, a reserve was established for the Mijikenda; it was divided into Northern Nyika Reserve and Southern Nyika Reserve. As Mambo states, "The southern Nyika reserve in Kwale district occupied 1934 square miles [5,009 square kilometers] out of a total area of 3052 square miles [7,905 square kilometers]. The difference, that is 1118 square miles [2,896 square kilometers,] was . . . set aside as crownland or for the use of 'non-natives.'"[55] Much of the reserve land in Kwale was, and still is, "unsuitable for crop agriculture," so the Digo left the reserve to settle in the more fertile areas closer to the coast.[56] This struggle over arable land became central to relations between settlers and the Digo (and throughout Kenya). Until 1926, reserve areas were redrawn in various ways to accommodate settler needs and, following the South African model, were "important landmarks in the development of rural segregation."[57] The South Nyika Digo Reserve area was gazetted in 1926. In 1930, a Native Lands Trust Board was established to administer the reserves, and it consolidated the various population movements into fourteen land units called "native reserves."[58]

In addition to the realities created by the establishment of reserves, how did the various ordinances issued during the early phase of British colonial rule affect the landownership situation on the south coast specifically? Most research on colonial rule in Kenya has focused on the highlands, and data about the coast is not as rich, especially when it comes to issues related to landownership. But several excellent studies allow for a better understanding of processes that structure these issues on the coast today. Karuti Kanyinga writes that the 1902 ordinance was not designed to regulate landownership on the coast "because it was assumed that private property rights had been institutionalized through the practice of Muslim law and Arab custom."[59] But over time, the various British ordinances, especially those of 1908 and 1915, greatly affected landownership on the coast as well.

First, crucial to understanding the early phase of British colonial rule and the emergence of the colonial economy on the coast, is the process that led to the disempowerment of both Arab and Swahili landowners and the local peasantry. As we have seen, the British state made an extraordinary effort to reach out to the local Arab and Swahili elite, some of whom became official and powerful collaborators. Other measures, however, challenged their economic status. The abolition of slavery (October 1, 1907) was certainly an effective public relations tool, but even though it came with all kinds of privileges for former slaveholders, who, for example, had the right to be reimbursed for their loss of slaves, it ensured that Arab and Swahili landowners "lost the ability to use that land through the control of a labor force."[60] Ultimately, by abolishing slavery, the British hoped to enable the emergence of a capitalist economy, and that abolishment did in fact facilitate massive shifts in production and ownership practices.[61] But—and here the situation on the coast of Kenya in the early part of the twentieth century foreshadows some of what occurred in postcolonial African countries—the process of capitalistic development remained slow.[62]

On the coast, squatters (often ex-slaves) and Mijikenda (among them the Digo) did not hold freehold titles to the land they farmed, and, as Frederick Cooper highlights, "the tension between title holders and squatters helped move the coastal economy into a state of paralysis."[63] Many slaves migrated away from the plantations to, for example, Mombasa, which—with its eminent port—had become a hub for colonial activities. Overall, freed slaves added significant numbers to the group of landless squatters. They were able to farm the land if they had permission of the landlords, but few owned the land themselves.[64]

Britain hoped to promote European development of the coastal area by issuing freehold titles to individuals.[65] Such titles were incompatible with the wide range of customary African land use practices and legal categories, which did not correspond to British notions of individual private ownership.[66] Importantly, however, in addition to communal land use, private use of land was also permitted and regulated under customary law.[67] According to Digo tradition, as recorded at the beginning of the twentieth century, "all land (*mitsanga*) belongs to God, grass (*vuwe*) belongs to the occupier of the land," that is, ownership was established through usage and regarded that which grew on the land.[68] Those who established ownership through usage at times rented out parts of their land.[69] While such records could have opened the door to a discussion over diverse conceptions regarding landownership, they instead essentially contributed to sustaining the myth that indigenous peoples had no system of landownership—notwithstanding the fact that under this system, which focused on land use, individuals owned the land they used according to regulations set up by elders. The notion that "land belongs to God" was especially cited often to advance the idea that locals did not have a concept of landownership comparable to European conventions.[70] The lack of written documentation also contributed to this perception.[71]

Pursuing the European capitalist script of development, the British sought to stimulate the economy by pushing for the privatization of land. Most important in our context is the effect of several ordinances, such as the previously mentioned Land Titles Ordinance of 1908, on the local peasantry. As Cooper writes, "the 1908 ordinance required the claimant to any plot in the coastal zone to produce documentary or oral evidence that he had obtained the land through purchase, clearing of bush, or inheritance, and that it had not been abandoned."[72] Cases brought to court by the Nine Nations and the Three Nations of Mombasa that argued for communal tenure, however, were overwhelmingly rejected.[73] After 1915, communal tenure claims were no longer permitted; only individuals were allowed to file claims. Indigenous groups were thus deprived of claiming the largest areas of land they used.[74] After several years of surveying, title hearings began in 1914. The approved titled land claims (mostly approved on the basis of inheritance, not through purchase) of the Nine Nations and the Three Nations were disproportionally low compared with those of other groups.[75] It is especially noteworthy in light of later developments that, as Cooper points out, "with the Twelve Tribes—more so than with Arabs—the tendency was to sell off farmland, undermining the potential for agriculture and self-sufficiency of these groups."[76] Most of the land was bought by Europeans and Indians. This tendency continued after independence and continues to this day and clearly contributes to the overall disempowerment of the local Mijikenda and other groups who traditionally lived off agriculture and fishing.[77] While, as Willis points out, in the eyes of "people at the time . . . the penetration of capital offered . . . welcome alternatives," some of the opportunities that were pursued, such as selling land, reduced the economic and social power base of locals in the long run—then as much as today.[78]

With conditions thus pitted in favor of individual landownership and against the communal claims of the Nine and Three Nations in Mombasa and the Mijikenda along the coast, the south coast saw new owners come into the area. Sales occurred even though the land on the south coast had not been surveyed.[79] The leading developer in the Diani area during the early decades of colonial rule was East African Estates Ltd., one of the largest British colonial companies operating in Kenya at the time. Cooper calls "the concession of 260,000 acres [approximately 105,000 hectares] of land south of Mombasa made by the Government to East African Estates in 1908 . . . the biggest embarrassment of all." This was embarrassing for the British government because much of the land was left uncultivated, was badly managed, and was "used by squatters."[80] In the early 1930s, Jomo Kenyatta wrote the following about the company: "One of the largest plantation companies in Kenya is the East African Estates, Ltd. It has a paid-up capital of £260,000 and owns 350,000 acres [141,640 hectares], including valuable land near the port of Mombasa. It also owns nearly the whole of the share capital of Central Coffee Nairobi Estates, Ltd."[81] Cooper's and Kenyatta's differing figures regarding the acreage allotted to the company reflect the fact that the company had to return 100,000 acres (40,469 hectares) in 1915, because "the lease was granted 'subject to native rights,' which were found to be so extensive that the grant was reduced."[82] Other companies who bought large areas of land along the coast were Magarini Estates, British East Africa Rubber, Cotton Estates, Boustead & Clarke Ltd., and the British East Africa Corporation.[83] Even "before the official grant of 250,000 acres [101,171 hectares], East African Estates was already cultivating rubber and sisal as far south as Shimoni. By 1913 the Gasi Rubber and Fibre Estates had 1005 acres [407 hectares] under rubber."[84]

East African Estates thus owned a vast area of land that "stretched [along] the entire south coast including most of Diani Beach."[85] In fact, the original concession amounted to about one-sixth of what was to become the South Nyika Digo Reserve, which closely matches with the area of today's Kwale County. In comparison, according to David Anderson, the area that was claimed from Europeans by the Kikuyus in the 1930s and that would later become the impetus for the Mau Mau Uprising against the British (1952–1960) comprised only 60,000 acres (24,281 hectares).[86] East African Estates was indeed still present in the memory of one of the older Indian inhabitants of Diani. The only person I interviewed who mentioned the name of the company, Alibhai Khan, was in his eighties when we spoke in 2012 (he died in 2014). He had grown up in Ukunda and suggested that the 1930s was the first significant period of development in Diani, although some activity had already occurred earlier, especially after the Land Titles Ordinance of 1908. According to Khan, East African Estates developed parts of the land, mostly along the beach and then from the beach inland, and sold it to white settlers in parcels of 12 acres (almost 5 hectares). In addition, "large tracts of land in Diani Beach were also leased to an Afrikaner, Johannes Theodorus Oberholzer, for agricultural purposes, on a 99-year lease."[87] According to another source, the person who was selling land at the time was a Mr. Rayner, a British man, who bought from East African Estates and then subdivided the plots.[88] During the 1920s and 1930s, a number of smaller residences for British settlers were built along the beachfront.

One measure of the role of East African Estates on the south coast and also for the limited nature of activities at the time are transactions recorded in the Kenya Blue Books.[89] Entries in the categories of, among others, "Return of farm lands and township plots granted," some of which were reverted to Crown Land, list a wide range of transactions each year from 1933 to 1938 in upcountry areas (such as Nairobi, Kisumu, and Thika) and fewer transactions for Mombasa and the north coast. Only two entries indicate transactions on the south coast during this period. Both times, the owner of the plot was East African Estates Ltd., which gave up one plot in 1935, in "Digo District," for the extension of a school in Waa, and another one in 1938, when it surrendered a plot for a "Wireless Station site in Likoni."[90]

One of the settlers who bought land in the 1920s was Maxwell Trench (1884–1969), a white Jamaican. He built what became known as the Diani Banda, which was turned into the Jadini in 1937, a hotel that still exists (but is currently closed) and is generally acknowledged as the first hotel in the area.[91] Maxwell and his son Daniel Trench (1919–1991) are mentioned in James Fox's *White Mischief* (1982), which chronicles the events surrounding the murder of Josslyn Victor Hay, Earl of Erroll, in 1941 and reveals the activities of the British upper crust in Kenya's "Happy Valley" during the colonial period.[92] In fact, Dan Trench made headlines again in 2007 when a tape he had recorded revealed the final bits of information that solved the murder mystery.[93] Development on the Diani coast is closely related to the creation of this hotel, which was, in turn, a first step toward the formation of the larger tourism infrastructure in the area. The next hotel to be built was the Sandy Beach (or Sandibay, both names were mentioned) Hotel, which later became the Trade Winds and was built by Corny Trench, a brother of Maxwell's, in the 1940s. The Trade Winds was used as a resting place for British marines during the 1940s. Diani Beach Hotel was also built in the 1940s and bought by a Mr. and Mrs. Fish, who were from South Africa and renamed the hotel "Two Fishes." The war disrupted further economic development, and at around 1946 Mr. and Mrs. Fish left the area, and sold their hotel to George Plumb.

Even before the war, visitors and tourists on the coast did not generally come from Europe, but rather from within Kenya and from East Africa and South Africa. Alibhai Khan suggested that the British did not want anybody to visit. He also recalled British attempts to introduce a version of apartheid through dress codes and other means. He remembered that wearing a suit was required at the cinemas in order to keep Africans and Indians out (but he also recalled situations when Indians and Africans dressed in suits and had to be allowed in). Khan's memory accords with what is known about the affinity of segments of Kenya's white elite for the South African model. The attempts to segregate Africans by moving them to reserves and the measures undertaken to deny them political representation were accompanied by license to violence on the interpersonal level, all of which echoed the extreme racism characteristic of South African practices.[94] The use of these practices in Kenya was to some extent facilitated by settlers with roots in South Africa, as this group made up a significant portion of colonial settlers in Kenya. As Brett Shadle points out, "especially in the early years many Kenya settlers hailed from South Africa and brought with them their own peculiar ideas about race and violence."[95] In fact, Robert Coryndon, the second governor of Kenya (1922–1925), was born in South Africa.[96] It is often forgotten that Indians (who by the 1920s outnumbered the white population by about 100 percent) were also affected by colonial racism and organized to challenge the British colonial system.[97] The white settler community, however, only intensified its ruthless rule over time. Even after World War II, as David Anderson writes, "the white settlers vigorously campaigned against enhanced political representation for Africans, pushed themselves into key roles in the management of the colonial economy, and tightened their grip over local and municipal government."[98]

By the 1930s, then, real estate development was well under way on the south coast, involving land that had been grabbed from the indigenous population; the fishing villages of Diani, for example, predate the real estate developments that began with the Land Titles Ordinance of 1908, and the descendants of their inhabitants are the original landowners of the area. The alienation of land in other parts of the country contributed to a growing crisis for Kenyans, who either lived on reserves or became squatters or worked as tenants for European settlers. Colonial reports from the period document the astounding disconnect between official discourse and local reality. As the acting governor wrote about one of his tours in the 1920s, "I was very much struck by the spirit of content and happiness which prevailed amongst all the native tribes."[99] But land alienation, settlement schemes, the establishment of reserves, taxes that forced Africans to work for colonial landlords, and insidious labor law policies attest to a different reality.[100] By the 1930s, the amount of dispossession of Kenyan farmers and the comprehensive oppression of African Kenyans and Asian Kenyans reached explosive levels. In 1932, the Kenya Land Commission assessed the situation in the colony, but the commission's 1934 report did not satisfy the demands of Kikuyus and others; rather, it confirmed European titles deeds and offered low-quality land in compensation to some. As Anderson writes, "Instead of righting the wrongs of earlier policies, as Kikuyus must have hoped, the Land Commission effectively extinguished all African claims to lands occupied by whites."[101]

What do we know about the Digo population in Diani at the time when the first touristic buildings went up on the south coast? According to figures in the 1933 Kenya Blue Book (based on the March 1931 census), the population in the "Digo area" was 54,772 in an area of 3,027 square miles (7,839 square kilometers) of land, with an additional 25 square miles (64.75 square kilometers) of water area. The "nonnative population" consisted of 27 European men, 9 European women, 346 Asiatic men, and 270 Asiatic women. The population density for Digo Land is given as 17.9 people per square mile (roughly 7 people per square kilometer).[102] Figures for "South Nyika and Digo detached areas" are given as 25,513 Digo and 23,005 Duruma living in a reserve of 1,903 square miles (4,929 square kilometers) of land area; that is, most of the indigenous population—according to these data—lived in the reserve area, which made up roughly two-thirds of the entire area, with the rest of the land, as previously noted, designated for settlers.[103] The area of today's Kwale County is 8,270 square kilometers and thus more or less corresponds to the area listed by the British as "Digo area." In 2009, 649,931 people lived in Kwale County, and the population density was listed as 79 per square kilometer.[104] However, historical evidence and colonial reports about Digo movement away from reserves toward the coast suggest that a significant concentration of Digo lived in settlements along the coast before and during the colonial period.[105] Gazi and other locations had been known as seats of local power and commerce for centuries. Archaeological evidence, such as the Kongo Mosque in the northern part of Diani and Kaya Kinondo just to the south of Diani, indicates settlement of the Diani area for more than five hundred years. The nature of the Diani beach (considered the most beautiful beach of Kenya), the fertile soil of the area, the fact of sufficient rainfall east of the Shimba Hills, and the advantages of the reef for fishing are factors that encouraged habitation of the area. Various sources document the existence of fishing villages in Diani before the beginning of British-driven development at the beginning of the twentieth century.[106] I restate this point here because in my interviews with German developers, I have come across some who were of the opinion that "there were no Digo" (da gab es keine Digo) in Diani, even when referring to the 1980s. When development began in the 1930s, the area had already been inhabited by the Digo, Swahili peoples, and other groups for centuries.

Political consciousness and a willingness to organize grew among the coastal peoples, and during the 1940s several advocacy organizations formed, among them the Digo Welfare Association, founded in 1945.[107] By the early 1950s, Kenya was embroiled in the struggle for independence, and while the Diani area was far away from the main activities, all Kenyans felt the repercussions of the hostilities, especially the state of emergency that lasted from 1952 to 1959. As A. I. Salim points out, however, even though "upcountry politics" echoed in the Digo area, "when the emergency was declared, only one Mdigo [Digo] was deemed deserving of arrest." Shortly afterwards, the political activities of the Utsi Society, a Digo organization that was founded in the 1940s to oppose colonial rule, prompted more arrests and attempts at intimidation, reflecting an increase in confrontation also on the south coast.[108]

Various measures that characterized the transition to independent Kenya, especially the outcome of land transfer schemes, affected developments on the coast as well, albeit in distinct ways. In 1960, Britain agreed to Kenya's independence, although the details of how it was to be achieved were still to be defined. One central issue concerned alienated land that white settlers occupied. When the British anticipated the end of their rule in the highly priced colony, they developed a plan that would ensure British settlers be "reimbursed" for their losses in real estate; they also exerted a tremendous control over population movements, which continues to haunt the country. The focus was the Kenyan highlands, known at the time as the White Highlands. Less than half of Kenya's land is arable, and about one-third to one-half of that arable land is in the highlands.[109] Most of the expropriated land that the British government had distributed or sold to Europeans (often for nominal fees and often after settlers had already occupied the land) was in that area, to the extent that a significant portion of arable land was in the hands of white settlers who made up less than 1 percent of the population.[110] Settlers did not want to give up their treasured possessions easily. As Christopher Leo describes the plans before independence: "in short order, the authorities set out to develop a government-assisted program for the transfer of land from European to African hands. The program evolved, in stages, into a number of schemes aimed at different groups and designed to meet different needs. The most important and best known of these was the massive Million-Acre-Settlement Scheme . . . which . . . subsequently became a corner-stone of post-colonial land policy."[111]

As Leo demonstrates, the first phase of this scheme, with Kenya still under colonial rule, benefited "those who had been loyal to the colonial regime." The second phase, which Leo identifies as "neocolonial," "expanded the scheme to offer benefits to Africans of all classes and political tendencies." The most shocking aspect of this land transfer is that it was financed as a "development project, an international aid program with funds from the World Bank and the Colonial Development Corporation (CDC). . . . Africans would be lent money to enable them to buy European [i.e., European-occupied] land."[112] Some of these loans were provided by West Germany.[113] The various loan programs enforced a massive debt on Kenya on the eve of independence; it made up more than "a third of all the foreign debt incurred between 1961 and 1969."[114] In addition to the effect on the national debt, the programs, which resettled about half a million people (about 4 percent of the population) on about 4 percent of arable land (some of it of low quality),[115] significantly affected interethnic relations: "The settlement program not only reaffirmed and hardened existing ethnic boundaries, but in fact reintroduced ethnic uniformity in areas where mixing had already taken place spontaneously."[116] In addition, the settlement schemes created the material basis for Kenya's political elite.[117]

Although some critics realized the future effect of the land settlement schemes at the time, others—especially those writing from a colonial perspective—were blind to the long-term repercussions. But soon after independence, the issue of land was raised again, and it has remained the most important topic in Kenyan politics, emerging as the root cause for much violent conflict.[118] Calls for reform of the status quo date back to the first decade after independence and highlighted the centrality of the issue.[119] Gary Wasserman stressed in 1976 that "consenting to the validity of land titles and to land transfers was the linchpin to the nationalists' acceptance of the continuity of the colonial system and their own role in maintaining that continuity."[120] Over and over, politicians, scholars, and writers warned of the consequences if the issue was not addressed. Report after report acknowledged the urgency of the issue. Political activists and writers of fiction, such as Ngugi wa Thiong'o, contributed to the discussion; autobiographies were another vehicle for voicing complaints, especially among those who fought in the Mau Mau Uprising. As David Maughan-Brown points out, "the desire for land is the one common denominator in all the accounts of 'Mau Mau' aims to be found in the autobiographies of the forest fighters."[121] All the while, postindependence land-grabbing practices, as will be seen, ensured that the issue continued to be the most sensitive one in Kenyan politics.

The situation regarding landownership at the coast, however, was different compared with other areas of Kenya. The status of the ten-mile strip, which was distinct because of the 1895 treaty with the sultan of Zanzibar, was negotiated separately. In 1961, Commissioner James W. Robertson submitted a report to the British secretary of state and the sultan titled "The Kenya Coastal Strip." The report was based on a significant number of interviews and reviewed the history as well as the current situation in light of the "constitutional development in East Africa."[122] The main question was whether the coastal strip was to retain separate status or was to be integrated into the emerging Kenya. The report acknowledged factors that were described as the "ingredients of an explosive situation" and recommended integration, albeit with a series of "safeguards" that included, among others, continued nominal sovereignty of the sultan (mostly for cultural reasons), a Coast Land Board, and several measures for ensuring the legal, cultural, and educational needs of Muslims.[123] Integration was in fact favored by the Mijikenda as well; as Mambo states, "growing African nationalist sentiment was opposed to seeing this strip handed back to the sultan," a stance represented most vocally on the coast by Robert Gideon Ngala, among others.[124] In his report, Robertson suggested that colonial rule had "created a sense of oneness of the Coastal Strip with Kenya"; at the same time, he also stressed that "there is a strong feeling on the coast that the needs of its people have received scant attention from the Government in Nairobi."[125] This sentiment was only to increase in postindependence Kenya. The coast was, as we know, integrated into Kenya, but most of the recommendations of the commissioner, some of which indicate an awareness of the distinct realities of the coastal population, were not enacted.

Gentrification 2: Postindependence

Perhaps the most astounding dimension of postindependence approaches to landownership in Kenya more generally—and here we can acknowledge the connection between larger developments and those at the coast—lies in the significant continuity of policies developed under the colonial regime and during the transition in independent Kenya, including certain legal restraints, settlement schemes, alienation of land, and landlessness among the peasantry.[126] Collectively, these four issues are the key contributing factors leading to the second phase of gentrification in Diani. First, after independence, the legal framework did not address the overall landownership issues resulting from British colonialism, especially shifts from communal tenure and customary notions of ownership to private ownership as defined by the British.[127] Second, new settlement schemes resettled individuals from one area of Kenya to another. These schemes were intended to turn landless into landowning individuals and communities, but repercussions often included tensions with those who greeted their new neighbors with ambivalence. Third, the government, from Kenyatta to the most recent period, alienated land and distributed it to various favorites, thereby increasing the economic power base of the new elite. Complaints about land grabbing became central to political strife. Fourth, the high number of landless peasants has remained a significant problem. All of these factors have been acknowledged as contributing to the violent clashes the country has seen, especially in connection with elections; a recent study by Kathleen Klaus provides much evidence for the connection between land rights claims and election violence.[128]

In the Diani area, these four issues have a visible effect to this day. Regarding the first (the insufficient legal framework), after independence, all titles on the coast were to be upheld. But large areas were not titled, so those who used the land were doing so without a title, setting the stage for various abuses. In fact, the delay in approaching the issue of landownership was significant; "as late as ten years after Independence, a committee was appointed that had to advise on land ownership in the ten-mile coastal strip."[129] Regarding new settlement schemes, two of the seven existing schemes in Kwale District are in Diani—the Ukunda Settlement Scheme (1968) and the Diani Settlement Scheme (1978). It is noteworthy that the plots distributed through the schemes did not go exclusively to local squatters; although the majority of the recipients were Digo from Diani, others came from adjacent areas, such as Tiwi and Mbuguni, but also from farther away in the Coast Province.[130] These schemes were part of the government's attempt to "cope with the increasing squatter problem and to bring mismanaged or unused tracts of land into use."[131] The intended outcome of land distribution was in most cases "to improve food security and alleviate malnutrition."[132] Several research reports highlight the benefits of the settlement schemes in terms of higher household income, decrease in poverty, and increase in food consumption.[133] In the case of the Diani scheme, which allocated plots as individual holdings, success was limited; many plots were left unoccupied "because two sides of the scheme border the access road to the local beach hotels and many plots were acquired for speculative purposes."[134] These speculative purposes, as we will see, involved a number of German developers.

In addition to the settlement schemes, transactions occurred during President Kenyatta's rule that allowed preferred parties to acquire beach plots and adjacent areas. According to John Kamau, "only Eliud Mahihu, the then Coast Provincial Commissioner, would identify and recommend those who qualified to acquire such plots. And as was expected, nearly all his nominees were highly placed members of the political class and a few well connected businessmen."[135] From Lamu to Malindi and Diani, Kenya's political and economic elite continued the land-grabbing tradition on the coast. There was even an attempt to integrate the sale of these plots and other plots "into the World Bank funded Million Acre Scheme—which was an illegality."[136] As it turns out, the Kenyan case proves what Frantz Fanon anticipated with astute clarity, namely, that the greed and other destructive qualities of the national postindependence bourgeoisie were to wreak havoc on the independent country.[137]

Along the Diani coast, beachfront plots were sold to influential upcountry players, and during this period villagers effectively lost their claims to such property. According to villagers, residents of Mwakamba, Mvumoni, Mwaroni, Mwamambi, Mkwakwani, and Magutu each used to claim beachfront land but lost access to that land first when it was distributed to various individuals after independence and then again when hotel development began on the stretch—when Leopard Beach Resort, Leisure Lodge Hotel, and other hotels were built. Villagers did not have title deeds for the land they had used for centuries. Kenya's beaches, however, are public, and the villagers continue to have access to the sea and continue to pursue fishing. They also sell carvings and other items to tourists on the beach and take tourists on their boats to the reef; to some degree, the beach remains divided among members of the various villages.

In my exploration to assess what remains in the collective memory of long-time Diani residents about the past, almost all locals were aware of the awarding of land to upcountry politicians. The recipients were, according to most voices, individuals who had been active in the Mau Mau Uprising, mostly allies of Kenyatta. Invoking Mau Mau memoirs in conjunction with claims to power and legitimacy has a considerable currency in Kenya, but fact and fiction are often hard to distinguish. While some beneficiaries of beach plots, such as James Njenga Karume, claimed a Mau Mau legacy legitimately, most of the recipients of the prime real estate had nothing to do with Mau Mau activities. As Marshall S. Clough points out, among the group of allies that Kenyatta formed in 1962 and 1963, "there was no one in this inner circle from the Mau Mau movement. . . . For the most part . . . Kenyatta would keep Mau Mau and the Kikuyu populism it represented at a distance."[138]

Despite considerable outrage, these land transfers nonetheless continued. In the 1970s, some of the plots that Kenyan politicians had acquired ultimately were turned into hot spots for the development of tourism. Interestingly, some of the favors also benefited former colonialists who had chosen to remain in Kenya, such as Jackie and John Bland, who acquired a plot in Diani and for years ran a deep-sea fishing business and rented out cottages to tourists.[139] On the southern end of Diani beach, Kenneth Matiba acquired several plots, including the land that contained the Jadini Hotel that had originally been developed by Maxwell Trench. The plot had been sold to Heath Robinson in 1969, and when Robinson died, Kenneth Matiba flew to London to meet with the executor of the estate and bought the Jadini in 1970.[140] In fact, he acquired the hotel together with Stephen G. Smith and Enoch Malmqvist, with whom Matiba formed Anglo-Kenya-Inns, which later became Alliance Hotels.[141] After a brief hiatus following Kenyatta's death in 1978, President Daniel arap Moi continued the policy of preferential treatment for those seeking beachfront property.[142]

I was interested to know how locals perceive and would comment on the land-grabbing practices, as well as the legal sales since independence. In addition to the connections residents generally made to Mau Mau fighters as beneficiaries of land transfers, longtime residents of the area were able to provide details, including names, regarding particular cases. Similarly, facts regarding controversial sales of land during the 1980s and 1990s, discussed below, are widely known, including names of key figures. Some narratives, however, reflect a certain degree of confusion, especially regarding the period immediately after independence. An older resident (in his eighties) had a relatively positive memory of Kenyatta. He claimed that Kenyatta "started to give land to local people. A surveyor would come, measure, then they would go to Kwale and get a title deed. And then the people would sell the land. Ninety-five percent sold their land. The surveyors sold a lot of the land for themselves, took the land for themselves. Often title deeds did not correspond to the size of the land. At some point Kenyatta put a ban on selling beach land." This recollection speaks to the propensity of local Digo to sell their land and also the abuses of the Land Registry, which are widely known. Another narrative of land alienation was offered by a fifty-year-old resident of Mvumoni, one of the original villages of the area, who suggested that "colonialists sold land to Kikuyu and some land was given to the home guards and others who had worked for settlers in various capacities." This man established a connection between collaborators of the colonial period and those who received beachfront and other plots (something I was not able to verify) and thus acknowledged the tremendous continuity that had been created through these land-grabbing practices between the colonial and the postcolonial regimes.[143] Despite the lack of available evidence for some of these statements, these and other testimonies show that locals are clearly aware that irregularities abounded, that most land grabbing was done by people from other parts of the country, and that alienation took more than one form and involved more than one group of players.

The situation of landless tenants—the last of the four issues related to land reviewed here—has not been addressed to this day, despite countless reports that have documented it and made recommendations. In 1978, a report about landownership on the coast stated that "the strip now has probably the largest single concentration of landless people in the whole country."[144] Thirty years later, a 2007 government report confirmed the lack of improvement of the situation: "The abuse of the Land Titles Act has had a great negative impact on coastal land leading to the area having the largest single concentration of landless indigenous people."[145] Repeatedly, grievances about irregularities in the Diani area made their way into parliamentary debates.[146] Ultimately, the question of landownership on the coast was never properly resolved, and the realities of landlessness and squatters, in combination with other factors, have now attained another level of urgency.[147] Today's secessionist movement, led by the Mombasa Republican Council, arises from these longstanding grievances of the coastal people. While contemporary Mijikenda secessionists have moved away from the position they held at the moment of independence (when they were clearly opposed to coastal autonomy), they could be said to harken back to older alliances, especially those between the Mijikenda and the Mazrui.[148]

While essentially nothing was done to remedy the land grabbing, in 2003 President Mwai Kibaki initiated steps to at least assess the situation. The resulting 2004 report of the Commission of Inquiry into the Illegal/Irregular Allocation of Public Land (also known as the Ndungu Land Commission, named after its chair Paul Ndungu) detailed the horrific extent of land-grabbing practices in postindependence Kenya, focusing on "public land," which generally includes government land. "Public land," "trust land," and "private land" were the basic categories of land in Kenya then; the 2010 constitution has since renamed trust land as "community land." The commission decided to consider trust land part of its investigation because abuses of trust land were widespread.[149] The commission identified a host of grievances in the more than two thousand pages of its report, but the details do not include any of the cases of illegal land transfer in Diani.[150] The only item directly related to Diani is an illegal allocation of land to President Moi associated with the Kongo Mosque.[151] Why are the known land-grabbing cases from the Diani area not mentioned? One explanation is tied to the role local politicians played over the years. As Roger Southall points out in his analysis, "extensive tracts of Trust Land have been illegally allocated, with county councillors having been the main beneficiaries. Whilst the Commission was able to provide some glaring examples of such abuse, it was hampered in its work by the failure or refusal of councils to submit relevant information."[152] The commission itself came to the following conclusion: "Instead of playing their role as custodians of local resources including land, county and municipal councils have posed the greatest danger to these resources. . . . In fact, the most pronounced land grabbers in these areas were the Councillors themselves. . . . The corruption within central government has been replicated at the local level through the activities and omissions of county and municipal councils."[153]

Given the known complicity of local leaders in Diani land-grabbing schemes, this grim verdict is not surprising and in part explains the absence of Diani grievances in the report of the Ndungu Commission, even as land belonging to the Ukunda Settlement Scheme and to a state-owned farm are involved in legal cases dating back to the 1980s (discussed below). The other, perhaps more relevant, reason for the missing Diani land grievances is that most of the land involved was neither public/government land nor trust land but untitled land that villagers had used for generations. That is, even this far-reaching report was unable to address the situation of the scores of landless squatters and those people unable to convert either a letter of allocation or their customary land use claim into a title. Landownership, however, is at the core of tensions in Diani.

The fact that the issue of landownership was not addressed at independence set the stage for four decades of gentrification in the Diani area. In particular, German developers, who are absent from the public debates and scholarship about land issues on the coast, played a significant role in this process: they operated in the overall climate of illegality that surrounded landownership; their actions were enabled by dominant practices that independent Kenyans inherited from the colonial period; and they contributed to the disowning of local peasants. At the same time, they created employment opportunities and significantly advanced infrastructure development.

Gentrification 3: German Development of Tourism, Business, Real Estate, and Beyond

German entrepreneurs appeared on the Kenyan scene during the 1960s and took on a significant role in the creation of the coastal tourism infrastructure. Until the 1960s, "the coast was the resort chiefly of upcountry expatriates who would hire beach cottages at low rates," but now hotels were being built that attracted international visitors.[154] One of the first hoteliers was Edgar Herrmann, also known as "Herrmann the German"; some have credited him with coining the slogan "Sun, Sand, and Sex," which corresponds to the dominant image of Kenya in German mainstream media. Many people mostly know Herrmann as an internationally recognized rally driver; he won the Safari Rally twice, in 1970 and 1971, and competed many times in this and other race car competitions. But he was also active in the tourism industry: from the early 1970s and into the 1980s, Herrmann, together with his Swiss partner Beat Frey, owned the Blue Marlin Hotel, which dates back to 1913 and is considered the oldest hotel in Malindi. Herrmann also owned a safari business called Windrose Safaris. When the Blue Marlin went bankrupt, it was bought in 1985 by the German Matthiessen-Kampa family, who also played a major role in the development of tourism in Diani. Malindi became Kenya's first resort town, largely because of German-led development during the 1970s and 1980s; a German-language newspaper, the *Malindi Zeitung*, which had a circulation of three thousand already in the early 1970s, is testimony to the involvement of Germans at the time. Since the 1990s, Italian developers and hoteliers have dominated the area.[155]

In Diani in the early 1960s, the German Karl Pollman bought Two Fishes, the third hotel built in Diani in the 1940s, from George Plumb. Around the same time, Pollman founded a safari company that continues to be one of Kenya's main companies in this area.[156] He was also one of the directors of the Robinson Baobab Hotel, which was built in the early 1970s. In 1972, Leisure Lodge Hotel was ceremonially opened by President Kenyatta. It was bought by a German company, Hobby Hotels Gesellschaft, in 1973. Wilhelm Meister, who was the lawyer for Hobby Hotels and also for Two Fishes, invested heavily in Leisure Lodge and in 1975 acquired the luxury hotel. Just south of Leisure Lodge, Leopard Beach Resort opened in 1974.

Hobby Hotels was key to the beginning of German hotel activities in Diani. According to one hotel owner, it was an *Abschreibungsfirma*, a company facilitating issues related to depreciation of capital, write-offs, and capital allowance in Germany. In addition to Two Fishes and Leisure Lodge, Hobby Hotels was also involved with the Whispering Palms on the north coast and with Nairobi Westwood Park. Generally, the company bought hotels and made them solvent again. When Hobby Hotels went bankrupt in 1973–1974, Gerhard Matthiessen, who had invested in the company, moved to Kenya and pulled Two Fishes and Whispering Palms out of bankruptcy. Meister did the same for Leisure Lodge. At the time, Matthiessen (who died in early 2012) was one of the major German figures active in the development of tourism in Diani. Initially, he was involved with Two Fishes and then opened Diani Sea Lodge in 1981 and Diani Sea Resort in

1991.[157] Those hotels are still owned by the family; Matthiessen's daughter, Silvia Matthiessen-Kampa, and her husband, Harald Kampa, also own Trade Winds, the second oldest hotel on the Diani coast, and until 2006 the Blue Marlin in Malindi.

Overall, the German share in hotel ownership and management in Diani was significant. Until the end of the late 1980s, Germans owned or managed most of the hotels on the south coast: eight of the ten major hotels of that period were under German management. Four of them were owned or partially owned by Germans or a German company.[158] Some of the hotels that were built during the 1990s were also owned or managed by Germans at some point (see table 1; appendix).

In 2013, only thirteen of the major twenty hotels were open, reflecting the overall decline of tourism on the south coast, and six of the seven that were closed were African Kenyan–owned or owned in partnership with African Kenyans. Four of the closed hotels were owned by Kenyan politicians, namely, James Njenga Karume (Indian Ocean Beach Club) and Kenneth Matiba (Jadini, Africana Sea Lodge, and Safari Beach Hotel). Karume, a major political figure of postindependence Kenya, died in 2012. Matiba was one of the major opposition figures during the Moi regime. In partnership with European Kenyan Stephen G. Smith, he developed three of the hotels that were particularly popular with Germans. After Matiba's incarceration in Kamiti prison in 1990, he ran as a presidential candidate and withdrew money from his hotels and other assets, contributing to the demise of the hotels. Two of them, the Jadini and Africana Sea Lodge, were sold in July 2012; Matiba and Smith still own the Safari Beach Hotel.

While African Kenyan ownership of hotels was down, Indian (Kenyan and otherwise) ownership was up. Of the thirteen hotels open in 2013, eight (61.5 percent) were owned by Indians. The high number of Indian Kenyans who own hotels today clearly stands out and is in line with the increase in Indian business ownership generally, in Kenya and globally.[159] Only one hotel (Kaskazi Beach Hotel) that operated at the time was owned by an African Kenyan; the others were owned by Germans (two), French (one), and a European Kenyan (one). Of the thirteen hotels that were open, four still had German management (Diani Sea Resort, Diani Sea Lodge, the Sands at Nomads [Austrian], and Leopard Beach). The German manager of Leopard Beach Resort has been one of the most successful in the area for close to four decades and worked as project manager and management consultant with the hotel's African Kenyan management staff.

It can be seen that the situation with regard to major hotels along the coast has changed dramatically since the late 1990s; Table 1 (see the appendix) shows how from the 1960s to today, German hotel management and ownership is down, and Indian and African Kenyan management is up. However, the area also features a host of cottages and boutique hotels, of which many are owned or managed by Germans; these cottages and hotels are part of the real estate boom, a development that is discussed below.

Many factors explain this drop in the German role in Diani's tourism industry. German operators moved out of Kenya especially after the 1997 election-related violence. The decline in the number of tourists was devastating to the local industry: only 140,000 tourists vacationed on the coast in 1998, compared with 550,000 in 1996—a decline of two-thirds. The number of tourists never again reached the peak of the mid-1990s: in 2011, 230,000 tourists vacationed on the coast, and in 2012, the number dropped to 190,000.[160] Tourism on the Kenyan coast has always seen fluctuations and is related to sporadic instances of rioting (especially since the late 1990s) and to larger infrastructure, social, economic, and political issues. While violence on the coast flares up particularly in conjunction with elections, it is also related to a broader set of grievances held by coastal communities that feel neglected by the central government (we return in particular to the question of landownership below). As mentioned in chapter 1, the most consequential infrastructure issue that hurts the tourism industry on the south coast is the slow development of the Dongo Kundu Bypass, which will allow traffic to flow from the airport without having to make a long and inconvenient ferry crossing at Likoni, which presently is the only connection between Mombasa island and the south coast.

Hotel-based tourism also generated the development of a second area of German economic activity in Diani, especially since the late 1980s. Germans own scores of small and larger businesses in Diani, among them safari tour companies, nightclubs, restaurants, cafés, massage salons, yoga studios, diving businesses, and shopping malls. Originally these outfits targeted tourists, offering supplemental services that the hotels did not. Today, they also cater to the growing residential community of the area. Many of these businesses flourish for only a short time; individuals come and go as they try and often fail to fulfill their dream of living in a beautiful tourist destination. Many do not have the kind of expertise that might ensure success, and they leave bankrupt and disappointed, unable to adjust to Kenyan business practices. The successful business owners are those who pursue one of two strategies: either they adjust to the Kenyan environment and work closely with a Kenyan partner (often a spouse), or they control every aspect of their business themselves, ideally as a couple or family business. Individuals who pursue the second approach, though economically successful, often show severe signs of burnout after a few years, primarily as a result of an overall lack of knowledge about the Kenyan business environment in combination with their attempt to hold on to German business practices (such as timeliness, planning, and reliability). None of the German entrepreneurs I interviewed spoke any significant measure of Kiswahili, even after decades of living in the country. Because of their overall lack of contextual understanding and the constant cultural disorientation they face, they often experience what is called *Tropenkoller* (tropical madness). This term was used during colonial times to describe the mental distress that affected colonizers in the tropics. In Kenya, one most often sees such distress manifest when Germans (and other Europeans) yell at their employees, often in a completely uncontrolled fashion, in both public and private spaces. Despite these challenges, several of the most successful businesses in Diani are run by Germans, and some of them have been operating for more than ten years.

A third area of German business activity is in the real estate sector. The 1960s and 1970s saw new residential development in Diani. Initially it was driven mostly by British citizens who either left the highlands to move to the coast or came first as tourists and then bought land. But Diani also attracted a wide variety of other European individuals, who left their home countries for a variety of reasons; investors and heirs were joined by adventurers and criminals, and often these qualities were combined in various constellations.[161]

Real estate development was slow, but in the early 1980s Diani experienced the first major postindependence land alienation scheme. In 1981, Wilhelm Meister (who owned most shares of Leisure Lodge Resort), Peter Ludaava (who had been employed at Two Fishes before he became Meister's "right-hand man" at Leisure Lodge), and a Mr. Shretta (a lawyer from Nairobi who owned about 20 percent of Leisure Lodge shares) founded an organization called Diani Agriculture and Research Development (DARAD). This organization bought land to the north and south of the connector road for various agricultural purposes. When DARAD bought the land, the relevant title deeds were already in the hands of a Kwale District member of parliament, Juma Boy.[162] Part of the area at stake was known among local Digo villagers as "Chidze," which means "outside" or "away from the village" in Chidigo. The land, which is closest to the area of Mwamambi Village, also served as agricultural land to the people living in the adjacent villages of Mwakamba, Mvumoni, and Mwaroni. These four villages are located in the area between the connector road and the Kongo River, and villagers used the Chidze area collectively as one of their farming areas (along with another area called Maweni). Villagers would live on their various agricultural plots in the Chidze area during the farming and harvesting seasons.

The loss of Chidze and adjacent areas was a significant blow to the community. Several villagers recounted the events with bitterness. They said that an alliance of local leaders that included the Diani chief, the area member of parliament Juma Boy (the father of Boy Juma Boy, who continues to be an active political figure and took over from his father also with regard to DARAD), and the area counselor "sweet-talked village elders," who then signed a consent, thus permitting the sale.[163] The money, however, went to the alliance of local political leaders, and the villagers received nothing. So the villagers turned to protest. One man recounted how he and his grandfather had been detained at the local police station after a protest against the sale of the land. Another man from Mvumoni remembered a fight in 1988 or 1989 outside of Club Willow on the north side of the connector road. The confrontation between DARAD, which wanted to subdivide the land, and the evicted former owners turned violent: a police car was burnt, one villager was killed, and a police officer was injured. These events, people often complained, were not properly covered in the newspapers at the time. During Moi's dictatorship, the press was censored and would identify incidents such as these as the actions of criminals. Villagers were not able to claim reimbursement for their land because they did not own title deeds for the land on which they had lived for centuries (and in most cases, throughout the area, villagers still do not own title deeds for their land, even though allotment letters exist). Villagers were mostly illiterate and unable to represent themselves effectively, especially once their own leadership had given in to the demands of more powerful players. All in all, according to one villager, of the ninety-six families that were affected by this particular land sale, only about three benefited financially.[164]

The officially authorized intent of DARAD (in contrast to its actual pursuits) was agricultural development; it also included a veterinary section. The organization experimented with and did research on growing cloves and other spices and also growing grass (*Grassversuchsfarm*, experimental grass-growing farm), for which DARAD is said to have received a loan from either the German Development Agency (Deutscher Entwicklungsdienst, DED) or the Society for Technical Collaboration (Gesellschaft für Technische Zusammenarbeit, GTZ).[165] DARAD also featured a large carpentry training program that was run by a German carpenter, a Mr. Krüger (a "Schreinerei mit Meister, ein Herr Krüger"). Krüger had previously worked for the DED on Lamu; evidently a flamboyant figure, he was known as the "King of Lamu." He made contact with some of the wealthy German and other expatriates on Lamu and, hoping for a more lucrative employment, terminated his contract with the DED and joined Meister in Diani. He ran the carpentry shop there, which evidently was funded by the German Center for International Migration and Development (Centrum für Internationale Migration und Entwicklung, CIM).[166] Some employees at Leisure Lodge are also said to have been paid with CIM money. While DED and GTZ were officially not supposed to work with private enterprises, CIM often collaborated with private companies and was evidently scandal-ridden at the time. DARAD also managed to secure two airplanes that were supposed to be used by Flying Doctors from the German development agencies. Meister, with his training as a lawyer, is said to have been savvy in organizing these monies. His supporting cast included the local member of parliament, the Diani chief, and other local stakeholders and government officials.

Over time, the truth about DARAD came to the surface. The *Grassversuchsfarm* turned out to be a development project for a golf course (construction for the golf course began with government permission in 1991, and it opened, after various delays, in 1997); the planes were used for safari tourism, not doctors; and the carpentry training program was in fact a successful privately owned furniture store, Diani Furniture, which made furniture for various hotels, among other things. When the misuse of German development funds was uncovered, the scandal broke loose, though apparently with no negative consequences for the Kenya-based players.[167] Meister was also tied to what became known as the Amigo-Affair in Germany. The Bavarian minister president, Max Streibl, who was forced to resign over a scandal involving favoritism of the kind described here, had been a frequent guest at Leisure Lodge Hotel.

The DARAD scandal and the Amigo-Affair were not the only time that German development and other governmental agencies made headlines because of their activities in Kenya: in 1998, one of the German project managers who oversaw forestry development projects was murdered in the area.[168] The DARAD scandal also was not the only case in which German development agencies funded projects related to tourism development; Kaskazi Beach Hotel, which was jointly owned by LTI Hotels (part of DER Touristik Hotel & Investments) and an African Kenyan, also received funds from a German development agency, evidently facilitated through connections that an LTI manager had to the relevant ministries.[169] Most likely, none of the funds provided by the German government for these instances of corporate development in Kenya were ever returned.

Struggle over the Chidze and adjoining areas continued, and even though DARAD was dissolved in the 1990s, the question of ownership of DARAD land remains contentious. With the aid of German development money, part of DARAD land has been turned into the golf course (which is still in use today; see map 1) and other parts have been sold to various developers. After Meister's death in 1993 (the year the Amigo-Affair became public), the new owners of the DARAD land realized that, as one man put it, "they had not dealt with the real owners of the land. They wanted to hand back the rest of the land which they did not use." But the land never went back to the villagers; local leaders had already sold off the land and continued to sell it, piece by piece, for private development. The situation was chaotic: often, two or three competing title deeds were used to prove ownership of the same piece of land. Modern houses and businesses sprang up, mostly along the beach road and the connector road, and the area became one of the more densely populated sections of Diani. In 1998, locals began to occupy part of the land, which in their view was taken from them against their will, and to this day, the conflict has not been resolved and construction continues to boom. In fact, local villagers have been joined by a motley group of developers and homeowners who insist that they acquired the land legally and have since erected private homes, apartment complexes, schools, orphanages, restaurants, and other businesses on both sides of the connector road and along the northern stretch of the beach road. As a result of the competing claims, several court cases have been filed since the 1990s, some of which are still pending. Some of these cases pit villagers against hotels, and in others hotels are suing developers or squatters who have moved onto land registered as the hotels' property.[170] Several people described the Kwale Land Registry as being complicit in all of these events; one villager called the office one of the main "culprits." Because so many title deeds have been forged over time and because of the high degree of criminal activity surrounding the sale and alienation of land, official records are not a reliable source (hence my decision not to pursue research at the Land Registry office).

Clearly, the manipulated sale of the Chidze land during the 1980s was only the first in a series of landownership changes that led to business and real estate development in Diani. An outright building boom began in the early 1990s. Upscale housing development previously had been restricted to beachfront property, but now enclaves of luxury villas began springing up throughout the Diani area. The entire area has been surveyed and is recorded on registration maps that indicate numbered rectangular plots that are often subdivided into smaller units. The various sections of the area are conceptually tied to the beach, which clearly indicates that beachfront property is valued the most: the first section is referred to as "Beachfront" property; the next section stretches to the beach road and is known as "Row 1." Afterwards, every 300 to 350 meters, another section is theoretically marked by another "road," but these roads, if they are identifiable, are not paved and often do not even cut across the entire area. As of the completion of my research in 2014, most of the development had occurred in Rows 2, 3, and 4. I have not heard anybody *refer* to Rows 5 or 6, even though development occurs all the way up to the Mombasa–Lunga Lunga Road and beyond. The total number of rows between the beach and that road should be eight or nine if the design was applied systematically (and of course, because the beachfront and the main road do not follow straight lines, the size of rows would differ across the area). Even local real estate companies and locals do not use the same language when they refer to the various sections from the beach going inland.

I divide the areas into "zones" based on the phase of development (see map 2, appendix): Zone 1 combines beachfront and Row 1, as this was the first phase of development up until the 1970s. Development in Row 2, here Zone 2, began in the 1980s. Building activity in Rows 3 and 4, which constitute Zone 3, started in the second half of the 1990s. Construction in the DARAD area also began in the 1990s. Building activity continues in all zones.

What drove the real estate push that began in earnest during the 1990s? Particularly consequential were the Structural Adjustment Policies imposed on Kenya by the World Bank and IMF in the early 1990s.[171] The many adjustments Kenya made during that period were celebrated in an IMF report from

1996: "Direct controls on domestic prices, internal marketing, external trade, and the exchange system have been eliminated, and the exchange rate and interest rates are now fully market determined. The government budget deficit (excluding grants) was reduced from 11.4 percent of GDP [gross domestic product] in 1992/93 to 2.5 percent in 1994/95; money supply growth was brought under control and confidence in the banking system was restored." The implementation of privatization and other neoliberal practices was promptly rewarded with an IMF loan.[172] As suggested in chapter 1, the fact that these policies failed is by now widely accepted. As elsewhere in the global south and also some regions of the global north, poor people got poorer, and rich people got richer: "In Kenya, people living below the poverty line increased from 46 percent in 1992 to 49 percent in 1997, and [increased] further to 56 percent in 2000."[173] In Diani, these policies made it much easier for foreigners to invest in and buy land in Kenya, resulting in substantial changes in landownership and the development of foreign-owned businesses in the area. Various practices made land available for development (discussed below).

German realtors were crucial in facilitating a consequential shift in landownership from villagers to settlers. One of the key agents continues to be Joe Brunlehner, who has received a lot of attention for his often contentious activities and who advertises widely: "Diani Homes—Seit 1983 Garant für Ihre Immobilien in Kenia" (Diani Homes—Since 1983 Guarantor for your real estate in Kenya).[174] Other German developers are less visible but have also acquired and resold a large number of plots. I interviewed Frank Neugebauer, an associate of Brunlehner's, in July 1999. Also present was his African Kenyan wife of ten years. Neugebauer had come to Kenya in 1985 and had started his career as a hotel manager. He confirmed that the building boom began when the situation changed in 1992 and "foreigners were allowed to buy property" without the previously existing condition that a Kenyan must partner with a foreigner for a ninety-nine-year lease. As of July 1999, the company had sold about 260 houses to about two hundred families in Diani and the adjacent Galu areas; some families, Neugebauer said, had bought two and even three houses. Ninety-five percent of the buyers were Germans, with 60 percent of those coming from the former German Democratic Republic in the eastern part of the country. Neugebauer said that most of these people had been high-ranking officials ("früher hohe Tiere") or younger individuals who had made money during the first few years after German unification. Rumor in Diani has it that many of these influential figures from the former East Germany had worked for the Ministry for State Security, or Stasi. Most of the plots were located in Rows 2 and 3. Prices for homes listed in 1999 ranged from 165,000 German marks upwards ($100,000 and upwards at the time).

Neugebauer said that Diani Homes Ltd. had been founded in 1989 (the current website points to 1983 as the beginning of real estate activities) and that the company's first projects had been on Chale Island, an area that continues to be in the news regarding controversy over its status as a marine reserve, national monument, or *kaya* (sacred area, homestead) or an area for development. Neugebauer claimed that "nobody lived there"—a statement I frequently encountered when Germans wanted to legitimize problematic land transactions. But use of the island by locals had already been mentioned in a travel account by Johann Ludwig Krapf that dates to the middle of the nineteenth century.[175] In 1993, Diani Homes began to prepare plots it had acquired for construction. Neugebauer explained to me that the land was leased for ninety-nine years (leasehold titles, as opposed to freehold titles, which are not restricted), and he compared the legal status of the land to the German concept of *Erbpacht* ("genauso wie früher in Deutschland"; the same as earlier in Germany).[176] In retrospect, his comment may not be correct, because, according to my findings, many Germans during this period did acquire freehold titles. Neugebauer said that for the most part the company does not build homes itself but consults and establishes contacts with contractors.[177] He said the company also provided contacts for homebuyers to get legal advice. He explained to me that those who buy property are automatically entitled to get Kenyan residency. In fact, one path to obtaining residency status in Kenya is through investment.[178] He also mentioned that the IMF and World Bank regulations had been crucial in this regard; credits to Kenya, he said, had been tied to stipulations that made it possible for foreigners to acquire property in Kenya. Neugebauer was clearly fully aware that the company's success was intricately linked to IMF and World Bank policies.

The company continues to operate in the area. In fact, online searches for real estate contacts in Diani almost always lead to Diani Homes. My attempts to conduct a follow-up interview in 2013, however, were fruitless. Too many charges of fraud have been brought against the company and its various representatives, one of whom, Volker Pullig, had to leave Kenya and now operates from Germany.[179] Most charges against the company concern properties that were sold at prices higher than actual value, problems concerning paperwork, and the fact that the company often sells subleases (which evidently often are not properly understood at the time of the sale).

All along the Kenyan coast, from Lamu to the north and Chale to the south, Joe Brunlehner has developed a tourism (Romantic Hotels)[180] and real estate empire of his own. Brunlehner (who supposedly had to leave Germany because of tax evasion charges) is known in Kenya and Germany as "Mombasa Joe," which conveys a sense of the aura he has acquired.[181] But Brunlehner and Pullig are only two in a series of controversial German entrepreneurs who are operating in

Kenya. Shakatak, a local discotheque that serves as a popular hub for prostitution, is said to be run by a former pimp from Hamburg. German criminals who evade the German criminal justice system by escaping to Diani may end up being taken advantage of by the local German mafia.[182] But the Germans are not alone in this regard; rumors circulate in Diani that explain the recent influx of Italians to the area as the outcome of a mafia rivalry that led one faction to abandon Malindi for Diani.[183] Beyond Germans and Italians, the Kenyan coast has been described more generally as an area "where people go to escape their pasts . . . [they] have all come to Diani to avoid alimony payments, charges of tax evasion, and disgruntled clients back home."[184]

While the early and mid-1990s drew a host of German entrepreneurs and speculators of all kinds to Diani, by the end of the decade another World Bank intervention had significantly affected the German settler community. This time the World Bank targeted Kenyan interest rates on savings. By the mid-1990s, Kenyan banks paid up to 20 percent on deposit rates on savings.[185] As one local German entrepreneur told me, Germans who had bought villas were initially also lured to Kenya by the prospect of being able to live off their savings. They invested, for example, 100,000 German marks or more in Kenyan savings accounts, and with the tremendous interest they received—and the low cost of living in Kenya—they were able to sustain their lifestyles. Some individuals who had invested high amounts were also able to pay off their villas. In response to this and other economic issues, the World Bank increased its substantial criticism of Kenyan economic practices and pressured the country to implement a number of reforms, including reducing the exorbitant deposit rates.[186] Rates decreased dramatically between 1998 and 1999 (a 10 percent decrease) and then more slowly over about five years until they were set at around 4 percent. This of course put an end to the glamorous lifestyle of those German immigrants who lived off their savings. Gradually, many of them returned to Germany or Switzerland. Some tried to sell their villas, only to discover that they could not sell even at the price they had originally paid. Several German investors, however, had the capital to buy up some of the land and property from those who found themselves in financial trouble or who realized life in Kenya was not as easy as they had thought it would be. Some of the owners did stay and are still waiting for things to change—for "the Chinese to get interested," or "the Australians," who are mining titanium in Kwale.[187] Some of the land that is still in German hands is now leased to other nationals, and many plots have been sold. Together with the election violence of 1997, the changing financial landscape is a key factor that led to a decrease in the number of Germans in Diani, be they tourists or settlers.

Though the German real estate boom in Diani peaked in the late 1990s, new private homes have been built continuously, and today, real estate is again hot. With this recent push we can perhaps identify the beginning of a fourth phase of gentrification in Diani. The designation of Diani as a resort town in the country's vision plan (Kenya Vision 2030)[188] and the prospect of the bypass that would circumvent the ferry at Likoni have brought new speculators to the area. But all over the world, a rush is under way for beachfront and near-beachfront property, and Diani is no exception. Prices for land on the south coast are still much lower compared with prices on the north coast, and Diani is the most coveted of the south coast area. But even in Diani, costs per acre, especially farther inland, are often as low as 10 percent of what those costs would be in, for example, Nyali on the north coast of Mombasa. While many real estate transactions occur through consulting firms and international companies (such as Knight Frank), the only company that is registered locally in Diani as a real estate company is run by a German couple. Baobab Holidays Homes (Kenya) Ltd. has been active since 2010, evidently very successfully, and clearly competes with Diani Homes and other consulting firms.[189] In an interview in November 2013, the owners, Sandra Nikolay and Frank Meininghaus, said that demand was high. In November 2013, Baobab Holiday Homes listed 170 properties, including homes, apartments, and plots of land—quite an impressive number. The properties are located mostly in Diani and Galu Beach, but also several other locations on the south coast and in Kwale. The company was recording about two hundred visitors per day on its website. Eighty-five percent of its customers came from Nairobi, among them officials of the United Nations, workers with INGOs, and businesspeople from various European countries. The owners also noted that, increasingly, African Kenyans made use of their services (a number they expected to increase in the future), which confirms the current trend toward upcountry-driven gentrification.[190] Nikolay and Meininghaus also said that they did not deal with land that indigenous villagers owned, because the legal situation was often too obscure. The law mandates that all family members have to agree to a sale, and in their view, tracking down every member of an extended family is too difficult; so they decided to stay away from these potentially conflict-laden situations.

The new 2010 Kenyan constitution revised the law regarding property ownership by foreigners, in what could be seen as an attempt to undo some of the changes that were introduced in the early 1990s.[191] One of the key changes concerns the status of the title; whereas it had been possible in the past couple of decades to acquire freehold titles, the new law mandates that foreigners may register their land only through leasehold titles for ninety-nine years. It seems, however, that despite a public appeal to foreign nationals owning property in Kenya to apply for this new status, few, if any, have done so. Furthermore, according to individuals who are familiar with the sector, even today, new sales often do not follow the new rules, and freeholds are still issued to foreign nationals. "Pwani si Kenya" (the coast is not Kenya), the slogan of the secessionist Mombasa Republican Council (see chapter 1), takes on a different meaning: the coast is not a part of Kenya, but owned—to a significant extent—by foreign nationals.[192] Germans continue to represent a driving force, both as realtors and buyers in the real estate market.

The developments in Diani, especially as they occurred in the 1980s and 1990s when German entrepreneurs dominated the area, occurred in the context of a general land-grabbing frenzy. As Paul Ndungu, the chair of the Ndungu Commission, has explained, "Our conservative estimate was that some 200,000 illegal titles were created between 1962 and 2002. Close to ninety-eight percent of these were issued between 1986 and 2002." He further stated that all kinds of lands were affected—"forests, settlement schemes established for the poor, national parks and game reserves, government civil service houses, government offices, roads and road reserves, wetlands, research farms, state Corporations' lands, trust lands, etc., etc."[193] Clearly, this overall lawlessness created a climate that facilitated the illegal transactions of land in Diani as well. This fact does not absolve German developers from their responsibility to know whether the transactions in which they were involved were legal or not; surely many of them were aware of areas of illegality. As one of the main real estate developers said to me, "Unter den Blinden ist der Einäugige König" (among the blind the one-eyed is king), whereby he meant to acknowledge that even though many Germans were not highly skilled (they were one-eyed) and might not have been able to succeed in Germany the way they did in Kenya, the Kenyan context was an ideal setting for their transactions.

It will be up to the National Land Commission of Kenya—which was mandated by the 2010 Kenyan constitution, created through the National Land Commission Act of 2012, and complemented by the 2012 Land Act—and perhaps also up to investigative journalists to uncover the extent of the complicity of German developers as well as the Land Registry, county officials, and other local players in the alienation of land from the Digo people.[194] In the meantime, local people have to cope with the consequences of the developments brought into their communities from abroad, and, more recently, also from upcountry.

Consequences for Locals

How have the largely German-driven developments of the 1980s, the outright building boom of the 1990s, and the continuing construction activities of the present affected the situation of local Digo villagers? How do they perceive these developments, especially amid the more recent real estate boom? And what were and are their actions and reactions to the changes in landownership; that is, how did they participate in and shape them?

To answer these questions, we must first acknowledge the legal dimension of the situation with regard to landownership. As we have seen, postindependence governments never resolved how much land should be allotted to indigenous villagers, but also squatters, of the Diani area. Apart from the fact that the community used larger areas of land collectively and individually for agriculture, ownership of plots that contain houses and perhaps an adjacent small yard is often not settled. Theoretically, Diani villagers have title deeds for their personal property, as the entire area has been surveyed, and government-registered "Green Cards" document the existing properties throughout the area. As a result of this process, most individual owners should have received "Letters of Allotment" that document the size of their property. But villagers often delay turning a Letter of Allotment into a title deed because they fear that their claim thus may be rejected and they would be evicted as a consequence. The process is also costly, which poses a further impediment to villagers. In addition, land that might be considered community property has been alienated throughout the entire area.

As we have seen, beginning in the 1980s and especially in the northern part of Diani, some villagers, usually those who were unable to document through title deeds their claim to the land they were inhabiting, were simply kicked off that land. In other cases, title deeds were forged by various parties and generally to the disadvantage of less powerful individuals. Other villagers sold their land to German and other developers voluntarily, especially beginning in the 1990s, but often they were not able to use the profit from the sale in beneficial ways. As German and other developers were eager to acquire land, villagers gradually sold plots of land, first alongside the beach road (beachfront and Row 1) and then farther inland. Usually the first step was to get their land titled. One of my research assistants, Bakari, told me that his family had controlled more than five acres of land (about two hectares). His great-grandfather had been a hard-working man who had become wealthy. He owned animals and used land for grazing. Bakari confirmed that landownership was established through usage: plots were allotted according to need and effort in cultivating it, and elders oversaw the process. Later, his father and uncle, who inherited control over the land from their great-grandfather, kept dividing and renting out the land to other locals. His father and uncle did not have a title deed for the land, and when they died and their children wanted to collect rent from the renters, the renters resisted. But the father and uncle had drawn up written agreements that outlined the expanse of the land and the terms of the rental contracts. So with that, the fourteen children of Bakari's father and uncle went to the Land Registry and got title deeds for all five acres. Then they began to subdivide the land and had title deeds drawn up for every single piece of land. "This way we were safe," Bakari said, vis-à-vis the renters, but also for future situations. However, the many leases created conflict in the family, and property was then divided among the family members. Afterwards individuals decided for themselves whether they wanted to rent or sell the land. As Bakari put it, "Now everybody can and has to deal with land grabbing on their own," thus acknowledging that the breakup of family solidarity brought opportunity but also made individuals vulnerable.

From the perspective of the villagers, they were paid significant sums of money for their land, but, as one man from Mvumoni put it, the villagers "ate the money, and now they have nothing." In only a few cases did villagers invest their money wisely—if at all. Not being accustomed to an investment-oriented environment, they often quickly spent all the money. Villagers whom I interviewed were clearly aware of the consequences of land sales. When I told Bakari in July 2011 about my interest in finding out about what happened to those who sold land, he immediately said that his family "was among the victims." I was struck by the fact that he used the word "victim." I asked him to track down individuals who were willing to talk about their experience or the experience of others regarding the sale of land, especially their economic situations. Here are a few of the stories he collected from Digo who grew up in the area:

- "One *mzee* [old man], he bought two *matatus* [minibuses], his sons ran them, another son built a video hall. All with the money [from selling land]. But the investment did not last, it was a mismanagement of funds, they did not know anything about this business. You can blame the sons, but the father also made bad decisions. Back then having a car was a big thing, they collected money, spent it, but kept no leftover for reinvestment; at the end of the day, the matatus were broken and the money was gone."
- "One young man was married to an Australian. She wanted to build a house, so the young man sold the wife his family land. Then the money he received from her for the land was used to build a house for the father, and then the couple also built their own house. Then they opened up a business; by now they have sold the first house and moved on."
- "One old man used to drive to Mombasa every morning, with a taxi, for a lavish breakfast. He kept spending his money like this until it was gone."
- "Some people lost the money they got from a sale because they succumbed to the many demands of the extended family and turned it all over to them. Some used their money to build themselves sturdier and bigger houses on their remaining land."
- "A young local man had a British girlfriend who bought land; the woman died later, he inherited the land, and built a house on it. Now, he had subdivided the land, one acre [0.4 hectare], into two halves. He sold one half to a foreigner, an Italian or German, with a local spouse. Now he is just using up his 2.5 million Kenyan shillings [KSh, about $25,000] that he received from the sale—just spending it. He bought some fishing nets and that's it. After fishing he goes drinking."
- "A man, when he was in his late forties—he is still living, is now in his sixties—sold land; before he sold the land he was working and running a

café; then he sold the land, in the area of Row 2 or 3, and had the idea of a two-story café. But it was built poorly, he used bad contractors, and then it was just abandoned. All his money was spent."

- "One young man who had some land built a house on it with the money of his French girlfriend."
- "Most people who sold land sold one of their plots, usually their agricultural land, what they used for harvesting, and kept one plot for their own house. But there are a few who have nothing left, no land at all. Or they kept a small hut on a big lot that they sold, and remained living there."

"Remained living there" basically means living as squatters on their own land. This statement resonates with the title of Okoth-Ogendo's incisive account of land tenure under British colonialism—*Tenants of the Crown*. As these vignettes show, selling land has had a range of repercussions for individuals and their families, depending on how they used the profits from the sales or used their land otherwise. Some benefited or at least did not lose everything, but others were left with nothing over time. As a result of these shifts in landownership, some of the individuals who were previously able to sustain themselves by growing food on their land (for sustenance and sometimes also for sale) and owned the homes in which they lived now pay rent and work salaried jobs, if they can find any. As acknowledged earlier, the propensity of coastal villagers to sell their land has been observed from the colonial period onward and continues to capture public attention.[195] The repercussions have been dramatic for the Diani villagers. In addition, as we have seen, the tourism industry has attracted large numbers of upcountry immigrants to the area, which has intensified the struggle over available resources.

In order to get a sense for the extent of the change that has occurred in the area, I spent many days walking around, or *dériving*, Diani with two research assistants for a period that totaled eight months but was spread over five separate stays.[196] I also drew on my memories, recounting the time when I had walked through Diani in the early 1980s, before the beginning of the real estate boom and then during additional visits in the 1980s, 1990s, and 2000s. On our walking tours, we moved in and out of a wide range of social, economic, ecological, and historical spaces, acknowledging the relationship between small and large, abandoned and occupied buildings; the swimming pools, schools, dispensaries, post offices, official government buildings, recently built modern commercial areas, makeshift restaurants and bars and fancier versions thereof; the water tanks and wells; the farming areas, gardens, age-old baobab trees, and lush vegetation; the stone harvesting areas; the airstrip that was plopped on land that is and was used for farming and villager housing; the goats, chickens, colobus monkeys, baboons, vervet monkeys, and bugs; and the myriad of different people, from all areas of

Kenya and the entire globe, who live in the area. We walked in one-hundred-degree heat and in the rain. We walked at various hours of the day, but at night, we drove. I learned to walk the more obvious paths myself, but my research assistants, Peter and Omari, continued to surprise me with new "shortcuts," although some of them meandered so far away from our intended destinations that they seemed to take longer than other paths. Along the way we often stopped to greet passers-by. Omari, who was born in the Mvumoni area, was more protective of people's privacy and walked with me only a few times. We also *dérived* in his taxi. Peter, who was more adrift and lived a more precarious life, was willing to share his knowledge with less hesitation.[197]

Walking through the Diani area, one sees the stark contrast between the new developments, the big villas built by tourists and immigrants, and the buildings of the villagers. The quality of a roof is a good indicator of the financial situation of the African Kenyan owner. Whether a house has a grass roof, a *makuti* roof (made from leaves of the coconut palm), an iron sheet roof, or shingles tells you whether a local or upcountry owner has made money from having sold land, has a salaried job, or perhaps is involved with a tourist or immigrant who paid for a more expensive roof. Basic buildings use poles from mangrove trees (which are insect resistant and very durable) and mud for construction and have either a makuti or grass roof. The next level up are houses that use a combination of concrete and coral stones or cinder blocks instead of mud but still feature a makuti roof. The most durable house has an iron sheet roof or shingles. A blue roof, I was told, usually indicates a German (or other European) sponsor or owner. More expensive houses have outside walls that are covered with a plaster made from mud or cement and sand; painting the house white is known as "whitewashing." In various areas of the original villages, mostly at the farthest point away from the roads, only few houses are plastered.

When walking through the interior of Diani one also encounters a number of ruins. In most cases the owner of the plot ran out of funds during the building process and was unable to complete construction. In all cases of ruins, I was told that the owner had been one of those villagers who had sold land but then spent too much too quickly such that when he turned to building a house for himself, he could not complete the project. I should add at this point that Digo women rarely own land by themselves or even in joint ownership, and thus in almost all cases, the profit from selling land would have gone to a man.[198]

The walking tours allowed me to see the physical evidence of how real estate development had encroached and continues to encroach on the original villages of the area, and how money available to villagers had brought new development to the villages. *Dériving* also made me aware of the patterns of development, from the beachfront area to Row 4 and all the way to the Mombasa–Lunga Lunga Road, whereby one moves gradually from essentially white residential areas through mixed and finally into almost entirely black neighborhoods. Everywhere, how-ever, were signs of the interaction between locals and Europeans that has oc-curred over the past few decades. While *dériving* with Omari one day, within the space of only about 2.5 square kilometers, we saw a primary school that was funded by a German individual after whom it was named Hermann School; we walked through the village meeting space in Mvumoni; we came upon an eco-logical project funded by Germans, a huge greenhouse, adjacent to farming areas used by Mvumoni villagers; we passed a new secondary school that is under con-struction with funds from Germany; we saw a dispensary that often receives do-nations from Europeans; we saw houses of all shapes and kinds of construction, from the most basic to the most extravagant; we saw the remnants of a cremato-rium that had been built by British residents of the area and that had created an uproar in the predominately Muslim community; we saw garbage dumps from hotels, which locals scavenge; and we saw walls (figure 2.1)—the worst of them the one that meanders around the contested golf course, an eyesore that cuts right through the area "like a huge freeway," as Omari put it. Omari and others often asserted that villagers like the development because it brings water and electricity to their homes. But the walls around compounds and the golf course were described as "irritating": "You think you will have a good neighbor but then the wall goes up. If the children play and the ball goes over, it is lost." These walls are a relatively new phenomenon, as people used to grow bougainvillea for privacy and perhaps put up a wire fence for protection. While the walls and the buildings behind them are the most visible symbol of the tension between Afri-can Kenyans and Europeans, other buildings and sites indicate the considerable level of interaction and cooperation.

But can we quantify such changes as well, after this more qualitative consid-eration? As of the completion of my research in 2014, Germans have been joined especially by Italians (some of whom have built extraordinarily extravagant villas in the northern part of Diani and often surround their compounds with tall walls and electric fences), British, and upcountry Kenyans in this massive gentrification process. The 2009 census population of Diani of close to seventy-five thousand does not include both tourists, who make up a significant portion of the people frequenting businesses, and part-time residents, many of whom came as tourists, made contact with the local population, sometimes got married, and now spend part of the year in Diani, often in a house that is co-owned with a Kenyan.

Figures for the number of Europeans, including European Kenyans (both residents and citizens) who are permanent residents in the area, are very dif-ficult to come by. The census has no subcategories for residents or ethnicity. The South Coast Resident Association had 295 members in 2011. The association does not represent the population proportionally but includes mostly European

Figure 2.1. Security wall in Diani

and European Kenyan members, and fewer African Kenyan and Indian Kenyan members, and also includes members who live beyond the boundaries of Diani. However, there are household memberships and corporate memberships. Together with the association's chair, I identified forty-six German members, many of whom were couples who shared a membership, of which some were mixed couples. Roughly, between sixty-five and seventy-five German individuals were members of the association at the time. This number, however, was only a fraction of those living in the area, full time or part time. Estimates by longtime residents regarding the European population on the entire south coast (from Likoni to Tanzania), a significant part of which is in Diani, were as high as 7,500 to

8,000. The largest communities among these expatriates and European Kenyans are British (often born in Kenya), German, and Italian. Another estimate suggested that Europeans who live along the south coast part time make up another 3,000 individuals. Regarding Diani proper, several interviewees suggested that between 1,000 and 2,000 Europeans live in the area full time and part time, with another 1,000 to 2,000 living in the Galu Beach area to the south of Diani. The Diani chief and his assistant were much more conservative in 2012: the first number they ventured was that 70 *wazungu* (whites) lived in the area, which they then revised to around 200 and then to 500. One Swiss resident mentioned that he knew from the Swiss consul that 900 Swiss citizens are registered in Kenya and that 450 live on the coast, including Mombasa. The question is: how can we verify these varied estimates?

Taking stock of housing sheds light on the number of residents. As we have seen, more than 250 villas that went predominantly to Germans in Diani and Galu had been built by the late 1990s (facilitated primarily by the first significant real estate company, Diani Homes). Some of these buildings changed ownership, but additional residential structures have gone up since. In order to get a sense of the housing situation, I systematically surveyed the area by foot and car with my research assistants, from the beach to Row 4 and in the more populated DARAD area. Europeans also live beyond this area, but in much smaller numbers, so the data regarding these scattered housing units is left out of this analysis. In addition to walking and driving tours, we used GIS tools and evaluated satellite images of the area. Not all areas are updated on Google Maps (some were updated over the course of the research); the information gathered during walking and driving sheds light on the more recent developments. On the basis of these various methods, and assuming a margin of error for areas that we were not able to access or apartment buildings where we had to estimate the number of units, we came up with figures for housing units, including villas, apartments, and cottages, that are owned or inhabited by the more affluent members of the community. We did not include those cottages or small hotels that would usually be rented out to short-term tourists (such as Asha Cottages), but we did include cottages that would be rented by part-time and full-time residents (such as Kijiji Cottages). We did not include housing for workers in the hotels or the huts of squatters; regarding the latter, probably around 100 to 150 huts are sprinkled throughout Rows 2 to 4, housing perhaps five hundred or more individuals. Locals call these areas "no smoking zones" because at times the huts are entirely built from grass and makuti leaves and thus are most vulnerable to fire. Housing that was and is being built in Rows 3 and 4 encroaches on the housing in the original villages of the area, especially Mvumoni, Mwamambi, and Mwakamba in the northern section. We did not count buildings that were under construction, and there were quite a lot of them, especially apartment buildings, which would account for at least another three hundred living units in the making. Among the units counted here are a wide range of houses (from extravagant villas to small cottages) and apartments of various sizes.

Our results show that in the area of the beachfront and Row 1 (Zone 1 on map 2), we counted (and estimated) 270 units (figures rounded to the nearest tens; see table 2). The percentage of Europeans and European Kenyans who live here and/or own houses is the highest, probably even higher than 90 percent. Included in this figure are also a small number of Indian Kenyans; even though the discussion thus far has not included Indian Kenyans in the analysis, they play a visible role in the tourism industry (as documented in table 1), own small businesses, and also reside in the area (with ownership exceeding residency by far). Socially they are more connected to European Kenyans and Europeans, rather than African Kenyans living in Diani. In the area of Row 2 (Zone 2), we counted 340 units. A good number of mixed couples live in this area, but the percentage of Europeans and European Kenyans (and again, some Indian Kenyans) is still about 80 percent. Ownership of housing is probably even higher, at around 90 percent, and here the percentage of Indian Kenyan ownership is more significant than the number of Indian Kenyans who occupy buildings. In Rows 3 and 4 (Zone 3), we counted 530 units. Again, a good number of mixed couples live in this area, and the percentage of European, European Kenyan, and Indian Kenyan occupancy and ownership is probably about 80 percent. In the DARAD area, which stretches along the connector road from Row 3 to about Rows 6 and 7, we counted 410 units. The largest percentage of mixed couples live here, and also a significant number of middle-class African Kenyans. The percentage of European, European Kenyan, and Indian Kenyan occupancy and ownership is probably around 50 percent.

The biggest challenge is to estimate the number of people who live in a unit. Most units are usually inhabited by either a couple living alone, a couple and a child or two, or a couple and one or two additional relatives or friends—resulting in (a conservative estimate of) an *average* of three individuals in a unit.[199] The resulting number of Europeans, European Kenyans, and Indian Kenyans, an estimated 3,432, living in this area is significant. Not all of them are present throughout the year, and the figure of those present at any one time is lower. But considering the activity in the most popular public spaces—such as supermarkets, banks, the post office, restaurants, and bars—and also taking into consideration the number of Europeans and European Kenyans who work in the various economic spaces of Diani, it becomes obvious that these figures describe the reality in Diani quite well.

I suggest that Germans make up about one-third of this group, about 1,100 individuals. Another third are European Kenyan and British, and the final third are Indian Kenyan and Europeans of Italian and various other nationalities and origin. These estimates are rough, and only a systematic census would shed more light on the issue. The official figure for registered Swiss citizens in Kenya is 924, and the number of Austrians is lower, at 174.[200] I was unable to obtain official figures for the number of Germans, but in light of the figures for registered Swiss (with most of them living at the coast, and a large percentage on the south coast), we can assume that several thousand Germans are registered in Kenya. Given that many of those who live in Diani off and on are not officially registered in Kenya, the cumulative figure of 1,100 for individuals from the three German-speaking countries who own or rent in Diani (one of the most popular places for Germans on the coast) is realistic.

While the absolute numbers may not seem significant in an area that is populated by close to seventy-five thousand people (a little more than 1 percent of the population), the effect of the German presence is substantial, especially in terms of landownership, business, and tourism, but also, as we will see, with regard to the structure of social relations. In addition to the presence of German settlers, we should not forget the significant number of German tourists visiting the south coast; tourism brings new potential settlers to the area every year. In addition, Germans are part of the larger community of European expatriates that is integral to the Diani economy and social life.

When one considers the larger picture, it becomes evident that the overall result of tourism and real estate development, especially for the indigenous population of the area, is overwhelming. If we exclude the area of Bongwe and focus on Gombatu and Diani, where most of the Europeans live, the figures highlight the inequalities within the community more starkly. The area of these two sublocations amounts to a total of 36 square kilometers, and the population totals 62,653 (2009 census). Approximately 4,650 affluent Europeans, European Kenyans, Indian Kenyans, and African Kenyans make up slightly less than 7.4 percent of the population of this area, but they own or occupy between 80 percent and 90 percent of the residential units located in the more coveted half of the area (beachfront through Row 4, plus some parts of DARAD; see map 2, Zones 1–3). Future investigations will show how much more of the as-yet undeveloped land is owned by these groups and increasingly also by upcountry Kenyans. My research assistant Omari suggested early in our conversations that only 20 percent of the land between Galu and Tiwi beaches "that once belonged to locals" was still owned by Digo; the rest was now in the hands of Europeans and people from upcountry. This figure, in light of the data collected over time, may turn out to be fairly accurate.

On July 11, 2012, I met with three village elders of Magutu, the chair and two committee members. All three were born in Magutu (in 1937, 1946, and 1955, respectively). Very quickly our conversation turned to the land issue. "Our land has been taken," they lamented. The villagers blamed upcountry people for most of the land grabbing: "People from upcountry come with their title deeds and grab the land. Because of this, people don't understand each other. Now they can't be working together, they are divided." They said that strife over landownership was the reason for division within the community, and they blamed elders for having sold their land. The government, they said, does not support the coastal people, especially with regard to health care, schools, and roads. "Independence came in 1963, but we have not seen freedom," said one of the villagers. But they also asserted that "the wazungu are not the problem." Tourism, they said, had been good for the local people because of the employment opportunities. This theme was continued in another conversation I had with three representatives of Magutu in October 2013, the vice chairman (born in 1948), the treasurer (born in 1951), and another committee member (born in 1955). Again, the main complaint was reserved for the government, which had alienated beachfront property and interfered in local dealings. Here, village committee members expressed that they felt they should be allowed to do what they want with their land; if they want to sell it to Europeans, for example, that choice should be accepted. "Europeans are not the problem, they just use their money, and if locals sell, they should sell." They claimed that the government interfered with their dealings with Europeans through all kinds of rules.

In approaching these comments we need to acknowledge that Magutu was not affected by the land alienation scandal connected with the golf course and the Chidze area. One should expect that villagers from the northern part of Diani, who are involved in several lawsuits over land grabbing, have a more historical understanding of the role of both Europeans and local political players in creating the current situation. Magutu also feels more of the pressures of upcountry Kenyans moving into the area, as much of the land being acquired by upcountry middle-class African Kenyans lies in the Magutu area and in other areas closer to the Mombasa–Lunga Lunga Road. European building continues to encroach in more dramatic ways on the villages located in the northern part of Diani. But local wrath for the government is widespread across Diani, including in the northern part (we will return to this question in chapter 3 and the epilogue), and it has been exacerbated by this more recent influx of upcountry individuals as well as the continued neglect of the larger area. This anger, which surfaced in many conversations over the years, contrasts with the generally benevolent view locals held of European developers.

Digo wrath at upcountry people is matched by upcountry disrespect for the Digo, who are considered backward, lazy, and uneducated by their fellow Kenyans.[201] Precolonial and colonial Digo had lived as farmers but also as traders, a life more independent from the famines and natural disasters that often affect those living upcountry. When the British arrived, the coast was ahead, economically speaking, compared with inland and upcountry areas, and Digo society was an integral part of the trading networks. Since independence, however, the Digo and other Mijikenda peoples indigenous to the coast have been overwhelmed by both Europeans and Kenyans from the interior, so that Kwale, and other counties along the coast, now lags behind many regions of Kenya on almost every level. Prejudice against Islam and lack of advocacy for coastal concerns among key political actors have certainly played roles in upcountry attitudes toward the coast; economic conflicts are aggravated by cultural and religious clashes, whereby these days, coastal Muslims share their ancestral lands with Christians. The long-term Digo frustration regarding the inaction of the Kenyan government and the influx of upcountry Kenyans is the main source of support for the Mombasa Republican Council, which advocates secession of the coast from Kenya. This is in blatant contradiction to the historical events around Kenya's independence when Mijikenda peoples did *not* support coastal independence, mostly because of the long-term resentment and distrust against coastal Arab landowners and slaveowners. The rallying cry "Pwani si Kenya" (the coast is not Kenya) was embraced increasingly over the time frame of my research.

I found it bewildering that many villagers throughout Diani, as well as political activists, the Kenyan media, and scholarship to date, do not establish a connection between European-driven real estate developments and the political, economic, and cultural situation on the coast. Even though villagers are aware that the tourism industry marks the beginning of the end of their traditional way of life and control over their own resources, they have decided not to blame the expatriates. In my interviews, many locals embraced the idea of modernization and development and insisted that they did not want to return to "wakati zamani," the good old days. Some, however, especially older men, clearly longed for days passed. But in both cases, locals perceived Europeans as offering solutions to local problems, while they saw upcountry people mostly as competitors over resources. Another factor that may explain the more benevolent local view of Europeans is rooted in the fact that tourism has brought jobs to the area, and locals hope that if tourism experiences another boom, they will benefit from this development. The consequences of the real estate expansion, which brought barely any new jobs to the area and in fact contributed to the demise of the tourism industry, are understood less well.

The Value of Land

In *The Wretched of the Earth* (1961), Frantz Fanon writes, "For a colonized people the most essential value, because the most concrete, is first and foremost the land: the land which will bring them bread and, above all, dignity." Fred Pearce, in his study of the global extent of land grabbing, also acknowledges that landownership is central to questions of identity and dignity.[202] In Diani, Digo language, culture, and history are tied to land, and as ownership of ancestral land diminishes, so does the cultural life of the Digo. The Digo who live in areas throughout Kwale County and into Tanzania do not feel their existence *as a people* to be threatened by what is happening in Diani; but a part of the larger Digo history that is tied to, among other sites, the kayas in the Diani area as well as the Kongo Mosque is threatened to disappear as lived culture.

In 1975, a 159-page report on proposed tourism development of the Diani area outlined a scheme that included a planned town for forty thousand people to the north and the south of the connector road, with residential areas, schools, a community center, a hotel training school, health centers, and more. The report pays significant attention to kaya land, mosques, forests, and village land and clearly advocates for a different kind of development as what actually occurred over time, one rooted in historical knowledge and respect for cultural rights and that presents a more sensible balance between economic development and community claims. The report correctly anticipated the challenges of the following decades, and, had it been turned into reality, it might have forestalled not only land grabbing but also increases in crime, drug use, prostitution, and sex trafficking.[203]

In the absence of large-scale approaches to preserve Digo land and culture in Diani, the process of gentrification that I have outlined here and that has occurred over more than one hundred years is bound to continue. And because the question in the end is not only one of landownership, Digo agency will not be enhanced by way of a certain percentage of Digo privately owning land in the area. Some villages, such as those in the northern part of Diani, continue to display a significant degree of cohesion, but private landownership will only divide the community further. All communities and cultures change, however, and privatization, new concepts of the family and labor, and the overall scope and pace of change in the area will create social energies that may also result in new communal practices. But in the meantime, the overall sense of loss and multiple grievances are articulated via the discourse on land, a discourse that addresses more than just landownership.

In his study on the land rights of indigenous peoples in Africa, Albert Kwokwo Barume identifies several reactions and strategies indigenous people use to fight for their land. He distinguishes between "immediate" and "long-term" reactions. Immediate reactions include "clandestine use and occupation, often sustained by small-scale violent actions," all of which Digo peoples have turned to. Among the long-term strategic reactions Barume counts legal challenges, lobbying and advocacy, and the revival of the community's history.[204] The Digo have pursued these strategies as well. For instance, reviving the community's history is reflected in the preservation effort of the area's kayas and in the general consciousness that people display vis-à-vis their history and culture, also as part of the Mijikenda. Most of these long-term strategies concern the community as a whole. (Even though the legal strategy of land titling results in private ownership, in the absence of communal titling options in Kenya, it is the only option for gaining legal control over land.)

But in response to their situation, individuals also pursue strategies that might not benefit the larger community. The most destructive of these practices are prostitution and drug use, in particular heroin use, which is currently exploding into an epidemic that is ravaging youth, especially unemployed young men. As elsewhere in the world, an increase in crime accompanies both drug use and prostitution. My discussion does not turn to these alarming matters, which a full account of Diani would certainly have to consider. Instead, I focus on two other practices that have developed—"charity" and "romance"—and that are problematic in their own ways. Like drug use, prostitution, and crime, these practices can be seen as survival strategies and coping mechanisms for addressing the economic and social pressures most members of the African Kenyan community face; however, they are clearly less destructive and at times display a considerable degree of empowerment. In Diani, the overall amnesia and cognitive dissonance I observed regarding the role of foreigners in creating precarious economic situations for Kenyans is to a great extent facilitated by these two social practices.[205] The following two chapters focus on how these practices structure social relations between African Kenyans—including not only Digo but also upcountry Kenyan immigrants to the area—and German-speaking residents and tourists in Diani, and on the role these practices play in negotiating economic and emotional precarity.

3 Charity

Then they talked at length of traders, Arab and European, wandering the African continent, propagating their faith, making gifts of their deities and beliefs (like present-day foreign aid), presents that the Africans accepted with little question.

　　—Nuruddin Farah, *Gifts*

[Gifts are] in theory voluntary, disinterested and spontaneous, but are in fact obligatory and interested.

　　　—Marcel Mauss, *The Gift: Forms and Functions of Exchange in Archaic Societies*

Gifts opened channels of communication here across boundaries of status and literacy. They gave expression to the highly strained but genuine reciprocity between unequals in the social and economic order.

　　—Natalie Zemon-Davis, *The Gift in Sixteenth-Century France*

Timeo Danaos et dona ferentes.
(I fear the Greeks, especially when they bring gifts.)

　　—Vergil, *Aeneid*

From *Utsi* to *Wakati ya dotcom*

Until the recent past, the Digo of the Diani area made frequent use of several institutions of solidarity through which individuals benefited from communal action and the community benefited from the collective actions of individuals. One of them, *utsi*, involved the entire village or a large part of it; another, *mweria*, addressed the needs of smaller groups of people.[1] Village elders would determine the time for an utsi, and a variety of collaborative activities could be carried out under the umbrella of utsi. Some involved the whole village community; some drew on all able-bodied men and others on abled-bodied women.[2] Utsi were announced for the purposes of harvesting coconuts (*kubwaga nasi pamoja*), hunting (*kuwinda*), fishing (*kuvua*), cleaning the beach or areas of the village (*kusafisha, kuosha*), planting (*kulima*), harvesting on communal land (*kuvuna*), and conducting weddings and funerals (*harusi, mazishi, mahanga*).[3] Another collective event that villagers I interviewed mentioned several times as an important example of utsi was a rainmaking ceremony (*kuomba mvua*), which the vice chair of Magutu, one of the villages in the Diani area, described in 2013 as follows: "Two men get a black cow, their clothes are also black. They walk with the cow in a big circle to Kaya Likunda, then along the beach, up again until Kibundani, until Bongwe, Shamu, and Musema Guo, and then back. Then the cow is slaughtered, and everything is eaten by the community. Then the rain comes." Villagers also recalled ceremonies to protect against illness (i.e., *uganga*, a term designating a healing ceremony) as forms of utsi.[4] There was also collective action against thieves (*wezi*).[5] Utsi involving women specifically were aimed at guarding against wild animals (*wanyama porini*).

Mweria, the term for the system of communal self-help involving smaller groups of individuals, was explained thus: "Today for me, tomorrow for you, it goes around." Ten people might come together to fix their roofs, one after another, or they might harvest or plant together on their individuals plots, renovate their houses, or dig holes for pit toilets.[6]

Today, both institutions are more or less extinct in most parts of Diani. Utsi for the purpose of collecting funds for a wedding or funeral still exist, but other examples of collective action carried out in the form of these two practices are rare. Some forms of utsi are no longer possible: hunting, for example, has basically died out, as much of the forest has been reduced and what is left is protected as a kaya (such as Kaya Diani and Kaya Ukunda). One middle-aged villager from Mvumoni said that he remembered utsi still being practiced when he was a child in the mid-1970s, but he could not attach a specific year to when he had last heard of its use. He recounted an event that he described as an utsi that led to the building of a primary school around 1970: in Mwaroni, a number of villagers with adjacent land all agreed to give up a slice of their property, and in the middle of that land they built the school. In 2013, the assistant chief of Bongwe, Ali Nassir Mwakubo, said that the last utsi he could recall must have occurred in 1997, a year of terrible drought. At that time, the council of elders decided to call for a rainmaking utsi. The last mweria that he remembered occurred more recently: in 2012 a group of people decided that they wanted to build traditional toilets in Vukani, and they dug holes for all members of the mweria group.

Conversations with elders in Mwaroni, Mvumoni, and Mwamambi in December 2014 shed more light on present-day practices of communal support. These villages on the northeast side of Diani are, in contrast to other parts of Diani, inhabited mostly by Digo. They resemble times past in that they follow some longstanding traditions and remain more tightly socially organized. The villages are free from the piles of garbage one sees in the areas of mixed population on both sides of the main road, areas that lack social cohesion. Though Muhammed (age eighty-eight) from Mwaroni suggested that these days people were not supporting each other as they did in old times ("hawashirikiana kama wakati zamani"), he stated that sometimes utsi and mweria were still practiced in Mwaroni ("baado iko," some are still here). Bakari (age sixty-seven) from Mwa-mambi provided several examples of mweria. It seems, however, that utsi and mweria, if they occur at all, are practiced mostly by the senior members of a community.

Cynthia Gillette, in her 1978 study, mentions two other forms of communal action that did not come up in my conversations but that Diani Digo may also have used. The first one is *wiri*, which Gillette defines as work groups; the second one is *kukumbana*, which brings together three or four families who work on one another's fields in rotation. While kukumbana, similar to mweria, were reciprocal, wiri "benefitted only the person who called it." Gillette asserts that these forms of communal support "are no longer operative."[7] She also describes various Digo practices of generating capital that are in fact indigenous forms of microcredit. She mentions forms of borrowing based on the borrower's posses-sion of tree crops, which provided credit under three different options. Another way to obtain smaller amounts of credit was through cash gifts (*msaada*, Kiswa-hili for "help") from the family or larger community.[8] It seems to me that this last method to raise funds also could have been conducted within the framework of an utsi. Gillette's discussion illustrates the ways kinship relations and lineage structured the various forms of communal support.[9]

Overall, these forms of communal solidarity have largely disappeared over the course of the past fifty years. Most younger Digo in Diani, especially those born after 1980, have never heard about utsi or mweria. Some villagers said the institutions vanished after independence, while others suggested their disap-pearance happened more recently, about twenty years ago. It seems that this dis-appearance was gradual, though the most significant changes occurred during the 1970s. The three village elders of Magutu with whom I met in July 2012—the chair (born in 1937) and two committee members (born in 1946 and 1955)—all clearly remembered participating in utsi. "When you had a problem, the local people solved the problem together," said one of the committee members, who remembered collective farming, fishing, and coconut harvesting. The elders also mentioned a number of other customs that existed previously but are no longer valid or followed, such as rules concerning illness (where and when not to farm if an illness is present; creating a sacred space for sick people) and slaughtering (performed ritually at a place designated for slaughtering in the area of Umoja). When I asked for their opinion on when most of these customs had been aban-doned, the three men agreed that things had changed during the 1970s. Up until then, the village was united, they said, and villagers talked about all kinds of things together.

In a conversation in November 2013, three women from Mkwakwani (born in 1951, 1953, and 1963) suggested that utsi and mweria stopped because of "bad decisions made by the village elders." What exactly those decisions were (and it is notable in this regard that women are not represented on village committees in Diani), I was not able to establish, but it seems that the village councils of the area must have, at some point, made decisions to stop harvesting together or stop fishing together. "Watu wanapendana zamani" (people used to like each other in the old days), suggested one woman, implying that they used to care for each other then. Today, the women complained, everybody was just looking after their own business; everybody just cared for themselves ("chako ni chako," "kila mtu mwenyewe," "kila mtu shauri yake"). They were especially vocal about their wrath against the area's young men. "Hakuna heshima" (they have no respect), the women said. "They don't take care of their families, not even their mothers; they are bad."

This sentiment also dominated a conversation I had the same year with three other village elders of Magutu: the vice chair, the treasurer, and another elder (born in 1948, 1951, and 1955, respectively). These men suggested that communal activities ended in the 1960s, after independence, for a number of reasons. "Watu walianza kufanya kazi" (people started working), they said, referring to the influx of salaried jobs, and "watu wamesoma" (people studied), referring to increased participation in formalized education. People wanted development, I was told, they wanted modernization, they no longer wanted to pursue the traditional ways (*utamaduni*), they wanted privacy. "Sasa hivi ni wakati ya dotcom" (today is the era of dotcom), they said, an expression that the female elders had also used and that was associated with the preeminence of privacy and doing things only for oneself. Village elders seemed torn between an endorsement of the desire for development and a longing for the traditional ways of doing things. The village elders also insisted that the government played a role in bringing about changes for the worse: today, one needed a permit for everything.

These conversations point to two main developments that contributed to the disappearance of communal solidarity: the increase of salaried employment opportunities and various top-down government interventions. The latter of these points evokes the issue of the detrimental effect of actions carried out under the *harambee* (let's all pull together) movement, which was intended to build on existing institutions of solidarity but in effect contributed more broadly to the demise of communal solidarity. In the immediate postindependence era, President Kenyatta identified harambee as a key concept to "mobilize local resources and . . . involve local participation in development." Yet over time, as Peter Ngau stated already in 1987, "harambee has become distorted, deviating from its traditional emphasis on basic production to the provision of large, costly social amenity projects." Ngau termed this development "departicipation," as it "reflects disempowerment at the grass-roots level."[10] The initial easy appeal of harambee is rooted in the fact that self-help institutions were central to most Kenyan communities; harambee was supposed to draw on these active forms of self-help. But whereas harambee was meant to inspire collaborative action and solidarity, the type of harambee projects pursued and the way they were managed turned the movement into a divisive system that led to polarization among the poorer segments of the population and the emerging elite.[11] Initially, harambee benefited especially the Kikuyu elite; after Kenyatta's death, President Moi deployed harambee for his own interests and, according to Stephen Orvis, "used *harambee* strategically to reward close supporters and weaken or divide enemies."[12] Overall, harambee became a vehicle for Kenya's elite to enrich itself, with an adverse effect on less powerful and privileged social segments and communities such as Diani. It seems that in the case of Diani, harambee and other governmental development initiatives contributed to the de facto demise of local self-help institutions, without offering an adequate replacement.[13]

The various sentiments Digo villagers voiced regarding the loss of utsi and mweria capture the tension between some sort of desire for development and modernization, on one hand, and the all-too-late realization, on the other, that some traditional institutions had merit. In conjunction with introducing harambee policies, Kenya's leadership embraced capitalist development. But communal systems of solidarity are incompatible with a capitalist economy based on individual ownership and salaried labor. Ultimately, utsi is an inherently political institution, which explains why it became a political concept during the struggle for independence. In fact, utsi and other practices of solidarity resonate with what Robert Mambo has described as an "apparent democratic practice" among the Mijikenda society in the nineteenth century.[14] As the discussion in the previous chapter showed, the Digo, in line with their earlier participation in anticolonial resistance, were increasingly involved in political activities after World War II.[15] The fact that one of their key political organizations during the years leading up to independence was called Utsi Society reflects the significance of utsi as a political institution.[16]

Utsi and mweria are centrally defined by the idea of reciprocity; that is, all members of the community have to invest in collective action in order to receive benefits. This aspect, as historian Steven Feierman explains, was also integral to precolonial forms of sub-Saharan philanthropy more broadly: "Sub-Saharan Africa, in the centuries before colonial conquest, was a region where voluntary giving was, in a majority of cases, grounded in reciprocity, and yet where inequalities existed, where kindly help was as double-edged as it is in the philanthropic West—a peculiar combination of caring and dominance, of generosity and property, of tangled rights in things and in people, all in a time and place where the strong would not let the weak go under, except sometimes." After reviewing various forms of philanthropy in precolonial Africa, Feierman stresses that "after colonial conquest, every one of the philanthropic institutions [that he discusses] . . . was transformed."[17] While utsi and mweria persisted throughout the colonial era, they did not survive the effects of postindependence political policies of the central government and its concurrent integration into capitalist development.

The disappearance of indigenous communal forms of support created a vacuum because both the Kenyan state and the capitalist economy, which in the narrative of modernization should have restructured those areas of social and economic activity that had been traditionally defined and organized by local communities, showed only rudimentary interest in the Diani community. The 1970s, which Diani villagers identified as the period during which utsi and mweria largely disappeared, is also the decade when tourist development began in earnest and when villagers first began taking salaried positions in the hotels. While the tourism infrastructure initially brought welcome change through salaried job opportunities, neither the state nor capitalist institutions were engaged sufficiently in developing the area. As a result, population growth and rising unemployment in Diani increased poverty and created an overall situation of need in basic areas of life, such as infrastructure development, education, housing, and health care. Over the course of fifty years, Diani went from being a self-sustaining community with a communitarian ethic to one in need of outside help.

Today Diani is characterized by a pervasive "culture of charity." This culture is shaped primarily by expatriate residents and repeat visitors who initially came as tourists, but its roots lie also in colonial charitable institutions, which perhaps explains why, locally, humanitarian activities are referred to as "charity." The culture of charity, in one way or another, structures most social and economic relations in Diani, for there is no family in the area that does not benefit from the formal and informal humanitarian activities of Germans and other Europeans. This culture of charity draws on ideas of human rights and humanitarianism that are perceived to be a virtue of Western modernity but knows nothing of indigenous forms of communal solidarity; as Bonny Ibhawoh points out, those forms of solidarity were "integrated within a system of rights and obligations, which gave the community cohesion and viability."[18]

Some of the key questions at the center of this investigation of developments in Diani concern the long-term effect of humanitarianism: Was the outside help that flooded into the area in the form of humanitarian activities a factor that not only addressed, but also engendered the loss of self-supporting institutions (in addition to top-down measures of the postindependence government and the economic effect of the tourism industry)? Does this influx of humanitarian support also help to explain why Kenyans living in the Diani area seem to be reluctant to devise new methods of communal action?[19] And in what ways is charity integral to neoliberal capitalism? In order to get a sense of the extent of various social practices that are structured by charity, I review four representative types of humanitarian activity in Diani, each of which is either led by or substantially supported by Germans. I then discuss these initiatives comparatively with regard to their effects on the state, the economy, and local African Kenyan communities of the area, which today include not only Digo, but African Kenyans from all regions of the country. First, however, a review of the German propensity to donate funds to projects in Africa will help explain the availability of monies and the eagerness of Germans, Swiss, and Austrians to get involved in charitable activities in Diani.

German Aid to Africa

Humanitarian aid to Africa is a prominent form of contemporary philanthropy, one that is central to the self-image of societies of the global north. According to the Deutsches Zentralinstitut für soziale Fragen (German Central Institute for Social Questions), in 2013 the total of all forms of private donations in Germany reached €6.3 billion.[20] More than 75 percent of private philanthropic organizations are active internationally; almost 80 percent of their work is designated as "humanitarian aid"; and the largest percentage of German donations for internationally active organizations supports humanitarian aid to Africa.[21] During the summer of 2011, appeals to donate in response to the famine in East Africa raised €91 million within four weeks.[22] In July of that year in Switzerland, one news organization reported that 7.8 million Swiss francs were raised in the course of only a few weeks.[23] In August, Swiss citizens donated 20 million Swiss francs through one particular donating platform for the famine in East Africa.[24] In 2013, the volume of private donations in Switzerland was 1.6 billion Swiss francs, exceeding the amount of giving per person in Germany (the population of Germany is 82 million, while that of Switzerland is about 8 million).[25] Austrians donated €510 million in 2013, slightly up from the €500 million in 2012. In light of the Austrian population of roughly 8.5 million, the per capita spending volume is not as high as that of Switzerland and Germany.[26] In 2011, €131 million were designated for "humanitarian and development purposes." Austria, then, sent less aid to countries of the global south compared with the aid Germany and Switzerland sent to those areas.[27] One report states that Austrians prefer to give to domestic projects.[28]

While per capita giving of Germans, Swiss, and Austrians is lower than, for example, that of Americans, the differential rates are tied in part to the fact that social inequality in those European countries is lower than in the United States and many of the initiatives supported by US donations are funded through different sources and mechanisms in Europe (e.g., religion and education). In the United States, the majority of donations address domestic issues (such as education, religious institutions, and other social issues), and international giving, at $19.1 billion, amounts to only 6 percent of total donations.[29] In contrast, the bulk of German and Swiss (less so Austrian) donations are designated for projects abroad, especially in the global south. The reasons for giving are complex; what donors self-report may not explain all of the dimensions at play. When self-reporting, donors tend to emphasize solidarity, identification with the organization or a specific cause, and ethical or other beliefs.[30] These factors certainly play a role, but self-interest, power, and guilt are additional motivations that guide donors and humanitarian activists, as we will see.

Historically grounded social norms are relevant as well. German humanitarian activities in Africa, when placed on a longer continuum and within the context of north-south relations, resonate with historical models of humanitarian activities, in particular those of the Christian missionaries who accompanied colonial expansion.[31] I have shown elsewhere that Albert Schweitzer, who spent decades of his life as a doctor in Gabon, epitomizes a form of individualized modern humanitarianism that was born of the Christian tradition and then was secularized. Alternatively, Henri Dunant, the founder of the International Red Cross, embodies the institutional dimension of modern humanitarianism.[32] Schweitzer's actions and writings have shaped German humanitarian discourse and activities (including fundraising patterns) to this day, and the ongoing connection to Schweitzer is quite visible, as will become evident when we turn to the activities of individual Germans in contemporary Kenya.[33] The figure of Schweitzer provides a tie to Africa that continues to appeal to many German humanitarians, but contemporary aid to Africa is also inspired by other traditions of philanthropy and solidarity. Welfare institutions sponsored by aristocrats, religious groups, and, later, political organizations such as the Workers' Welfare (*Arbeiterwohlfahrt*) were the most common forms of philanthropy before the modern welfare state and certainly provided models for international aid.[34] Annett Heinl and Gabriele Lingelbach have shown that West German giving to organizations that operated abroad emerged in the 1950s in the context of development aid (*Entwicklungshilfe*) activities and discourses.[35] The economic, political, and social situations of "Third World" countries have attracted growing public attention since that time. Human rights advocacy in particular relates German philanthropic activity in Africa to what Lora Wildenthal has identified as one of the four usages of the "language of human rights," namely, "activism on behalf of foreigners." In the former West Germany, this activism can be traced back to the Society for Threatened Peoples (Gesellschaft für bedrohte Völker), which, according to Wildenthal, began as the Biafra Aid Campaign (Aktion Biafra-Hilfe) in 1968 and soon thereafter "broadened its scope to any 'people' (Volk)."[36]

Activities on behalf of foreigners can also be placed within the context of two even larger currents that distinguish German culture. First, the longstanding identification of Germans with Native Americans, which Glenn Penny brilliantly discusses in *Kindred by Choice: Germans and American Indians since 1800* (2013), educated the German public about the consequences of colonial rule for indigenous peoples. Second, critical discussions of the Shoah in Germany (and elsewhere) facilitated a broader debate of genocide and human rights. Together, these developments contributed to the emergence of humanitarian initiatives and new legal norms relevant to humanitarian responsibilities.[37]

In Germany and other areas of the Western world, humanitarian activities are distinct from forms of charity and philanthropy that focus primarily on alleviating suffering at home, though structural similarities exist and are increasing in tandem with the growing social inequality in the Western world, as the aftermath of Hurricane Katrina has shown.[38] While faith-based humanitarianism continues to play a significant role in global humanitarianism, the much broader mobilization of what Austin Sarat and Javier Lezaun call the "humanitarian impulse" has become a cornerstone of politics.[39] "Humanitarian reason," as Didier Fassin suggests, informs a "new moral economy," the roots of which can be found in the longer history of missionary work, charity, and philanthropy, and which, as Andrea Muehlebach has shown, is integral to the functioning of neoliberal capitalism.[40] In the new millennium, Schweitzer has been replaced by the likes of Bob Geldof, Bono, Oprah Winfrey, Angelina Jolie, and even swindlers like Greg Mortenson.[41] In the German context, celebrities such as the late Karlheinz Böhm, Herbert Grönemeyer, Wolfgang Ambross, and Philipp Lahm have popularized humanitarian work in Africa.[42] The star power of film, music, and sports celebrities imbues "good works" in Africa with a glamorous distinction, and concepts that are popular topics in the media, such as the advancement of human rights and democracy around the planet, buttress the idealist legitimacy of humanitarian deeds.[43] The pervasiveness of the discourse of human rights in Western culture has been the focus of numerous studies, which have collectively created a kind of metadiscourse on the subject that by itself calls for analysis in the context of global power relations.[44]

Humanitarian organizations that focus on Africa are ubiquitous across Germany and can offer support across the continent or to specific groups (such as children or people with disabilities), countries, and regions. Often, several organizations exist that address a specific country or even town, such as Ukunda.[45] German donors and the organizations they fund influence African societies in substantial ways. With regard to Kenya, German humanitarian activism is closely tied to the significant role Germans played in creating Kenya's tourism sector, as a result of which a large number of Germans have visited and also settled in the country since the 1960s. Overall, economic interaction between the countries is significant, but in Diani, tourism specifically was a crucial factor in generating humanitarian activity. The effect of tourism on local communities differs from case to case; examples from around the world range from utter destruction of environments and communities to modes of coexistence between locals and visitors/part-time residents and, more recently, sustainable ecotourism projects.[46]

As we saw in the previous chapter, the tourism-dependent economy of Diani, as it developed over the past fifty years, is unable to sustain the African Kenyan community that surrounds it. The case of Diani documents that failed, lacking, and ineffective planning and infrastructure development resulted in the economic precarity of the local community, which in turn led to the creation of a pervasive culture of charity. In Diani, charity fills the gap that was created through the disappearance of communal forms of support but, arguably, also contributed to their disappearance. Although charitable actions address needs that were previously attended to through various forms of communal social action and also tackle new areas of need and want, they differ from utsi and mweria in terms of notions of accountability and reciprocity, which are key elements in creating not only coeval relations, but also sustainable forms of social and economic action.

Charitable activities initiated or supported by Germans operate according to distinct approaches to the local community, and all of them embrace the jargon of human rights and humanitarianism. In categorizing these activities, it seems sensible to acknowledge basic structural differences. Whether key organizers are based locally or abroad plays a central role, as does the relationship between Diani-based initiatives and donor networks or other forms of institutionalized funding in Germany, Switzerland, and Austria. Four different modes of charitable activities are representative of the range of endeavors in the Diani area: (1) activities of foreign (in this case, German) individuals who have a donor network abroad but are not registered in Kenya and who also pursue diverse projects; I call such individuals "contraband humanitarians"; (2) educational institutions that are run by expatriates and registered in Kenya but also draw on a donor network abroad (such as Diani Maendeleo Academy, which was founded by a German woman); (3) Kenya-registered charitable organizations whose history often dates back to the colonial era and that address a range of needs (such as the East Africa Women's League, which is dominated by women with British backgrounds but also draws on support from Germans); and (4) initiatives in the health-care sector (such as the Kwale District Eye Centre) that are run and supported by local and foreign personnel and donors and tied to internationally recognized INGOs (in this case, Germany-based Christoffel Blindenmission). I present examples for each mode of humanitarian activity, paying attention to three main points: (1) the relationship to the Kenyan state, (2) the effect on the economy, and (3) the involvement of the community and questions of reciprocity. I then discuss the projects comparatively and tie the overall culture of charity in Diani to local economic precarity and consider its relation to transnational economies of aid and volunteering.

Case Studies

Contraband Humanitarians

Tourism is frequently the contact zone for humanitarian activity. Once tourists realize that even small sums of money can have a tremendous effect, many of them pursue philanthropic activity with great enthusiasm. Initial contact is often made in a hotel at which visitors stay or at a restaurant, bar, or beach. In the late 1990s, I conducted my first study on German repeat visitors who vacationed on the Diani coast and learned about the extent and nature of their interactions with the local population. I distributed questionnaires to 110 German repeat tourists and interviewed 28 of them. These repeat visitors had vacationed in Kenya in some instances more than twenty times. Most tourists came to Kenya for an average of two weeks, but repeat visitors generally stayed for longer periods, especially if they were retired. In all cases there was significant contact between the local population and the tourists. The questionnaires showed that 70 percent of the repeat visitors had visited Kenyans in their homes; 49 percent had exchanged letters with Kenyans since their last visit; and 70 percent had brought presents for locals. Among those I interviewed, an even larger number of individuals, 80 percent, supported Kenyans materially in one way or another. They paid education fees for different types of schools, such as primary and secondary schools, language institutes, and driving schools; they bought school supplies and uniforms; they took care of hospital bills and paid for other medical needs; they brought clothes, household items, and electronic appliances; and they even helped people build their own homes.[47]

For some of the tourists these measures of support were a first step toward becoming a committed "contraband humanitarian." I use this term because most of the activities of contraband humanitarians occur outside the official structures of development (be they governmental or nongovernmental) and at times include outright illegal activities. In Diani, contraband humanitarianism is the most widespread form of humanitarian support. Locals actively inspire tourists and European residents to take on the role of the humanitarian, and Europeans eagerly accept this role and often also initiate the interaction. I suggest that the practice is so widespread because it successfully responds to both Kenyan and German (and other European) needs. Kenyans see economic gain; and Germans benefit primarily in terms of their emotional need for recognition, power, and a certain degree of adventure and excitement that Europeans experience when traveling to and acting in African countries. Back in the mid-1980s, I met a German woman, Helene Niedermeyer, who, every afternoon at around 4:00 p.m. would pull up a chair in the same place on the beach and wait for people to bring their requests to her.[48] From paying school fees and hospital bills to resolving marital disputes, Niedermeyer, who was in her early seventies, tried to address every request. She operated as an effective contraband humanitarian, creating a donor network back home in southern Germany that allowed her to pursue projects of significant scale. The nonprofit organization she established held regular fundraisers, and Niedermeyer, who vacationed two to three times a year in one of the five-star hotels of Diani Beach, brought the proceeds of the fundraisers to Kenya, distributing the money to various locals who had succeeded in attracting her attention.

By founding a donor network in Germany, Niedermeyer had essentially created the type of organization that journalist Linda Polman calls a "MONGO," or "My Own NGO," a term that highlights the subjective and perhaps haphazard dimension of this type of NGO.[49] Niedermeyer, who died a few years ago, was not the only repeat visitor drawing on the support of a network at home; the larger Diani area is crowded with schools, water tanks, dispensaries, nurseries, houses, toilets, and wells that were built for locals with the funds of contraband humanitarians. There is not a single public or private school in the area that does not have a sponsor, usually European, whose name is stamped on school desks or acknowledged on the entrance wall of the building (figure 3.1). Every larger family in Diani has been touched in one way or another by the activities of contraband humanitarians.

The stories of two contraband humanitarians who have been active in the area over the past twenty years shed light on the tremendous extent and effect

Figure 3.1. Donated benches in a Diani school

that such individuals can have on a community. I first heard about Gustav Müller from a local musician who had received his guitar from him and who indicated that Müller was sponsoring various projects in the area. Fortunately, Müller was visiting Diani at the time, and I was able to meet him and his wife, Bertha.[50] Our initial conversation in January 2010 gave me a sense of the extent of the Müllers' humanitarian activities and was followed by several meetings with Gustav Müller during the summer of 2011 and again the following summer.[51] The Müllers have been traveling to Kenya since 1991. They first pursued their aid activities alone but eventually established a support network in Germany (their MONGO) that is raising ever-increasing sums of money. Müller said that in 2009, his network had raised more than €25,000 and that he expected the sum to rise to €100,000 in 2011. As of May 2010, the association, which is also loosely connected to a larger and more visible network, was registered as a nonprofit organization (*eingetragener Verein*) in Germany. A core of about twenty active members draws on a constantly growing donor network; overall membership had grown to eighty-two individuals by the end of 2014. Fundraisers take place at weddings, birthdays, concerts, schools, and other public events.

The explicit goal of the organization, as expressed in its constitution, is to "improve the living conditions of human beings in Africa," with a focus on education and health care. The organization emphasizes that it is guided by principles of self-help, which demonstrates once more that amateur humanitarian organizations of this type are fluent in the language of development and have adopted the discourse of humanitarianism in their publications. Beginning in 2005, the main focus of the Müllers and their association has been Kijiji Village, which is located at a significant distance from Diani. About twelve thousand individuals live in the area connected to the village. Among the various humanitarian projects, including some in locations outside of this particular village, are the following:

- Replacing defunct water pumps
- Building toilets and shower stalls
- Sponsoring school children (in 2015, Germans paid fees and bought supplies for 116 children; in 2011, the Müllers' organization had sponsored 48 children)
- Supporting primary and secondary schools, both public and private (funding the building of new structures and toilets, supplying books, providing a meal program for, in 2015, seventy-five children, and erecting water tanks)
- Supporting the Kwale District Eye Centre (through donations of cash and equipment as well as by collecting used eyeglasses and buying and reselling items from the Eye Clinic Charity Shop)
- Supporting orphans (three children from Kijiji Village were taken to an orphanage in another location)

- Building water tanks in various places (to date, nine water tanks have been built in Kijiji Village alone)
- Providing mosquito nets (in 2008 the initiative distributed more than one thousand nets)
- Building a maternity ward (a €65,000 project)
- Supporting health dispensaries (the organization provides a significant amount of medications, particularly in support of an epilepsy network)
- Creating employment (through the support of seamstresses, woodcarvers, and musicians) and supporting various children in an SOS Children's Village.

Funds for the Müllers' organization are raised in Germany. Initially, the couple relied on their private network, and over time their association reached a substantial number of supporters in their hometown and the surrounding areas. The Müllers have been savvy with regard to the handling of money. Funds for schools and other initiatives are transferred directly into bank accounts in Kenya, and the Müllers collaborate with several individuals who keep the books. Gustav Müller, now retired, can draw on his professional experience as a former member of the management team for a company that employed one thousand individuals. Bertha Müller previously worked as an office administrator. Together they have the know-how to deal with various aspects of their humanitarian initiatives. Gustav Müller travels to Kenya several times a year, sometimes accompanied by his wife or other members of the organization. During these stays he moves around the area in an impressive SUV, checking on his various projects, not unlike a county commissioner. This may seem like a reasonable method for his monitoring the status of the various initiatives, but the image of Müller as an inspecting officer brings up questions about his role and that of his organization within the Kenyan context. While some of their activities, such as the building of toilets, require government approval (in this case, from the Ministry of Health), none of the planning occurs in collaboration with state institutions. As a result, almost none of the organization's activities are coordinated with Kenyan governmental agencies, a situation that would be unthinkable if, say, the flow of such activity were reversed: Would Germany, for example, allow Qatari or Chinese humanitarians to fix dismal situations in its areas of urban poverty without any oversight or involvement?

To give me a sense of the extent of his activities, Müller invited me in July 2011 to spend a day with him visiting a number of the projects he had sponsored or was in the process of sponsoring. The account of this day-long journey is instructive as it provides insights into the activities of one individual who clearly emulates historical models, such as that of Albert Schweitzer. Müller has carved out a space and a role for himself that affects the lives of hundreds of Kenyans, although his activities, for the most part, occur without any knowledge or involvement of the Kenyan state or any kind of INGO.

Müller, who usually stays in one of the most expensive hotels at the coast, had rented a large SUV. Similar to other charity workers in the area, he seemed to have no problem with this display of wealth—an aspect that does not go unnoticed by locals. As one Digo man once said to me, "At least the missionaries of old used to live with us in the village." We left Diani at around 8:30 a.m. On our way out, we picked up various people, among them a doctor who works at a dispensary that we later visited. Others were waiting along the road to hand their requests or contractor quotes to Müller. For instance, one contractor provided Müller with a quote for a toilet to be built next to another dispensary still under construction. Just before Kijiji Village, we stopped at a borehole in the area of Umoja Village. In 2009, Müller, noticed that the old pump was defunct, so he decided to replace it and also improve the installation and reach of the pump. Materials and labor had cost only about €1,000, so with relatively little money Müller and his organization were able to support the livelihood of the approximately four hundred people who benefit from the borehole. Without the functioning pump, villagers would have to walk more than two hours to the next borehole. Closer to Kijiji Village we stopped at another borehole. Müller had replaced this pump in 2010. He also built a trough to catch the dripping water from the pump, which is now drunk by thirsty cows and also nurtures a few banana trees that villagers planted on the moist soil at the end of the trough. Because cows had eaten some of the bananas, the village chair wanted to build a fence, and during our visit he asked Müller for a kilogram of nails. At this and other boreholes we visited, locals recognized Müller and engaged in friendly conversation with him.

We then arrived at a private primary school in Kijiji that enrolls 160 children, 40 of whom, I was told, are orphans—a number I found exceedingly high, as the area has not been afflicted by famine or war recently and AIDS rates are low in the coastal area. I was wondering whether this inflation reflected an attempt on the part of locals to secure funding for scholarships from Müller's organization. The school includes the three levels of kindergarten and eight classes of primary school. It employs fourteen teachers, including the school's principal. The school was founded in 2008; Müller came into the picture in 2009. The Müllers and their network donated desks and a cupboard for the office, which they commissioned from local carpenters. Müller insisted that involving small businesses in the country is to be preferred over, say, exporting large machines into existing factories in Kenya: "That only destroys the local infrastructure," he pointed out to me. He also commissioned the construction of a water tank for the school. The tank catches rainwater from a couple of roofs and provides water for cooking and drinking. The government regularly inspects the water quality.

Müller proudly drew my attention to the cleanliness of the schoolyard. He explained that this was part of the agreement between him and the school, namely, that the compound had to be kept in good shape. His organization also built a new toilet (and here, getting a permit from the Ministry of Health was mandatory)—only one toilet for 160 students, but still an improvement over the previous installation. His group furthermore provided a high number of mosquito nets for the children; this visit alone they had brought five hundred. A local doctor helps distribute the nets and also documents everything for the donors. The principal showed us the results of the last state-administered tests and was excited to point out student improvement from the previous year. He was also proud of the fact that eight of eleven eighth-grade graduates had continued on to secondary school. "This would not have been possible without the books you provided," he told Müller. Adjacent to the primary school is a vocational school. Here, Müller was given a "request for assistance," which asked for nine mechanical sewing machines and three boxes. Müller has supported this school before, and he accepted the request for consideration.

Our next stop was the Kijiji dispensary. The building, which was originally built in 1990 with funds from several non-Kenyan organizations, consists of five small rooms and serves a community of roughly fifteen hundred individuals each month. The services include outpatient treatment, testing and treatment for tuberculosis and HIV, immunizations, prenatal care, child welfare, laboratory services, and family planning. Here, Müller and his organization supplement resources provided by the government. The government restocks the dispensary every three months, but according to a doctor who works at the dispensary (and who was clearly uncomfortable with my presence, perhaps worrying that I was in a position to challenge her accounts and activities), the clinic usually runs out of supplies about halfway through a cycle, and the additional supplies are much welcomed. In February 2011, Müller funded the installation of solar panels on the roof, which now supply electricity. Apart from the availability of light during, for example, night-time deliveries, the electricity also enables the dispensary to maintain a refrigerator for medications. A staff house was also equipped with solar panels. "We bring only contemporary technology, nothing outdated," Müller explained. During our visit, Müller received a request for repair and painting of the building. Presumably, the government had been delayed in allocating funds for building maintenance, although the doctor said that the government just devised a new scheme, called Hospital Services Funds, which was supposed to provide support. The doctor insisted that the fee of twenty Kenyan shillings collected from each patient (and which in some cases is waived) and assistance received by the government do not cover the expenses. Salaries, medical supplies (such as cotton pads and gloves), and medications, let alone building maintenance funds, exceed the available resources. There are other needs in addition to the renovation of the building: the existing water tank, for example, is not sufficient, and the nearby borehole does not function.

Our next stop was another private primary school, this one founded in 2005. In the summer of 2011, it enrolled 187 children. With three kindergarten levels and grades one through eight, the school employed eleven teachers, two cooks, one watchman, and one guard. Müller and his organization were sponsoring thirty-nine children with a scholarship of €150 per year, which covers most of the expenses. They had also built two water tanks and a toilet. In 2010, the school was running despite the fact that it was not yet registered with the Ministry of Education (which occurred in early 2014). What was still missing in 2011, according to government guidelines, was a permanent structure with a proper foundation. Constructing this permanent building with four classrooms was one of the projects Müller was supporting in 2011. A building for the administration, including rooms for the principal and teachers, was also planned. Much of this had been accomplished by 2015.

Next we visited a public secondary school. It was built about a decade ago on a compound that featured an unfinished school structure that had deteriorated into ruins. Inspired by personal contact with one of the villagers, a German woman had taken on the project and had the structure rebuilt. The school opened in 2000, and when I visited in 2011, it was in excellent shape on well-maintained grounds. The school enrolls eight hundred students; six hundred are girls who stay on the campus as boarders, while the boys live off campus. Müller and his organization replaced the existing but defunct water pump. They installed a submersible pump and drilled a very deep hole, after which the pump began to deliver 2,500 liters per hour. The water is potable, and Müller was very proud to show me how clear it runs. The pump is running on a generator, as the school has no electricity. For the near future, Müller was sponsoring the building of a pipe to water tanks located higher up on the school grounds, as well as pipes that would bring water to other buildings. Next door is a public primary school, and Müller was planning another project that would deliver water to it as well. The plan was to run a pipe from the secondary school to a 5,000-liter-capacity water tank to be built at the primary school. During my visit a discussion—brought on by some of my questions—occurred about the contribution of villagers to the project. After some resistance from the principal and only in the vaguest of terms, it was agreed that villagers will support the building process with their labor, as a kind of matching donation. While we were visiting, Müller was presented with a handwritten request for assistance. Written on college-ruled paper, it spelled out the various aspects of the water pipe and water tank projects.

On our way back to the Diani area, we passed by another borehole where the organization had replaced and enhanced the pump. Our last stop was a large public primary school that employs forty teachers and enrolls about fifteen hundred children in kindergarten through eighth grade and that recently added a first level for a secondary school. The principal explained that many of the children are orphans (again, the high number of orphans is puzzling), and the school also has a unit for mentally challenged children. Müller's organization installed a 250-meter water pipe, added electricity for a submersed water pump, installed a water tank, built a tower for the new tank, renovated the nursery, bought toys, added an outside veranda, and built an indoor kitchen (an improvement over the previous outdoor cooking facility). It also supports a feeding program for the kindergarteners and for the first level of the secondary school; the local representative of the organization delivers food two to three times a month. In addition, the organization was building twenty toilets, in four phases. The first phase had been completed, and Müller proudly presented the five new toilets, a dramatic improvement over the two long-drop toilets that had served the school's children until recently (the teachers had access to another set of two toilets). The principal and others call Müller "Papa," a clear expression of the role he is playing at this school. He would often pick up one of the children and walk around with a child in his arms. At two of the schools, the children sang for us. Müller's style of interaction with the various people we encountered was jovial. He adopted the local style of bantering very well and is visibly comfortable in his role. His English skills are not perfect, so at times he is not able to communicate verbally with quite the politeness he apparently intends, but his gestures and mimicry support the generally warm affect that he exudes.

The range of Müller's projects is substantial, and when he surveys his projects in the area, his public appearance is reminiscent of that of a Kenyan official or a United Nations development officer. Müller's organization is not registered in Kenya (and only recently in Germany), and Müller has never visited Kwale's county (formerly district) commissioner, education officer, or development officer. At some point Müller considered registering his network as a local organization, but he felt this would inevitably lead to conflict with his Germany-based organization: "Because then we have two organizations with different goals," he explained. Müller went through official channels—such as when a sanitary unit attached to a dispensary had to be approved—in only a few cases, and most of the time these interactions were initiated and carried out by his local contacts. Müller admitted to me that at one point a representative of the Ministry of Health had approached him and asked him to stop importing and handing out medications free of charge, as this interferes with the local pharmaceutical market. Müller recounted that on one occasion he had brought in twenty thousand tablets for epilepsy in response, as he insisted, to the absence of a functioning governmental program. But it seems that the prohibition to import medications illegally had no effect on Müller's choices: as he confided to me in 2011, on that visit alone, he had brought two hundred kilograms of supplies, including medication, first aid kits, a wheelchair, and a bicycle. In 2013, the cargo amounted to seven hundred kilograms. Interestingly, some airlines fly cargo for various charitable organizations for free, thereby becoming complicit in the transport of contraband charity items. The activities of Müller's organization raise a host of questions regarding its role within Kenya's political, economic, and social landscape.

My second example of a contraband humanitarian active in Diani in recent years is a Swiss woman, Anna Bäumler, who over time has significantly contributed to infrastructure development in the area and has also directly helped select individuals.[52] She first came to Kenya in 1988 and slowly got to know people through contacts she made with hotel staff. Those staff members took her to their homes in the villages of Diani, and she gradually became familiar with the living conditions and needs of various people. She initially brought children with her to the hotel and then began to pay for the education of certain ones. Soon she expanded her range of activities, establishing an organization in Switzerland to serve as a fundraising platform to support projects in Diani. She advertised her initiative in newspapers, on the radio, and on television. Sponsors included individuals from all walks of life, as well as faith-based organizations. Some donations were as large as 10,000 Swiss francs. One of her most successful projects, dating back to this early phase of her activities, is an elementary school that in 2012 provided about seventy scholarships to select students. She also provided funds that enabled older students to attend secondary school and placed disabled children in an orphanage.

Bäumler's educational background does not extend beyond middle school (ten years of schooling in the Swiss system); she speaks no Kiswahili and only rudimentary English. Her work experience was as a salesperson in a department store. Considering her lack of knowledge of language, culture, and history, she moves across the area with amazing confidence, which, however, is rather typical for German and Swiss settlers in the area. Bäumler is articulate in a matter-of-fact and persuasive way and also has a keen sense of the emotional dimension of human suffering—qualities that enabled her to mobilize the empathy of hundreds of donors for her projects.

In the early 1990s, she fell in love with one of the hotel employees and in 2001 left her husband and Switzerland behind and relocated to Diani. Bäumler was forty-eight when she made this life-changing decision. She had had "secure employment" in Switzerland, she told me, but she was not content with her life there. "I always had to do what the boss told me to," she said. "I wanted to be the boss for a change and show what I am able to do." Once she moved to Diani, her level of charitable activity increased. She raised funds to dig wells, repair roofs, and build toilets and three large water tanks (figure 3.2). She took drug addicts to the treatment program of the local Catholic church and began caring for a child whose mother had died of AIDS and who himself was infected with HIV. She

Figure 3.2. Water tank in Diani

is trying to adopt the boy, but the process seems to be very difficult; it had been under way for about three years at the time I talked with Bäumler in 2013. All of this, Bäumler said, was done without asking for reciprocity; it was done out of a good heart ("alles ohne Gegenleistung, von gutem Herzen").

Without my asking her to elaborate on her motivation for helping in Diani, Bäumler offered the following explanation for her activities: "I always loved Africans. On Epiphany I was dressed as an African" (Ich hab die Afrikaner immer lieb gehabt. An Dreikönig war ich als Afrikaner verkleidet). The Catholic feast day of Epiphany commemorates the three kings who are said to have visited Jesus after his birth. It used to be one of the few occasions in which ordinary Germans, Swiss, and other Europeans would come into contact with a positive image of Africans, as traditionally one of the three kings would be represented as being black. It is easy to imagine that the notion of an African as king and having a special relationship to Jesus Christ could inspire the imagination of children and adults alike. In addition, in some areas of Switzerland, Epiphany is celebrated as the beginning of the Carnival season; as Bäumler said, as a child, when asked to choose her costume, she had opted to be a black queen.

Her strong identification with and affection for Kenyans was disturbed significantly when she discovered that her lover had defrauded and cheated on her. His name is on the title deed of their house, so she had to move out and de facto lost the property. One Digo man, commenting on the affair, said: "She is a good woman but the man was too clever . . . . The lady really was very kind, everybody in the village knows her." Subsequently, Bäumler stopped most of her charitable activities (though the school and the water tanks still exist), and today she has barely enough money to survive and take care of the African Kenyan child who lives with her. When I interviewed her in 2012, she was bitter and visibly exhausted (she had suffered two strokes in the previous few years and told me she had been depressed for more than a year). She complained that after all the years she had spent helping others, nobody had come to her assistance when she was in need, not even to offer emotional support. By 2013, she seemed to have found her bearings again and seemed more balanced than she had been the previous year, but she was still disappointed about the lack of support she had received from those whom she had helped over the years. In 2014, she reported that she was receiving pension payments from Switzerland and her situation was more stable again. Overall, her experience illustrates the disconnect between contraband humanitarians and the community. My interviews with her revealed that she had a limited understanding of Diani and of Kenya more broadly.

What are the implications of this contraband charity? For contraband humanitarians, proof that their work is meaningful is easily established: providing for education, improving sanitation and health care, and taking care of orphans are actions that correspond to the goals of the United Nations and other development agencies and accord with widely acknowledged concepts of human rights. Financially, all of the projects supported by Müller and Bäumler, as well as those supported by others who are active in similar ways in Diani, depend on funds flowing to Kenya from Germany, Switzerland, and Austria (and other European countries). Without this donor support, none of the projects would be able to survive; the erected infrastructure would quickly crumble without funds to support its maintenance. Nevertheless, Müller's and Bäumler's investments have the potential to produce long-term effects.

Contraband humanitarians achieve their goals with a minimum of bureaucracy and overhead costs, and they track the outcome of their aid through long-term personal contacts. In many ways, these activities seem more effective than what results from what Dambisa Moyo calls "systematic aid—that is, aid payments made directly to governments either through government-to-government transfers (in which case it is termed bilateral aid) or transferred via institutions such as the World Bank (known as multilateral aid)."[53] As Carol Lancaster has shown, "aid agencies themselves have often lacked the technical experience, local knowledge, staff, and appropriate processes to manage such projects and programs effectively."[54] In contrast, Müller and Bäumler seem more effective than the agents of systematic aid and also those who work for INGOs, which have been criticized for large overhead costs, ineffective management, problematic political effects, and questionable outcomes.[55] Müller and Bäumler, and other contraband humanitarians, work directly with and in response to requests by locals, which suggests a collaborative dimension to this form of charity.

What, then, are the main objections to contraband charity? Despite the seemingly obvious beneficial dimensions of this kind of aid, there are long-term repercussions that most contraband humanitarians are not prepared to grasp. Because such aid functions independently from governmental institutions, weakens the local economy, and fosters dependence more than reciprocity, contraband charity, more than any other form of aid discussed here, is part of, and has further built, a culture of charity that has detrimental effects on various levels. I return to these issues in the discussion below.

Educational Institutions

VERKAART DEVELOPMENT TEAM AND MEKAELA ACADEMIES

While contraband humanitarians build and sponsor schools in informal ways, a large number of the schools in the Diani area are sponsored, run, and owned by Europeans who have officially registered their institutions with the Ministry of Education. Although generally more integrated into the social fabric of the area and aligned with Kenyan-designed educational initiatives, German activism on behalf of education in Kenya struggles with many of the known challenges that are integral to international humanitarianism.

The most visible sponsors of education on the south coast of Mombasa are two Dutch citizens, Jan and Ans Verkaart, who founded the Verkaart Development Team (VDT) in 1991.[56] Their organization is registered in Kwale County and works in close collaboration with the Ministry of Education.[57] VDT is also active in the area of health, disability, and infrastructure development. The organization identifies itself as a "private charity foundation" and, apart from two employees in Kenya, works exclusively with volunteers. It insists on representing a model of "development cooperation" rather than "aid." As of 2016, VDT has built *more than seventy* public primary schools, four public secondary boarding schools for orphaned girls (with more than two thousand girls enrolled—but again, we have to question the orphaned status of these children), ten dispensaries, a dental clinic, and two polytechnic schools on the south coast. The organization states that the seventy schools serve seventy thousand children and employ seven hundred teachers. Other VDT projects address the needs of disabled children (150 mentally and physically disabled children live in a boarding school), albinos, and abandoned boys. It is unlikely that the Ministry of Education has had a comparable track record in Kwale County during the same time frame.[58]

Sponsors of the organization are encouraged to travel to Kenya to visit the projects onsite. Tours are offered twice a year, in March and October, but additional tours can be arranged for large groups. On VDT's website, the tour is described as a "festive event: You can visit our projects, meet your orphan/s, and discover a different world." But the trip to Kenya will not focus only on charity projects: "Often the project visit is combined with, for example: a visit to one of the nature parks, such as Serengeti, Masai Mara, Tsavo and Shimba Hills; a visit to the city of Mombasa; visits to Wasini Island, Zanzibar, and Lamu; sports activities like snorkeling and scuba diving, motorbiking, quad biking, golfing, kite surfing, mountain biking etc."[59] The organization thus promotes what is known as "voluntourism," in this case a voluntourism that is clearly directed at a most affluent group of European sponsors. In addition to the tours for sponsors, foreign volunteers contribute to the projects by working on the ground in Kenya.

In several conversations I had with African Kenyans and Europeans, the VDT was mentioned as one of the organizations that attached considerable stipulations to its sponsored projects. When I interviewed representatives from the local Department of Health and the Department of Education in 2011, several officials, and also teachers, described Jan Verkaart, the central figure of the organization, as "bossy": "He acts like a king, is not even in consultation with his own group." An individual who worked in the education sector told me that Verkaart had decided to support building a secondary school in Waa, but during the building phase, the school's principal accepted a donation to build a mosque on the school compound. When Verkaart found out, he was enraged and pulled all support from the school. He also retaliated against the school's principal and had her transferred to a different school. Students were infuriated and protested on behalf of their principal, and their criticism of Verkaart was widely publicized, but to no avail.

Others said that Verkaart interfered in decisions that governmental representatives considered their domain, such as the staffing of schools. The degree to which an expatriate from the Netherlands is involved in Kenya's public education is astounding. It is not surprising that a figure who runs such an influential organization should be perceived as a competitor to Kenyan governmental officials. Verkaart has a command over resources that can't be matched by what local representatives of the Ministry of Education have at their disposal. The case of Jan Verkaart and VDT brings into focus the challenges that come with privately run foreign aid, especially as regards its relationship to the state.

While the VDT is unmatched along the south coast in terms of the scope and scale of its activities, a wide range of educational institutions are run by expatriates from other European countries as well. The Diani area has a high number of private schools; fewer private schools are found farther inland, which illustrates the connection of the Diani schools to the tourism-related infrastructure closer to the beach. Several of Diani's private schools were founded and are now maintained by Germans. The most visible institutions in this regard are the four schools known as Mekaela Academies, which serve a significant portion of the population of the larger Diani area. The organization was founded in 1993 in

Germany as Watoto e.V., a nonprofit organization in accordance with German laws.[60] Over the years, founding members Frank Muether, Micki Wentzel, and Stefan Wentzel have overseen the building of three primary schools, the Manuel Alexander School, the Likunda Primary School, and the Heshima Primary School (built with support from the German foundation Eine Welt Stiftung), and a secondary school, the Lulu High School.[61] Enrollment as of 2014 was considerable: 277 at Manuel Alexander School, 385 at Likunda Primary School, 77 at Heshima Primary School, and 251 at Lulu High School. The total number of boarders was 267, most of them high school students (251). About half of the children enrolled in the schools receive scholarships through the organization's fundraising network.

Students enrolled at Mekaela Academies have been highly successful, and test results documenting their achievements stand out in nationwide comparisons. Student performance in national exams in 2013 is a case in point: the primary schools produced most of the top ten candidates in Kwale County, the highest score being 421 out of 500. Lulu High School ranked first in Msambweni District (one of three administrative units of Kwale County). Twenty-eight graduates qualified to attend college. Among the various services offered by Mekaela Academies are "free basic out-patient medical coverage for all students" and "career guidance and counseling."[62] In 2011, an agency was set up to help unemployed parents and relatives of students locate permanent employment with good working conditions. The schools build on their credibility and on the sustained relationship with parents to vouch for the employees' reliability, trustworthiness, and overall character. About fifty employees are employed through Noble Domestic Agency; this, as co-owner Micki Wentzel said, "is although we are not doing any form of massive advertising. A lot of our reputation is due to word-of-mouth. Clients also like the idea that we are a not-for-profit organization. Any financial surplus which is generated is utilized for uniforms, an annual bonus for each employee, etc."[63] Mekaela Academies permanently employs almost 160 people (such as teachers, gardeners, kitchen staff, and security) and is thus one of the larger employers in the area.

Mekaela Academies pursues several projects that are designed to increase the sustainability of the schools. Two farms, comprising an area of about twelve hectares, provide grain and vegetables for students. Solar power generates part of the schools' electricity needs. Students and employees are encouraged to assist in saving energy by, for example, switching off lights when not needed. Mekaela Academies has its own workshop for repairs (including welding and carpentry as well as a tailor shop). Elements of reciprocity and community involvement are rudimentary, but promoted. When parents apply for sponsorship, volunteering is identified on the reverse side of the application form as one of the terms of condition: "It is expected that parents of sponsored children offer voluntary services to the school. In every term, one parent should be available for one half day to render his/her services to the school on the headmaster's request. Such services are to be provided for no other than the school's benefit." It is thus mandatory for parents of sponsored pupils to contribute some labor, such as slashing grass, sweeping the school grounds, and cleaning up. Generally, such volunteering lasts for only a half hour or one hour. Another purpose of mandatory parental involvement is to create opportunities for parents to interact with one another and with teachers; in this way they are also encouraged to follow up on their children's progress. As Micki Wentzel suggests, however, involving parents who themselves often have very little schooling is not an easy task, and lack of parental involvement often affects the performance of a child. Noteworthy in this regard are also four famine-relief missions during 2011 and 2012 to the drought-stricken province Turkana in the north of Kenya that consisted of volunteering parents and teachers.[64]

The organization has a tremendous fundraising capacity. An illuminating example of this is the swift recovery after a fire destroyed Lulu High School and parts of adjacent Likunda Primary School in 2013. The schools were "provisionally operational with lots of improvisation" only two weeks after the blaze, and "after two months the schools operated normally. Although much construction was still taking place, several classrooms were already in a condition that allowed us to use them for regular lessons."[65] Less than 50 percent of the funds for rebuilding came from insurance reimbursement; the rest of the money needed to rebuild the schools, €150,000, was raised in Germany. In light of its considerable enrollment, placement, fundraising capacity, community involvement, and the wide range of social services, Mekaela Academies stands out among the schools within Kwale District and the larger Diani area.

DIANI MAENDELEO ACADEMY

Since early 2010, I have been following Diani Maendeleo Academy, a private secondary school for girls. When I first met its director, Ingeborg Langefeld, the school was still in the early stages of development, which allowed me to observe the challenges that emerge in establishing an educational institution in Kenya.

Langefeld, who was employed in Germany as a social worker (*Sozialpädagogin*), moved to Kenya with the specific plan to create opportunity for girls. At the time, no such institution existed on the advanced level in the Diani area, which is predominantly Muslim. Diani Maendeleo Academy is the result of her efforts. As the managing director of the school, Langefeld has an investor's permit in the area of education, which includes both work and residency permits. Similar to what we have seen with regard to contraband humanitarians and Mekaela Academies, the school is supported by a Germany-based association: the NGO Girls' Hope e.V. promotes the project and raises funds for scholarships, school supplies, and construction and maintenance of buildings.[66] Langefeld is the chair of the German NGO, which increased its membership from twenty-eight in 2010 to thirty-eight by 2014. The relationship between the German NGO and the Kenyan school is regulated through a contract. Buildings constructed with money from Girls' Hope belong to Girls' Hope, which holds first buyer's right for buildings that belong to the school but were not built with funds from Girls' Hope.

The Diani Maendeleo secondary school was founded in 2004 and opened in 2005; its academic reputation has increased every year. Between 2010 and 2013, enrollment fluctuated between eighty and ninety-five students, and in early 2014, one hundred students were enrolled. The school is located in the area of Mwabungo, about seven kilometers from Diani. It serves Diani and the larger area; about 80 percent of the girls come from nearby Ukunda and other Diani locations; other girls come from Mwabungo, Msambweni, Tiwi, and even Kinango, which is more than an hour's drive away. The school is accredited by the Ministry of Education, but as a private school with a donor network, it is 70 percent to 80 percent financed by donations. Most of these funds are raised through the German NGO and are used to pay for student fees, building construction and maintenance, salaries, and supplies. To provide financial transparency, the German NGO posts the complete financial annual reports of itself and the school on the web, which is not at all a common practice among these types of charitable institutions.[67] The total amount raised by Girls' Hope over the years has fluctuated between €50,000 to close to €100,000. Maendeleo secures additional funds through school fees and also local donations. Over time, local donations for specific projects have made it possible for a kitchen to be built, for example, and a school bus acquired.

Girls' Hope raises money mostly in Germany; it initially drew on Langefeld's personal networks in Gelsenkirchen and Mühlheim and then broadened its geographical range over time. Funds are obtained in various ways, including the fundraising platforms Bildungsspender and Betterplace (the latter received a substantial donation from the Buscher-Stiftung in 2010).[68] Fundraising went well in 2010 and 2011, despite the recession; Langefeld interprets this fact as a sign that the school maintained credibility in the eyes of donors. In 2012, however, the decreasing value of the euro posed substantial challenges for Langefeld, who compensated for losses by paying some expenses out of her own pocket. Funding, however, went up again in 2013. In 2010, Girls' Hope supported 51 of the 80 students at Diani Maendeleo through fellowships; by 2014, 78 of 100 girls were sponsored through fellowships. The four classrooms each have a capacity of 45, allowing for a total enrollment of 180 students. Increasing enrollment is one of Langefeld's goals, as it would make the school more sustainable.

Conceptually, the school is inspired by human rights demands in the area of education and gender equality. In a conversation with me in February 2010,

Figure 3.3. School bus of the Diani Maendeleo Academy

Langefeld emphasized that learning is a "human right: everyone has the right to learn." "Modern Education based on Traditional Roots" (figure 3.3) is printed on the school bus, along with, "No one can go back and make a new beginning / But anyone can start from now and make a happy ending."

This call for individual agency but also solidarity is reflected in another school slogan: "Many small people in many small places who take many small steps can change the face of the world." The school aims to promote the full participation of women in Kenyan society. Overall, Diani Maendeleo Academy is explicit in its support of gender equality, better education, self-empowerment, solidarity, and ecological thinking. The school provides free breakfast and lunch for all students. This policy developed after the realization that girls from poorer backgrounds were often arriving to school hungry. In the school's 2013 report, Langefeld wrote, "We consider good meals as just as important as good academic instruction."[69]

Part of the school's identity is its support of academically weaker students. Langefeld is adamant about accepting students who do not necessarily score high on tests. She insists that in contrast to other private schools in the area, her goal is to be inclusive and to create a school for all members of the community. Because the school accepts weaker students, Langefeld suggested, the ratings are not as high in comparison to, for example, the Mekaela Academies, which are said to target high-achieving students. Langefeld's principle, she explained, was to accept one academically weak girl per every strong or average girl. In 2011, she accepted two girls into the boarding school who had been abandoned by their parents and who were academically low achievers. In 2012, she graduated two girls who were mentally challenged. She also explained that according to Kenyan educational guidelines, schools are not allowed to order a student to repeat a class. The pressure to perform well is incredibly high: Langefeld pointed out (and media reports corroborate the statement) that every year a few students who do poorly on the exit exams of their primary school, and who thus do not have a chance to enter secondary school, commit suicide. In addition, the age of girls (and boys) who enroll in secondary schools is often high; it is not unusual for a seventeen-year-old to embark on secondary education. That delay is a result of the fact that children are often kept at home when parents are unable to pay for books, uniforms, or transportation to the nearest primary school, let alone pay fees for private schools.

Despite Langefeld's policy of accepting weaker students, the school's reputation has not suffered. In July 2012, the Ministry of Education presented Diani Maendeleo Academy with the "District Most Improved School" award for secondary schools in what was then Msambweni District (now a subcounty of Kwale County), which gave it a considerable distinction among the then five private and fourteen public secondary schools in that area.

Langefeld has made a tremendous personal investment in the school. Her monthly salary amounts to KSh30,000 (about $300 in 2016), and she does not own a private car. As of 2016, she continues to live in a small and rather simple apartment in Ukunda, the center of the Diani area, just a few yards from the main road. The rent for the apartment is KSh10,000, roughly $100. She explained to me that she will eventually move to a more comfortable place, but she knew she could be successful only if she kept her own expenses as low as possible for the first few years, rather than allotting herself a generous allowance—a practice that has often led to the demise of nonprofit projects. Her living situation stands in stark contrast to that of many contraband humanitarians who lodge in some of the five-star hotels on the coast or who have been able to secure a substantial allowance for their own needs.

I first visited the school grounds in July 2011 and have returned every year since. Langefeld owns the 2.2 hectares on which the school is built. The school association used the compound rent-free for five years; since 2009, the rent has been KSh200 (about two dollars) per student per year, which is clearly a nominal fee, a gesture rather than income. Apart from one building that came with the compound when Langefeld bought it, the various school buildings were constructed with funds from Girls' Hope. Three separate buildings house the four classrooms (one for each grade), a laboratory, and a storage room. The office building contains the main office, the teachers' room, an area in which food is passed out, a Muslim prayer room (60–70 percent of the girls are Muslim), a storage room, a library (containing, in addition to Kenyan school books, donated materials from the United States), a small classroom, and another storage space. Two buildings are named, reflecting associations that donated the funds for their construction: the Sternstundengebäude (named after the Sternstunden Foundation) consists of a room for the teachers, a computer room, a dining hall, and a study hall, and the Buscher-Haus (funded by the Buscher-Stiftung) is a dormitory where thirteen of the girls board. During my first visit in 2011, twelve of the boarders were rather crammed into two rooms, while one slept in a bed in the kitchen and a teacher slept in another room of the building. "We desperately need a sleep hall," Lange-feld said. At the time, the compound also had one water tank (a second one was under construction, with funding from a German chapter of Soroptimists),[70] a makeshift open-air kitchen, a duck coop, and a goat stable. Charcoal is produced on the grounds, and gardeners grow vegetables and take care of fruit trees. Wild pigs and monkeys diminish the harvest, minimizing the profit, so the school is trying to devise better strategies to protect the crops. In 2011, Langefeld proudly showed me the foundation for a permanent kitchen—a donation from the Stern-stunden Foundation.

Another 2011 acquisition was the school bus, which seats thirty-three and was purchased with support from the Futura-Stiftung and local donations. The bus picks up girls from Ukunda; students who come from farther away use other forms of transportation, either to the first stop of the bus or directly to the school. Painted brightly in yellow and red, the bus publicizes the school more effectively than any advertising campaign. Langefeld received the bus, at a significantly reduced price, from a local dealer, Associated Motors, whose owner was a member of the local chapter of the Rotary Club. Additionally in 2011, the school had entered a competition called "Lebensräume—Lebensträume" (Spaces to live—Spaces to dream) in collaboration with a school for handicapped children in Germany. They won the €20,000 prize, and shared it with their German partner school.

Enhancing the school's sustainability has become a priority for Langefeld. In order to secure the food for school meals, she acquired a greenhouse in 2012. In 2013, she added a fishpond to generate income from the sale of fish. The fishpond is funded by the Ministry of Fisheries Development, which runs a program encouraging Kenyans to farm fish. Upon approval of the request for participation, the ministry provides a plastic tarp, nine hundred small fish, fish feed, and consultation free of charge.[71] The first harvest was relatively small (flamingoes and water evaporation are among the challenges that Langefeld continues to face), but the project is in its infancy. The greenhouse comes with its own trials in the form of pests and unreliable watering systems. Langefeld also grows *sukuma*, a type of spinach, and cassava on a field behind the school, though the fight with wild pigs is ongoing (at times involving charges of witchcraft that staff members and neighbors voice; witchcraft is also evoked in other situations that beg for explanation). All roofs have been equipped with water spouts for rainwater collection. Solar panels have been added to several roofs. Recycling practices are integrated into the curriculum. For one project, students made greeting cards out of recycled paper; for another, they built musical instruments from a variety of items found at trash sites; and they are generally encouraged to collect glass and plastic bottles.

The environment was also the focus of a series of events that students organized at the end of the 2013 school year. Langefeld explained that it was important to provide opportunities for students to engage in activities that the girls themselves structure. The traditional Kenyan approach to education, she suggested, rarely fosters students' creativity and initiative; here, the girls discussed the benefits of solar and wind technology, produced a newspaper, made soap from neem leaves, and staged a theater and a musical performance. Occasionally, the school organizes field trips, for example, to Shimoni, a site connected to the slave trade on the coast. The teachers also take field trips once a year (reminiscent of the German convention of *Betriebsausflug*, or company outing), usually to historically and culturally relevant sites.

In 2013, Langefeld submitted several applications for funds that would help her build a boarding house. In addition to offering a more appropriate living space for current boarders, the house would allow Langefeld to increase boarding student enrollment, as students who live farther away in areas without a secondary school and who are also unable to commute would be able to attend. Many parents, even those who live within commutable distance, will opt for the boarding school option, as it often shows better results with regard to overall learning, retention, and graduation rates. In December 2013, after a long wait, Langefeld received notification that her grant application for funds from Global Care, a foundation connected to the Knorr-Bremse Group, had been approved.[72] The grant totaled €50,000. Half of the funds were designated to buy computers, fund solar panels, and build ecologically friendly toilets. The other €25,000 facilitated construction of the boarding house. The plan was to increase capacity to provide boarding for one hundred girls, which allowed Langefeld to raise enrollment, stabilize income, and thus increase overall sustainability; in 2016, that goal was reached.

Since its inception, fifty German interns have worked at Diani Maendeleo Academy, and their presence has often been a mixed blessing. The process of recruitment involves several stages. Candidates first submit a statement of purpose, a résumé, and letters of reference. Then selected candidates, who must have completed at least four semesters of higher education, are screened in a two-hour interview by an associate in Germany. The internships last between one and three months; in a few cases they are longer. Interns have to pay for their flight to Kenya and cover their own room and board. Some interns are able to secure internship fellowships through organizations such as Weltwärts, a global service program comparable to the Peace Corps that is initiated by the Bundesministe-rium für wirtschaftliche Zusammenarbeit und Entwicklung (the German devel-opment ministry) and cooperates with approximately 180 partner organizations (*Entsendeorganisationen*—the German term retains the connection to the idea of a "mission").[73] The German Academic Exchange Service also provides oppor-tunities.[74] Langefeld provides a detailed guide covering work conditions, health issues, and local living conditions, among other aspects, which gives interns a sense for the challenges and rewards of the internship. An FAQ document pro-vides additional information.[75]

Despite the guide's frank description of the challenging work and living en-vironment and the contract's equally concrete conditions and stipulations, many interns view their service in Kenya as an extended vacation.[76] Diani, with its spectacular beaches, and Kenya, with its opportunities for wildlife safaris, moun-taineering, and more, offer many distractions. To Langefeld's dismay, her interns often turn into "voluntourists." Interns typically go through several phases dur-ing their stay; initial enthusiasm is often followed by confusion and lethargy, mostly as a result of the failure to integrate the overall challenges of working in an unfamiliar environment. Another challenge for interns is their interaction with the local population. Langefeld says that interns have to be able to navigate local culture without being overwhelmed by it. In Diani, once personal contact is established, locals expect foreigners to help them financially. Often, interns feel used after they realize that a friendship or romantic relationship in which they engaged left them broke and that they did not properly understand the economic dimension of the interpersonal connection (see the next chapter). It is impor-tant, Langefeld says, for interns to balance emotional closeness and distance, and those who immerse themselves without understanding the local context leave the country feeling frustrated and disappointed. She is critical of interns who come to Kenya primarily to have a tourist experience, and clearly, she is aware of some of the problematic dimensions of voluntourism.

Langefeld does not use local interns because she says Kenyans would not work without pay. Kenyans would consider the fact that her German interns pay for room and board and travel expenses to be unacceptable working conditions. Langefeld suggests that this is especially true of Kenyan university students or graduates—the social group equivalent to the German interns—and even more so if they come from rich families.[77] However, many local and international or-ganizations in Kenya do draw on unpaid or modestly paid Kenyan interns and volunteers. Perhaps Langefeld's hesitance to recruit local interns speaks to her unfamiliarity with certain aspects of Kenyan society and the fact that she is not networked sufficiently. An additional explanation for a preference for foreign in-terns in projects such as Diani Maendeleo Academy may be that such interns af-ford foreign-born owners of enterprises with familiarity and support from their own culture; humanitarians in charge of organizations can draw on a personal staff with whom they can speak in their own language, and collectively they form a power block vis-à-vis the local staff members, such as teachers in this case. The question of how much to involve locals and at what level was crucial also in colonial contexts, and the relationship between humanitarians and their local collaborators resonates with the social, cultural, economic, and political dimensions of the colonial experience.[78] The English-only policy at Maendeleo (with, of course, the exception of the use of Kiswahili during Kiswahili lessons) also speaks to this aspect. Even though English-only policies will enhance the students' literacy and fluency in the language, and such policies are also practiced at institutions that are run by Kenyans, in this particular case (and in similar cases) the use of only English makes it easier for Langefeld, who speaks only little Kiswahili, to manage her environment. This dynamic between humanitarians/foreign interns and locals all too often reproduces colonial structures.[79]

In mainstream culture, however, international volunteering seems to be beyond critique: it is sponsored by governments (through programs such as the Peace Corps and Weltwärts), churches (through building houses in Mexico, for example, a favorite spring break option for many Midwestern high school students),[80] and INGOs alike. The message that "volunteering for a worthy cause can be fun, fulfilling, and an adventure you'll anticipate year after year" is broadcast by a wide range of advocates of volunteerism.[81] Scholars such as Katherine Borland and Abigail E. Adams, who critically study voluntourism in Central America, insist on the overall beneficial potential of international volunteerism: "Although critical of much current practice, the authors affirm the importance of cultivating cosmopolitan values and acting to promote social justice in a profoundly unequal world."[82] Perhaps international volunteering evolves in distinct ways in different regions of the world. Central and South America, for example, can draw on longstanding traditions of solidarity and community-based activism that may structure voluntourism from a local perspective. Yet the economic and social effect of international volunteering is complex. Voluntourism has created an industry that is generating substantial economic volumes; expenditures related to voluntourism globally are estimated to be between $1.66 billion and $2.6 billion a year, involving 1.6 million voluntourists annually. Volunteering also has commercial dimensions that are more pronounced in some cases than in others. As Angela Benson writes, "Whilst many of the volunteering opportunities are often linked to charitable organisations, it is also evident that some of the growth in this sector is by profit-making companies, and whilst some of these can be linked to social entrepreneurship others are purely commercial."[83]

There is little research on the effect of international volunteering on host community economies. Volunteerism represents an economic factor similar to remittances and the informal economy, the latter of which is estimated to have averaged around 20 percent of Kenyan gross domestic product between 1970 and 2005.[84] The phenomenon of interns in countries like Kenya raises serious questions. Like other factors of aid, volunteerism devalues local labor, especially in economies with already high unemployment rates, and thus stifles national economic development. In addition, the psychological dimensions are profound, especially with regard to the way unemployed and underpaid Kenyans perceive foreigners who do "their" work free of charge. The Kenyan cases exemplify this global phenomenon: volunteerism highlights the detrimental effect of this industry, as labor is donated in a country that has a substantial unemployment rate but also a large group of high school and college graduates in addition to uneducated workers who would be able to do the jobs foreign volunteers perform. The lack of local knowledge that foreign volunteers display, in almost all cases, also makes them less qualified than a Kenyan employee would be, despite the occasional expertise that volunteers might have to offer.

Volunteer labor is part of the increasing reality of unpaid labor across the globe. Unpaid and paid internships have increased the economic precarity of young people in both the global north and south, with volunteerism especially pronounced in the global south. But the effects of unpaid and paid internships are also felt by countless individuals who are part of the labor force. As Ross Perlin writes, "In a time of chronic high unemployment, internships are replacing untold numbers of full-time jobs."[85] Volunteerism devalues local labor, intensifies social inequality, and decreases opportunities for paid labor. What seems like a noble gesture on the part of affluent members of the global community amounts to a reduction of employment opportunities for the less fortunate while foreign interns increase their employability back home. International volunteerism may be effective in specific situations, such as legal representation or targeted medical services, but its potential to amplify global inequality is considerable.[86]

With so much voluntary aid and services coming to Diani from Germany, how then does the local community get involved in projects that foreign philanthropists develop for the benefit of that community? Does Diani Maendeleo Academy, for example, incorporate community involvement the way it is practiced at Mekaela Academies? Does the school ask for forms of reciprocity especially from those parents whose children are on scholarship (and who, in fact, often lobby tirelessly to find sponsors for their children from among the tourists and local residents)? Langefeld complains that her attempts to commit parents to contribute their labor to improve the school grounds on so-called working days have been fruitless. Nothing, she says, is being done without money, and that includes collaboration with other public schools, sports competitions, and medical camps as well as between teachers and parents. Without remuneration, Langefeld reports, nobody contributes to school activities, even if their children are on scholarship, and village elders are of no help. On top of this lack of support from parents and the larger community, she at times faces outright hostility from neighbors whom she suspects of poisoning her dogs and who often approach her for money. She mentioned one exception: a community-based organization for troubled children that collaborates well with her. Despite the fact that Langefeld pays attention to the needs of the local community—for example, by accepting weaker students—the community is evidently not willing to reciprocate. Does this unwillingness of locals to volunteer amount to an intuitive or conscious resistance to the contradictions of capitalism? Is it a resistance to an economic order that monetized a society that used to be built on social actions performed without monetary exchange? Is such resistance an expression of historical aware-ness of a colonial system that forced Kenyans to work without pay?

Langefeld is key to all of the school's operations. She oversees financial trans-actions, manages the fundraising, hires and supervises the teachers (eleven in 2016) and other staff (six permanent, plus several workers for agriculture and other manual labor), supervises the interns, controls aspects related to the cur-riculum, and even personally passes out food supplies. As of 2016, her school provides secondary education to 130 girls and, with the completion of the board-ing house, potentially to more in the future. Diani Maendeleo Academy is part of the local fabric of Diani, and yet, like other projects supported by donations and interns from abroad, it is also part of a transnational economy of exchange that poses a range of important questions regarding the culture of charity, questions I return to in the discussion below.

Kenya-Registered Charitable Organizations: The East Africa Women's League

Scholars have only recently acknowledged how missionary and charitable work were two main areas through which nineteenth- and early twentieth-century women were able to play a pronounced public role. Elizabeth Prevost states that "overseas evangelism was driven in large measure by female organizers, mission-aries, and converts" and points out that in the British empire, "by the turn of the twentieth century, the majority of missionaries operating in the field were women." Prevost stresses the connection between "mission work and broader civilizing missions."[87] As regards nursing, Lora Wildenthal has shown that it "was second only to missionary work as a social role for German women in the colonies, predating even marriage and motherhood. Years before colonialists urged German women to become wives and mothers of settlers, nurses and the women who raised funds to dispatch them had a secure place in the colonialist movement."[88] Nursing is a characteristic area of charitable activity, and the con-nection to fundraising resonates with contemporary practices of humanitarian work. Wildenthal explains that the beginning of women's colonial activism dates back to the early phase of German colonialism, the 1880s, and in both the British and the German cases, women's missionary and charitable activities increased in scale during the first decades of the twentieth century.[89]

The East Africa Women's League (EAWL), which includes several Germans in its chapter on the south coast, was founded in 1917 by colonial settler women, right around a time that saw a general increase in women's institutions in the colonies. The organization's first aim was to secure East African women's right to vote, which was accomplished in 1919. At that point the league concentrated on "improving the lives, physical, moral and mental, of all women and children in the country whatever their race or religion."[90] Historian Deanne van Tol has explored in detail the more political rather than charitable origins of the organization.[91] In the historical context of the Kenyan colony, the right to vote initially was granted only to white women, and only white women could be members of the league. As van Tol writes, "the question of admitting members from African and Asian communities was not discussed in a serious way until the 1950s and not enacted until Kenyan independence in 1963."[92] Even today, EAWL, at least in its South Coast chapter, has few African Kenyan members. When in 2010 I asked members of the South Coast Branch why there were only two African Kenyans in the local chapter (there were three in 2013), one woman suggested that most African Kenyan women "would not be able to afford the membership fee" and that those who could afford it were "busy working."[93] However, a good number of wealthy African Kenyans live in the area, some of whom are members of other charitable organizations. Perhaps the lack of African Kenyan members in EAWL speaks to the culture of an organization with roots in the colonial period, when the relationship between colonial and indigenous women was hierarchical and certainly complex.[94] The diverging realities and objectives of colonial and indigenous women stifled the emergence of forms of solidarity that would consider indigenous perspectives, even as some EAWL members who were active during the colonial period, such as Isabel Ross, were advocating equality and inclusion.[95] To this day, political views of league members have been far from unified.

Since membership meetings are held during the day and during the week, rather than on weekends, participation is indeed more difficult for working women, which also explains the average age of about sixty among EAWL members. Clearly, and in line with the historical roots of the organization, membership is based on a certain level of affluence; the chair, for example, has to be able to host membership lunches, and EAWL members draw on their own money when organizing various events.[96] As one EAWL chair put it, "You pay for the privilege," which sums up the fact that an active league member has to commit a baseline of resources.

The South Coast Branch is one of twenty-four chapters; I was not able to establish when the chapter was founded. The history of the nearby Mombasa

Branch dates back to 1926, yet the Diani area showed no significant white settlement until the 1960s, making it likely that the branch was founded in the 1960s or 1970s.[97] The South Coast Branch, at the beginning of 2010, had forty-three paying members, and over the past few years, this number has essentially remained the same. About 25 percent of the members live overseas and are in Kenya only part of the year. In 2010, five of the paying members were German or Swiss. While the role of Germans in EAWL has fluctuated over the years, the organization is considered here as representative of one type of several locally based charitable organization that operate in the area and are supported by Germans. Money is generated through membership fees and, more important, fundraising: the South Coast Branch organizes bake sales, garage sales, lunches, bingo games, and similar events. The largest fundraiser is a goat derby, held annually at the local golf club and drawing a crowd of about seven hundred to eight hundred people. In October 2009, the derby brought in KSh950,000 (equivalent to about $13,000 at the time), quite an astonishing sum for a one-day goat-racing event. The 2010 event raised even more money, more than KSh1 million. In 2012 and 2013, the figure continued to rise, to roughly KSh1.5 million (about $17,000) and KSh1.88 million (about $22,000), respectively. The high amount in 2012 was partly due to a donation of KSh1 million from the Commercial Bank of Africa; the event also benefited from massive media coverage through KTN, one of Kenya's main news channels. I was told that the success of the 2013 goat derby had made members "lazy," and therefore there had been fewer additional fundraisers that year. The total amount of money raised annually by a local EAWL chapter, including the membership fees, initially goes to the umbrella organization, from which it is dispensed centrally. The individual chapters then decide which initiatives they will support with the money they receive.

EAWL supports a wide range of projects. In the area of health care, for example, it built a maternity ward at Mbuwani; a Swiss woman, along with others, brought the project to a successful conclusion. The Kwale District Eye Centre (discussed below) always receives funds; in 2010 and 2011, the center received a considerable KSh250,000; in 2013, it received KSh200,000. Most of those funds go toward the Poor Patients Fund. EAWL also supports an epilepsy clinic (with about KSh100,000 in 2010); the monies mostly help to buy medication and sponsor five children who suffer from epilepsy. Until recently, a leprosy village in the area received funds annually. EAWL also contributed to a lunch program, "Child for Child," and for a period provided daily lunches for about fifty children.[98] Sanitation is another area of need addressed through EAWL funds. In Ukunda, for example, the organization commissioned a block of toilets that have septic tanks rather than a long-drop structure. The league also supports sustainability initiatives: it has, for instance, built chicken houses (at the Kwale School for the Deaf and elsewhere), which are prime examples of sustainable projects. In early 2010,

EAWL donated KSh200,000 toward a posho mill for Fioni Village, a poor village in the area, so that villagers could grind maize. In 2013, I was told that the mill was successfully in place, allowing villagers to process the maize they grow into the flour and grits that are among the staple foods in Kenya. In 2011, EAWL also sponsored an orphanage, Diani Children's Village, as well as Nimuyumba Primary School, which has a unit for intellectually challenged students. At that time, the league was building a workshop for these children, which now essentially functions as a classroom. The children are taught beadwork and various life skills that will enable them to generate some form of income; the beadwork is taught in ways that teach children to count, sort colors, and remember patterns and structures. EAWL buys the results of this labor, such as a kind of doily that is used to cover drinks and food, protecting them from flies. Also in 2011, a calendar titled "Characters of Diani" was produced and sold; it featured long-term and mostly European Kenyan and European residents of the area, thus providing a documentary history of this group.

Although the lunch program is no longer operational and both the leprosy village and the Diani Children's Village lost support in 2013, other initiatives continue to receive funds (such as the primary school, the local epilepsy clinic, and the Kwale District Eye Centre) and new projects have been added (such as support for the Kenyan Society for the Protection and Care of Animals). Sometimes the support acquires very personal dimensions. League members, for example, found a boy who was evidently hyperactive and couldn't be managed by his parents and consequently had been tied to a tree. The members secured a place for him in a boarding school with a special needs unit.

Overall, EAWL supports projects in the areas of health care, sanitation, education, and food security. Usually, if somebody comes to the organization with a proposal for assistance, members will consider it. I asked EAWL chairs about the criteria for acceptance; they said that "sustainability is the main criterion," demonstrating that the "language of development" is part of EAWL vocabulary. Clearly, league members have no interest in investing funds in programs that do not have a long-term effect. In principle, EAWL supports the idea of matching funds, matching efforts, or any form of reciprocity. I am not aware, however, of any project sponsored by EAWL that insisted on reciprocity.

In 2013, two EAWL members described what amounts to a substantially new approach. The league was planning to collaborate with a local community-based organization, Community Social Responsibility, which was running a microcredit program for women. One of the bankers from a local bank, an African Kenyan who was to be an EAWL member, would help identify projects. EAWL would then review and approve the applications. League members said they hoped this would provide opportunity, especially to groups of women. If this type of sponsorship proves to be successful, it will take the league in new directions.

EAWL exemplifies a charitable organization with roots in the colonial era that continues to reflect features developed during that period but also increasingly embraces innovative approaches to philanthropy. Projects initiated and funded by EAWL are visible throughout the Diani area and beyond. In explaining the league's relationship to the African Kenyan community, one EAWL chair said, "We want to help them to help themselves." When asserting the league's commitment to sustainability, she was also very critical of other charity projects, especially with regard to how funds go astray. In fact, corruption or graft never came up in any of my conversations with EAWL members or with Diani residents who commented on the league. The planned collaboration with Community Social Responsibility would signal a new approach toward the community. Yet that organization, despite its extensive local knowledge, keeps a distance from those who benefit from its charity. EAWL is also not thinking substantially in terms of systemic change or political and human rights. Even though the league's various initiatives address some basic human rights (health, education, food, and housing), the idea of rights never entered the conversations I had with various EAWL members. The league is not the only, but it is perhaps the most visible and successful organization of its kind in the Diani area. Second to it is the Rotary Club, which also draws on the support of local Germans. The historical tradition in which EAWL stands may be paternalistic, but the types of projects it more recently supports signify a move away from traditional forms of charity (such as the lunch program) and are increasingly oriented toward community self-help and sustainability.

Initiatives in Health Care: Alternative Approaches?

CHRISTOFFEL BLINDENMISSION

The various aid initiatives reviewed so far are led by or composed of individuals who lack educational and professional backgrounds in humanitarian assistance. None of the contraband humanitarians I interviewed were trained in development or humanitarian aid, and none came from the nonprofit sector. While some of the school owners and directors have social work or education backgrounds, most of them have not undergone any substantial form of preparation in the area of nonprofit work in the development sector. Similarly, EAWL is composed of volunteers who collectively bring broad knowledge to the table but have not been exposed to professional discussions of, for example, best practices in development aid. In addition, the European-born humanitarians tend to know next to nothing about Kenya's history, cultures, and languages.

Sometimes, of course, the lack of professional training can have a devastating effect on the intended beneficiaries of help, but lack of formal training does not mean that humanitarians are completely ignorant of the issues at stake or have not acquired the knowledge necessary to run their initiatives.[99] Even contraband humanitarians tend to be fluent in the basic vocabulary of development, such as the idea of sustainability and "Hilfe zur Selbsthilfe," the German phrase that emphasizes the agency of aid recipients (aid that empowers individuals to help themselves). Indeed, most of the initiatives thus far reviewed are successful by some of the standards commonly used to evaluate development projects in terms of their outcomes, effects, sustainability, capacity building, and other measures.[100] Nevertheless, the critical discussion of development and aid has in the past decade placed a greater emphasis on the active involvement of targeted communities in the planning and execution of projects. Critics have pointed out that projects that lack this component tend to sustain *humanitarians* and *their* needs rather than benefit the communities they intend to help.[101] Also, the notion of an entitlement to enforceable "rights" is almost entirely missing from the conceptual framework of contraband and other humanitarians active in Diani. In this regard, the initiatives discussed here are devised according to traditional and generally paternalistic models of aid. For the most part, the organizers do not involve communities in significant ways, even if attempts are made, for example, to engage parents in matters relevant to schools and to put agency into the hands of aid recipients (such as EAWL's recent microcredit initiative). The contraband humanitarians in particular make almost no attempt to request that the communities or individuals they support contribute something to their project. At times villagers may be asked to do some of the manual labor needed to dig a well or build a school; but in most cases, donors will simply pay for labor and consider these payments a form of support to the local labor force through job creation. This approach, which places little value on collaboration and devises no mechanism of reciprocity, is contrary to approaches that have been developed over the past decade and are slowly catching on in the professional sector of the aid industry.[102]

One organization that embodies a community- and rights-oriented approach to aid is Christoffel Blindenmission (CBM), a vast INGO with projects in Asia, Africa, Latin America, and the Middle East. In 2012, CBM was active in 73 countries and involved in 714 projects in collaboration with 624 partner organizations. Two years later, the number of countries (65) and projects (672) was down, as CBM decided to focus on areas of largest need. Worldwide in 2015, 38.9 million individuals received services in one form or another through CBM.[103] The organization originates in the work of the German pastor Ernst J. Christoffel, who in 1908 in the Turkish town of Malatia founded an institution for children and orphans who were blind or had other disabilities. Christoffel established several institutions over the course of his lifetime, all connected to the umbrella organization Christliche Blindenmission im Orient (Christian Blind Mission in the Orient). After his death in 1956, the organization was renamed Christoffel

Blindenmission in honor of its founder. Gradually, it expanded to become the worldwide institution it is today. While the organization was born within the tradition of Christian charity and still retains its Christian identity, it has clearly departed from the original charity framework. Today, it is profoundly structured by principles tied to human rights, collaborative partnership, and sustainability. While these keywords pop up in a wide range of INGO documents declaring goals and principles, CBM puts significant effort into pursuing these principles on the ground according to a set of distinct priorities.

I interviewed CBM representatives at the organization's headquarters in Bensheim, Germany, in August 2011. Both Wolfgang Jochum and Dominique Schlupkothen vehemently rejected the idea of "charity": "Charity is always top down," Schlupkothen said. He emphasized that CBM was inspired by an entirely different concept of humanitarian work, which is outlined in the organization's publications.[104] Our conversation circled around several key themes: CBM's philosophy of partnership, community-based rehabilitation, consciousness-raising, and the notion of rights and political work.

One of the organization's key principles is its philosophy of partnership. CBM generally moves into an area only if local partners are already active on the ground. Disability activist organizations are crucial in this regard. Collaboration with communities and local activists is paramount to CMB's approach, especially in the planning stage. "CBM serves as a consultant to people who want to pursue specific projects," Jochum said. The initiative and the original planning have to originate locally. When a new project is proposed, CBM holds a workshop with community members and local activists, who provide feedback on the proposed project. Advocacy groups of the disabled play an important role in the process. Another key concept is the notion of community-based rehabilitation, a concept central to principles declared by the World Health Organization concerning disability and rehabilitation.[105] The ultimate goal of CBM, according to Jochum and Schlupkothen, is to become unnecessary. Before CBM withdraws from a project, it assesses where the partner organization stands in terms of self-sustainability and to what degree the community is involved. Contributions from CBM patients, among other factors, are essential for a project to become self-sustaining.

Jochum and Schlupkothen acknowledged that when it comes to the issue of publicity work that is designed to raise consciousness, they are often faced with a contradiction. In order to inspire individuals to donate, they have to appeal to popular expectations and ideas about disability. These popular images, however, are in contrast to what they aim to achieve with regard to consciousness-raising, namely, to articulate and disseminate a new understanding of persons with disabilities as individuals whose true impediment lies in the exclusive attitudes of the societies in which they live, rather than in the limitations that they experience as a result of their disabilities. Raising consciousness to educate the public with regard to a deeper understanding of disability is an important objective for CBM, but the obstacles are substantial. The book *Hilfe—100 Jahre Christoffel-Blindenmission: Ein Bilderbuch* (2007) that was produced for CBM's one-hundredth anniversary serves as a good example of this apparent contradiction, as the appeal of the images in the book works strictly on the level of affect and draws on stereotypes about not only disability, but also cultural difference. The reality of the partnerships on the ground would not have the same marketing effect as these stylized representations of disability. The contradiction between communication with the public (through various media) and the actual work on the ground is thus often substantial.

The question of rights has increasingly become essential to CBM. "Ten years ago we did not consider our work to be political," Jochum said, but today CBM embraces the fact that it advocates rights. A page on the CBM website is dedicated to discussing areas of political activism. Understanding the relationship between poverty and disability, for example, is identified as one area in which political activism must occur in order to advocate effectively for persons with disabilities. CBM argues that the objectives expressed through the United Nations' Eight Millennium Development Goals are unattainable unless the situation of persons with disabilities is addressed. Inclusivity emerges as one of the key concepts of CBM's political advocacy.[106] Overall, the principles articulated by CBM representatives demonstrate a high level of awareness regarding the various traps of humanitarian work, as well as a thoughtful articulation of goals and principles that are based in collaboration with communities and political advocacy.

In August 2012, I had a second conversation with CBM representatives, this time in Kenya, at the organization's Nairobi branch office. Jack Muthui, then country coordinator for Kenya, and Eddah Wang'ombe, interim administration manager, described the types of initiatives that CBM supported in Kenya, which are mainly in the areas of health and education. The main themes that had emerged in my conversation with representatives in Germany were central again, but with a local flavor. Muthui and Wang'ombe foregrounded the partnership philosophy that was pivotal in my previous conversation. As Muthui said, "The goal is that, ideally, CBM should exit one day, and the government should take over." He also stressed the importance of local activism in the area of disability advocacy, which has become quite vocal over the past two decades. Muthui furthermore pointed to the centrality of community involvement and contribution. He gave me an example of community-based rehabilitation: in a typical case, a community screening would "mobilize" (the technical term used by CBM in Kenya) an individual who needs surgery. A social worker would then consult with the patient about how to pay for the surgery, and someone from the community would stay at the hospital with the patient. Wang'ombe reinforced the idea that if the surgery were offered without any charge, it would be of no value, so some form of contribution was essential. She asserted that CBM was critical of organizations that did not require contributions from individuals. Resource mobilization was crucial; funds should come from the community. The CBM representatives stated that this was a fairly new concept but that they had been pushing it for the past three years or so. The repercussions of the "free help" model had created passive attitudes among members of the community, and the new approach of required contributions was designed to remedy that.

With regard to the question of consciousness-raising, the Kenyan CBM representatives agreed that the main obstacle in this area was culture. Disability continues to carry a stigma in Kenya; some disabilities face greater discrimination than others, but generally, persons with disabilities struggle to be treated with respect and to be given equal opportunities.[107] The question of status led to the question of rights. According to Muthui and Wang'ombe, not enough funds are mobilized to put into practice theoretical goals regarding the improvement of the situation of persons with disabilities. Even though Kenya passed the Persons with Disabilities Act in 2003 (it was enacted in 2004), enforcement of its principles is still in its beginning phase.[108] CBM representatives in Nairobi were concerned that disability was "not high enough on the agenda" of the government, that the "spirit" was lacking to vigorously protect the interests of people with disabilities. Advocacy, education, and enforcement remain key issues. As an example, incentives are available to Kenyan employers, but often, both employers and people with disabilities do not understand them. Though employers receive a tax benefit when hiring disabled employees, most are not aware of this provision, and they are also not aware of the fact that, as Muthui emphasized, they "don't have a choice, they need to employ"—that is, the law, at least theoretically, protects disabled individuals.[109] In practice, however, persons with disabilities remain highly vulnerable to discrimination.[110]

These comments from CBM representatives in Kenya reveal that the umbrella organization's general principles are also embraced in the Kenyan context, but they are met with a host of local challenges. This dimension becomes even more obvious when we turn to a project on the ground that is supported by, among others, CBM and that embraces core CBM principles—but also struggles to actualize them. The main impediments are tied to dominant practices that structure the overall culture of charity, locally and internationally.

KWALE DISTRICT EYE CENTRE

The Kwale District Eye Centre (KDEC) is located about halfway along the road between Mombasa and the Diani area.[111] The center is a natural partner for CBM because of its focus on sight-related illness. Even more, though, it is a natural partner because ophthalmologist Helen Roberts, who founded the clinic in 1993, places great emphasis on involving and educating the community and on physically going into the field to interact with members of the community. KDEC is supported by various international and local charities, companies, tourists, residents, and contraband humanitarians who are based in or connected to the Diani area, and Diani is among the areas KDEC serves. Since 1996, CBM has been one of the main sponsors of the organization, and in the past few years, support levels have been at 15–20 percent of KDEC's annual budget.[112] Even though KDEC's chief fundraising organization, Eyes for East Africa, is based in the United Kingdom, several German ophthalmologists have played a key role at KDEC over the years, and—as the list of recent donors demonstrates—a large percentage of donations is supplied by German tourists, repeat visitors, and contraband humanitarians.[113] Funds are raised internationally and locally; an annual fundraising event, "Diani Rules," not only brings in funds (KSh600,000 in 2013; roughly $7,000 at the time) but also serves as a consciousness-raising and publicity event.[114]

Roberts, who was born and trained in Britain, founded KDEC in response to the fact that one of every one hundred people living in Kwale County is blind because of diseases that are 80 percent curable or preventable but mostly because of poor nutrition. KDEC quickly grew into a successful operation, expanding from its original single room into a large facility, with the number of patients growing exponentially: while in 1995 fewer than one hundred surgeries per year were performed, by 2005 this figure had risen to more than fifteen hundred annually. The figures speak for themselves: as noted on the center's website, between KDEC's founding in 1993 and 2016, the clinic registered 90,000 new patients, although "this figure does not include all the patients we see, as many need to return for ongoing follow up and care. Many thousands of patients, who have walked through our doors, are still receiving support and eye care services both at base, in schools and in the field." The clinic reports seeing more than 500,000 patients in the field and performing more than 35,000 eye operations, "most of which were sight-restoring cataract operations." The center can provide only "short-term help" in the remotest parts of the country, where it has nonetheless treated more than 24,000 patients.[115]

KDEC works closely with the Kenyan Ministry of Health and trains ministry staff but receives no governmental funding and has maintained financial independence through creative fundraising strategies inside and outside the country. One key reason for the center's successful mobilization of the community is the fact that its workers go out into the field; of the forty-nine people KDEC employed in 2009, eighteen were fieldworkers (including rehabilitation officers and vision therapists) and other community-based staff members.[116] In addition, almost the entire staff is Kenyan, which seems to be central to facilitating successful community-based work.[117] KDEC is keenly aware of the factors, particularly cultural ones, that typically keep people from seeking medical help.

It addresses this cultural and psychological dimension by sending its fieldworkers directly to villages to educate people and identify patients. Staff members hold public awareness meetings and conduct screenings. As Roberts and other staff members suggested, the willingness to engage with traditional healers has allowed KDEC health workers to become accepted and respected within the communities in which they work. KDEC staff members have developed creative ways of collaborating with traditional healers; for example, they bring healers to the operating theaters and explain what happens during surgery. They have devised a referral system based on collaboration in which they educate traditional healers to distinguish between diseases that the healers can treat successfully and those they should refer to the clinic. Staff have also developed a lexicon that is geared toward diminishing local fears. Rather than using the word "surgery," for example, they use the Swahili word *kusafisha*, which means "to clean" (the eye), in order to describe what will happen during surgery.

In June 2007, I attended a health screening in the Tiwi area.[118] Such screenings are held once a month in various locations assigned to a particular fieldworker and are announced a few days before through loudspeakers and pamphlets. They consist of three components: registration, visual testing, and examination of the inner parts of the eye. Following registration, in which a person's name, address, age, and gender are recorded, the individual undergoes a vision test; a chart with letters is used for people who are literate and one with symbols for people who are illiterate. The final step for determining whether an individual needs treatment is the eye exam. Those requiring treatment and surgery (typically about five to fifteen people) are brought to the clinic immediately after the screening. About 95 to 120 people are screened in one day. It should be noted that the Ministry of Health also offers such screenings, but the trip to its assessment center in Kwale is too expensive for many individuals; thus, KDEC reaches the population more effectively than the ministry. Both the high figure documenting treatment in the field and the high number of surgeries and treatment at the center can be attributed to KDEC's successful community-based approach.

Unfortunately, the global recession of 2008 hit KDEC hard; several regular sponsors reduced their funding levels, and many one-time donors gave less. The biggest hit came when UK-based Sightsavers pulled out in early 2010. Despite the fact that the number of surgeries had increased dramatically since the mid-1990s, Sightsavers had wanted KDEC to scale up even more. This was not possible at a time of reduced donation levels. So Sightsavers decided to give more directly to governmental agencies, which, as Roberts says, is "the right thing to do in the long run."[119] Here, the action of Sightsavers as well as Roberts's general endorsement of the organization's principles signal a turn away from charity to a rights-based approach that is enforced by the state. However, "Kenya is not ready for this stage," Roberts said in November 2013. She added that "even though many areas of the health-care sector have improved, things have to build up slowly." Though she did not spell it out, Roberts was clearly referring to the overall lack of resources in the health-care sector; she also may have had in mind issues of corruption and graft. KDEC is still connected to Sightsavers, which advises and provides consulting services and in return benefits from the insights that KDEC communicates. Roberts points out that "the need to collaborate in the eye world, and share information is very strong."

The reduction of support from Sightsavers, however, in combination with an overall reduction in donations resulted in significant changes for the organization, in particular with regard to KDEC's interaction with the community. During the first half of 2010, the number of field screenings was halved; a KDEC brochure said that "all training and visits to village health committees, women's groups and social development assistants" were stopped, and the targets for patient screening and surgeries were reduced by 20 to 30 percent.[120] In 2013, the number of staff was down to forty, almost entirely a result of the scaling-down of the fieldwork program (from eighteen in 2009 to only eight). The number of surgeries went down as well. While more people come to the clinic themselves (rather than KDEC staff going into the field), people also come less often, from less far away, and often with less serious diseases—that is, because of the reduced amount of onsite work in the field, more people outside the clinic's immediate area remain blind or severely vision-impaired.

Despite the funding challenges, KDEC shows continuing resilience and creativity. In May 2010, another branch office was opened in Mwatate, in Taita and Taveta County. "It was an obvious move to expand into the next district," Roberts said. "The biannual surgical safaris into the area were not enough, and did not serve the needs of the community properly. Many low-vision children are still underserved because there is not enough funding to provide for the community." In addition, the charity shop that has existed in the Diani Shopping Center since 2005 was repurposed to also serve as a base for conducting eye exams, fitting glasses, and performing other exams and consultations. The shop's medical office, which opened in May 2013, serves mostly the residential community of Diani and tourists. In 2015, KDEC responded to the increasing need in the Diani area by opening an office in Ukunda. Community work remains central: in 2013, in addition to the thousands of patients who were seen at the hospital and community screenings, eighty "awareness creation meetings" (reaching 8,624 people) and twenty-five "school awareness meetings" (reaching 3,671 people) were held.[121]

Roberts clearly acknowledges the potentially detrimental effects that can occur when charity is provided without contributions from patients and communities. She maintains that "you undermine efforts" if services are provided for free. Here, Roberts addressed the tension between work done locally by Kenya-based health-care workers (both private and governmental), who generally charge some sort of fee for their services. Charity that is provided through the international donor community ends up competing with locally based services; if those international organizations treat patients at no charge, the locally based infrastructure is negatively affected and cannot grow. When I asked Roberts in 2014 how KDEC addressed the idea of reciprocity in the field, she described a new approach: "Now we are charging for glasses. More people are willing to pay." In most cases the patient contribution does not cover costs, but "the gesture is important." Again, she repeated the negative effect of cost-free charity: "If something is for free, it is less valued." This statement addresses the problems of a country that has low employment and high poverty rates (a poverty rate of 45.9 percent in 2005)[122] and consequently little tax revenue and limited options for creating the social net associated with a welfare state. The challenge for humanitarian workers is how to address real need without engendering passive and fatalistic local attitudes. Consciousness-raising among community members is crucial but also challenging. For KDEC, the persistent stigma of disability in Kenyan culture factors in strongly, but in addition, locals have gotten used to the culture of charity that is prevalent in the area, whereby services and goods are provided for free and their own contributions are not expected.

Roberts acknowledges that she feels her clinic has reached a considerable level of sustainability, a goal she cares about deeply: "I am pleased that I reached a stage when I can hand over, have trained enough people, and I can walk away." Clearly, if she walked away things would change in unpredictable ways, as she is in many respects the heart and soul of KDEC. But she has a long-term vision that, more often than not, is lacking in other humanitarian organizations and humanitarians, especially of the contraband type. "We need to imagine what may be in one hundred to two hundred years," she says. "Current affairs are interesting, but it does not tell us much about long-term developments." Roberts maintains that "doing good in developing countries is difficult." Most humanitarians are unable "to see the big picture, but you have to; there are ripple effects to your work. We also made mistakes; you have to be careful and listen." She clearly recognizes the importance of coordinating efforts, in this case, in the health-care sector. Roberts describes contraband humanitarians as those people "who want to do it their way." She is critical of what she calls the "dreaded passions" of humanitarians: "The rules are different from what they expect in the countries where they want to help." The experience that Roberts has been able to gather and reflect upon over the past two decades enables her to envision a future of rights- and community-based health care, in Kenya and beyond.

KDEC offers a paradigm of Western-based medicine that aims to involve communities, works within given cultural parameters, and even reserves a space for traditional indigenous medicine. Though it has evolved in its own right and according to its own philosophy, KDEC corresponds in key areas to the main principles outlined by CBM, especially through its fieldwork, community-focused activities, and consciousness-raising work. The reality of the Kenyan health-care system, with its lack of funds, corruption, and persistent areas of mismanagement, suggests that it would be premature for KDEC to integrate into the national health-care system at this point.[123] Culture-based impediments, especially regarding the status of people with disabilities in the Kenyan context, continue to pose a challenge as well. More political work, including advocacy for disability, is needed.

Discussion: The Culture of Charity

Supporting an individual through education or a village through water tanks may seem to be constructive actions beyond criticism, but the various initiatives reviewed here produce larger-scale effects that are less tangible and not easily understood in terms of their overall repercussions. Humanitarians are active in areas that in most countries of the world are understood to be primarily the domain of the state, such as education, sanitation, infrastructure development, and health care. Philanthropic institutions indeed complement state activities around the world, and local philanthropic institutions are part of the energies a society can mobilize to address social justice issues. Philanthropy becomes questionable, however, when it glosses over or enables systemic social injustice—which is, as critics such as Didier Fassin and Andrea Muehlebach have argued, in fact what much of the philanthropy enacted in the contemporary neoliberal world does.[124] This is true locally and with regard to transnational humanitarian interactions. In Kenya, scale matters crucially when it comes to evaluating the cumulative effect of humanitarian action; humanitarians are affecting and interfering with local affairs in Kenya in ways that raise the question as to whether humanitarian activities are beneficial or whether they produce dimensions that undo or counteract the benefits.

The effect of humanitarian aid is the subject of controversy in scholarly and public debates. What does this review of representative cases of humanitarian work in Diani reveal? How does it contribute to the existing debates over the value of humanitarianism? What does this study about Diani show about the cumulative repercussions of activities that are propelled by various kinds of humanitarians and humanitarian organizations and that affect the state, the economy, and local communities?

The State

As I suggested in chapter 1, I take as a starting point for my evaluation the views of Kenyan citizens, who conceive of their ideal state as a form of welfare state (in contrast to, for example, views held by many citizens of the United States, but closer to those of Europeans). These views were voiced in Diani and environs repeatedly during my interviews, but they are also part of the larger discourse in Kenya, as it emerges, for example, in the media. Kenyans complain about the abuses of the state and relentlessly express their expectations regarding the state's responsibility. In more than one way, the constant lament about the failures of the *serikali*, the government, explains why many Kenyans turn to nongovernmental, mostly non-Kenyan actors.

And indeed, INGOs in Africa and other areas of the world developed out of frustrations resulting from severe shortcomings of state-controlled services, including corruption, mismanagement, graft, and political oppression. But the initiatives led by nonstate actors, including the various forms of humanitarianism reviewed here, produce their own problematic outcomes and in some cases undermine the potential for governmental institutions to be effective. Some critics, such as Gregory Mann, have suggested that the heavy involvement of external players in the affairs of African states in particular has been on a continuum with colonial rule.[125] In part, my research confirms the findings of other critics who have illustrated the negative repercussions of INGOs and NGOs in Kenya.[126] The work of contraband humanitarians represents the most extreme case of humanitarian activities that all too often contribute to disabling the Kenyan state rather than pushing for more accountable practices. Gustav Müller and his organization, for example, operate almost entirely outside of the official administrative framework. As I have already pointed out, the reverse situation—Kenyans involved in infrastructure development without state approval in Germany or elsewhere in the Western world—would be unthinkable, and the structural imbalance smacks of colonial paradigms where different laws ruled colonizing and colonized countries.

I interviewed several governmental officials in Msambweni, Kwale, and Mombasa about their views on charity, including contraband charity.[127] The officials were unable to provide any data or quantify the level of humanitarian activity by any measure. One official complained that, for the most part, schools "are not willing to give out any information" when it comes to external support. Overall, the opinion of these officials was that informal charity and other forms of humanitarian activity interfere with the planning of their respective offices. Most of the time the education office is bypassed. One official said that this situation "has been a serious challenge." A tourist might, for example, build a school in an area that already has enough schools, while the biggest need might be in another part of the county. The education officer would have a better sense than the tourist of which areas in the county need support. The education office does routine checkups and is aware of the condition of buildings and supplies. Donors, however, "may support a school that has no need and others who are deserving do not get the support," said the official. She added that monitoring such activities "is a challenge. We don't know how much is coming and how much is provided."

Officials also commented on the question of uncoordinated and unchecked donor activities: "We encourage them to work through school committees, but in some cases the office is only told about an initiative when, for example, the school is already built," complained one representative (Müller's organization illustrates this uncoordinated approach). The office then evaluates the situation and sends a teacher if there is a justifiable need and possible enrollment in the area. The school has to be built on public land (and in instances where this rule is ignored, serious problems arise). At times, donors want to be listed as trustees and insist that their names appear on the title deeds of public schools, which also conflicts with Kenyan law. Another officer said that generally, the office wanted donor organizations to achieve their goals, "but what if the organization does things that are not needed?" He referred to a case in which several foreigners were building classrooms. "And that was good," he said, "even though the education department was not aware of it." But in addition, "those people wanted to teach the lower-level classes, Standard 1 and 2, themselves. So foreigners were teaching in a public school without permission." The case, which is now settled, exemplifies the degree of entitlement that some donors feel in their efforts to improve the Kenyan educational system. One officer did admit that some organizations with a significant level of foreign participation collaborate well with his office: "We give them guidelines, and we have had a good working relationship."

All in all, one official summarized, the activities of donors "undermine the state; we don't know how much money is pumped in; and donors want to control aspects of education that they should not get involved in, such as appointing teachers." On the other hand, she continued, "the community appreciates the support, so we are torn. The intentions are good, but the approach is wrong and affects the results." Governmental officials thus did not outright reject humanitarian work, including contraband charity; they granted that the area benefits from the improved infrastructure. Donor support creates challenges, but in light of, for instance, the great demand for development in the educational system, the office has no choice but to cope with the existing situation. "I understand that we still need more schools, so we close our eyes and allow the schools to start," said one officer.

My conversations brought into focus the extent to which governmental officials have little control over the actions of tourists and other humanitarians in the area. Considering the case of Jan Verkaart, the Dutch industrialist who has built, among other projects, more than seventy public primary schools over the past twenty years, and factoring in the omnipresence of private schools funded by foreign donors, the percentage of schools built or funded with foreign funds in the same time frame may be larger than those exclusively funded by the Kenyan government. This scenario highlights the extent to which the Kenyan educational system is structured by the actions of foreigners.[128] While foreign humanitarians feel legitimized in their paternalistic actions by reports about graft and corruption, contraband humanitarianism in particular may actually buttress the inaction of government employees. Their work, after all, is being done by someone else. State funds can disappear without major consequences, as schools, dispensaries, toilets, and wells are still being built. Thus, governmental employees feel less pressure to create a functioning infrastructure. As with other forms of aid, contraband charity in particular "props up corrupt governments."[129] These charges apply also to areas of humanitarian activity that are legal and officially sanctioned. Scale matters significantly, but charges of corruption in all sectors of the Kenyan government are high, including in the Ministry of Education.[130] Funds can disappear because foreign donors will compensate. In addition, funds may not even be allocated to, in our case, the coastal areas that receive informal foreign aid, as governmental agencies in Nairobi are aware of the phenomenon. I suggest that the dependence of the coast on external sources of support (and the lack of internal assistance) is a crucial factor in explaining the alienation coastal residents feel toward the central government.

If initiatives of contraband humanitarianism are problematic, do the private schools, such as the Mekaela Academies and the Maendeleo Academy, offer better models to enhance educational opportunities in the area? They are, after all, part of the fabric of Kenyan life; their owners are Kenyan residents and even citizens; and even though the majority of students would not be able to attend them without scholarships from abroad, they do not, as far as I can tell, feed corruption. Ingeborg Langefeld has many frustrating stories to tell with regard to her interactions with Kenyan officials, but she insists that she is not willing to pay bribes and displays a significant amount of determination and awareness regarding the repercussions of corruption. While these private schools, in contrast to contraband humanitarian projects, are more integrated into the official framework of Kenyan social institutions and clearly provide much needed educational institutions, they also release the Kenyan state from its responsibility toward its citizens (and Kenyan communities from taking initiative; see more below). In this regard, even the private schools become part of the "NGOization" of Kenyan society, whereby mostly foreign-based or foreign-supported organizations complement, but more often interfere with, the responsibilities of the state and local communities. Once more, the situation also encourages the central government to care less about, and invest less in, development in the coastal region.

The actions of contraband humanitarians affect the health-care sector in similar ways. The importation of expired medications and medications that are passed out for free (and then often sold under the table by doctors or nurses) interfere with the work of the government and thus create grey zones that make it more difficult for the government to be held accountable.[131] One health official stressed that "many INGOs are not aligned with what we think about health" and that "they do not follow the standards" of the Ministry of Health. The health-care activities of EAWL, on the other hand, take place within the framework outlined by the Ministry of Health, and the league has secured a space from within which the governmental framework can be reformed and improved. KDEC also coordinates with the Ministry of Health and, more important, builds exemplary structures through its emphasis on community work and consciousness-raising. Both EAWL and KDEC thus present models of successful collaboration between the state and communities, despite being funded to some extent from abroad.

Contraband charity is clearly the most detrimental form of humanitarian activity affecting state institutions in Diani and beyond. The notion of "human rights" can provide some people with a sense of entitlement regarding intervention; contraband humanitarians seem to believe that "human rights" override "citizenship rights" and state laws. Local organizations such as EAWL, Mekaela Academies, Maendeleo Academy, and KDEC, on the other hand, operate within the framework outlined by the Kenyan state; and despite their potential to enable the inaction of state institutions and their dependence on support from abroad, they play a complementary and educational role as models for and within the Kenyan educational or health-care sector. In addition to the various complex effects that German-supported and other humanitarian activities have on the functioning of the state, the actions of foreigners have a psychological component. From the perspective of the average citizen on the coast, foreigners are more attentive to their needs than the central government, which has certainly increased the antagonism between coastal residents and their government.

The Economy

As regards the economy, contraband charity again emerges as the most problematic form of humanitarian activity in this area. Gustav Müller and his organization and Anna Bäumler, for example, both feed and impede the growth of local industries. They employ people to construct buildings and buy many items locally; but the cargo they bring into the area from Europe is problematic. As I have already mentioned, several airlines (such as Condor and Air Berlin) transport goods for approved charitable organizations at no charge, which can facilitate the import of outdated and defunct items. Cargo is inspected at Kenyan airports, but much that a county health commissioner, for example, would deem useless, passes through customs. In Kwale during a conversation in 2012, a Ministry of Health official complained about the following examples of useless donations:

- Germans sent baby bottles that the Ministry of Health neither needed nor wanted because the country promotes breastfeeding, abiding by World

Health Organization policy. The ministry's representative accepted the donation "to be polite" but came to "regret" that acceptance because an entire storage room was filled with the useless bottles. It had cost the German donor €9,000 to transport them to Kenya.

- Donors brought a machine they claimed was an x-ray machine, but it turned out to be an ultrasound machine that was missing an essential part. The missing part would cost KSh200,000 ($2,000). The machine was also outdated (it was more than ten years old) and sat uselessly outside a Ministry of Health building in Kwale. A donor paid for the expensive transport.
- DHL ships medicine for free if the medicine will be available at no cost in the country of destination; however, no mechanism exists that requires quality control.
- A donated x-ray machine was missing a fuse; although the repair would be cheap, the part had not been found, and the machine in 2012 had already been sitting in storage for three years.
- A woman shipped thirty used hospital beds from Europe; she spent $6,000 for the shipping container and paid additional fees and bribes. The same money would have bought a higher number of brand new hospital beds locally.
- An expensive bed for cosmetic surgery was flown in (by Air Berlin) from Germany, but no surgeon in the area would use it. It was stored in a shed, unused.
- Coca Cola shipped a container filled with toys for hospitalized children. "We didn't know about this, and we didn't ask for it," the ministry official said. "By the time we found out, the port was charging KSh2 million [$20,000] for storage overstay and release." Five years later, the container was still sitting in the port.

What results in convenient tax write-offs for German and other Western companies and individuals might end up merely taking up storage space or becoming an eyesore on the Kenyan landscape.[132]

Just as donated defunct equipment poses a problem, donations of medications have significant consequences. As medications are delivered to government dispensaries without any effective mechanisms for controlling the volume and nature of the donations, the reselling of donated drugs has become widespread.[133] Donors are usually unaware of the black market for drugs and medical supplies.[134] They operate with an image of doctors and other medical personnel that is based on the relative affluence of these professionals in European countries. It may be inconceivable to these donors that a doctor they befriended would sell donated medications under the table. Illegally imported medications particularly undermine the growth of the local pharmaceutical market.

Ingeborg Langefeld, on the other hand, uses the funds she raises abroad and in Kenya to buy locally almost exclusively and to employ a large number of Kenyans at Maendeleo Academy. In this regard, her activities are an integral part of the local economy. Similarly, EAWL buys and commissions locally. KDEC employs Kenyans almost exclusively. Contraband humanitarianism is the most detrimental form of humanitarian activity, but the effect of volunteers, such as those who contribute to both Maendeleo and KDEC, also undermines the local labor market. In addition, the heavy dependence on funding from abroad leaves various projects extremely vulnerable, with a low level of sustainability. In this regard, the actions of Maendeleo Academy, in its attempt to use raised funds to increase self-sustainability, are exemplary.

Local Contexts and Local Communities

How humanitarians interact with their local contexts and how their actions shape local communities are two important aspects of humanitarianism.

The practices of contraband humanitarians are the most controversial with regard to the *local contexts*. The ignorance of these humanitarians of local culture and language makes them vulnerable to many kinds of schemes. They depend on their local confidants and usually do not suspect them to be complicit in illegal operations or untrustworthy. One organization claimed that it had a foolproof system of reconciling expenses, which entailed bringing all of the involved parties to the table to compare figures. "One hundred percent of our money goes to Kenyans!" the representative of the donor organization proudly assured me. It is certainly true that a much higher percentage of these aid funds arrive in Kenya than is the case with, for example, systematic development aid, where much of the aid remains in the donor country and large sums disappear into various pockets. With contraband charity, however, all of the money may arrive in Kenya, but not all of it necessarily reaches the aid projects that humanitarians are supporting. What this particular donor representative did not know (and what I was told by one of his local contacts and also knew from interactions over the years) was that everyone but him had already agreed on the figures in advance of the meeting; receipts can be forged easily in Kenya, and the representative was thus cheated collectively by all the contractors and collaborators.

In addition, my research showed that Müller's organization, for example, pays significantly more to contractors and other contacts than the various projects call for. Another organization did not suspect that individuals with whom it interacted, such as the principal of a school, were known to be corrupt. Bäumler, who speaks little English, depends entirely on her local contacts and has been cheated on numerous occasions. Her disastrous romantic relationship deprived her of most of her financial resources. She does not understand the Kenyan legal system and is in no position to help herself. Since her pension is too small for her to live in Switzerland, she is no longer able to return to her home country. Her case is not unusual in the area. Müller also has insufficient knowledge of local language, culture, and customs. Even after two decades of travel to and living in the area, he does not speak the local language and his English skills are not good enough to communicate adequately. Müller is unaware of the fact that he often comes across as rude and bossy. In this regard, both he and Bäumler continue the paradigm of the colonial settler interacting with the indigenous population in reductive and reduced language that is devoid of the nuances that intelligent conversation allows. Local African Kenyans are often offended by these crude linguistic interactions, but they also know how to exploit and negotiate these situations creatively.[135]

There are additional questions related to Kenya's educational and health-care systems that beg to be answered. For instance, with regard to the practice of donating funds to schools that are not registered: Who checks on the qualifications of teachers? What are the indicators that children have received a proper education? And what is the mechanism for establishing that a child is indeed an orphan? Often based on whim and not having a system of checks and balances, contraband charity is ignorant about many aspects of Kenyan society and encourages a culture of betrayal and graft. While deceit and fraud are subversive strategies of the less powerful (and often are the only ones available to them), they tend to sustain rather than alter power structures.

In contrast, the three other types of initiatives Germans support in the Diani area constitute, in one way or another, a more integral part of the local fabric. Although all expatriates have lessons to learn, these organizations' leaders are generally savvy with regard to the political, economic, and social contexts of Kenyan life. Noticeably, however, most of them also do not speak the local language, suggesting a continuation of colonial practices. Of the initiatives reviewed here, only KDEC successfully engages with dimensions of local culture (such as the beliefs regarding persons with disabilities and the network of traditional medicine). EAWL's microcredit system, depending on the actual terms of the microcredits, may be a step in a new direction. But the lack of local knowledge that contraband humanitarians display and the inability of Maendeleo Academy or Mekaela Academies to successfully engage the local community reveal the limited success of these initiatives to generate reciprocity, community empowerment, and ownership.

The most consequential dimension regarding the effect of neoliberal charity on *local communities* is that it has contributed significantly to the destruction of indigenous systems of solidarity and self-help, as we saw at the beginning of this chapter regarding utsi and mweria.[136] These local institutions, which humanitarians have never even heard about, are basically extinct. For the most part, the younger generation of local Digo has never participated in these activities; they have grown up in a context that taught them to rely heavily on outside assistance.

The overall culture of charity that is observable in Diani is enabled by tourists (mostly repeat visitors) and resident expatriates, the lack of interest of the Kenyan government in the coastal region, and various social practices of Digo and other African Kenyan societies.

Tourism brought a large number of affluent Europeans to the area, and what started small and perhaps already drew on colonial patterns of charity evolved over the years into a network whereby today *every large family in the Diani area can be tied to some sponsor from (primarily) Europe*, be it through school fellowships, health-care facilities that function with European donations, volunteers who do work Kenyans could do, or personal contacts, some of them romantic (see the next chapter). It is not unusual in Diani for African Kenyans to approach a tourist by calling out "can you sponsor me?"—even when the "sponsorship" consists merely of buying a banana, a coconut, or a leather bracelet. Children seek attention with their hands stretched out; most of them ask for *peremende*, sweets, but others ask directly for money. Locals have wised up to the sensibilities of their visitors: questions such as "Hast Du ein Hitlerherz?" (do you have the heart of a Hitler?) and "Bist Du ein Rassist?" (are you a racist?) will cause German tourists to open their wallets and buy the offered goods. African Kenyans write letters, send emails, make phone calls, and advocate their stories passionately. Sometimes they don't remember the version of a story they told before: one man, for example, explained to me he was a single father because his wife had run off. The next year, his story expanded into a dramatic tale in which his wife had died in a car accident while she had been on the way to visit her brother in a hospital. When introducing me to his daughter, whom he claimed to have raised alone, the "child" curiously looked more like the man's older sister. Another man also told me that his wife had abandoned him; a year later, he told another person that his wife had died in a car accident and that he was now a single father taking care of two children. Evidently locals had decided that the tale of the single father was more effective than that of the abandoned husband.

I do not recount these stories to accuse impoverished Kenyans of lying; their true stories are difficult and their situations precarious, but for reasons that a tourist is unable or unwilling to comprehend. If Juma told Brigitte that he had lost his property because of land graft in Kenya, would his German friend grasp what that loss means? Or if Muhammad told Sebastian that his employment opportunities are dim because the Structural Adjustment Programs of the IMF caused the real estate boom in the Diani area that is now stifling the development of other industries, would Sebastian be moved? Or if Binti told Helmut that her educational choices as a Muslim girl are slim because the government neglects the coastal region, would Helmut understand? Most African Kenyans are acutely aware of the reasons for their poverty, and their true wrath is reserved for the central government. They see foreigners as a solution to local problems. The younger

African Kenyans I interviewed were especially insistent that they were glad for the support they received from international donors; they complained that the government was not helping them and that it was better to receive aid from German and other individuals and organizations. These attitudes point to the generational conflicts that plague Kenyan society, in which younger men and women feel immobilized by the gerontocratic and socially hierarchical power structures of the society. Traditionally, older and more powerful members of a community are expected to help others; yet the younger generation feels abandoned by the older generation in power. Their expectations for support, which would traditionally be directed at older and otherwise resourceful members of the African Kenyan community, have now shifted to Germans and other humanitarians. In addition, the repressive and corrupt nature of Kenya's postindependence elite has led to disenchantment with state institutions, and on the coast, this disenchantment is additionally justified by the government's neglect of the area since independence.[137] Avoiding or diverting the conflict with their local and national elders, the younger generation turns to outside assistance—including assistance that comes from sources that support the equally alienated youths of Somalia.[138]

As we have seen in the discussion of social institutions such as utsi and mweria, developments in the Diani area indicate that the age-old structures of communal support and philanthropy are no longer in place, and I suggest that they are in part being reconstituted through relationships that African Kenyans develop with humanitarians. Few institutions exist that organize communal self-help, informally and formally. While networks of support within distinct families and through religious affiliation may work to the advantage of individuals, the larger issues of the Diani area are not addressed collectively. The number of registered community-based organizations, another form of organized self-help, is quite low; as of summer 2012, for example, twenty-nine organizations were registered in Kwale County, with their activities ranging from raising poultry to eradicating poverty.[139] Certainly, a significant disconnect exists between community-based organizations of all kinds (registered or not) and the international and local aid industry; this issue affects Kenya more broadly.[140]

The paternalistic model of charity shifts responsibility for a wide range of social concerns to non-Kenyans. It encourages Kenyans to manipulate and exploit the aid industry, seemingly pursuing opportunity but clearly not considering the long-term detrimental effects of such manipulation. Can we find merit in the fact that Kenyans use various strategies to commit humanitarians to address their needs? The Digo of the Diani area have a reputation for not wanting to work for others; their reasons are grounded in the history and stigma of slavery. As Roger Gomm wrote in 1972: "The Digo concept of dignity, *heshima*, is closely bound up with the notion of being freeborn, a status which is inherited matrilineally. Being hardworking, bearing abuse without redress, and lacking autonomy, are all marks of slavery: leisure, influence and authority indicate being freeborn."[141] But that is not the only reason for the persistence of the charity model. As long as coastal and other Kenyans delegate responsibility for their well-being to foreign humanitarians (either out of necessity or simply for the sake of opportunity) and as long as humanitarians continue to make careers of charity and fail to ask for reciprocity from communities, this paradigm will not likely change.

From *Wakati Ya dotcom* to Where?

This discussion has revealed a significant difference between "professional" forms of humanitarian activity and those activities that I term "contraband humanitarianism," which has a questionable effect on the social dynamics of the communities it targets. Germans and other Europeans who live in Kenya (and often are Kenyan residents and citizens) and engage with their contexts daily are aware of economic, ecological, political, and social factors that outside actors rarely comprehend. African Kenyans in Diani benefit from the various forms of informal and formal aid on a large scale, and the tremendous economic benefit that comes to the area through humanitarian activity explains its resilience amidst modest government and private sector investment. But a disconnect continues to exist as long as African Kenyans are passive recipients rather than active contributors (and this holds true with regard to their views of the state as well: the kind of welfare state Kenyans seem to favor requires engaged citizens). While African Kenyans in Diani may show resilience in securing a piece of the charity pie, forms of reciprocity and community contribution may open the door to greater degrees of independence from outside humanitarians.

What are the possible options? I hesitate to make large-scale recommendations, but some suggestions do emerge from this study. If we take Kenyan calls for a more active role of the government as a guiding principle, then more governmental oversight is needed to regulate the activities of contraband humanitarians. The government should ensure that Kenya is not a "dumpsite" for the likes of old hospital beds, unwanted baby bottles, and outdated machinery that doesn't work; in addition, regulations regarding the export of goods and services in the donor countries ought to be stricter. Donors should employ locals and buy from local companies; nothing, or little, should be provided for free, which devalues labor and destroys the local economy. International volunteerism is a case in point, and should perhaps be curtailed and strictly controlled. In addition, a wide range of community stakeholders could address various areas of need were they to pool resources, as was modeled by the Kwale Health Forum until 2007.[142]

Diani is not representative of all of Kenya. Kenyan social activists such as Wangari Maathai, Boniface Mwangi, and many lesser-known individuals successfully engendered grassroots mobilization beyond the humanitarian paradigm.[143] But Diani is representative of key areas on the coast, and on the coast, humanitarianism covers up the detrimental effect of governmental neglect of the area, including the situation of landless squatters and unresolved title deed questions, as we saw in chapter 2. Currently, Kenya's economy is booming, particularly in terms of foreign investment in the search for natural resources. Here, larger systemic issues tie philanthropy in Africa, as exemplified in Kenya, to globalization in intricate ways. German and other philanthropic activities in Kenya increased around the same time that neoliberal practices were introduced—practices that, as has now been shown, impoverished many Kenyans over the past thirty years, though the trend seems to be reversing slowly.[144] It is doubtful that the present push for globalization, which occurs in Kenya and across the continent as part of a "Second Scramble for Africa," will lead to a significant improvement of the livelihoods of the majority of Kenyans. Globally, remittances, private philanthropy, and private investment are more consequential to the economies of poor countries than the aid extended by the governments of rich countries, and they jointly operate as crucial cornerstones of neoliberal capitalist economics.[145] We should be mindful of the ideological and material function of philanthropy in the context of these larger economic and political developments. Although philanthropic activity in general aims to address areas of social inequality and alleviate the suffering that results from it, in many cases it may ultimately ossify the structures that are responsible for social inequality and suffering. In fact, INGOs have undermined the sovereignty of African states in a way that, as Gregory Mann, Maurice Amutabi, Peter Buffett, and others have suggested, puts these external actors on a continuum with the history of colonial rule.[146] The case of aid to Africa demonstrates this clearly; humanitarian aid that is *not* accompanied by large-scale economic and political reforms will not address the root causes of, in this case, Kenyan poverty. While political reforms need to tackle issues of corruption, favoritism, and impunity, economic reforms need to focus on current debt and currency policies, the agricultural subsidies of Western nations, and tariffs on products from Africa (all of which tilt the economic advantage toward the richer nations), while simultaneously allowing Africa to implement trade barriers to level the playing field.[147]

All too often philanthropy serves the needs of those who give, not those who receive. On the level of the individual humanitarian, philanthropic activity in Africa is frequently born of the discomfort that wealthy or wealthier individuals feel in light of the poverty they encounter around the world; that anxiety may be related to the subconscious knowledge that their riches are gained on the basis of structural economic, social, and political injustice. As Simon Schama observed for the Dutch elite of seventeenth-century "Dutch Golden Age," "riches seemed to provoke their own discomfort, and affluence cohabited with anxiety."[148] Philanthropy that is rooted in a guilty conscience and not in an understanding of the reasons for the poverty it strives to remedy results in actions that do not address the root causes of destitution. Such misguided gifts of philanthropy often turn out to be Trojan horses. As the TV comedy series *The Samaritans: Aid for Aid* shows, there is indeed public awareness of this fact.[149] The question remains: What to do about it?

4 Romance

A white lady is like gold for us.
> —Peter aka Mody aka Sawa

Kuingia Harusi, Kutoka Matanga.
(One enters [Mombasa] for a wedding, and gets out in a coffin.)
> —Swahili proverb

That the native does not like the tourist is not hard to explain.
> —Jamaica Kincaid, *A Small Place*

Today I believe in the possibility of love; that is why I endeavor to trace its imperfections, its perversions.
> —Frantz Fanon, *Black Skins, White Masks*

Precarious Romance

Mombasa yapapasa, Mombasa is comforting; *Mombasa raha*, Mombasa is pleasure, *na Lamu tamu*, and Lamu is sweet. Just as coastarians—a word used in Kenya to describe people from the coast—take pride in the natural beauty and culture of the area and just as upcountry Kenyans see the coast as a place of idle pleasures, tourists have flocked to the Kenyan coast not only to enjoy its historical sites, the beach, and the area's lush vegetation, but also its people. Since the 1960s, when tourism to Kenya became an international attraction, vacationing on the coast has been associated with sex. As mentioned in chapter 2, the slogan "Sun, Sand, and Sex" is said to have been coined by Edgar Herrmann, one of the first German-born tourism entrepreneurs, and by the 1980s, this image was deeply engraved in the imagination of Germans and visitors from other Western countries. Sex tourism in Kenya frequently makes the news in Germany, Switzerland, and Austria, and accounts of the sexual behavior of foreigners and stories involving pornography and prostitution are featured regularly on Kenyan news stations as well.[1]

Indeed, sex tourism is a thriving business along the Kenyan coast; Wanjohi Kibicho, who has written the most comprehensive study on the topic, suggests "a figure of 20,000–25,000 self-styled CSWs [commercial sex workers] in Kenya's coastal region," which includes the ugliest side of the sex trade—forced sex and child trafficking for sex and pornography.[2] Kibicho reports that "there are approximately 3,000 child CSWs in Kenya's coastal region, serving both international and local clients." Prostitution is especially pronounced in the centers of tourism, with encounters between tourists and prostitutes, including children, often facilitated by hotel staff members.[3] Kibicho's discussion, which focuses particularly on Malindi but also provides data about the sex trade and tourism more broadly, sheds light on the social context and conditions that produce and enable contact between sex workers and international as well as domestic tourists.

To date, scholars who have explored interactions between tourists and Kenyans have focused on prostitution and assessed questions related to culture, economic factors, and health.[4] Some studies have documented other modes of interaction with tourists by focusing on tour leaders, safari guides, and entertainers.[5] Sex relations between Kenyans and tourists/expatriate residents, however, also fall into a variety of patterns that are distinct from prostitution and range from different kinds of unmarried relations to marriage. Similar to situations in tourist centers in countries around the world that have high poverty rates, the boundaries between different types of relationships in Kenya are often blurred.[6] Scholars have acknowledged romance tourism and intermarriage, both significant phenomena since the 1980s,[7] but the varying modes of romantic interaction between Kenyans and tourists/expatriates have not been researched systematically.[8]

Beyond the Kenyan context, marriage is often discussed in relation to mail-order bride schemes, which facilitate a "flow from the poor to the relatively affluent countries" and is generally seen as a phenomenon that oppresses women.[9] Several studies acknowledge that marriage to tourists is pursued by sex workers who want to leave their home countries for a better life in the (mostly) global north.[10] Lacking, however, are investigations that more broadly tie romance tourism to the contemporary north-to-south lifestyle and retirement migration, aspects that are crucial to trends in Kenya. While accounts exist on sex tourism (in locations such as Thailand) and romance tourism (especially the Caribbean), and the past decade has also seen analyses of retirement and lifestyle migration of mostly European and North American citizens, the intersection of these various phenomena has not been explored (to the best of my knowledge). This chapter addresses this apparent gap in scholarship and, more broadly, adds to the discussion of "love in Africa."[11] It focuses on north-south romantic relations in Kenya that are *not* perceived as prostitution by either partner and that carry on over several years, sometimes in the form of marriage.

In Diani, most romantic relations between Kenyans and tourists or expatriates share one aspect: they are born of a nexus of emotional and economic precarity (granted the variations inherent to individual histories). Economic need is the main factor explaining the growth of forms of prostitution studied by Kibicho, who convincingly demonstrates the salient correlation between increases in unemployment and poverty levels and the growth of both the tourism industry and the sex trade.[12] The precarious context is clearly the vehicle through which most romantic relationships emerge in Diani as well. While "charity" addresses the existing lack of opportunity and economic need through actions that are, for the most part, initiated by or made possible because of outsiders, romantic relations are primarily a result of the agency of Kenyans. Even though Germans and other expatriates are fully conscious of the possibilities for romantic relationships in Kenya and also actively pursue their opportunities, it is more often a Kenyan who takes the first step toward establishing a relationship. But why are Germans motivated to engage intimately with African Kenyans? And for Kenyans, does the appeal of these relationships extend beyond the economic dimension? What are the scope and scale of the economic and sociocultural effects of such relationships, which, I suggest, may be as high or higher than the number of commercial sex workers, on communities along the coast and in Kenya more broadly?

After a brief review of the German-language discourse on mostly north-south binational relations, which comments on and perhaps even fuels the phenomenon in Kenya, I discuss data resulting from an analysis of thirteen years of marriage licenses kept at the Office of the Registrar of Marriages in Mombasa. Then I discuss insights I gained from interviews and through participant observation in Diani. I first sketch profiles of four representative couples and then focus on factors that stabilize the relationships (such as community support, fluid kinship relations, and sex) and those that pose challenges (such as age gaps, cultural differences, and psychological tensions). Finally, I acknowledges the relationships in terms of their implicit objective, namely to address emotionally and economically challenging situations.

German-Language Discourse on North-South Romance

While Kenyan liaisons with foreigners are picked up regularly by news stations, television, and digital and social media in Kenya, the popularity of the topic in German-speaking countries is unparalleled in terms of its pervasiveness.[13] The ubiquity of the discourse, I argue, can be correlated to the scope of Kenyan-German and other north-south romantic relations. In the late 1990s, the phenomenon of Kenyan-German relations attained mainstream attention in Germany, Switzerland, and Austria through a flurry of wildly popular nonfiction and fiction texts and films. The large number of publications with a focus on Kenya documents the extent of contact with the country that is facilitated through tourism;[14] it also builds on a preexisting Western discourse of the country as a location of adventure and romance that dates back to the beginning of the twentieth century. Ernest Hemingway's *Green Hills of Africa* (1935) and *The Snows of Kilimanjaro* (1936), Karen Blixen's *Out of Africa* (1937), and Elspeth Huxley's *The Flame Trees of Thika: Memories of an African Childhood* (1959) are among the most well-known novels and autobiographies that have popularized an image of Kenya as exotic fantasy. The movie version of *Out of Africa* (1985), starring Meryl Streep and Robert Redford, is said to have done more to enhance the development of tourism in Kenya than any other factor, and its release date coincides with a period of rapid expansion of the industry.

The most widely circulated story in Germany, Switzerland, and Austria about a Kenyan-German romance is Corinne Hofmann's 1998 autobiographical account *Die weiße Massai* (The White Masai), which narrates her relationship, marriage to, and divorce from a member of the Samburu ethnic group. The book was tremendously successful: it has sold four million copies and been translated into more than thirty languages. In 2005, it was made into a movie of the same title.[15] A more self-reflective account is Miriam Kwalanda's 1999 book *Die Farbe meines Gesichts: Lebensreise einer kenianischen Frau* (The Color of My Face: Life Journey of a Kenyan Woman) (co-written with Birgit Theresa Koch). This autobiography also tells the story of a cross-cultural marriage and divorce, but here the subject is approached from the perspective of a Kenyan woman. After working as a prostitute and sustaining a series of romantic relationships, Kwalanda married a German man and moved to Germany. The marriage also ended in divorce, and the autobiography clearly represents the author's attempt to come to terms with her life and the situation she and her three children are facing in the new country. Both autobiographies were preceded by Stefanie Zweig's *Nirgendwo in Afrika* (*Nowhere in Africa*, 1995); the film version (2001), directed by Caroline Link, won an Oscar for Best Foreign Language Film in 2002. While the novel and movie do not feature romantic love between Germans and Kenyans, the relationships between the child protagonist and her Kenyan playmates and those employed by her parents (particularly a man by the name of Owuor) are deeply affectionate, thus conveying a poignant emotional intimacy between Germans and Kenyans. Since then, a number of documentaries (such as RTL's *Der Traummann—Liebe ohne Grenzen*; Man of Dreams—Love without Borders) and feature films (such as *Paradise: Love* [*Paradies: Liebe*, 2012], by Austrian filmmaker Ulrich Seidl) explore dimensions of sex and romance tourism in Kenya.[16] The 2013 TV reality show *Wild Girls—Auf High Heels durch Afrika* is set in Namibia and is yet another testament to the popularity of fantasies about sex and romance in Africa.[17]

These texts and films are part of, but also key catalysts for, a flurry of German-language publications on intercultural relations more broadly, and with Kenyans specifically; in fact, a great number of autobiographies and self-help literature about intercultural relationships have been published in the German language since the end of the last millennium.[18] In addition, numerous accounts on the topic have been translated from other languages into German.[19] Books, blogs, forums, and websites about relationships with Middle Eastern and African men are particularly popular and reflect a wide range of experiences and views on the topic.[20] The website "Eintausendundeine Geschichte" (One Thousand and One Stories) is one of the most visible sites offering support to women who have had disappointing or abusive economic, physical, or emotional encounters with (mostly) African and Middle Eastern men.[21] This recent proliferation of discussions regarding relationships with men from areas to the south and east of Europe builds on publications that date back to the 1980s. One of the most spectacular of those was Betty Mahmoody's autobiographical account *Not without my Daughter* (1987), which sold two million copies in its German translation (*Nicht ohne meine Tochter*, 1988) and popularized a paradigm whereby Western women had to flee and protect their children from abusive Middle Eastern (and other) men.[22]

Sensationalist texts and movies were paralleled by social activism addressing the very real issues that binational, especially north-south, couples faced in Germany at the time: as Julia Woesthoff has shown, the Alliance of German Women Married to Foreigners (Interessengemeinschaft der mit Ausländern verheirateten Frauen), for example, played a decisive role in advocating the rights of both foreigners and women.[23] Overall, the larger discourse on binational relationships speaks through a number of venues, from fiction fantasy to self-help guides and discussion forums, that are—to some extent—grounded in the reality of interactions between Germans and Africans (and partners from other nations). The pervasiveness of the discourse in a wide range of German-language textual and visual media may have normalized a type of relationship that was once considered highly unusual and thus contributed to the increase in the number of Kenyan-German romantic relations since the mid-1990s.[24]

Setting and Conditions of North-South Romance in Diani

If the German discourse can be considered a push factor, Kenyan agency is a pull factor in the establishment of north-south romantic relations. In Diani, local Digo and upcountry women and men will approach tourists or expatriate residents at the beach or in various restaurants, hotels, bars, and discotheques with the goal of establishing a long-term or longish-term relationship that will serve as a solution to economic pressures and provide a pathway to greater personal independence. In some cases, the Kenyan partner will have a stable job, as hotel manager, waiter, or salesperson, for example, and is not necessarily in a situation of economic insecurity. Relationships also develop between humanitarian aid workers and locals. Sometimes the visitors or residents initiate the relationship, but the agency lies predominantly with Kenyans. These romantic relationships, as already suggested, are different from instances of direct prostitution that Kibicho explores. She focuses primarily on direct and on some cases of indirect prostitution, though she also acknowledges that the line between direct and indirect prostitution is blurry.[25]

"Beachboys" are usually associated with sex tourism in Kenya, but they generally do not consider themselves to be prostitutes and will not ask for money in exchange for sex directly. Over the period of an encounter with a tourist, beachboys (and their female equivalents, though the term "beachgirl" does not exist) elicit substantial sums of money from the visitor. The 2012 feature film *Paradise: Love* (*Paradies: Liebe*) by Ulrich Seidl explores the short-term relationships that are examples of indirect prostitution in Kenya and addresses the high number of female sex tourists who get involved with beachboys and other individuals like those Kibicho identifies.[26] The relationships featured in Seidl's film are similar to those studied by Amalia Cabezas. About her research on sex and tourism in Cuba, Cabezas writes: "Before long, I realized that the unified object of my research, the 'sex worker,' did not exist, was ambiguous, or at the very least was quite an unstable subject. Furthermore, most women in Cuba did not identify as a sex worker or a *jinetera*."[27] These observations also hold true for the Kenyan situation; especially Kenyan men who seek out and are sought out by female tourists—and at times extract large sums of money from them—do not see themselves as prostitutes. Indirect and to a lesser degree direct prostitution tend to be condoned by the African Kenyan community, an aspect that resonates with Cabezas's study of Cuba and also with an earlier study by Luise White on prostitution in Nairobi during the colonial period.[28]

Some distinctions are certain: in Diani, the term *malaya* (Kiswahili for prostitute) is clearly used for those who provide sex for cash; all other forms of sexual relations, regardless of their economic benefit, are not, in the view of locals and visitors alike, associated with prostitution. But the boundaries between prostitution and other relationships are fluid, and many relationships display various degrees of the kind of normativity associated with romantic relations in both Kenya and Europe. Some of the Kenyan partners I interviewed may have practiced direct or indirect prostitution before becoming involved in a more stable union, and several of the couples met on the beach or at a nightclub. The relationships discussed here range from long term (several lasting more than ten years) to short term (five lasted fewer than two years). Only four were married relationships, yet overall, marriage is a significant feature of Kenyan-German romantic relations. Data gleaned from an analysis of marriage certificates kept at the Office of the Registrar of Marriages of Mombasa shed light on the comparatively high frequency of Kenyan-German marriages and their nature with regard to age difference and economic status.

Data from the Office of the Registrar of Marriages in Mombasa

When one visits the Office of the Registrar of Marriages in Mombasa, one is likely to see couples made up of a European and a Kenyan partner, with the European partner, regardless of gender, usually ten to thirty years older than the Kenyan partner. White wedding dresses are not very common; rather, there is a casual tone to most festivities, especially in the absence of large groups of family and friends. Only a fraction of all couples marries at the registrar's office: many British and other tourists marry each other at their vacation hotels. These marriages constitute a large portion of the overall certificates; between a quarter and a third of all marriage licenses kept in Mombasa represent marriages between UK nationals who combine marriage and honeymoon on their vacation in Kenya.[29] Kenyan-Kenyan couples may also come to the office to register a marriage that was concluded in an officially recognized religious ceremony. In addition, a few Africans from other countries (such as Sudan, Tanzania, and Uganda) marry Kenyans each year; marriages between local members of the Indian community and Indians who live abroad represent another significant block.

Marriage licenses are expensive for locals: couples pay KSh10,300 ($116 in 2014) if the wedding takes place at the registrar's office and KSh15,000 ($170) when it is performed at another location (such as a hotel). The fee equals an average monthly paycheck of many Kenyans working in the coastal region (e.g., as waiters, household help, and night watchmen). Registering is thus prohibitive for most people in the lower and lower middle classes. Two main reasons encourage some Kenyans to register their marriages: state employees typically need proof of marriage in order to secure benefits for spouses, and many of the Kenyan-Kenyan licenses I reviewed involved soldiers and police officers. The second reason is travel: Kenyans who marry foreign nationals may register the marriage as a first step toward acquiring a passport.

I first turned to marriage licenses as a relevant source of information in the 1990s when I became aware of the ubiquitous phenomenon of Germans marrying Kenyans. Reviewing licenses for the years 1994 to 1998 confirmed anecdotal evidence that a trend was under way: in that five-year period, marriages between Kenyans and foreigners had increased by 64.3 percent and between Kenyans and Germans by 56.4 percent.[30] The increase for all German-speaking tourists (Germans, Swiss, and Austrians) who married Kenyans ranged from 68.2 to 77.4 percent of all foreigners.[31] The total number of 433 German marriages to Kenyans for the years 1994 to 1998 (out of a total of 587 marriages to foreigners) may seem low, but a marriage to a foreign national involves the entire extended family, and thus, in light of the growing frequency of these unions, a large number of people, especially in the greater Mombasa area (including areas to the south and the north), have been affected by these marriages over the years. We return to this aspect below.

For the purpose of the present study I analyzed a total of thirteen years (2000–2012) of marriage licenses kept at the Registrar of Marriages in Mombasa that reflect marriages concluded in Mombasa and in areas to the south and the north of Mombasa.[32] I also perused the licenses kept at the Registrar of Marriages in Kwale, the capital of what is now Kwale County, which is closer to Diani than Mombasa. Between 1991 and 2009, however, only thirteen German-Kenyan couples were married there (no Swiss or Austrians were among them), and the data are not statistically significant.

In 2009 and early 2010, I evaluated the ten-year period between 2000 and 2009 (close to nine thousand licenses) and found that of all the non-African and non-Indian foreigners (mostly Europeans, Canadians, US citizens, and Australians) who married Kenyans during this period, Germans make up 59 percent, for a total of 1,302 couples (see table 3). The total number amounts to a 50 percent increase compared with the data from 1994 to 1998. British marriage partners (397 in number) constitute about 17.9 percent of total marriage partners, with the rest divided among various nationalities (23.2 percent; tables 3, 5, and 7). Overall, the percentage of German-speaking marriage partners out of all foreign marriage partners has decreased by more than 10 percentage points from the earlier 73.8 percent that was recorded for the 1990s and can be directly correlated to an increase in marriages between Kenyan and British partners (from 10.1 percent in 1994–1998 to 17.9 percent in 2000–2009). The percentage of German-speaking marriage partners remains considerable, especially given that these marriages are closely related to tourism and that the number of German-speaking tourists during this time decreased significantly to about half that of British tourists (84,704 from Germany, Switzerland, and Austria and 163,084 from the UK in 2009).[33]

In 2013, I reviewed the years 2010 to 2012 (with an eye toward a possible fallout from the election violence in 2007 and 2008). While the number of German-speaking marriage partners remained relatively constant in total numbers, increasingly Kenyans married people of other nationalities (see tables 4, 6, and 8). These figures are related to the changing face of the tourism market, whereby Eastern Europeans and other nationalities constitute larger groups of visitors. While the total number of German-speaking tourists has dropped by half since the 1990s, the number of marriage partners has been steady, which raises the questions: Is there a special relationship between Kenyans and German-speaking visitors, and if there is, why?

More German-speaking men than women marry Kenyans. In the years 2000–2009, 68.6 percent of German-speaking marriage partners were male, and 31.4 percent female. In 2010–2012, the gap between male and female partners grew, with 72.8 percent for men and 27.2 percent for women. In comparison, British marriage partners are more equally divided between male (56.7 percent and 56.1 percent) and female (43.3 percent and 43.9 percent, respectively). Ratios are thus distinct for the various nationalities, a dimension that is grounded in aspects of gender and cultural, social, and religious identity and begs for closer comparative analysis. While the preference for German-speaking over British marriage partners is, from the Kenyan perspective, sure to be grounded in colonial history and the appeal of the strong German economy (a topic that came up repeatedly during interviews), Germans enable the relationships through various factors, as the following discussion will demonstrate. The gender differential, however, is more difficult to explain.

Demographic information gleaned from the marriage documents sheds additional light on age difference and economic status. In 2012, the average age of a German man at the time of marriage to his Kenyan partner was fifty-two and for a German woman forty-three, while the average age of their Kenyan partners was twenty-nine and thirty-two, respectively (table 9). The average age gap between German men and their Kenyan partners was twenty-three years, and between German women and their Kenyan partners, eleven years. About one-third of the ninety-three German men were thirty or more years older than their Kenyan wives. Similarly, one-third of the German women (fourteen of forty-one) were twenty or more years older than their Kenyan husbands. Fifteen percent (fourteen of ninety-three) of the German men were ten or fewer years older than their Kenyan spouses (a lower number than that for 1998), while 41.4 percent of the German women were ten years older or less than their Kenyan husbands.[34] Most foreign-born marriage partners are thus significantly older than their Kenyan spouses; only four Kenyan women and eight Kenyan men were older than their German spouses. The age gap between Kenyan women and German men is the most noticeable. Overall, this age gap far exceeds the average age difference in Western societies, in which the median age gap for different age groups stays mostly below ten years, and it is rare to see women who are significantly older than their spouses.[35] I have not had access to data about the age gap in Kenya; however, anecdotal evidence suggests that in first marriages the median age gap also stays below ten years, while in polygamous second and other marriages, the gap increases.

Twenty of the ninety-three German men listed professions predicated upon some sort of college education, such as engineer, IT specialist, or teacher (among them two retirees, table 9). Twenty-one of the men were retired and did not provide information about their professions. Considering that some of the retirees had a background in higher education and that some professions listed may have been based on a college education (such as "businessman"), it is reasonable to assume that about a fourth to a fifth of the German men had a college education. (Note that professions that require college in Kenya or other countries would not require college in Germany because of Germany's vocational educational system.) Most men listed professions such as electrician, packaging officer, factory supervisor, cashier, sales agent, pilot, prison warden, and toolmaker. Nine of their Kenyan spouses identified themselves as "students" or "college students," and three worked in professions that may have been preceded by a college education (e.g., "lab technician"). Many Kenyan women identified as hairdressers (eight) and businessladies (twenty-nine). About a quarter of German women had professions that require a college education (eleven), such as teacher, social worker, and therapist. Others identified as nurse, saleslady, postmaster, waitress, and clerk. From the available evidence, I would conclude that six of their Kenyan partners had a college education (manager, scientist, and hotelier), although the four who identified as hoteliers could also be waiters or on the administrative staff of a hotel and, as some of the others, may have had some vocational education past secondary school. (Since the information is self-reported and not specific enough, there is, in some cases, no way of telling what kind of actual profession it refers to.) Artist, seaman, driver, businessman, tour operator, and police officer are among other professions listed.

Compared with data from 1998, 2012 data show a slightly lower number of Germans working in professions that require a college degree. While most of the Germans marrying Kenyans are of working-class and middle-class background, these data do not clearly indicate the financial situation and economic status of the individuals; generally, however, Germans from these social classes tend to be financially stable. Many of the male Kenyan partners are economically vulnerable; while a waiter may have a contracted salaried position, a "boat operator" or "businessman" may in effect be one of the scores of individuals who try to make a few shillings a day by offering goods and services to tourists on the beach. Similarly, "hairdresser" and "businesslady" (the most frequently named professions among the Kenyan women) signals that a Kenyan woman does not have a regular income; the business, for example, may be selling *khangas* (a local wrap) on the beach. Overall, the data show that these marriages are not necessarily correlated to the social status of the individuals involved, as the marriage partners come from all walks of life, and at times, the partners have a comparable professional status within their respective societies (e.g., a Kenyan hairdresser marries a German hairdresser). Nevertheless, economic factors, as we will see, play a significant role in the dynamics of the relationships.

As noted before, many people who marry do so in order to acquire the papers that would allow a Kenyan partner to move to the home country of his or her non-African partner. Some of the female marriage partners may in fact be trafficked, though this is difficult to assess, since, as Kibicho asserts, "Kenyan bureaucrats are often in cahoots with traffickers, helping to provide false documentation for a fee" and "the majority of trafficked Kenyan women enter Germany or the UK through Eastern European countries," that is, not via a marriage to a German national.[36] A Diani resident estimated that about 80 percent of those who marry a European move to Europe; that estimate is corroborated by the figures about marriages registered in Germany, Switzerland, and Austria (see tables 10, 11, and 12). Couples who want to live in Europe would have to register their marriages in the respective country, using their Kenyan or other marriage certificates for that purpose.

The official statistics kept in Europe thus contain data about marriages concluded in Germany, Austria, and Switzerland as well as those concluded elsewhere.[37] As indicated, not all couples who marry in Kenya move to and register their marriages in Europe. Accordingly, the number of marriages registered in Switzerland is consistently higher than the number registered in Mombasa, as it includes marriages concluded in other locations in Kenya and in Switzerland (see table 11). Similarly, the number of marriages registered in Germany is considerably higher than the number recorded in Mombasa (table 10). The same is true for Austria (table 12). While the figures for marriages registered in Europe include data about couples who originally married in Nairobi and elsewhere in Kenya, contact between Kenyans and German-speaking tourists occurs mostly at the coast and thus accounts for a significant percentage of the overall German-Kenyan marriages. Considering that getting married in Kenya is cheaper and easier than getting married in Europe, the estimate that 80 percent of those who get married in Kenya move to Europe seems reasonable.

These couples, however, represent only a fraction of the larger group of north-south couples that are engaged in various forms of long-term romantic relations. Most of the couples who live along the coast are *not* married. While the total numbers of *marriages* between Kenyans and Germans are low, the larger phenomenon of intercultural relations has had a considerable cumulative effect on specific communities in Kenya, such as Diani, over the past thirty years. Overall, in every larger African Kenyan family that is indigenous to Diani, it is common for at least one family member to be or to have been either married to or living with a German or other European locally or in Europe. Generally, a salaried person in Kenya is estimated to provide, in one way or another, for ten to twenty individuals; as my research indicates, similar assessments can be made with regard to Kenyans who are in a relationship with expatriates and benefit from the relationship financially. Given the absence of comprehensive figures for marriages registered in Kenya, if we take the official data from Germany, Switzerland, and Austria as a starting point and assume an average of 250 Kenyan-German marriages per year over the past twenty years, then the resulting five thousand couples affect or have affected the lives of between fifty thousand and one hundred thousand Kenyans for the duration of these unions (and beyond, if the marriages led to the buying of land and building of houses or other support that continued beyond the marriage).

If, additionally, we assume that the marriages account for about 10 percent of all romantic relations with Germans that last more than a few months (an estimate that I venture on the basis of my research), the number of Kenyans whose lives have been affected by these unions grows to half a million to one million. Considering the overall number of marriages to foreigners (the figures from Mombasa are a starting point, with German-speaking partners in 2012 making up 38 percent of the overall foreign marriage partners; see tables 3–8) as well as other types of romantic relations, the number grows again, to perhaps one to two million people or more over the course of a couple of decades—that is, a significant portion of people living on the coast (3,325,307 for the entire Coast Province [2009]) are directly affected by romantic relations with foreigners. Many Kenyan marriage partners come from other areas of Kenya but live on the coast most of the year; they and their expatriate partners may, however, also extend financial support to in-laws who live in other areas of the country. The support may come in the form of remittances sent from Europe or be extended by couples who live in Kenya.

More research is needed to arrive at a better quantitative understanding of the effect of marriages and long-term romantic relations on the coast and other areas of Kenya, but the data given here show that it is of significant proportion. In addition, further research would better elucidate the overall economic (and cultural) effect of Kenyan interaction with tourists and other foreigners, be it through employment, for example, in the tourism and mining industries, humanitarian activity, or prostitution, particularly on the coast. More than twenty thousand foreigners are registered in Kenya as permanent residents, and hundreds of thousands come to Kenya each year as tourists or humanitarians, or in pursuit of business.[38] Their effect on Kenyan lives is considerable. Among a population of 44.35 million (estimated for 2013), the official figure for wage employment in Kenya in 2013 was 2,265.7 individuals; the figure is six million according to other sources.[39] In addition to remittances, the effect of the informal sector, including the economic transactions discussed in this book in the realms of humanitarianism and romance, is substantial.

The fact that a significant percentage of married couples and practically all of the unmarried couples live in Kenya challenges assumptions prevalent in the media and scholarship that north-south romantic relations are synonymous with a south-to-north or poor country–to–rich country movement. The image of the mail-order bride has helped to ossify the notion of the economically and culturally oppressed Third World woman whom Western men take advantage of.[40] Binational marriages are thus studied primarily in countries of the global north; binational couples living in Ghana or Morocco, however, have received only scant attention.[41] Yet similar to the Kenyan case, significant pockets of settler communities have sprung up around the world, especially near resort areas in places such as Tunisia, Ghana, Panama, Costa Rica, Thailand, and Turkey, that are distinguished by a high frequency of north-south couples.

The data gleaned from the analysis of the material available at the Office of the Registrar of Marriages in Mombasa sheds light on frequency, age, and social background that distinguish one type of union—marriage—between Kenyans and Germans. The interviews I conducted with couples and individuals in Diani provide additional insight into the nature of romantic relationships—their strengths and their challenges.

Kenyan-German Couples in Diani

At the beach, on matatus, in shopping centers, restaurants, the post office, banks, hospitals, hotels, and villages, mixed couples are an integral part of everyday life in Diani. Tall Masai men and pudgy German women, young Kikuyus and Swiss pensioners, rasta-haired Digo men and European widows, poor Nairobians and rich Swabians, upcountry managers and Austrian restaurant owners—individuals with distinct and complex histories create bicultural unions that provide a multitude of both opportunities and challenges for the involved men and women as well as their families and friends. One day I watched a group of two European women and two African Kenyan men who were close in age walking on the beach (figure 4.1). One of the African Kenyans put his arm over the

Figure 4.1. German-Kenyan couples on Diani Beach

shoulder of one of the white women and started playing with her hair, whereupon she also started playing with his hair; the other couple followed suit.

One can imagine the conversation they were having, and the scene might have been moving to some degree, suggesting a perhaps innocent exploration of very real physical differences that are part of the attraction between white and black bodies. But this attraction comes with a history of exclusionary laws, violence, and exoticization, and this moment of seemingly innocent romantic interaction happened in a context of tough economic conditions that have been shaped by the long violent history of black and white encounters. African Kenyan and German partners are vulnerable in distinct ways, with economic need a predominant motivator for African Kenyan agency and emotional need a predominant motivator for German behavior, though both factors play a role for both sides. The success and failure of these relationships are related to how the partners negotiate their individual vulnerabilities and needs.

In 2009 and 2010, I conducted thirty initial interviews with thirty-six individuals who are or were partners in relationships lasting from three months to thirty-nine years. Most of the interviews were conducted with only one of the partners; in six cases I interviewed the partners together, and in one case, I spoke to the partners individually.[42] Data thus reflect information about twenty-nine couples—a total of fifty-eight individuals (see table 13). Conversations lasted between thirty minutes and two hours, and in several cases I interacted with couples and individuals repeatedly. After these initial interviews, I stayed in close touch with nine couples over the following years and was able to observe the course of their relationships (nos. 2, 4, 5, 7, 13, 18, 22, 24, 29; table 13); eight couples I heard from more sporadically (nos. 12, 14, 16, 20, 25, 26, 27, 28). Two have separated as of 2014 (nos. 20, 22), and one Swiss man died in 2012 (no. 25). Five couples had already split up at the time of the interview (that is, the interview partner spoke about a relationship that had already ended; nos. 3, 9, 16, 17, 21). I did not maintain contact with seven couples (nos. 6, 8, 10, 11, 15, 19, 23) and do not know whether they are still together.

I also took notice of the views voiced by members of the Diani community (approximately forty individuals) who commented on these relationships. Considering "gossip" and the views of as many people as possible became crucial to my research. Self-representation, especially in emotional matters, is a tricky thing. Complementing and corroborating through additional conversations and observations what individuals said about themselves helped me to fill in the blanks and balance the self-representations of the people I interviewed.

The couples differed in terms of legal status, the place of birth of Kenyan partners, the residency of German partners, employment, and the number of children. Only four of the couples were married (13.8 percent), though several people mentioned marriage plans. The average duration of the relationship at the time when I first conducted interviews was 7.9 years for those couples involving Kenyan women and 5.9 years for those involving Kenyan men. Confirming data from the analysis of marriage certificates, a considerable age difference structures most relationships; the German partners are generally older than their Kenyan partners, with the margin being larger for German men than for German women. In the group that I studied, the age difference averaged 25.4 years for unions involving German men and African Kenyan women and 13.7 years for those involving German women and African Kenyan men (table 13). German men and women were older than their Kenyan partners, except in one case in which the Kenyan was older and another in which the partners were the same age. The significant age difference, as will become evident, affects the emotional, social, and economic aspects of the relationships.

The more stable relationships are those in which both partners live in Diani most of the year, although in one case, the German partner had been visiting three times a year for the previous ten years, staying for about one to three months during each visit; he also built a house in Diani (couple no. 4 in table 14). Generally, if the German partner lives in Germany most of the year, the relationship will end after a few years or the Kenyan partner will move to Germany. Most of the German partners who live in Diani own property in the area or have built or contributed to the building of a house in other areas of Kenya. Some move back and forth between Kenya and Germany, and the house in Diani can be considered a second home, similar to what has been observed with regard to German retirement communities in other locations, such as the Canary Islands.[43]

Noteworthy is the fact that most of the Kenyan women were not from the coast; only three women were from the traditionally Muslim Diani area, while thirteen were born in other areas of Kenya. Eight of the Kenyan men were from the coast, five from upcountry (table 15). Eight of the men had stable employment (waiter, politician, police officer, cook) or were self-employed (owner of a shop, boat, or cab); five were basically unemployed and worked odd jobs or mainly looked for opportunity on the beach. Two of the Kenyan women worked in shops owned by or co-owned with their German partners; others worked as waitresses (two), hairdressers (one), housekeepers (one), sold *khangas* on the beach (one), or owned a small shop or restaurant (three). Six women did not work (table 16).

Five couples had one child together, and one German man talked about a miscarriage with apparent emotion; the experience clearly had created a commitment to his Kenyan girlfriend (table 17). Approximately two-thirds of Kenyan men, Kenyan women, and German men had children from previous relationships. This was true for half of the German women. Some of the Kenyan men and women may have had children whom they did not acknowledge in the interview or whom their German partners did not know about.

Reviewing the stories of four select couples serves as an entry point to the analysis of the emotional and economic ecology of these relationships.

Profiles

FATIMA AND ERWIN[44]

Erwin (born 1940) had always wanted to travel to Africa, but his first visit to the continent, to South Africa, had been disappointing. Kenya, however, with its varied natural and cultural attractions, matched his fantasies and expectations. At age sixty-five, when he first visited in 2005, he acquired his diving license. More important, he also met Fatima (born 1981) at the beach: "Saw the beauty from afar" (Sah die Flocke von Weitem).[45] Fatima shared her own romantic version of love at first sight: she had always waited for an angel to save her, and lo and behold, the man's last name was Retter, which is German for "savior," so her wish came true. When Fatima met Erwin, she "had no house, no place to sleep." Erwin, she says, saved her. Erwin usually comes to Diani two to three times a year for extended periods of one to three months. For his age, he is agile and physically fit; he has been working hard on the house that he has built for Fatima and himself. He is a skilled worker with professional training in plumbing and roofing and has remodeled scores of homes. For many years he was employed as a technician and consultant for a large roofing company. He received his advanced professional degree (*Meistertitel*) by taking evening classes. At that point, he had developed a liking for studying and continued on to also finish tenth grade (the second of three possible exit exams from public school in Germany, the third one granting access to college), which he had not had a chance to do before: "My brain wanted to learn more," he explained.

Fatima has lived all her life in the Diani village of Mwaroni. She completed primary school but did not go on to secondary. She used to support herself by singing a genre of music called *taarab* at local bars and had evidently been quite popular. She told me that she is unable to conceive children, which may be one reason why she was open to a relationship with a foreigner—something that is not common among the Muslim women of the area. Fatima's family owns a piece of land, and when the couple decided to stay together, they began to build a house on the plot. Erwin said he first located the direction of the wind in order to determine where the windows should go. He then built the house, from the foundation up, with help from a couple of Fatima's cousins and one of her brothers. During every stay in Kenya he completes another part of the house. Over time, the bare structure that I saw when I first visited in 2010 developed into a plastered and painted building with a kitchen equipped with a stove and refrigerator—unusual for the area. The house and plot are modest compared with the villas of other Europeans, but in Mwaroni, the compound is a little gem. Fatima has planted a lush garden, with fruit trees, decorative bushes, and vegetables; in June 2016, during my last visit, the trees had matured enough to provide plenty of comforting shade. Erwin did well figuring out the effect of the wind; for those sitting under the trees in the yard, a cool breeze takes off the edge even in the hottest and most humid weather. In addition, Erwin has had a well dug and a water tank installed; neighbors come to fetch water, which Fatima sometimes sells and sometimes passes out for free. The access to water clearly gives her a special status in her neighborhood.

Erwin, who has been divorced twice, also owns a house in Turkey. While Fatima has not visited him in Germany (where, as she emphasized once, she would prefer to live), she spent two months in 2011 with Erwin in Turkey on what was her first trip abroad. He clearly enjoys his worldliness, and indeed, considering his humble background, the fact that he owns property in three countries and is able to adjust to culturally distinct environments is quite impressive. He insists, however, that he would not live in Kenya permanently: "One is safest as a tourist." He said that he would advise people against paying the high fees for residency visas, because if one were to run into trouble, those with residency would have to deal with the Kenyan state, whereas those on a tourist visa would be represented by Germany. It seems that part of his pleasure lies in the nomadic dimension of his existence. His language skills are limited: his command of English is rudimentary, as is Fatima's, and his knowledge of Kiswahili is even more limited. Fatima has accommodated him by acquiring some basic proficiency in German, which has now surpassed her English proficiency. Although their options for communication are constrained, Fatima seems to have a sense for the odd humor of her at-times caustic lover, who clearly enjoys talking and offering witty remarks about everything and everybody.

Erwin went through a drawn-out and stressful litigation during his second divorce. He is estranged from his three children, and Fatima has never met any of his relatives, although Erwin is well acquainted with Fatima's relatives and friends in Diani. The two come across as a harmonious couple; she puts up with his antics and somewhat commandeering tone, and he does not seem to be bothered by the fact that some aspects of Fatima's world remain obscure to him. It seems that what they know about each other and the degree to which they care for and respect each other are sufficient to create a stable emotional connection. Fatima stated repeatedly that Erwin took good care of her and that she loved him. Several of Erwin's comments displayed his deep affection for his lover. He shared his outrage with me regarding the clitoridectomy to which Fatima had been subjected. Visibly agitated when he talked about it, he was frustrated and angry that it was not in his power to undo the procedure, and his compassion for Fatima was moving. "Fatima alone is my happiness" (Fatima ist mein ganzes Glück), he said. In 2012, they shared plans about building another house in a more remote area:

"Not a single white person around," gloated Erwin. "I would be in the middle of the village." He takes pride in living in the village and is critical of other Germans (especially a couple he referred to who comes from the former East Germany) who are hostile toward their Kenyan environment, especially the people.

In November 2013, shortly before my departure, I dropped in on Fatima to say good-bye. When I knocked at the door, a young African Kenyan man who was roughly her age opened it. Fatima was not home, he said, so I left, asking him to give her my regards. I had seen the young man once before during an earlier visit to Fatima; he had entered the house, but she had quickly sent him outside. At the time I thought that he was one of the many villagers who buy water from Fatima, but my research assistant, who initially had introduced me to Fatima and knew her well since childhood, told me that the young man was Fatima's boyfriend "when Papa Erwin is not around."

ESTHER AND WERNER[46]

When I first interviewed Esther and Werner in January 2010 in Esther's small restaurant in the middle of Ukunda, they were visibly besotted with one another. She was forty-seven and he sixty-six at the time (born in 1963 and 1944, respectively). They had met only a few months earlier but were ecstatic about their plan to get married in October. Werner, who comes from an area east of Frankfurt, is a retired butcher and in his youth had been a boxer on the German national team. His arms were tattooed, and he wore a stud in one of his earlobes. He is rather short, as is she, so, as Werner pointed out, they made a good fit. Esther, a Luo, was from upcountry and had worked in various professions in the Diani area for more than two decades. Both of them have two children; Werner's children are adults (ages forty-six and forty-five in 2010), and Esther's daughters were seventeen and eighteen years old and lived in the area. Werner said that he was divorced, and Esther said that she was separated. Esther is very assertive and emphasized that she liked to have her own money, to have her own business, and to do things her way. They planned to live in Kenya; she did not want to move to Germany, and Werner was very enthusiastic about living in Kenya. While Esther had not met any of his family members, Werner knew some of her local family: "They are happy with him," she asserted. Her commitment to her family seemed very strong. She recounted how she had supported her siblings and children over time. "Everybody looks at me for support," she said, and she expected the pressure to rise, now that she was involved with a *mzungu*, a white man who was expected to be wealthy. He, on the other hand, expressed how much he enjoyed the interaction with Esther's family ("not a bad word is said" [kein böses Wort wird gesprochen]) and with people in the area in general ("I get along well with people"). He spoke barely any English, and she knew only a few words of German at the time; nevertheless, he said, "I can communicate well, she really helps me a lot" (ich kann mich gut verständigen, sie hilft mir ja sehr).

After my research assistant and I had parted from Werner and Esther, whose positive energy was contagious, my assistant told me that Esther had once been a police officer and for a while had sold marihuana out of the trunk of her police car—"wholesale," he kept repeating. Eventually, she was arrested and lost all the money she had made from the illicit business as well as her job. As it turned out, her luck would run out again, this time with Werner.

When I returned to Diani in 2011, Esther contacted me and said she and Werner needed my help. Something had gone wrong with the automatic deposit of Werner's pension check into his Kenyan account. He had returned to Kenya in December 2010, and since then, no money had arrived in Kenya (they also never followed up on their plan to get married). I met with him several times to try to understand the situation and figured out that he was being scammed by a German resident, a "friend" who was evidently collaborating with a local banker, and a German contact to whom Werner had given power of attorney. He had been told that his German bank had closed down his account and that he had been declared dead in Germany. Werner's pension was probably deposited into someone else's account, and my suspicion was that the German "friend" was the beneficiary. Esther was visibly stressed by the situation. They had had to move out of the house they had rented and were living in a small room on the outskirts of Diani that was furnished with only a bed and a small table. As Werner kept telling stories that revealed his confusion and how he was being taken advantage of by an entire army of crooks of all nationalities, I wondered whether he had the skills to survive in Kenya. Werner and Esther still seemed to like each other a lot, but the "honeymoon" was over.

Then when I returned in 2012, Esther told me the last act of their story, which had, by then, turned into a tragedy. Werner had cheated on her, evidently with prostitutes, and had been unable to pay their rent for almost a year (though one may wonder why Esther did not continue running her restaurant, a question I failed to ask); the couple had been arrested and jailed in November 2011. Werner was bailed out quickly by a German fellow and deported to Germany. But Esther had stayed in jail until April and was now living "in the bush": a friend of her mother's had taken her in, offering her a home in a small village about fifteen miles from Diani. The older woman was running a palm wine business, but according to Esther she was not a good businesswoman and was drinking her product herself. Esther had taken over the operation: "I am all about business," Esther said proudly. "The old woman sold ten bottles a day; I am already at forty-five." She had plans to expand the business; a bar was already open. "I am happy now," she said, "no stress in the bush." I asked her how she felt about Werner, who, according to Esther, had cheated on her, gone after prostitutes, and turned out to be a disappointment. "I learned a lot," she said. Clearly, she was resilient and knew how to pick herself up again.

In July 2012, I visited Esther in her new location. Her *jua kali* (literally, "hot sun"—slang for informal economy) business, the bar, was located in a simple structure made of wood and mud that was roofed with *makuti* leaves. Several fishermen were sitting on benches drinking *pombe*, palm wine. Esther also served *changa'a*, the local brew. She showed me how and where she made her liquor and described the process of distilling in detail. She worked from dusk to dawn, but I could see that she would soon be able to build herself a little house and turn the bar into a more respectable building. Considering how hard she was working, it is not surprising that especially younger women are dreaming of obtaining a shortcut to a better life through a relationship with a European.

As to Werner—in 2013 I heard that he was back in Diani, living with another woman.

THOMAS AND BETSY[47]

Thomas fits the cliché of the successful German entrepreneur who moves up through hard work. His family owned a small business in southwestern Germany, but when the industry went through a financial crisis in the 1990s, he decided to leave Germany for Kenya. "I came here to survive" (Ich kam hier zum Überleben), he said. He had visited Kenya from early childhood and had fallen in love with the country. He made the move in 1997 and slowly built a little empire in Diani, where he is one of the most successful businessmen, with investments in shopping centers, grocery stores, cottages, real estate, and a touring company. Thomas met Betsy in a clothing store in Mombasa owned by her sister's husband, a Kenyan of Italian origin. After a short period of courtship, she gave up her employment and moved with Thomas into a Diani villa that he had built with the considerable profits from his local businesses. He was forty-one years old and she was twenty-six when they met in 2001. Betsy is a self-confident woman who has a son (born in 1997) from a previous relationship with an African Kenyan. Thomas has no children from his marriage to a German woman that was dissolved before he moved to Kenya. Together, Thomas and Betsy have one son (born in 2005), but they have remained unmarried.

During my first conversation with Thomas in 2010 it became obvious that he felt conflicted about his relationship with Betsy. "I have a good wife," he said initially, but then added, "I would never be in a relationship with an African again." He said they often fought and had been through a number of emotional crises; because of their child, however, he wanted to stay in the relationship. When I asked what the main disagreements were about, he offered a number of generalized observations concerning cultural differences between Europeans and

Africans: "Europeans always want to move forward," he said, "while Africans are content with what they have. To look toward the future is impossible for them." He also complained that Kenyans never take responsibility for their actions; others—"or God," he said—were always at fault. "I would love to take my child to Germany," he said. "A child who grows up here does not have a chance in the Western world." Some of the differences seemed to lead to very tense situations: "An African will provoke until it gets physical," Thomas said. "Then I have to leave. If we argue and we are in the kitchen and she has a knife or hot oil, I leave." He got quite aggravated when he described such scenarios, and also referred to a German neighbor who regularly was beaten up by his African Kenyan wife. I asked Thomas why he does not end his relationship with Betsy; he answered that he had tried to get her to leave the house, but to no avail.

Two weeks after our first interview I ran into Thomas, who surprised me with the news that he had moved out of his house. He was considering his legal options. A few days later, after he learned that Betsy was entitled to a considerable share of his wealth because they had lived together for almost a decade and also had a child together, he was visibly upset. He felt trapped: he did not want to share his wealth or to leave his son. Eventually, he moved back in with Betsy, into a bigger house he had built that gave him more personal space. Thomas is known to explode in public, be it with his employees, a guard at a supermarket, or workers at his house. He is famous in Diani for his temper tantrums, and one day, one of the hawkers on the beach volunteered a humorous imitation of him. Thomas is aware of this weakness; "I get easily testy," he said. "I just can't wait; I am actually a patient person." When I considered his behavior, the term *Tropenkoller* from the German colonial period came to mind (see chapter 2). Thomas displayed the nervous behavior of Europeans who are unable to cope with the combination of social and physical disorientation that can result from life in an unfamiliar culture and climate.[48] "Colonial neurosis" affects both colonized and colonizers, and the nervousness that was and is displayed by Europeans in the tropics is a testimony to colonial and neoliberal contradictions.[49] Thomas is a prime example of this type of expatriate. His wife, however, is also known for dramatic scenes in which she threatens to "beat up" those who come onto her turf. Together, Thomas and Betsy fuel gossip and seem to provide entertainment for the local community.

Although Thomas has struggled with health problems over the past few years, his relationship and business seem stable. He has slowed down a bit, gained weight and then lost it again, and seems less emotionally volatile. He continues to expand his business, at times making questionable architectural choices that upset other residents: "He thinks he owns everything here in Diani," commented one embittered salesperson who works in a store that has become almost invisible from the street because Thomas blocked it with a new building in which he moved one of his offices. Thomas is not the only German whose economic prowess has changed the face of Diani, but he is one of the most powerful.

RITA AND JAMES[50]

Rita (born in 1954) came to Kenya in 2005 with her then-husband Karl (born in 1939). They had decided for years that they would leave Switzerland once Karl retired. They had visited Kenya off and on over three decades and had fallen in love with the country's natural beauty. The history and culture of its people, however, were rather unknown to them. When Karl's retirement approached, they were ready to turn their dream into reality. Karl left first in order to find a house; Rita stayed in Switzerland for nine months, selling their house and furniture and packing belongings into boxes for storage. But there was more to this process than packing boxes: Rita had married Karl when she was in her early twenties, and now, for the first time in her life, she was on her own, making her own decisions and living according to her own schedule. By the time she joined Karl in Kenya in January 2006, she had changed: Karl seemed too dominant; he criticized her initiatives, curtailed her creativity, and interfered with her newly acquired feeling of independence. Into this atmosphere of alienation came James (born in 1965, eleven years younger than Rita), who sold handcrafted wooden curios at the beach. She had met him on one of her daily walks along the ocean. Rita said that talking to James instantly made her feel understood (even though her English is limited); the way he listened and paid attention to her reminded her of her grandmother ("Ich kriegte mein Omagefühl"). One day, they saw a fantastic rainbow in a cloudless sky, and Rita, who is always on the lookout for propitious signs from the universe, took this as confirmation that she had found the love of her life.

James, who was born in the Akamba area of Kenya and had been hawking in Diani since the late 1980s, left his modest one-bedroom place in Ukunda and moved into the magnificent house, overlooking a private beach and surrounded by a lush yard, that Karl and Rita had rented north of Diani. The three shared this paradisiacal space for several months, but the area has a reputation for being unsafe, and sure enough, the idyll was disrupted by two violent robberies. During one of them, a visiting friend was seriously wounded; after the second incident, Rita and James decided to move out. When I met the couple, they were living in a handsome though small two-room house south of Diani surrounded by a well-maintained yard. James, who has no professional training and has not completed secondary school, continued to sell curios to tourists on the beach, but made little money. Rita began to support his son Martin (born in 1996), even though she was dependent on a monthly allowance from Karl, who by then had started a relationship with his housekeeper, Anna (born in 1982). "Since she has become my girlfriend," Karl confided, "I am paying her a bit more." Anna is forty-three years younger than Karl and is blind in one eye. In 2012, Karl paid for surgery to replace the lens and improve her face aesthetically. To this day, Karl maintains the relationship with Anna and also provides for her daughter (born in 2000).

Rita became increasingly frustrated with her economic dependence on Karl (who was sustaining a total of three families at that point: his first family in Switzerland, Rita and the Kenyans connected to her, and Anna and those connected to her) and also began to feel exhausted from aspects of daily life in Diani, such as the heat, the seasonal rains, diseases, robberies in the area, and what she experienced as a lack of community. When one of her two sons announced that he and his wife were expecting a child, Rita decided to return to Switzerland—with James. In an elaborate effort that counters widespread perceptions about the presumably insurmountable difficulties for foreigners to land a residency permit, let alone work permit, in Switzerland, she succeeded in securing both for her Kenyan lover. The file she put together included a letter from her then-still husband Karl in which he certified that his wife and her lover had lived with him and that he had been paying their rent, thus assuming financial responsibility for both. Rita and James moved to Switzerland in 2010, and both landed stable but also physically exhausting jobs; for the most part, they stocked shelves, and in addition, Rita (who has trained as an insurance agent and also has worked in various offices) took on some secretarial duties. James sent most of the money he made to his parents in Kenya, in support of building a house for him and Rita, who also contributed funds. One development that Rita had not expected was the increasing contact with Salome, the mother of James's son. Rita had been under the impression that the relationship had been long over and insignificant, yet evidently Salome played a bigger role in James's life than she thought. (James also has a daughter with a French woman; the daughter was eighteen years old in 2011 when James saw her for the first time as a result of efforts Rita undertook to reunite the family.)

In late October 2012, I received an update on the couple's one-month visit to Kenya. Rita and James had spent the first few days on the coast with Karl; after three days, James had gone upcountry to his ancestral village. When Rita followed him a week later, she was shocked to find Salome in the house that he and Rita had financed. Rita said she was angry; James's explanation—that according to the traditions of his ethnic group, the Akamba, the mother of his child was entitled to live in the house (which is not true if the couple was never married or is divorced)—did not appease her. In the end, James convinced Rita that he would lose face with his family if she would not accept the situation. Interestingly, the two women had worked out a modus vivendi over time, and Rita said that in the end she was grateful for Salome's presence, especially because the expectations of the larger family would have been difficult for Rita to meet alone: "Salome cooked for all of us, I never would have managed. . . . She was very sweet, after all, it really was extremely good providence" (Salome hat für alle gekocht, ich hätte das nie geschafft . . . Sie war ganz liebevoll, es war dann doch eine supergute Fügung). The word "providence" is quite telling here, because it implies that "fate" or even God had played a role in arranging the events and is indicative of how Rita approaches life more generally. In the end, Rita even bought a bed and a mattress for Salome, evidently for the third, and, as she said, last time.

I visited James and Rita in July 2014 in their home in Switzerland. Rita and Karl divorced in 2013, which simplified matters on various levels and helped diffuse tensions between Rita and James. A couple of months earlier, however, James had fallen seriously ill and almost died from a burst appendix that went undetected for three days. He was clearly a changed man when I saw him in Switzerland; he was no longer the positive, cheerful man I had encountered four years earlier. Rita also seemed drawn, and the two bickered constantly. "You won't turn me into a Swiss person," he barked at one point. Clearly, they had underestimated the challenges of immigration for James. He had lost his job even before he had gotten ill, and after applying for scores of positions, he felt that the prospects of his finding new work were dim. In addition, the bond between James and Salome seemed to have grown; Rita complained that James often talked to her on the phone and that their emotional connection seemed to have intensified while James was in the hospital. James and Rita felt stuck; economic pressure and the increasing effects of cultural differences had begun to erode their trust in one another. By the end of 2015, however, James had been working again for about a year, had gotten his driver's license, and was in good health. The couple spent most of October 2015 in Kenya, first with the family of James upcountry and then on the coast with Karl. By that time, James was no longer seeing Salome, as she had defrauded him of a considerable sum of money. During a Skype conversation in October 2015, Rita told me: "We are happy. Things have never been as good as they are right now."

The stories of Fatima and Erwin, Esther and Werner, Thomas and Betsy, and James and Rita may seem peculiar by some standards, but they are representative of basic types of long-term romantic relationships that one can find in Diani. Despite the differences between the various couples, there are shared points of connection that distinguish all couples in one way or another, regardless of whether the German partner lives abroad part of the year, the couple moves overseas, or both live together in Diani. These points of connection include stabilizing factors such as community attitudes, fluid kinship patterns, and positive sexual experiences. Among the challenges are the consequences of age differences, cultural differences, and psychological tensions. Perhaps the most relevant point of connection is the larger matter of what motivates the individual partners to engage in the relationship, a question related to the emotional and economic precarity of the partners.

Stabilizing Factors for German-Kenyan Couples

COMMUNITY ATTITUDES

Support from local communities and Kenyan relatives is one of the key aspects that allows interracial relationships in Diani to flourish. Analyses of intercultural couples in European countries, the United States, and a wide range of other locations across the globe point to the embattled status of binational, but particularly biracial, couples within their communities and families. In Kenya, however, unions made up of Europeans and African Kenyans are generally accepted within the African Kenyan environment. Reflecting this lived reality, interracial relationships are increasingly discussed positively in the Kenyan public sphere, as news reports about marriages of African Kenyan and Europeans or other whites illustrate.[51] Generally, African Kenyan–German couples who live in Diani concurred that, in Kenya, being in an intercultural and biracial relationship did not create any problems for them, other than, as one German man said, the envy

Figure 4.2. Kenyan-Swiss couples in Diani, Christmas 2009

of other African Kenyans. Most couples, however, emphasized that they felt accepted within the various African Kenyan communities. Erwin and Fatima, for example, live in the middle of Mwaroni and have never encountered problems with their neighbors, who are exclusively African Kenyan. Other couples who live in various parts of the area also said that they had not experienced hostility from neighbors. Mixed couples are able to walk about with no trouble in Diani, and nobody mentioned ever having been accosted by African Kenyans.

When I asked Kenyans *not* involved in an intercultural relationship about their views of mixed couples, Kenyan men were almost unanimously supportive of them. Older as well as younger men from all walks of life, be they village elders or waiters in hotels, agreed that a relationship with a European woman or man was perfectly acceptable, even if the European woman was older than her Kenyan partner. Some women, however, especially those from the local Digo community, were rather critical of younger men's relationships with older European women. Scores of local Digo men are engaged in sexual relations with women who are at times older than their mothers, and disgust was clearly visible on some faces and was communicated through dismissive gestures during conversations about the topic. Relationships of Kenyan women with older men, alternately, did not elicit negative responses, as they are in line with patterns of traditional polygamy, whereby second, third, or more wives may be significantly younger than their husbands.

When partners' families live in Diani, interaction with them occurs regularly. But some families live upcountry, and many Germans have traveled long distances to meet the relatives of their partners. In some cases, the connection is rudimentary. Thomas, for example, has visited Betsy's home village only once in fourteen years, whereas some of her family members visit often. Some Germans have never met the family of their partners; however, others have developed close connections. An African Kenyan woman, who was twenty-six years old in 2010 and had been in a relationship with a sixty-three-year-old German for the previous four and a half years, said that he had met most of her family and that some relatives were living with them; others visited often. Along these lines, a German woman said that "for his family I am his wife." One Swiss man, who was seventy-seven in 2010, was married to a woman who was forty-two years younger than him and had a three-year-old child with him. They lived in a beautiful house in Magutu that was larger than most houses in the area, though not as ostentatious as some of the villas closer to the beach, and was surrounded by a well-maintained garden. Her two children, ages sixteen and fourteen at the time, were living with them, and he said that he had visited his wife's family several times and that he enjoyed his new big family. "They are my parents," he said about his wife's parents. He said he only has "one white friend, who is a German." His own son from a previous marriage (forty-eight years old at the time) was "very happy to have a little brother." In 2012 I heard that the man had died and that he was buried according to his wish on the ancestral land of his Akamba wife.

Acceptance by the Kenyan family, however, does not mean that the relationship with in-laws is without conflict. Some Germans reported that the visit up-country was challenging for them ("I would never do that again") or that they did not get along well with some of the in-laws ("I don't like her brother"). Especially when it comes to financial matters, relations are strained from the perspective of the German partners. It is exactly this financial dimension that ensures the support of the African Kenyan family (and community more broadly), but it also creates tensions for Kenyan family members. In particular, other wives have to reconcile themselves with a challenging situation (the question of multiple families will be addressed below). Even those relationships that involve older German women and younger Kenyan men will not face outright resistance, but German women and men often are not aware of the hostile thoughts that some of their Kenyan in-laws or community members may harbor. Nonetheless, the African Kenyan community tends to appreciate the economic benefits of the interracial unions and thus ultimately condones them.

German in-laws are often less accepting than Kenyan relatives. Especially in those cases in which an older woman marries or lives with a much younger man, the German family is often hostile or at least initially reluctant to be supportive. One Swiss women, who was eighty-two in 2010, had been married to a local Kenyan politician thirty years her junior. She was widowed in 1995 and married her Kenyan partner in 1999. She had not been back to Switzerland for ten years and seemed entirely integrated and at ease in the local environment. Her son, she said, had been shocked initially, but he, as well as her two sisters, had gotten used to the situation and were visiting Kenya once or twice a year. Yet another Swiss woman stated that her sister was "very disappointed" in her choice of relationship. "You are not following the rules," her sister had told her. One German man reported that his son didn't like Kenya; he found it "too dirty." Others described that their German relatives had become more accepting of their relationships over time, with regard to both age and cultural differences.

Germans noted that the local British community (including members of the East Africa Women's League, which was specifically mentioned by two women who were active in the league) was hostile toward Europeans who were married or otherwise romantically involved with Kenyans. Some conflict was also reported with other German residents who were not involved with African Kenyans. Almost unanimously these Germans will say that African-German unions never work out, and almost everybody has a repertoire of stories that prove the point. The bulk of these examples refer to cases in which the German partner had been cheated out of money. One woman recalled a time that she had been at a restaurant when suddenly an older man got up and screamed, "I lost all my money! She took everything!" A Swiss man mentioned the case of a woman who went to Germany to visit her family, and when she returned after a few weeks, the locks had been changed on her house and—more significantly—it was occupied by new owners. All of her belongings were gone, and with them her Kenyan partner.

Interracial couples who live in Germany, Switzerland, and Austria often speak of discrimination and a hostile environment and complain of the resulting challenges in their lives. Every seventh marriage in Germany is binational, and every third child is born to parents of differing nationalities.[52] Figures for Austria and Switzerland, where every fourth or third marriage, respectively, is binational, are even higher.[53] Figures for the number of interracial marriages, which are much lower, are difficult to come by, but according to one study, race plays a lesser role than religion in creating obstacles to binational relations in Western Europe more broadly.[54] (Curiously, in predominantly Muslim Diani, religion was never a topic of discussion.) Despite the high frequency of binational relations, the mainstream environment in Germany, as an example, continues to be hostile to such relations, even if less so today than a few decades ago. According to various studies, even in the more recent past, one-third of Germans would object to intermarriage between German women and foreigners, and "more than 60% of respondents admit that they would be troubled with an asylum seeker marrying into the family."[55] Self-help books and counseling websites and initiatives generally acknowledge the challenges that interracial couples experience in German-speaking countries, despite the rising trend toward interracial, intercultural, and binational relationships.[56] It is interesting to note that the situation of German-Kenyan couples in Kenya is thus different in terms of their status within local communities. It is safe to say that the problems that Germans may experience with their partners in Kenya are not primarily related to any critical or unaccepting attitudes within the African Kenyan community.

Yet not all types of mixed relationships are condoned in Kenya. Marriages between African Kenyans and Asian Kenyans, for example, are still very rare and have encountered significant resistance from both communities in the past; the extensive coverage in the summer of 2014 of the case of a Hindu woman marrying a Bukusu man documents how rare these instances are.[57] Marriages with British partners are also less tolerated; nonetheless, as we have seen, they are increasing (see tables 3 and 4). In both cases, colonial memory certainly plays a decisive role, in addition to the persistence of blunt racist attitudes among the Asian communities of Kenya. Interethnic relationships among members of Kenya's various societies, though common, are also contested; incidents of interethnic violence, which break out mostly around election time, are a testimony to these attitudes. Interracial relationships between Kenyans and Europeans and most other whites, on the other hand, are accepted more widely; here, the economic benefits of these relationships outweigh the resistance that can be observed in other cases of exogenous marriage.

FLUID KINSHIP PATTERNS

The second factor that has a stabilizing effect on Kenyan-German relationships are fluid kinship patterns that are, to some extent, accepted in both German and Kenyan societies. Rita, as we have seen, continued to be married to Karl for seven years while involved with James, with Karl during this period embarking on his relationship with Anna (who may have had another African Kenyan partner). James maintained his relationship with Salome, the mother of his son, until 2014. Rita, James, Karl, Anna, and Salome are not the only individuals who live in constellations of fluid kinship relations. Given that the majority of German women who get involved with Kenyan men are beyond childbearing age, they are often willing to live with the fact that another wife and children are part of the deal. Several of the older German women I interviewed explained to me that one had to simply embrace the fact that a Kenyan man will want to have children. One Swiss woman (age seventy-six) was very frank when she mentioned that her Kenyan partner (age sixty-one), to whom she had been married for twenty-two years at the time, had another family: "You have to accept that; if the marriage is good, you remain number 1. If the man has no children, he won't have any respect here" (Das muß man akzeptieren; wenn die Ehe gut ist, bleibst du die Erste. Wenn der Mann keine Kinder hat, hat er keinen Respekt hier).

While women were frustrated if their partners (both African and German) frequented prostitutes, some German women are quite content with their role as older wife or, at times, grandmother. Women who live most of the year in Germany have at times met the local girlfriend or wife of their lovers. Some take health precautions: one woman has her Kenyan lover checked for venereal disease at a hospital at the beginning of each of her stays in the country. Relationship patterns differ: as one African Kenyan man put it, "It is better to have two girlfriends than to go to a prostitute." Local African Kenyans confirmed that many Kenyan partners in north-south relationships also have a local family. African Kenyan women often enter the relationships with one or more children from previous partners (table 17). African Kenyan men tend to have a local family that either preexisted the relationship with the German partner or developed later. When I inquired once about a local man who lives in Germany most of the year and is married and has children with his German partner, I was told that he was, in fact, in Diani at that time, staying with his "African wife."

But Germans often maintain their previous relationships as well. In one—admittedly unique—case, a German man sustained three families: one in Germany, one in Kenya, and one in Thailand. Because of his substantial wealth, he was additionally able to support the children of his Kenyan wife's sister. Though an economically unique case, it is perhaps not so unique in terms of its non-normativity, as a number of relationships defy mainstream (both Kenyan and German) expectations about romantic relationships. One day, one of my research assistants pointed out a Kenyan-German couple to me and explained that the German woman came to Kenya twice a year with her German husband. At the airport, they were met by a Kenyan couple, and then switched partners for the duration of their stay. Evidently they had acted on this agreement for a few years. One local Digo man, Bakari, recounted a situation that also challenges ideas of what is thought to be acceptable in a European marriage: he had taken up a relationship with a British tourist fifteen years his senior. He met her husband, who was initially not told about the sexual relationship Bakari had with his wife, and was even invited to visit and stay with them in Liverpool. He spent a few months in the city, and eventually, the husband was informed about the relationship, but evidently he accepted the situation. The British woman built a house in one of the villages of Diani and spent part of the year with Bakari. She fell sick and died of cancer while still in her fifties; both husband and lover, as well as some of Bakari's family members, took care of her during her last days. Cases of older European residents who live out their last days in Diani and are nursed by their Kenyan lovers and their families are not unusual. The notion of a "global care chain" has been used to describe the interdependence of peoples across the globe; the care extended by, for example, Kenyans to older Germans whose families are paying the school fees of the children of those Kenyans who tend to the older Germans exemplifies this concept.[58]

Kenyans are often more interested in getting married than their German partners. James, for example, was clearly exasperated when Rita was still married to Karl: "How do we call it now? What am I now?" he grumbled. At the time that he made this passionate plea in support of marriage I did not know that he was still involved with Salome, the mother of his second child; it seems that his desire to get married was structured both by an economic motif and by polygamous practices. Other Germans also reported that it was primarily their Kenyan partner who wanted to get married; especially African Kenyan women were keen on getting married and moving to Europe, which their partners sometimes condoned ("it would be better for the child") and sometimes deemed unrealistic and unfeasible because of the hostile German environment and also the perceived inability of Kenyans to adapt to German culture (because they lack education and the German way of life is so different; "mangelnde Bildung," "andere Lebensform"). Accepting the children of their partners and having children together is another stabilizing dimension of relationships. As table 17 demonstrates, one-third of the German men have a child with their Kenyan partner; German women, who tend to be beyond childbearing age, often help raise the children of their partners, as do German men. While the children of the Germans tend to be adults, many Kenyans bring small children to the relationships. Often Germans made a point of saying that they were embracing the responsibility: "I treat her children like my own," said one German man.

To some extent, polygamous practices that are normative in Digo and other Kenyan societies and that are grounded in both customary and Islamic practices structure these north-south families, but changed German attitudes toward marriage and family are also contributing factors. Traditionally, Digo marriages are based on economic factors that are closely tied to ideas of social status, not primarily to notions of romantic love. The fact that elopement was frequent, however, indicates that romantic passion has played a role in the past as well.[59] It has certainly gained currency more recently; in 1972 Roger Gomm wrote that "young Digo, no doubt influenced by east African pop-culture, see the ideal marriage as a love-match."[60] Even though romantic love has gained greater significance today, the age-long connection of marriage to economic and social dimensions facilitates the acceptance of relationships with foreigners through which the economic status of the Kenyan partner is raised.

Various studies of Digo marital practices have pointed out that relationships are loosely structured and "rates of divorce and remarriage are high in Digo society."[61] Scholars have offered various explanations, including the originally matrilineal organization of Digo society, the Digos' low social and economic status on the coast, and the fact that Islamization, while placing a high status on marriage, also "provided an easy and socially accepted means of ending marriages" through divorce.[62] Gomm explains that "the main social rewards of Digo life are not related structurally to *stable* marriage"; in fact, dissolution of marriage to avoid conflicts was often preferred as a means to strengthen stability in the larger community.[63] Even multiple husbands were common until recently and reflect the coexistence of Islamic and customary practices.[64] Mohamed S. Mraja's discussion of the attempts of a Muslim cleric to reform marital practices among the Digo on the southern coast of Kenya is further evidence for the loosely structured nature of local marriage practices.[65] While Gomm's study from the early 1970s suggests that "divorce, separation and remarriage have always been common" in Digo society, the same study also acknowledged a number of trends, including a tendency by which "young to middle-aged women leave their husbands for a life outside any permanent or semi-permanent cohabitation, in which state they exchange sexuality for cash and kind with a great deal of individual freedom."[66]

These various studies of marital practices among the Digo of the southern Kenyan coast reveal that multiple and changing partners were and are common, as well as economic motives for marriage. Upcountry Kenyans who enter this social and cultural space, and who make up a significant number of partners in north-south relationships, hail from various ethnic communities, and while each community has distinct practices, some aspects are shared. Polygamy is wide-spread and continues to be broadly condoned in Kenya, and customary practices coexist with Christian, Islamic, and Hindu norms.[67] The legal system accommodates all of these practices.[68] A huge billboard ad that was displayed at the Likoni ferry in Mombasa in early 2010 showed a handsome African Kenyan man and read: "I am a father, I get tested for HIV regularly." Contained in the innocuous adverb is an acknowledgment of reality: married men and unmarried fathers are not expected to be monogamous. More importantly in our context, however, economic motives as driving factors for entering a relationship are accepted in Kenya.

Changing attitudes in Europe also contribute to facilitating and strengthening north-south relationships. A study that compared data from the United States and various European countries (among them Germany and Austria) concluded that "over the entire 1988–2002 period, public opinion moved away from traditional notions of marriage and children in most countries."[69] Other indications of changed attitudes toward traditional marriage in Germany include German legislation in 2001 that recognized same-sex unions as civil unions (in German, "eingetragene Lebenspartnerschaften," registered life partnerships), the overall increase in such partnerships among the general population, and a simultaneous decrease in the number of traditional marriages.[70] In addition, the significant financial strain of divorce engenders acceptance for various kinds of nontraditional relationships.[71] Infidelity is also widespread and enjoys a certain degree of social acceptance.[72] While economic motives for marriage are stigmatized on the surface in Europe (marrying "just for the money"), they in fact play a significant role in the choice of partners as well.[73]

On the surface, the Kenyan situation is distinct from European conventions, as polygamous practices are still widely accepted and also legal. But in essence, German and Kenyan practices are not as different as they at first seem. As Sherry Ortner writes in her discussion of sexual relations between Himalayan Sherpas and mountaineers: "The idea that people have their own historically sedimented frames of reference, and come at events with their own ways of thinking and feeling, means that people across cultures are different, but not necessarily radically Other."[74] Perhaps those Germans who enter an intimate relationship with a Kenyan do not reflect dominant German norms regarding the choice of partners, but entering into relationship constellations that involve multiple partners is still compatible within the spectrum of social practices in Germany.

POSITIVE SEXUAL EXPERIENCES AND MODIFIED GENDER ROLES

Another area that emerged as a positive factor for relationships is sex, with sexual attraction, however, rooted in a subjective perception of behavior, not in specific physical features. Some Kenyan men suggested that German women enjoyed sex more. One man said that German women were "free, they kiss and touch without shyness" while "African women are shy, not free." Another Kenyan man said that with a German woman "you need to make strong romance, two to three hours romance, you enjoy the exercise." An African woman, he said, would enjoy sex "only thirty minutes, maybe one hour, then she is okay." But he liked "a long romance" and so enjoyed being with German women. One African Kenyan woman also stressed that her lover was "good in love-making" and that she did "not want to have an African." German men, for their part, appreciated that Kenyan women were "more free and relaxed." It is noteworthy that both Germans and Kenyans looked in a partner from another culture for the aspects that they believed were missing in their own culture. If there is a form of racialized sexual desire in these relationships, it seems to be grounded neither in physical features nor in general cultural behavior. Factors related to economic and emotional precarity, as we will see, play a far greater role in motivating sexual attraction.

In addition, expectations regarding gendered behavior were often, but not always, accommodated in Kenyan-German relationships. Some Kenyan women reported that they felt German men treated them better than African men; they found it appealing that German men cooked and helped around the house. In other cases, gender roles were enacted according to more traditional notions, and some Kenyan women felt too controlled by their German partners. One German man prided himself for not beating his Kenyan wife, which, he said, was the norm in Kenyan relationships. Overall, Kenyan-German relations seem to create a space that allows both sides to escape normative cultural structures.

Challenges for German-Kenyan Couples

Acceptance by the community, fluid kinship relations, and a positive experience of sexuality (and to some extent, modified gender roles) have a stabilizing effect on Kenyan-German unions and allow the participants to manage areas of challenge regarding age differences, cultural differences, and psychological tensions.

AGE DIFFERENCES

Apart from two instances, the German-speaking partners I interviewed were older than their Kenyan partners and spouses (see table 13). The age difference averaged 25 years for unions involving German men and African Kenyan women and 14 years for those involving German women and African Kenyan men. These data are comparable to the average age gap of 23 and 11 years, respectively, found from the analysis of marriages registered in Mombasa in 2012 (table 9). The African Kenyan men I interviewed who were not involved with European women usually accepted significant age gaps, while some African Kenyan women freely expressed disapproval. One Kenyan woman ridiculed young women who were involved with older European men: "I am thinking: is it your grandfather?" Europeans in Diani who are not involved with African Kenyans are also mostly critical of the age difference that characterizes most mixed couples. For them the issue is further proof that money is the true motivation for African Kenyans to engage in such relationships. Traditionally, it would be acceptable for an older man in Kenya to marry a younger woman, but some Kenyans disapproved of young men pursuing older women and very young women pursuing *much* older men.

Partners in mixed relationships tend to downplay or simply embrace the age difference. When asked about the gap, interviewees consistently said that it was not a problem for the relationship. Kenyan men went out of their way to insist that the German women looked beautiful to them. One forty-two-year-old man who was involved with a very slim and fit fifty-six-year-old woman said, "She looks like a young girl to me." One African woman whose partner was thirty-eight years her senior said, "Age is no problem, he is a *mzee* [a respectful Kiswahili term for an older man] but I love him." One retired sixty-six-year-old Swiss man stated enthusiastically that having a young girlfriend had helped him enjoy sex again. He pointed out, "You can have a twenty- or twenty-three-year-old girlfriend here, something that would never happen back home." He said that he felt rejuvenated through this relationship and was visibly happy with his twenty-eight-year-old girlfriend of two years.

In a few cases partners did identify the age gap as a cause of conflict. One Kenyan woman, who was about forty years younger than her German partner, complained about his lack of interest in participating in social events, such as dancing. Another woman whose Swiss partner was also almost forty years her senior remarked that she did not enjoy being mostly confined to the house. On the other hand, a German woman whose African Kenyan boyfriend of sixteen years was twenty-three years younger described their evenings at home as pleasurable and stated that she didn't feel like seeing her partner every day and that he was free to live his own life. Another fifty-seven-year-old German, however, worried that his twenty-seven-year-old partner might leave him. At the same time, he emphasized that he came with advantages that African Kenyan men lacked: he treated his girlfriend well, he cooked, and he helped around the house. In addition, he had built her a house in her ancestral village. Based on my research it seems that German and Swiss women are more at ease with giving their partners space to pursue their own interests than older German men, for whom this issue was more unsettling.

CULTURAL DIFFERENCES

In advice literature and studies of bicultural relationships, differences rooted in distinct cultural conventions and norms are often identified as a major source of potential conflict. Among the issues that strain German-Kenyan relations are conflicting expectations regarding ecologically minded behavior, time, and planning.

Thinking and acting in an ecologically responsible manner is important to many Germans, and behavior that reflects ecological ignorance becomes a source of conflict in Kenyan-German relations. The actual cause for tension can seem trivial. Several German men, for example, complained that their partners wash the dishes under running water and use too much dishwashing soap. A Kenyan man lamented that his Swiss girlfriend used to have fits when he washed dishes under running water. Several German men and women complained that "nothing gets recycled" (nichts wird wiederverwertet) and that garbage piles up in outdoor spaces ("the garbage in the bush is awful" [der Abfall im Busch ist furchtbar]). In fact, it is not unheard-of for German tourists to take the many plastic bags they acquire when shopping in Kenya back home to Germany to recycle them there. Despite a growing public discourse in Kenya about ecology and the environment, as well as the admirable work of pioneers like Wangari Maathai, Moses Ojwang, and Ikal Angelei, most Kenyans do indeed display a low level of ecological consciousness and simply drop plastic wrappers, napkins, and plastic bottles wherever they are.

Often tied to their ecological consciousness, Germans have a reputation of valuing order and cleanliness. Rita's former husband Karl once said: "With me, everything is organized; Africans will still have to learn that. And cleanliness" (Bei mir ist Ordnung, das müssen die Afrikaner noch lernen. Und Sauberkeit). A German who received national and international attention for sweeping the streets of Ukunda every day exemplifies this blend of care for the environment and a focus on cleanliness and order.[75]

A perceived lack of planning emerged as another conflict area for Germans. One man complained that he kept telling his wife that she should make a "to-do" list ("leg dir die Sachen parat, schreib auf"). Another man suggested that Kenyans were unable to think about the future. The clash of culture could not be more pronounced in this area. Germans are used to living in a predictable environment, on every level. Kenyan everyday life, however, is full of unexpected shifts and changes. A good example are the roads: a driver has to know every pothole and adjust to new ones that emerge overnight or over the course of several days. Street construction is such that dirt roads are used alongside roads that are being built; finished parts are opened in segments, and people swerve in and out of dirt, feeder, and tarmac roads, taking turns under freeways (in Nairobi) and suddenly facing oncoming traffic for just a second until the next turn appears (and all of this without street lights at night), adjusting to the ever-changing flow of construction. Transportation also has to be undertaken in flexible ways; matatus do not arrive on a predictable schedule, so one has to be prepared for delays and perhaps be ready to use a motorbike, known as a *piki-piki* or *boda-boda*, or a small three-wheeler, a *tuk-tuk*. Food supplies and food prices are also not predictable and affect the lives of the average Kenyan in dramatic ways. Power cuts and water rationing are still part of Kenyan everyday life. Especially lower-class Kenyans adjust to these shifts without much complaint, but as a result, short-term and long-term planning are put on the back burner: managing *today* is the priority. If an opportunity arises, one has to embrace it and drop other commitments. As a result of these and other challenges and a mode of prioritizing that is not always accessible to Europeans, many Kenyans have a flexible relationship to time, appointments, and other commitments—to the chagrin of many a European. Germans, on the other hand, experience security in all of these areas in their home countries. Perhaps one could even say that the fact that their lives are so overly predictable and secure explains their attraction to a fundamentally opposite environment. But while Kenya's unpredictability is appealing for awhile, the excitement usually wears off, and many Germans grow increasingly annoyed with what they perceive as the unreliability of Kenyan life and people.

Other cultural habits emerged as sources of contempt or complaint. Germans often mentioned as an area of conflict the apparent lack of their Kenyan partners to learn. "You can tell them something twenty times, but they will still forget," complained one German man who was especially angry that his partner had tried to open a can with a knife. He also lamented, "People complain, but they don't take initiative." One man recounted how a Nigerian girlfriend he lived with in Switzerland would sweep the house with a straw broom even if a vacuum cleaner was available. One man took particular issue with the fact that African Kenyans sit on the floor for many activities, such as eating or doing handicrafts. This was incomprehensible to him: "I am a locksmith, I just want to scream" (Ich bin Schlosser, ich krieg einen Schreikrampf). He also wondered why Africans did not use brooms with longer handles: "Why does an African always have to bend down?" (Warum bückt sich ein Afrikaner immer?). One Swiss woman complained that her Kenyan lover didn't sit properly at the table when they visited her friends.

Kenyans, on the other hand, also complain that Germans are not willing to adjust to and learn about, for example, local food and other practices. Several African Kenyan women described how they had to learn to prepare meals according to *German* recipes because their partners would not eat any of the local dishes. Germans usually speak only rudimentary English, and often their partners learn German, with some of them mastering the language quite well. But not a single German I interviewed spoke Kiswahili or any other Kenyan language beyond a basic vocabulary of about thirty words. Consequently, communication between the partners is distinguished by a lack of politeness and nuance and often leads to a rather rude style of interaction. In addition, Germans' knowledge of Kenyan history and politics tends to be minimal, while Kenyan men (more than women) have an acute sense for current politics. African Kenyans will complain that their German partners are bossy and push them too much. "I am a tractor but you want to turn me into a helicopter," was how one African Kenyan man put it when he complained to his German partner about her efforts to make him more proactive about various matters. Another African Kenyan complained that his German girlfriend tried to control him too much: she wanted him to quit smoking, told him what to do around the house, and even asked him to clean the bathroom, which he found unacceptable.

Another topic that came up, but only a couple of times, were attitudes toward work; one German man and one German woman referred to their Kenyan relatives as "lazy," but generally, the cliché of an African reluctance to work was not mentioned in terms of relationship dynamics.[76] Finally, religion was never identified as a source of conflict. Considering that about half of the Kenyan partners I interviewed are Muslim, this fact clearly defies clichés about German attitudes toward Muslims.

Surely, the kinds of conflict areas observed here—such as distinct ideas about ecological behavior, planning, and cleanliness as well as linguistic limitations—are predictable.[77] In addition, African Kenyans who are involved with Germans tend to come from rural areas (with only very few exceptions), while Germans are mostly used to a modern urban lifestyle. While these issues play a role in relationships more broadly, including those involving partners from the same culture, the severity of the conflicts is aggravated by an increased scale in the differences. Those bicultural couples who succeed in staying together have usually worked out a modus vivendi regarding the differences with which they struggle.

PSYCHOLOGICAL TENSIONS: NERVOUS CONDITIONS

"White skin is money" (weiße Haut ist Geld); "money is always an issue"; "it is all about money"; "everybody sees the money" (alle sehen das Geld); "when the money is gone, one has no chance" (wenn das Geld weg ist, hat man keine Chance); "when the money is over, love is over"; "money always gets in between" (das Geld kommt immer dazwischen). These quotations demonstrate that money is clearly a key source of conflict between couples. While Germans vehemently complain about the role of money in their relationships, Kenyans grumble about the pressure they feel from their families. Because white people are seen as "magnets of money," as one Kenyan man put it, the "color of money" makes families gravitate toward the couples and beleaguer them with various requests for support. "Stop the relatives right away," advised one Austrian man. Germans often fight with their Kenyan partners over how much money should go to Kenyan relatives.

Conflict over money is one, but not the only, factor that leads to shouting matches or even physical conflict. Distrust between partners is widespread: "There is no trust," said a German man. Germans complained about "lies" and "rumors" and suggested that Kenyans would all stick together against them in the event of a conflict. One German woman summarized her view of Kenyans in the catchy slogan "Guten Morgen, schon gelogen" (roughly translated as "Good morning, already lied"). "They are all Oscar-worthy actors," she scoffed. In addition, German residents in Diani often either don't understand or are unable to reconcile themselves with aspects of the sociocultural environment they have entered, and various dimensions of the lives of their Kenyan partners remain hidden from them. One German man said that "many [Germans] are surprised to see that their children [with their African partners] are so black" (Viele wundern sich, daß ihre Kinder so schwarz sind). The *Tropenkoller* that seems to regularly take hold of Thomas exemplifies the inability of many Germans to process the myriad emotional, cultural, and economic challenges they face.

The tensions can lead to violence. A Swiss man who has married twice in Kenya said that his first wife had tried to kill him three times: "She tried to strangle me, poison me, and once she was sitting on my chest until I could not breathe." Two German men reported that Kenyan girlfriends and wives often beat their German partners; "husband beating" is not uncommon in Kenya more broadly but may be affecting non-Kenyan men disproportionally.[78] Shouting is more common; two Kenyan women complained that their partners yelled at them and had bad tempers. Interestingly, German self-critique regarding how Germans struggled with their emotions was pronounced. Many Germans, including women, admitted that they would get loud easily and blow up more often and more quickly than they would in their home countries ("ich explodier schon mal"; "fahr ich manchmal aus der Haut"). They said they got angry and found themselves to be cranky and testy.

During my stays in 2009 and 2010, stories were circulating about the deaths of several Germans. One German man had either killed himself or been killed by his Kenyan girlfriend; another had committed suicide by sticking his hand into a tank filled with snakes. Yet another had killed himself first by slashing his wrists and then, when that failed, poisoning himself the next day with gas. A Swiss woman and a Swiss man had died of AIDS; four other Germans had died of heart attacks, cancer, and malaria. All of these individuals, and many others, had died within the previous couple of years and been younger than sixty years old. While only a few of these deaths were directly related to the volatile nature of Kenyan-German romantic relationships, they demonstrate the overall physical and emotional precarity that distinguish many such relationships and the situation of Germans living in Diani more generally.

Emotional and Economic Precarity: Romance, Charity, and Land

As we have seen, while age differences, cultural differences, and emotional tensions pose challenges to German-Kenyan relationships, acceptance by communities, fluid kinship structures, and positive sexual experiences may enable partners to negotiate these and other trials. The aspect that best explains why these relationships exist in the first place, however, is the underlying emotional and economic precarity of the partners.

Many older German women and men indicate that they come to Kenya in order to escape loneliness and also what they perceive as narrow-mindedness at home. In Kenya they feel liberated from social pressures. A widowed German woman, who was sixty-nine years old in 2010 and had been involved with a Kenyan man twenty-three years her junior for the previous fifteen years, said that she felt alive again in Diani. She was fifty when her husband died in a car accident and said she felt she was often the "fifth wheel on the car"—no longer invited to social events with friends and increasingly isolated. In Germany, she lived in the countryside and felt oppressed by social constraints. She first came to Diani as a tourist with her sister, and she began a new life after she met her boyfriend: "With him, after the death of my husband, I learned to laugh again." She is content with her life, physically active, and enjoys surfing, all of which would have been unthinkable in her previous life: "Here, nobody would ask me, that is my story, nobody's business." Similar views were articulated by other women and men. One sixty-nine-year-old man said to me, "In Germany I am old iron [that is, useless], here I am still respected" (In Deutschland gehöre ich zum alten Eisen, hier respektiert man mich noch).

In Diani, one can see European men in their sixties riding motorcycles with their young Kenyan girlfriends, wives, or children seated behind them. This image captures essential facets of an ideal of old age that includes vitality, sexuality, physical power, and self-actualization. In discussing Americans, Kevin E. McHugh identifies the "busy ethic . . . as the *raison d'être* and moral foundation for retirement in American society, a later life substitute for the work ethic" that is often linked to a notion of "deferred self-actualisation" and "leisurely living."[79] In Kenya, however, the emphasis is more on leisure, self-actualization, and social contact rather than a "busy ethic." German residents in Diani mentioned climate ("the weather, the warmth"), the natural beauty of the country, and a sense of freedom as reasons for moving to Kenya. "I wanted to get out of Germany," explained German men and women repeatedly. Germans emphasized receiving attention, being with somebody who has time for them and listens, as an important factor explaining what attracted them to Kenyans. Such desire for more meaningful human contact constitutes an aspect rarely considered in discussions of lifestyle migration, which, as Michaela Benson and Karen O'Reilly have argued, are often not "fully inclusive in grasping the complexity of this trend."[80] It seems as if especially the vulnerabilities of age—which tend to affect men and women differently, in particular with regard to sexual capital (with men generally being assigned more sustained sexual power) but also in terms of the increasing loneliness of old age—are more equalized in the Kenyan context. Money, however, is a factor as well; the lifestyle that a small pension in Kenya can afford includes appealing features, such as living close to a beach in a warm climate and eating well. Some pensioners who would have trouble surviving on their limited incomes or disability payments in Switzerland, Germany, or Austria find that Kenya offers a solution to their problem.[81] The fact that Kenya, among other countries, offers a residency status especially for retirees indicates how established age-related north-to-south migration has become and how a "burgeoning retirement industry" is emerging in many areas of the world.[82] That retirement industry is economically stratified, however; some retirees cannot afford official residency status.[83] In those cases, individuals move back and forth between Kenya and Europe or have their visas renewed in other East African countries. Other immigrants (including retirees) stay in Kenya illegally. Overall, the explanations that Germans who are romantically involved with Kenyans provide for their decision to live in Kenya overlap with those identified for other migrant communities in the global south.[84]

Kenyans made an effort to represent their interest in their German partners as primarily romantic, though some Kenyan women volunteered that they also appreciated the economic dimension and security the relationship provided. Fatima's story—she said that Erwin had saved her from a life on the streets—is rather typical. In most cases, however, Kenyan women chose not to speak about a prior history of economic or emotional struggle, including prostitution. Kenyan men are even more guarded and strive to present their interest in the relationships as being motivated by love; in no instance did a Kenyan man indicate that his German partner had "saved him" economically. On the other hand, both men and women volunteered information that brought the financial dimension of some relationships into focus. One Kenyan man freely talked about the monthly payments he received from his German lover, who wired KSh50,000 or KSh20,000 whenever he requested it ("when I ask, she sends it"). In an economy where even many salaried working-class Kenyans have to make do with KSh10,000 a month, these are considerable amounts of money. But even in this case, which is not unusual but is an exemplar especially for those relationships where the German partner lives most of the year in Europe, the man tried to downplay the financial side of his relationship; he presented it more as a bonus rather than a crucial element of the relationship. The self-representations, in this regard, provide clues but do not yet render a deeper understanding of relationship dynamics.

Considering how Kenyans and Germans speak about their motivations for engaging in romantic relationships, what others have to say about these intercultural couples, the history of gentrification in Diani, and the poverty in Kenya in general suggests that economic need is the main motivating factor for Kenyans. As one Kenyan African put it, "Most people value the money, not the love; they are fishing for something." Emotional needs, such as a personal history of abuse, a desire to control partners, or the desire to lead a life that allows for more personal choices, factor in as well and are ultimately also closely related to economic precarity. The economic dimension is relevant for African Kenyans who are indigenous to the area, for the Digo, and also for those who originate from other, mostly upcountry, areas of Kenya. One of my research assistants captured the essence of the economic dimension when he said, "A white lady is like gold for us."

As economic need is usually not addressed directly, the larger "culture of charity" in Diani provides the vehicle for financial assistance and thus also shapes romantic relations in substantial ways. The Kenyan partner often initiates the activity, but Germans are quite determined in their desire to help and provide assistance to extended families and the general community in all basic areas of need that exist in Kenya: in addition to building houses and buying land, they pay for the education of the children they have with their Kenyan partners, their partner's children, and even the children of their partner's relatives; they cover medical expenses and hospital bills; they buy water pumps, solar panels, and water tanks; and they supply equipment. Only rarely do they pass out cash. They tend to invest in ways that they have come to perceive as sustainable initiatives; comparable to what we observed with regard to contraband humanitarians, these activities demonstrate that the public debates on development aid influence and structure their choices. Often, however, Germans assume positions that mirror colonial patterns of interaction: Rita, for instance, who was building a house with her partner James, complained that James's brothers were not willing to work unless she was around to make them do so. Not knowing much about colonial history or the larger context of north-south relations, she was unaware that by insisting that James's brothers work on her schedule (after all, she was paying), she had stepped into a deeply ingrained pattern and taken on the role of the colonial settler, a part often played today by the (professional and self-appointed) development aid worker.

The economic benefit of many of these relationships is particularly visible in the area of housing. This became obvious to me during my walking tours through the area—and brings us back to the question of landownership. While I was *dériving* through Diani, my research assistants and other locals pointed out houses that had been built with the money of German partners, who often had also bought the land. A walking tour in the southern part of Diani, following a road behind the Diani Shopping Center that leads to the airstrip, revealed that every villa (this being the affluent area of Diani, in Row/Zone 2; see map 2) was occupied by a mixed couple: an African Kenyan woman and a British man, an African Kenyan woman and a Swiss man, a French-Swiss woman and an African Kenyan man, a Somali man and a Swiss woman (followed by a Belgian-sponsored primary school, a Belgian-sponsored dispensary, and a Belgian-Dutch-Kenyan–sponsored orphanage that evidently facilitated adoptions ["rich people come here to buy children," said my assistant]), a German man and an African Kenyan woman, and so forth. Other areas are primarily inhabited by European couples or individuals (such as in the so-called Italian quarter across from the Southern Palms Hotel or in parts of the German quarter across from the Neptune Hotel in the Galu Beach area south of Diani), but many houses are jointly owned by African Kenyans and Europeans, including Germans.

The airstrip remains the divider between the lavish houses and the poorer houses in the villages that spread out to the Mombasa–Lunga Lunga Road. But even in this less affluent area, we see an increase in building activity as a result of mixed relationships. Here, as we saw in chapter 2, a blue roof usually indicates that a German or other European built or sponsored a house. Germans who build houses and shops in this area are themselves not as wealthy as Europe-born residents who have property closer to the beach. In some cases, the (mostly) Digo owner of a property lives in Germany, Austria, or Switzerland. African Kenyans are also part of this development boom and usually hail from upcountry. Kikuyu and Kisii are prominent among the newcomers to the area, and some are Akamba, who were reimbursed by the titanium mining company, Base Titanium, for their land in the Kwale area and moved to Ukunda. Their stronghold is Kona ya Musa, but Akamba-owned houses also exist in Maskrepu, Magutu, and other areas. Much land has changed ownership, and the tendency of local Digo to sell their land continues (see chapter 2). Evidently they prefer to sell to non-Digo: "Digo do not sell to other Digo," said an upcountry man. But scores of Digo have built on plots they already owned and also have acquired new land.

On various walking tours through the area between the airstrip and the Mombasa–Lunga Lunga Road, and including some parts to the west of the road, that is, in areas predominantly inhabited by African Kenyans, I took note of the following (as described by my assistants):

- The house of a Digo man who owns three houses; he is in a relationship with a "very old German woman"; she lives in Germany, he "hangs out on the beach."
- The large house of a Swiss woman and her Kisii lover that includes a grocery store.
- The large house of a Digo man who lives in Switzerland; he rents out single rooms.

- The house of a man who owned five houses; he was described as a "hard-working Digo"; he had been married to a German woman and lived in Germany, then they separated, he lived alone for a while and eventually died; his mother is now taking care of the houses.
- Two houses of the brother of the previous man; he also has a German girlfriend, he is "twenty-seven or something, she is fifty or sixty."
- A house built by a German couple for their daughter and her Digo husband; for the past ten years they have lived in Berlin and the house is rented out.
- A four-story apartment building owned by an Israeli man who lives with a Digo woman.
- Three houses of a Digo man who had them built for him by three different women—one German, one Swiss, and one British; he lives off the rent he receives from his tenants.
- The house and shop of a classmate of one of my assistants; he also owns two bigger houses and had "many *mzungu* [sic] girlfriends,"[85] even three at the same time who didn't know each other (from Spain, Germany, and the United Kingdom); he also owns some cars and has three matatus.
- The shop of a Digo or Giriama woman who is married to a Greek man.
- The two-story house of a Digo man who worked in a hotel.
- The house of a Digo woman from Tiwi who is married to a Swiss man.
- Three houses of one Digo family who have been sponsored by a European.
- The house of a Digo man who has a girlfriend in Germany.
- One residential building and one shop owned by a local Digo man who lives in France with his girlfriend.
- The house of a man, who was about thirty-eight years old in 2012 and originally from Kwale, who had bought plots from his uncles in Ukunda with money earned at the Kenya Port Authority; he worked in one of the hotels and had various girlfriends: a US girlfriend in 1996 (he met her in Kwale; her brother was an English teacher there), then an older woman from the Netherlands who supported him "just a little," and then another from England in 2007 whom he met in the hotel. Over the years, he built two houses: one has five rooms that he rents and one room for himself, and the second is for his mother and sister.
- The house of a Swiss woman and a "very young Digo man."
- A small house that had been built with money from a German family. The young man who owned the house was a friend of the family; he had had an accident and needed surgery so he had emailed them and they sent him money. He built the house with the leftover money.
- The small house of a Digo woman who lives "with a white man."
- The houses of a Luo man in relationships with two older women, one German and one Swiss, each living in a different house; the man also has three vehicles (two matatus and one personal car).

These houses constitute a small sample of buildings that have been built with funds from German and other expatriates.

In some areas east and west of the Mombasa–Lunga Lunga Road it seemed as if one out of five houses had a European sponsor; however, as opposed to the areas in Zones 1 through 3 that were discussed in chapter 2, ownership here is mostly in the hands of African Kenyans, both Digo and other groups. In many cases both land and house are titled to Kenyan partners, and in some instances, the German partners lost claim to the property after the relationships fell apart. Sometimes the land had been owned by a local Digo, and the German or other partner helped build a house on the plot. In other cases, Kenyans bought a plot with help from an expatriate lover. As we saw in chapter 3, a high number of schools, boarding schools, orphanages, and clinics in the area would also not exist without non-Kenyan sponsors. Considering charity-based and romance-based building activity together provides a more complete accounting of developments in Diani.

Overall, romantic relations clearly significantly affect housing and landownership in Diani and beyond—as many couples build houses in the ancestral villages of Kenyan partners in other areas of Kenya. Romantic relationships allow African Kenyans to gain and maintain ownership over their ancestral land, buy land in a new location, or build on land that they or their family own.

Romance as Opportunity and Material Reality

Romantic relationships are one way for Kenyans to actively enhance their economic situations and to attain a degree of control and power over their lives. For some, economic pressures are excruciating and become the driving factor motivating their actions, whereas others pursue these opportunities simply because they exist. German partners are brought to their romantic relationships primarily by emotional needs, such as loneliness resulting from old age, the death of a spouse, or divorce and a need to gain some measure of control and power. Economic considerations, however, also play a role, especially for retirees. Regardless of the bare facts of economic necessity and emotional needs, partners in these relationships generally consider, and certainly present, these relationships as legitimate romantic relationships. In some cases, they last for many years. As with comparable cases from around the world, and also at different historical moments, where mostly economic necessity caused and continues to cause prostitution and various types of short-term and long-term romantic relations, local communities in Diani and other areas of Kenya support biracial and bicultural north-south relationships.[86] The fluidity of kinship relations in both contemporary Kenya and German-speaking countries in Europe provides the kind of stability that allows these relationships to thrive and to address questions of both economic and emotional need. In this regard, German migration to and tourism in Kenya and the resulting romantic relations do not necessarily create new social structures, but they are enabled significantly by existing patterns.[87] Partners often struggle to resolve the strain that arises from their different cultural backgrounds and to cope with the repercussions of age differences. Europeans move to Diani to escape various forms of emotional precarity, and at times also financial worries, but many do not have the emotional intelligence, cultural competence, and factual knowledge needed to navigate the unfamiliar environment. Diani consists of more than just white sand, sun, and palm trees; it comes with people who have histories and their own ways of doing things. New forms of emotional vulnerability arise for both Germans and Kenyans as a result of mismatched expectations and insufficient cultural and historical understanding, which can sometimes lead to the dissolution of relationships.

However, the humanitarian activities of Germans, whether they occur in the context of their extended Kenyan families or the larger community in Diani and beyond, are one vehicle to not only fortify relationships, but also enhance their status within families and communities—and in the eyes of the Germans themselves. Building houses, buying land, and paying for school fees and hospital bills contribute to strengthening the ties between Germans and their Kenyan partners and uplifts their role in the larger community; such actions are also indicative of the larger culture of charity in Diani.

The overall economic effect of Kenyan-German romantic relationships is significant. I have suggested that hundreds of thousands and perhaps millions of Kenyans experience some form of economic benefit from these and other transnational romantic relationships. The sociocultural repercussions are equally significant for both partners; Kenyans and Germans (and other Europeans) form extended kinship relations that bring culturally and socially diverse groups of people into contact. Kenya, with its pronounced ethnic and religious diversity, is experiencing a small wave of immigration, mostly from Europe, that, desite its insignificant numbers, affects many areas of life—from landownership to interpersonal relations. In Germany, Switzerland, and Austria, the ties to Kenya are part of an increased trend toward north-south relations and marriage, which play an essential role in the creation of multicultural societies and reflect economic and emotional dimensions of global mobility. While the movement of global capital is discussed widely, romance and marriage ought to be acknowledged as crucial vehicles facilitating both emotional and economic transnational flows.

Epilogue

Je, Vitaturudia? *Will They Return to Us?*

W HEN I TRAVELED to Diani to wrap up research for this book in December 2014 I wasn't sure what to expect. Tourism collapsed after Britain and the United States issued travel advisories in May and June of that year in response to multiple attacks that had occurred over several months on the coast, in Nairobi, and in the northeastern part of the country and had been linked to terrorist organizations. Especially damaging to Kenya's tourism industry was Britain's decision to evacuate most of its tourists in May, just a day ahead of a couple of bombings in Nairobi. Other countries also issued travel warnings, though Germany, among others, did not join this trend, even after two European tourists were shot in Mombasa's old town in July.[1] International tourism dropped to minimal levels, and cancellations forced hotel operators and feeder industries to reduce staff. Thousands of people lost their jobs.

When I arrived in Diani, scores of rooms were available for rent, and the staff quarters of big hotels were empty. Many of the upcountry people had left. By some accounts, up to 20 percent, and even 40 percent (though that seems unrealistic), were said to have moved back to Nairobi, Kisumu, and rural areas across the country. Surprisingly, a similar exodus did not occur among the white population, whether Kenyan-born or European-born. Some had indeed left and put their properties up for sale, but according to a range of people, from European realtors to African Kenyans who worked with tourists, this was due to generational turnover and financial pressures more than to a fear of terrorism. Aging Swiss and German residents had moved home to be closer to their children and more reliable health care. Italians, it was said, were selling property because of the poor economy in Italy. In addition, the annual residency fees were increased in 2014 and had become a significant burden for some Europeans. Tanzania, among other locations, seemed to be emerging as a cheaper (and "cleaner," as one Swiss woman suggested) alternative.

My last visits in December 2015 and June 2016 confirmed some of these trends. While December is the peak of the high season and Diani was bustling with visitors from (mostly) upcountry and abroad, June is the end of the low season, and economically, the area was hurting hard from the slump in tourism at that time. Poverty had increased even further, and incidents of mob violence, including lynchings of drug addicts, occurred on a regular basis (four in one week during my visit). In June 2016, there were visibly fewer Europeans in the area; the continued warnings of terrorism, the anticipation of violence in the year before the elections, the closing of Imperial Bank in 2015 and Chase Bank in 2016, as well as other economic factors and toughened visa regulations described above increasingly motivated Europeans to stay away. A smaller expatriate community would have a significant economic effect on the larger population in Diani; it remains to be seen how matters will develop.

But even if some of Diani's European residents were leaving and others were staying away for longer periods in order to gauge the security situation, for the time being, the usual mix of local and international was still intact. Sex tourists and those looking for romance could still be seen walking the beach, prostitutes were in their usual spots in the beach bars, and discotheques were open for business. People moved around as usual in Diani. I did not detect an increased hostility against tourists or white people in general. In fact, African Kenyans in Diani and Mombasa alike were keenly aware of the effect of government policies and media coverage abroad and put extra effort into making people comfortable. Among the Kenyan-German couples whom I had followed over the years, no new separations had occurred. One German, who has established families in Germany, Kenya, and Thailand, had moved to Germany with his Kenyan wife after the German wife died (he moved primarily for business reasons, as he had been involved in speculative real estate transactions). As far as I was able to gather information about other bicultural couples in the area, things were as they had been over the previous few years.

For the time being, the charity sector is the clear "winner" amid this economic downturn in the tourism industry on the coast. As one charity worker explained, the effect of pity (*Mitleidseffekt*) resulted in larger donations. In June 2016, Ingeborg Langefeld, the director of Diani Maendeleo Academy, reported that 130 students were now enrolled (80 in 2010; 100 in 2014), with 92 of them sponsored (51 in 2010; 78 in 2014). An emergency fund had enabled families affected by the layoffs to keep their daughters in the school. A significant donation from Knorr-Bremse was already producing visible results: ecologically friendly toilets had been installed, and the dormitory was completed. Not only charitable organizations, but anybody with a connection to Europe had seemed able to mobilize additional funds. Scores of African Kenyans in Diani, if not the majority, are surviving and in some cases doing quite well on money wired from Europe. For the most part, these transfers are not remittances from ex-pat Kenyans to Kenyans but from white Europeans to black Kenyans. Contraband humanitarians are as active as ever; it would be revealing to consult Western Union and other money-transfer services to get a sense of the amounts that have been flowing to the Kenyan coast since June 2014.

Despite the economic downturn that brought the hotel industry to its knees, other sectors of Diani's economy are experiencing an economic upswing. Construction activity is high, with new commercial and residential buildings going up in many places. Apartment buildings with several stories, a larger shopping mall, and several strip malls were being built. New restaurants, bars, and cafés have opened and are about to open. The road between Mombasa and Lunga-Lunga is in better shape than ever. The road was built by Base Titanium, a mining company located close to Msambweni, about half an hour south of Diani. The company is also responsible for new employment that draws on young men in Diani and other locations. Another source of new jobs is the sugar factory Kiscol in Ramisi, just south of Diani. Some money that enabled private building activity was said to be coming from remittances, sent by those who worked in Dubai, Qatar, Saudi Arabia, and other Gulf states. The beach town of Diani (or Ukunda, as the town is generally referred to) is a city in the making, and—despite the downfall of the hotel industry, the original development factor in the area—its growth creates job opportunities. Diani/Ukunda may yet emerge as one of the "secondary cities" that play a more prominent role in poverty reduction than is often acknowledged.[2] And though hotels and resorts are struggling, tourism is not dead; rather, according to the real estate company Baobab Homes & Holidays, the tourism industry is changing, moving more and more to a "cottage" model. Demand for real estate continues to be high, but the clientele is changing; in June 2016, Baobab reported that only few Europeans were buying—most buyers were either mixed couples or Kenyan citizens.

As far as county-initiated development is concerned, Diani is beginning to see some. While Governor Salim Mvurya initially focused more on the hinterland, an area entirely neglected during previous decades, many sections of Diani are now for the first time connected to the electric grid and have water lines built to homes.[3] The central government continues to invest more heavily upcountry, though construction on the vital Dongo Kundu Bypass has begun. As we have seen, once completed, the bypass will have substantial economic consequences for the south coast.[4] New ferries for the crossover at Likoni will increase traffic and economic activity.[5]

But behind the façade of things-as-usual and a partial economic upswing in Diani is a story of internecine fighting and poverty. Too many people living in the area do not have sufficient incomes and do not have access to the benefits of economic development. Such poverty and alienation, however, have not led to unified political action. Instead, radical and moderate Muslims (who are often said to be collaborating with the government) are targeting each other, and ten community leaders were said to have been killed on the south coast over the course of 2014. The assistant chief of Bongwe had been shot just a few days before I arrived in Diani in December of that year. He survived the assassination attempt, but other community members had not been as lucky. Another spate of violence involving returnees from the militant group Al-Shabaab occurred in May and early June 2016.[6] Various groups accuse each other of collaborating with Al-Shabaab or with the Kenyan government. "Amongst ourselves, this is a very cold war," said Juma, a middle-aged longtime resident of Diani. Again I heard complaints about a government that protects only preferred groups of Kenyans and neglects the coastal population. "Maybe, one day, it [the political situation] may cause one thousand people to die," Juma ominously predicted.

In 2014, I met with elders in Mwaroni, Mvumoni, and Mwamambi to hear their views on the current situation. A high percentage of people in these villages are unemployed, and even though they can partially survive on their agriculture and fishing, there is little money for school fees, hospitals, and clothing. "Although minerals are being mined, people still don't have three meals a day," complained Salim (age sixty-three) from Mvumoni. The male elders I talked to supported secession and generally the ideas of the Mombasa Republican Council. ("suluhu ni kujitenga," [the solution is to secede]) Devolution was seen as positive and as an opportunity for self-governance ("ugatuzi ni kitu kizuri, ni bora"). "We will wait for our time, it will come (tunasubiri wakate wowote, itarudi pale); rights never sink (haki haizami)," suggested Bakari (age sixty-seven) from Mwamambi. In contrast to what Juma had suggested, the elders rejected the idea of violence in Diani, saying, "there is no terrorism here." They said they wanted to talk, that they wanted dialogue. "Nobody wants to go through what they have experienced during Kaya Bombo," said Selimu (age forty-eight), a villager from Mwaroni referring to the aftermath of the election-related violence in 1997.[7] Again, the men reserved their wrath for the central government, while wazungu were seen as sources of employment and help. "The government banned NGOs because they help us," suggested Salim, referring to the recent shutdown of five hundred NGOs ordered by President Kenyatta.[8] When I pointed out that not all whites played a positive role in Kenya, Salim said that those wazungu who grabbed land are from colonial times, while today they bring development and, as Bakari emphasized, marriage. He even said that it would be better for the people living at the coast if colonialism came back ("kurudi tena ukoloni"). When I argued that some wazungu in Diani were useless drunkards and drug addicts, Salim said, "Well, then we take what falls out of their pockets when they are drunk." Muhammad (age eighty-eight, from Mwaroni) agreed that some wazungu get worse over time, but generally, these men, and other villagers, were adamant about whites being preferable to upcountry people. "Wazungu are more human than our fellow Africans," Muhammad said. The government is not supporting the Digo, Salim said, because it knows that whites are taking care of them.

Salim's statement and the comments of other elders confirmed one of the main theses of this book: a high degree of connection has emerged between the coast and Europe, and this connection is not a mere matter of perception but is grounded in and sustained by material support. Salim and other locals, however, are blind to the role Europeans have played in buying and alienating land and developing the real estate market. As I have shown, several Germans have been key players in shady real estate deals and collaborated with powerful African Kenyans to the detriment of the indigenous Digo population. The unwillingness of most Digo to acknowledge the negative effect of the activities of German and other Europeans on their lives can only be explained through the interpersonal relations that exist between African Kenyans and Europeans in the area. While some Europeans have significantly advanced the gentrification and larger economic processes of Diani, others—and sometimes also the economic developers themselves—have paid for education, health bills, and housing. And they have become relatives of many African Kenyans.

Though they did not blame whites for the loss of land, all I talked to lamented that loss. "I can't afford a lawyer, so I have no power," said Muhammad. "The rich take the land and then claim that they have bought it from the government." Acknowledging the consequences of private over communal ownership, Bakari said, "The community is now divided because of title deeds." Salim complained that if he went to the bank with his title deed, he would be denied credit, but if an upcountry person (such as the Kikuyu who owns the restaurant Rongai in Diani) went to the bank, he would get KSh10 million right away. Salim said that unless the Digo had their own money, they would not be able to fight upcountry development. Bakari also claimed that Digo did not sell their land voluntarily; they were simply kicked off of it—in contrast to the reality that many Digo had in fact sold voluntarily. (The other explanation several people offered for Digo selling land is that if they did not sell, they would be evicted, so they avoid eviction by selling, which may in fact be closer to reality in many cases). The rich, however, also invest, Muhammad said, so development continues, and in the end, that is also good because it creates jobs.

This pragmatism regarding development was mostly confirmed by the women I talked to. Aisha (age fifty-six) and Fatouma (age fifty-two), both from Mwaroni, acknowledged that the younger generation had received an education, had salaried jobs, and even owned cars. When I asked the women questions about politics, they said they had no opinion ("MRC? Sina."). They also mentioned new forms of solidarity, the self-help groups that are registered at the chief's office—a modern way of doing mweria, as they suggested. "Development is good" (maendeleo ni mazuri), Aisha said. "We have come out of poverty, also with the help of wazungu. Some benefit and some are destroyed by the developments." She thus acknowledged the complexity of the changes associated with development; but, in her eyes, not all was bad.

In contrast to the views of these women, male elders lamented very much the loss of power they once had. Bakari enthusiastically recalled the days when the *dzumbe*, the leader of the kaya, called upon the counsel of elders to decide matters related to the community. The government, he said, interfered with the rule of the kaya elders; it imposed people who changed the direction of things, and by now, the kayas no longer serve their original function. And indeed, in Diani kaya forestland has been developed, forcibly, and reduced to small areas. Most of the land surrounding Kaya Diani and Kaya Likunda has been grabbed, and the villagers have not been compensated. Since 1992, after villagers succeeded in gaining attention through protests, the remaining forest has been protected as a national monument. But encroachment continues. Traditions that were once regulated by male elders no longer exist, and the role of *wazee* (old men) in their communities has changed profoundly.[9] The elders' grievances are based in the loss of power more than any other factor. "Elders" have become "the elderly." The economic dimension has caused discontent among the youth (and no employment also means no social power, so in that sense, their complaints are also about power), but male elders have lost the most. Women in Diani, on the other hand, whether young or old, have gained somewhat in terms of social power (more of them receive education through secondary school, and more of them have their own income), though in small increments and not in a way comparable to developments in Nairobi.

The dream of regaining control over Digo land remains among young and old, male and female. But the Digo of Diani are not united in their goals and motivations in their insistence on the centrality of landownership (which is true for other areas in Kenya as well). In fact, the talk about land emerges as a discourse that betrays a wide range of distinct grievances and various goals. Landownership has become a mythical metaphor that stands for these multiple grievances and goals: the loss of power, melancholy over times past, the hope of economic power, the dream of living a modern lifestyle, the pursuit of more independence, the longing for community, and the desire for peace. The fact that motivations and goals are so diverse perhaps explains the lack of unified action; Digo (and other Kenyans) pursue their own interests according to Antonio Gramsci's idea of "common sense." In addressing their precarious situations, disempowered Kenyans make what Gramsci calls "spontaneous common sense" decisions (such as engaging with Germans and other Europeans through the charity model), as opposed to the "good sense" (or "new common sense") of collective action.[10] Collective action in the form of an uprising seems unlikely in light of the available opportunities that individuals are able to pursue, and perhaps the promises of devolution will address at least some of the causes of distress and injustice.

Alamin Mazrui's poem "Vitaturudia" powerfully expresses the melancholic sentiments I heard from villagers;[11] unsurprisingly, villagers along the coast are said to recite the poem, which they feel represents their cause. Its vision resonates with the grievances of indigenous peoples who have to give way to economic development around the world, especially in beachfront areas. Whereas, as Oisin Suttle suggests, distributive justice is "inevitable" on a global scale, it is unlikely that land will be returned to Digo (or comparable communities in the Caribbean, Brazil, Panama, Ethiopia, or Thailand) on a significant level; and whereas the issue of landownership, at this point, does not capture the multiple challenges the community is facing, the powerful vision put forth in this poem concludes this account.[12] It is a vision that not only evokes control over land, but also—perhaps more importantly—conjures up ideas connected to community, history, and solidarity.

VITATURUDIA	THEY WILL RETURN TO US
By Alamin Mazrui	*Translated by Ken Walibora Waliaula*

Kwa sisi wanao habibu	For us your beloved children
Kwa wale wengi, wengi mno, wanaosulubu	For the many, very many, who toil
Kwa wale wenye nyoyo zilojaa ghadhabu	For those with hearts full of rage
Na kwetu sisi warithi tulionyang'anywa	And for us disinherited heirs who are
tuloungana kama bawabu	as united as hinges
Kwetu sisi sote	For all of us . . .
Vyote vitakuja	All the things will come
Vitaturudia pamoja	They will all come to us together
Vitakuwa vyetu tena siku moja.	They will be ours again some day.
Mashamba ya wahenga wetu	The fields of our ancestors
Mabonde na miteremko yetu	Our valleys and slopes
Milima inayovutia nadhari zetu	Mountains that arrest our attention
Vyote vitakuja	All of these will come
Vitakuwa vyetu tena siku moja.	They will be ours again some day.
Ardhi yenye manukato ya rutuba	Our land endowed with the
	fragrance of fertility
Nyasi ziliosimama wima kwa kushiba	Grass that stands erect with
	satisfaction
Misitu ilosongana kwa mengi mahaba	Thick forests replete with affection
Vyote vitakuja	All of these will come
Vitakuwa vyetu tena pamoja.	They will be ours again some day.
Mito kwa furaha ikimiminika	The rivers that flow with joy
Maziwa yaliyokitwa yakakitika	The lakes with firm foundations
Na bahari zipovukazo katika zake haraka	And seas that move with speed
Vyote vitakuja	All these will come
Vitakuwa vyetu tena siku moja.	They will be ours again some day.

Kwa wale wanaoweza kungojea
Kwa wale wanaoweza kuvumilia
Kwa wale wenye majaraha, waloumia

Walothamini usiku wa baridi
  uhuru kuupigania
Kuliko mwezi na nyota kuzifurahia
  hali ni watumwa, watu kuwatumikia

Kwa hao wote . . .
Vyote vitakuja
Vitawarudia pamoja
Vitakuwa vyao tena siku moja.

For those who can wait
For those who can endure
For those with injuries, those who were
  hurt
Those who appreciated the cold night
  the freedom we fought for
Instead of enjoying the moon and the stars
while they are slaves, serving other
  people
For all those . . .
All these things will come
They will return together
They will be ours again some day.

Appendix: Maps and Tables

Map 1. Aerial view of the Diani area, showing villages, the airstrip, the golf course, and DARAD area (Diani Agriculture and Research Development)

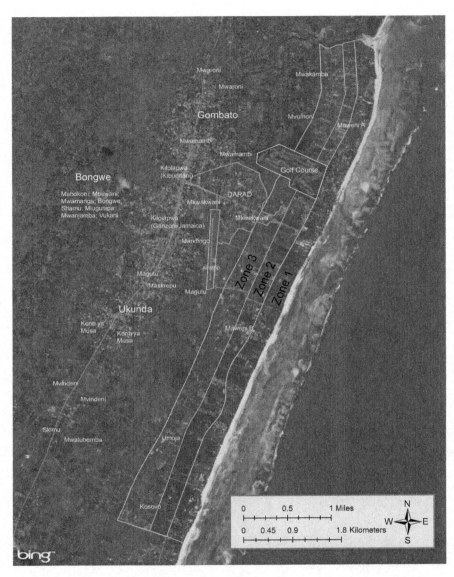

Map 2. Three zones of development in the Diani area

Table 1. Hotel ownership and management, 1960s to 2013

	Name of hotel (year of first opening)	Initial ownership	Change in ownership; current	General management
1	Indian Ocean Beach Club (1992)	African Kenyan	Closed October 2013	African Kenyan; closed
2	Southern Palms Beach Resort (1992)	Ismaili Kenyan Indians	Same	First British; various European, one Indonesian Dutch since 2006
3	Golden Beach Hotel (1980; only open for a short period)	African Kenyan	LAICO (Indian Kenyan), rebuilding into apart-ment complex Indian Kenyan	Swiss earlier (Hans Wittwer); no longer a hotel
4	Diani Reef Beach Resort and Spa (1972; org. Diani Beach Reef Hotel)	Changed hands sev-eral times; Israeli (Mr. Bernin)	Indian Kenyan	Used to have German man-agement (Siggi Jogschart); African Kenyan
5	Leisure Lodge Resort (1972)	Mostly owned by Germans (Wilhelm Meister); some African shares	Now Ismaili Kenyan (since about 1996); came out of receivership in 2001	Used to have German manag-ers, even after 1996; now African Kenyan (John Mutua)
6	Leopard Beach Resort (1974)	Italian	Sikh Kenyan	African Kenyan manager in consulting partnership with German manager (Chris Modigell, freelance consultant)
7	Swahili Beach (2012)	Sikh Kenyan	Sikh Kenyan	South African

(continued)

Table 1. Hotel ownership and management, 1960s to 2013 (*continued*)

	Name of hotel (year of first opening)	Initial ownership	Change in ownership; current	General management
8	Kaskazi Beach Hotel (1991)	LTI jointly with African Kenyan	In receivership 1991–2012; again owned by African Kenyan	Used to have German management; now African Kenyan
9	Trade Winds (1940s)	Government, African Kenyan	Now German (Kampa/Kampa-Matthiessen); presently closed (2013)	Formerly African Tours and Hotels (Kenyan), now German; presently closed
10	Diani Sea Lodge (1981)	German owned	German owned (Kampa/Kampa-Matthiessen)	German management
11	Diani Sea Resort (1991)	German owned	German owned (Kampa/Kampa-Matthiessen)	German management
12	Two Fishes (1940s)	Until after WWII Mr. and Mrs. Fish; then George Plumb; 1960s Karl Pollman	Various Germans until early 1990s; then African Kenyan; burnt down 1997 or 1998	Used to have German management; closed as hotel, run as beach bar and restaurant (Kim4Love, leased)
13	Africana Sea Lodge (1978)	African Kenyan and European Kenyan (Kenneth Matiba and Stephen Smith)	Sold in 2012 to Indian Kenyan (after being in receivership for 12 years)	German and African Kenyan; now closed
14	Jadini (1937; reopened 1973)	African Kenyan and European Kenyan (Kenneth Matiba and Stephen Smith)	Sold in 2012 to Indian Kenyan (after being in receivership for 12 years)	German and Kenyan African; now closed

15	Sands at Nomads (2005)	European Kenyan (Patricia Bonam)	Leased to Italian and European Kenyan	Austrian
16	Safari Beach Hotel (1986)	African Kenyan and European Kenyan (Kenneth Matiba and Stephen Smith)	Same	German and African Kenyan; now closed
17	Ocean Village Club (1987)	Italian owned	Changed hands several times; French	Portuguese
18	Papillon Lagoon Reef (1987; used to be Lagoon Reef Hotel)	Indian Kenyan (Reef Hotel Ltd.)	Goan (Mr. Correa); acquired by REX group in 1999	African Kenyan
19	Robinson Baobab (1974; then Baobab Beach Resort and Robinson Club, added Maridadi and Kolekole)	Used to be 100% German owned (Karl Pollman; Swiss; TUI)	Indian Kenyan (from Tanzania, Mr. Moledina), based out of UK; TUI still owns 10–20% or more	German and Swiss management; now African Kenyan
20	Shaanti (1998; then Galu Retreat Hotel; Afrika Pearl since Dec. 2013)	Indian Kenyan	Still Indian Kenyan but since Sept. 2013 leased by French, Africa Safari Adventure	Shaanti—Goan couple; now French management

Source: Table information is based on interviews conducted by the author from January 2010 to November 2013.

Note: The hotels are listed according to their north-to-south geographic order along Diani Beach.

Table 2. Occupancy and ownership of housing in the eastern part of Diani, beachfront through Row 4 and including DARAD, December 2014 (approximate figures)

	Beach/Row 1 (Zone 1)	Row 2 (Zone 2)	Rows 3 and 4 (Zone 3)	DARAD	Total
No. of housing units (incl. apartment units, rounded up)	270	340	530	410	**1,550**
Percentage of European/European and Indian Kenyan ownership	90% (243 units)	90% (306 units)	80% (424 units)	50% (205 units)	**76%** **(1,178 units)**
Percentage of European/European and Indian Kenyan occupants	90%	80%	80%	50%	
No. of Europeans/European and Indian Kenyans living in the area, full or part time (assuming an average of 3 occupants per unit)	729	816	1,272	615	**3,432** **(of 4,650** **total)**

Table 3. Kenyan marriages with German, Swiss, Austrian, and UK citizens, 2000–2009 (Mombasa)

Year	German		Swiss		Austrian		German-speaking			UK			Total licenses[a]
	M	F	M	F	M	F	M	F	Total	M	F	Total	
2000	87	33	8	12	4	1	99	46	**145**	22	11	**33**	(ca. 800)
2001	65	26	9	8	2	5	76	39	**115**	17	9	**26**	734
2002	72	17	10	7	4	4	86	28	**114**	18	16	**34**	804
2003	77	22	13	4	8	1	98	27	**125**	19	22	**41**	680
2004	63	41	8	4	5	1	76	46	**122**	20	11	**31**	703
2005	76	33	15	11	5	1	96	45	**141**	29	10	**39**	1,044
2006	68	38	11	3	7	3	86	44	**130**	26	26	**52**	1,100
2007	70	36	13	12	6	5	89	53	**142**	22	20	**42**	1,119
2008	71	39	13	9	8	1	92	49	**141**	26	25	**51**	913
2009	83	24	5	6	7	2	95	32	**127**	26	22	**48**	1,024
Total	**732**	**309**	**105**	**76**	**56**	**24**	**893**	**409**	**1,302**	**225**	**172**	**397**	**ca. 9,000**

Source: Marriage licenses in the Office of the Registrar of Marriages, Mombasa.

Note: Margin of error with regard to German last names (if citizenship was not indicated); some of the foreigners may be Kenyan residents or citizens. M indicates male; F, female.

[a]Reflects all licenses kept at the Registrar of Marriages.

Table 4. Kenyan marriages with German, Swiss, Austrian, and UK citizens, 2010–2012 (Mombasa)

Year	German		Swiss		Austrian		German-speaking			UK			Total licenses[a]
	M	F	M	F	M	F	M	F	Total	M	F	Total	
2010	69	24	7	8	7	1	83	33	**116**	24	26	**50**	1,098
2011	73	20	13	4	8	3	94	27	**121**	27	19	**46**	1,110
2012	74	32	15	6	4	3	93	41	**134**	36	23	**59**	1,090
Total	**216**	**76**	**35**	**18**	**19**	**7**	**270**	**101**	**371**	**87**	**68**	**155**	**3,298**

Source: Marriage licenses in the Office of the Registrar of Marriages, Mombasa.

Note: Margin of error with regard to German last names (if citizenship was not indicated); some of the foreigners may be Kenyan residents or citizens. M indicates male; F, female.

[a]Reflects all licenses kept at the Registrar of Marriages.

Table 5. Kenyan marriages with select groups of European, Israeli, and US citizens, 2000–2009 (Mombasa)

Year	Italian M	Italian F	French M	French F	American M	American F	Norwegian, Swedish, Finnish, Danish M	Norwegian, Swedish, Finnish, Danish F	Belgian M	Belgian F	Dutch M	Dutch F	Israeli M	Israeli F	Total
2000	3	2	6	4	3	2	4	5	3	0	7	1	2	0	42
2001	7	1	3	5	2	1	5	0	3	0	0	0	3	1	31
2002	5	3	9	3	3	1	2	2	5	0	1	0	5	0	39
2003	3	3	3	5	5	2	5	1	4	1	2	1	5	0	40
2004	5	3	1	3	6	1	7	5	3	3	4	0	2	0	43
2005	2	5	5	4	8	1	9	0	6	0	6	0	2	0	48
2006	5	6	4	2	6	3	6	0	8	1	4	3	1	0	49
2007	3	4	2	1	5	5	5	0	8	2	3	4	0	0	42
2008	5	0	2	3	4	3	4	2	2	1	3	3	1	0	33
2009	7	1	3	2	3	5	3	1	7	2	7	3	1	0	45
Total M and F	45	28	38	32	45	24	50	16	49	10	37	15	22	1	
Total	73		70		69		66		59		52		23		412

Source: Marriage licenses in the Office of the Registrar of Marriages, Mombasa.

Note: Margin of error with regard to Scandinavian and French/Belgian last names (if citizenship was not indicated); some of the foreigners may be Kenyan residents or citizens. M indicates male; F, female.

Table 6. Kenyan marriages with select groups of European, Israeli, and US citizens, 2010–2012 (Mombasa)

Year	Italian		French		American		Norwegian, Swedish, Finnish, Danish		Belgian		Dutch		Israeli		Total
	M	F	M	F	M	F	M	F	M	F	M	F	M	F	
2010	14	5	3	2	8	3	10	1	0	1	9	2	3	0	61
2011	11	11	5	1	14	5	8	9	1	4	4	2	0	0	75
2012	33	46	2	4	5	8	14	4	8	1	7	3	1	1	137
Total M and F	**58**	**62**	**10**	**7**	**27**	**16**	**32**	**14**	**9**	**6**	**20**	**7**	**4**	**1**	
Total	**120**		**17**		**43**		**46**		**15**		**27**		**5**		**273**

Source: Marriage licenses in the Office of the Registrar of Marriages, Mombasa.

Note: Margin of error with regard to Scandinavian and French/Belgian last names (if citizenship was not indicated); some of the foreigners may be Kenyan residents or citizens. M indicates male; F, female.

Table 7. Kenyan marriages with other Europeans, Canadians, and Australians, 2000–2009 (Mombasa)

Year	M	F	Total
2000	3	2	5
2001	2	1	3
2002	2	2	4
2003	3	4	7
2004	5	2	7
2005	7	2	9
2006	5	5	10
2007	12	5	17
2008	12	7	19
2009	16	7	23
Total	**67**	**37**	**104**

Source: Marriage licenses in the Office of the Registrar of Marriages, Mombasa.
Note: Some of the foreigners may be Kenyan residents or citizens. M indicates male; F, female.

Table 8. Kenyan marriages with other Europeans, Canadians, and Australians, 2010–2012 (Mombasa)

Year	M	F	Total
2010	6	7	13
2011	6	9	15
2012	12	11	23
Total	**24**	**27**	**51**

Source: Marriage licenses in the Office of the Registrar of Marriages, Mombasa.
Note: Some of the foreigners may be Kenyan residents or citizens. M indicates male; F, female.

Table 9. 2012 licenses: profile of partners

	German men–Kenyan women					Kenyan men–German women				
	Men's ages	Women's ages	Age difference	Men's professions	Women's professions	Men's ages	Women's ages	Age difference	Men's professions	Women's professions
	49	29	20	Driver	Saleslady	28	51	23	Self-employed	Engineer[d]
	41	24	17	Security officer	College student[d]	23	27	4[b]	Businessman	Businesslady
	37	26	11	Businessman	Businesslady	27	31	4[b]	Equipment operator	Unemployed
	70	33	37[c]	Retired	Businesslady	39	43	4[b]	Artist	Marketing[d]
	49	21	28	Bookkeeper	Receptionist	30	30	0[b]	Tour guide	Administrator
	45	25	20	Security officer	Supervisor	47[a]	36	11	Self-employed	N/A
	63	32	31[c]	Retired	Waitress	42	63	21	Farmer	Nurse
	71	34	37[c]	Teacher[d]	Sales/marketing	32	60	28	Businessman	Retired
	43	29	14	Businessman	Sales representative	32[a]	27	5[b]	Businessman	Sales woman
	43	31	12	Plumber	Salonist	31	59	28	Businessman	Retired
	38	28	10[b]	Engineer[d]	Animator	23[a]	20	3[b]	Hotelier[d]	Teacher[d]
	36	33	3[b]	Quality inspection officer	VCT (voluntary counseling and testing) counselor	31	51	20	Self-employed	Headmistress, music school[d]
	60	39	21	Cashier	Hairdresser	43[a]	32	11	Hotelier[d]	Teacher[d]

41	22	19	Physio-therapist[d]	Student[d]	28	47	19	Wireman	Nurse
52	28	24	Driver	Businesslady	40	41	1[b]	Driver	Dental assistant
30	20	10[b]	Purchasing manager[d]	Self-employed	29	38	9[b]	Animator	Postmaster
62	31	31[c]	Economist/gastronomy	Unemployed	25	38	13	Fine artist	Unemployed
64	26	38[c]	Retired	Student[d]	24	63	39[c]	Unemployed	Hostess
42	23	19	Businessman	Hairdresser	34	59	25	Boat operator	Pensioner
58	25	33[c]	Manager[d]	Artist	28	50	22	Businessman	Businesslady
52	36	16	Retired	Businesslady	29	47	18	Musician	Retired
51	31	20	Salesman	Manager	22	42	20	Artist	Coach
49	29	20	Engineer[d]	Ticketing	25	26	1[b]	Manager[d]	Psychologist[d]
61	31	30[c]	Retired teacher[d]	Veterinarian assistant	26	31	5[b]	Hotelier[d]	Hairdresser
59	23	36[c]	Farmer	Waitress	35	61	26	Fisherman	Nurse
60	38	22	Pensioner	Saleslady	29	58	29	Animator	Cook
43	29	14	Sales agent	Businesslady	50[a]	46	4[b]	Police officer	Flight attendant
53	46	7[b]	Engineer[d]	Unemployed	35	51	16	Musician	Employed
68	38	30[c]	Retired	Self-employed	22	27	5[b]	Businessman	Clerk
26	22	4[b]	Train driver	Hairdresser	42	45	3[b]	Hotelier[d]	Teacher[d]
67	32	35[c]	Retired	Businesslady	33[a]	27	6[b]	Beautician	Child attendant
48	25	23	Technician	Animator	29	30	1[b]	Scientist[d]	Health counselor

(continued)

Table 9. 2012 licenses: profile of partners (continued)

	German men–Kenyan women					Kenyan men–German women				
	Men's ages	Women's ages	Age difference	Men's professions	Women's professions	Men's ages	Women's ages	Age difference	Men's professions	Women's professions
	52	26	26	Civil servant	Businesslady	25	33	8[b]	Animator	Secretary at local court
	49	30	19	Draftsman	Lab technician[d]	29	48	19	Artist	Waitress
	41	31	10[b]	Electrician	Self-employed	34[a]	22	12	Seaman	Nurse
	49	23	26	Painter	Self-employed	54	74	20	Driver	Pensioner
	54	39	15	Printer	Tour guide	37[a]	22	15	Animator	Therapist[d]
	57	21	36[c]	Factory supervisor	Unemployed	32	48	16	Tour operator	Clerk
	57	46	11	Businessman	Businesslady	20	53	33[c]	Artist	Social worker[d]
	67	30	37[c]	Pensioner	Teacher[d]	33	53	20	Businessman	Nurse
	56	29	27	Packaging officer	Animator	35	40	5[b]	Sailor	Teacher[d]
	23	28[a]	5[b]	Chef	Hairdresser					
	37	22	15	Store logistics	Student[d]					
	50	40	10[b]	Retired	Businesslady					
	65	30	35[c]	Retired pilot[d]	Student[d]					
	68	33	35[c]	Pensioner	Businesslady					
	59	23	36[c]	Retired	Businesslady					
	39	24	15	Technical project manager[d]	Businesslady					

35	22	Banker[d]	13	Hotelier
47	24	IT specialist[d]	23	Professional writer
57	22	Businessman	35[c]	Businesslady
43	21	Horse trainer	22	Student[d]
48	33	Designer[d]	15	Hotelier
66	47	Retired	19	Businesslady
60	20	Mechanic	40[c]	Student[d]
75	28	Retired	47[c]	Unemployed
41	32	IT engineer[d]	9[b]	Hairdresser
65	30	Retired	35[c]	Businesslady
23	27[a]	Student[d]	4[b]	Student[d]
66	28	Retired	38[c]	Businesslady
63	28	Pensioner/retired	35[c]	Unemployed
27	28[a]	Unemployed	1[b]	Room steward
55	29	Supervisor	26	Secretary
64	27	Retired	37[c]	Businesslady
48	32	Electrician	16	Businesslady
67	31	Advisor	36[c]	Businesslady
56	37	Technician	19	Businesslady
63	38	Driving teacher	25	Businesslady
66	24	Retired	42[c]	Unemployed

(continued)

Table 9. 2012 licenses: profile of partners (*continued*)

| | German men–Kenyan women | | | | | Kenyan men–German women | | | |
Men's ages	Women's ages	Age difference	Men's professions	Women's professions	Men's ages	Women's ages	Age difference	Men's professions	Women's professions
59	24	35[c]	Investment agent[d]	Saleslady					
57	28	29	IT systems administrator[d]	Businesslady					
41	20	21	Cook	Student[d]					
45	42	3[b]	Prison warden	Businesslady					
49	31	18	Mechanic	Unemployed					
43	34	9[b]	Mechanical engineer[d]	Cashier					
61	21	40[c]	Electrician	Businesslady					
53	32	21	Retired	Businesslady					
45	28	17	Work tool maker	Beautician					
57	24	33[c]	Electrician	Artist					
49	29	20	Businessman	IT assistant[d]					
67	21	46[c]	Retired	Unemployed					
45	19	26	Retired	Unemployed					

56	32	24	Accounts manager	Housekeeper	
52	27	25	Tiles casual	Businesslady	
68	34	34[c]	Retired	Hairdresser	
49	36	13	Mechanic	Businesslady	
47	32	15	Supervisor	Unemployed	
56	28	28	Civil engineer[d]	Unemployed	
46	23	23	Technician	Businesslady	
65	26	39[c]	Bus driver	Businesslady	
55	36	19	Engineer[d]	Hairdresser	
43	33	10[b]	Mechanic	Hairdresser	
43	47[a]	4[b]	Gardener	Businesslady	
Average 52.04	**29.34**	**22.70**	**32.00**	**42.68**	**10.68**
Median 52	**29**	**22**	**31**	**43**	**9**

[a] Kenyan partner is older.
[b] Age difference ten years or more.
[c] Age difference thirty years or more.
[d] College or university education likely.

Table 10. Marriages between German and Kenyan nationals, as recorded in Germany, 2000–2012

	German man–Kenyan woman	German woman–Kenyan man	Total
2012	179	30	209
2011	143	20	163
2010	183	37	220
2009	207	35	242
2008	178	23	201
2007	165	28	193
2006	180	25	205
2005	140	30	170
2004	155	36	191
2003	151	28	179
2002	169	33	202
2001	154	51	205
2000	164	41	205
Total	**2,168 (83.87%)**	**417 (16.13%)**	**2,585**

Source: I thank Liliana Frey from the Statistisches Bundesamt Germany for her assistance in compiling this data.

Table 11. Marriages between Swiss and Kenyan nationals, as recorded in Switzerland, 1997–2013 and 1987

	Swiss man–Kenyan woman	Swiss woman–Kenyan man	Total
2013	25	11	36
2012	35	8	43
2011	29	21	50
2010	31	9	40
2009	39	10	49
2008	36	20	56
2007	44	31	75
2006	38	18	56
2005	26	16	42
2004	52	18	70
2003	41	20	61
2002	41	24	65
2001	36	22	58
2000	30	5	35
1999	35	6	41
1998	31	4	35
1997	26	5	31
Total	**595 (70.58%)**	**248 (29.42%)**	**843**

Source: I thank Corinne Di Loreto of the Eidgenössisches Departement des Innern, Bundesamt für Statistik, Sektion Demografie und Migration, for assistance in compiling this data.
Note: For comparison, total marriages in 1987: 17; total Swiss men: 15 (88.24%); total Swiss women: 2 (11.76%).

Table 12. Marriages between Austrian and Kenyan nationals, as recorded in Austria, 2000–2013

	Austrian man–Kenyan woman	Austrian woman–Kenyan man	Total
2013	13	4	17
2012	18	2	20
2011	28	1	29
2010	18	4	22
2009	19	3	22
2008	19	3	22
2007	9	0	9
2006	10	3	13
2005	13	8	21
2004	1	2	3
2003	5	4	9
2002	9	0	9
2001	11	1	12
2000	9	0	9
Total	**182 (83.87%)**	**35 (16.13%)**	**217**

Source: I thank Anita Mikulasek from Statistik Austria for her assistance in compiling the data.

Table 13. Profile of partners: Age and duration of relationship, in years, as of 2009–2010

Couple no.	Men's age	Women's age	Age difference	Duration of relationship
German men–Kenyan women				
1	44	28	16	1.5
4	67	29	38	7
5	67	27	40	3
7	50	36	14	9
10	58	29	29	2.5
11	49	23	26	3
16	65	34	31	0.25
17	52	32	20	3.5
18	65	55	10	26
20	62	26	36	4.5
21	50	22	28	1
22	66	47	19	0.5
24	67	67	0	39
25	77	35	42	5
28	70	50	20	18
29	66	28	38	2
Average	**60.9**	**35.5**	**25.4**	**7.9**
Kenyan men–German women				
2	44	55	11	3.25
3	27	42	15	1
6	50	37	13[a]	2
8	30	54	24	5
9	30	45	15	3
12	46	69	23	15
13	48	56	8	7
14	52	82	30	13
15	24	26	2	3
19	35	44	9	1.5
23	29	46	17	3
26	48	68	20	10
27	48	65	17	10
Average	**39.3**	**53.0**	**13.7**	**5.9**

[a]Kenyan partner is older than German partner.

Table 14. Residency of German/Swiss/Austrian partner

Couple no.	Diani		Europe most of the year	
	Women	Men	Women	Men
1		X		
2	X			
3			X	
4				X
5		X		
6			X	
7		X		
8			X	
9				
10		X		
11				X
12	X			
13	X			
14	X			
15			X	
16				X
17				X
18		X		
19	X			
20		X		
21				X
22		X		
23			X	
24		X		
25		X		
26	X			
27	X			
28		X		
29		X		
Total	**7**	**11**	**6**	**5**

Note: As of 2014, couple no. 2 has moved to Switzerland.

Table 15. Origin of Kenyan partners

Couple no.	Coast		Not coast	
	Women	Men	Women	Men
1			X	
2				X
3		X		
4	X			
5			X	
6		X		
7			X	
8		X		
9		X		
10			X	
11			X	
12		X		
13				X
14		X		
15		X		
16			X	
17	X			
18			X	
19				X
20			X	
21			X	
22			X	
23		X		
24			X	
25			X	
26				X
27				X
28			X	
29	X			
Total	**3**	**8**	**13**	**5**

Table 16. Employment of Kenyan partners

Couple no.	Coast		Not coast	
	Women	Men	Women	Men
1			None	
2				Sold curios on beach
3		Owns a cab		
4	None; used to be singer			
5			Sold khangas on beach	
6		Cook; owns boat		
7			None	
8		None; beach		
9		Beach; boating trips		
10			Waitress	
11			Hairdresser	
12		Owns small shop		
13				Odd jobs
14		Politician		
15		Cook in hotel		
16			Owns small shop	
17	None			
18			Owns shop	
19				Police officer
20			Works in pharmacy; beautician	
21			Waitress	
22			Owned restaurant, now bar	
23		None; beach		
24			Co-owns stores	
25			None	
26				Waiter in hotel
27				Owns small store
28			Waitress; retired	
29	Housekeeper			

Table 17. Number of children

Couple no.	Children together	Other children of Kenyan partner		Other children of German partner	
		Women	Men	Women	Men
1	1	—	0	0	0
2	0	0	2	2	0
3	0	0	2	0	0
4	0	0	0	0	2
5	0	0	0	0	0
6	0	0	1	0	0
7	1	1	0	0	0
8	0	0	—	2	0
9	0	0	2	2	0
10	1	—	0	0	1
11	0[a]	0	0	0	2
12	0	0	—	0	0
13	0	0	2	1	0
14	0	0	2	1	0
15	0	0	—	0	0
16	0	1	0	0	—
17	0	1	0	0	2
18	1	2	0	0	1
19	0	0	1	0	0
20	0	2	0	0	4
21	0	1	0	0	2
22	0	2	0	0	2
23	0	0	—	2	0
24	0	2	0	0	0
25	1	2	0	0	2
26	0	0	2	1	0
27	0	0	—	0	0
28	0	2	0	0	1
29	0	1	0	0	2
Total	**5**	**17**	**14**	**11**	**21**

[a]Miscarriage.

Notes

1. Multitudinal Coastal Entanglements: Pwani si Kenya—Pwani ni Kenya—Pwani ni Ujerumani (na Italia na kadhalika)

1. The Coast is not Kenya—The Coast is Kenya—The Coast is Germany (and Italy and so forth).

2. Nurse and Spear, *The Swahili*; Mazrui and Shariff, *The Swahili*; Horton and Middleton, *The Swahili*; Hoorweg, Foeken, and Obudho, *Kenya Coast Handbook*.

3. "The total contribution of Travel & Tourism to employment (including wider effects from investment, the supply chain and induced income impacts . . .) was 589,500 jobs in 2013 (10.6 percent of total employment)." World Travel and Tourism Council, *Travel & Tourism*, 4.

4. Scholarship on the Digo more broadly is scant. Some of the earliest known references in European languages date back to the mid-nineteenth century (e.g., Krapf, *Reisen in Ostafrika*). Several anthropological studies were conducted between the 1950s and 1970s; I refer to them in individual chapters of this book. Apart from several article-length analyses of various topics, no comprehensive study exists that focuses on the Digo of the Diani area.

5. For an overview of scholarship on German East Africa and the German colonial period more broadly, see Berman, Mühlhahn, and Nganang, "Introduction."

6. See Lekan, "Serengeti Shall Not Die."

7. The show was produced by Ivan Tors between 1966 and 1969. It was preceded in 1965 by the feature film *Clarence, the Cross-Eyed Lion*. The movie (filmed mostly in California) familiarized viewing audiences with the East African setting and featured main characters (including a lion and a chimpanzee) who became quite popular in both the United States and Germany.

8. See, for example, "Ferien '86"; "Kenia"; "Ob Malediven"; "Begegnungen in Kenia"; "Reise: Camping in Kenia"; "Reiseziel Sex"; "Wickelkinder der Wildnis"; and "Deutschland, deine Touristen."

9. For a brief overview of literature and films relevant to the German imagination of Kenya, see Berman, "Tourism," 179–184, and chapter 4 of this book.

10. The website of the German embassy in Nairobi recounted the fifty-year history of collaboration on the occasion of Kenya's independence anniversary in 2013. Embassy of the Federal Republic of Germany Nairobi, "50 years."

11. Figures based on publications by the Kenya Ministry of Tourism, Kenya Association of Tour Operators, the Kenya Tourist Board, and the Kenya Association of Hotelkeepers and Caterers. For data and a discussion of tourism during the 1990s, see Berman, "Tourism," 175–212, 219–233.

12. Ministry of East African Affairs, Commerce and Tourism, "Tourism Performance Overview 2010." Unfortunately, I was unable to get updated figures from the Kenyan ministry.

13. World Tourism Organization, "Kenya: Overnight Stays," table 5. The statistics of the World Tourism Organization consider all arrivals and do not distinguish between different types of visitors.

14. Berman, *Impossible Missions?*, 186.

15. For an overview of key aspects relevant to gentrification and case studies, see Levy, Comey, and Padilla, "In the Face of Gentrification"; Lees, Slater, and Wyly, *Gentrification Reader*; and Brown-Saracino, *Gentrification Debates*. For a case study on rural gentrification, see Nelson, Trautman, and Nelson, "Latino Immigrants and Rural Gentrification."

16. Atkinson and Bridge, *Gentrification in a Global Context*, 1. See also the discussion in chapter 2, "Land."

17. Ghertner, "Why Gentrification Theory Fails," 552.

18. Okoth-Ogendo, *Tenants of the Crown*, 11–12.

19. Cynthia Gillette writes, "In Digo society, individuals gain rights over land by receiving it from other persons, by clearing vacant land or by purchasing land, but legitimate occupation and ownership is not recognized without some visible sign of cultivation." "A Test of the Concept of Backwardness," 123.

20. Okoth-Ogendo, *Tenants of the Crown*, 41–44.

21. Ibid., 44.

22. Cooper, *From Slaves to Squatters*, 205.

23. Okoth-Ogendo highlights the continuity of basic principles of law and governance in the rural sector. See "The Continuity of Agrarian Law," in Okoth-Ogendo, *Tenants of the Crown*, 137–167, and "Development and the Legal Process in Kenya."

24. The Constitution of Kenya, ch. 5, part 1. In Laws of Kenya, rev. ed., 2010.https://www .kenyaembassy.com/pdfs/the%20constitution%20of%20kenya.pdf.

25. Leo, *Land and Class in Kenya*, 94, 96, 100. The Colonial Development Corporation was renamed the Commonwealth Development Corporation in 1963, with the acronym conveniently unchanged.

26. Kamau, "Seeds of Discord," 6–7.

27. Mathai, *Report of the Select Committee*, 1.

28. Republic of Kenya, *Sessional Paper No. 3*, articles 184–186, 39; quoted in Mghanga, *Usipoziba ufa Utajenga Ukuta*, 17.

29. Boone, *Property and Political Order in Africa*, 2, xiii.

30. The first study for this road was commissioned to a British civil engineering firm by Kenneth Matiba in the late 1960s, with the aim to assess the viability of a bypass around the port. Plans have been discussed ceaselessly since then, but it took more than forty years for the project to be approved.

31. This finding is similar to what Kenda Mutongi discovered in her study of attitudes toward the former British colonizer. See Mutongi, *Worries of the Heart*, 2–3.

32. Scott, *Seeing like a State*; Ferguson, "Seeing like an Oil Company."

33. Information on the film can be found at the Impacto Films website, http://www.impacto films.com/.

34. Jesse Freeston's documentary *Resistencia: The Fight for the Aguan Valley* (2014) records another struggle of peasants against developers, in Honduras.

35. Cultural Survival, "Ethiopia"; Rahmato, "Perils of Development from Above." The literature on land grabbing in Africa is vast, but the issue is global. For a glimpse of neoliberal land grabbing around the world, see Hall, "Hotspots."

36. Hatton and Williamson, *Global Migration and the World Economy*.

37. Heisler and Schmitter Heisler, *From Foreign Workers to Settlers?*; Goss and Lindquist, "Conceptualizing International Labor Migration."

38. A seminal study is Piore, *Birds of Passage*.

39. Sassen, *Global City*.

40. Breuer, "Retirement Migration"; Papademetriou et al., *America's Emigrants*; Sunil, Rojas, and Bradley, "United States' International Retirement Migration"; Benson and O'Reilly,

"Migration and the Search for a Better Way of Life"; Morales, "US Citizens Retirement Migration."

41. MacCannell, *The Tourist*, 1; Urry, *Tourist Gaze*, 4.

42. Jamaica Kincaid's *A Small Place* is one of the most poignant accounts of the affinity between postindependence tourism and colonialism.

43. For overviews on different approaches to the study of tourism, see, among many others, Urry, *Tourist Gaze*, 7–15; Wahab and Pigram, *Tourism, Development and Growth*; and Mowforth and Munt, *Tourism and Sustainability*. The idea of the empowerment of local communities has produced a flurry of studies; see, among others, Sofield, *Empowerment*; and Ruiz-Ballesteros and Hernández-Ramírez, "Tourism That Empowers?"

44. Swamy, "Kenya"; World Bank, *Kenya: Re-Investing*.

45. See, for example, Moyo, *Dead Aid*, 19–22; Stein, *Beyond the World Bank Agenda*; Rono, "Impact of the Structural Adjustment Programmes"; Kang'ara, "When the Pendulum Swings Too Far"; Thomas-Emeagwali, *Women Pay the Price*; Avery, "Stealing from the State"; Sparr, *Mortgaging Women's Lives*.

46. Patterns of foreign investment in Africa are discussed in scholarly literature, but impact studies are largely restricted to exploring the effect of foreign investment on the *volume* of national economies, and only a few studies assess the ways in which different segments of the population benefit or do not benefit from these developments. See, for example, Taabazuing et al., "Mining, Conflicts and Livelihood Struggles."

47. Visser and Hoogendoorn, "Decade of Second Home Tourism Research," 122.

48. See contributions in Keller and Bieger, *Real Estate and Destination Development*; Barkham, *Real Estate and Globalisation*; van Noorloos, "Residential Tourism"; Velásquez-Runk, "Indigenous Land and Environmental Conflicts in Panama"; Casas-Beltrán et al., "Turismo residencial y migración de jubilados extranjeros en México."

49. These companies include Bellevue (Germany), Buy Global Homes (US), Global Property Guide (US), Savills (UK), Le Groupe Barnes (France, global), NAI Global (375 offices worldwide), Qatari Diar Real Estate Company (Qatar), and Juwai (China).

50. McGuire, "House Hunting." What postures as a critical analysis turns out to be in effect an ad for a company, the Paradise Property Group, whose contact information is listed at the end of the article.

51. *The Love Boat* aired 249 episodes between 1977 and 1987. *Das Traumschiff*, produced by ZDF, was first aired in 1981, with 75 episodes as of July 2016.

52. Pearce, *Land Grabbers*, 62, 61.

53. Barume, *Land Rights*, 55.

54. China Scherz (*Having People*) shows how local expectations regarding charity and development, in this case in Uganda, defy sustainability goals of development workers. She relates these local conventions as rooted in long-term ethical practices of interdependence, a genealogy quite distinct from what I observed in Diani.

55. For examples of mutuality as a guiding principle in initiatives across Africa, see contributions to the special issue on mutuality in Rodima-Taylor and Bähre, "Mutual Help."

56. Discussions of humanitarianism generally consider the shorter time frame, even though several studies highlight the connection to colonialism and imperialism. See, for examples, Barnett, *Empire of Humanity*; Rist, *History of Development*. Bornstein and Redfield make a connection to early critiques of the sixteenth-century conquest of the New World but emphasize a genealogy of contemporary humanitarianism that "has its more obvious roots in European experience from the eighteenth century onwards" ("Introduction to the Anthropology of Humanitarianism," 13).

57. Surrealist Group of France, "Murderous Humanitarianism."

58. Berman, "Civilizing Mission."

59. Penny, *Kindred by Choice.*

60. Rothberg, *Multidirectional Memory*; for a discussion of the new concept of the "Responsibility to Protect," see Hilpold, *Die Schutzverantwortung (R2P).*

61. Representative publications from the Swiss and German contexts are Aktionskomitee Zürcher Entwicklungshilfe im In- und Ausland, "Antworten"; and Erler, *Tödliche Hilfe.*

62. Fassin, *Humanitarian Reason.*

63. See, for example, Polman, *Crisis Caravan*; Whitworth, *Men, Militarism, and UN Peacekeeping*; Orford, *Reading Humanitarian Intervention.*

64. For select studies, see Redfield, *Life in Crisis*; Moyo, *Dead Aid*; Easterly, *White Man's Burden*; Lancaster, *Aid to Africa*; Kabou, *Et si l'Afrique refusait le développement?* The literature arguing for the success of aid is also vast. One of the most visible proponents is Jeffrey Sachs; a synopsis of his arguments is provided in his "Case for Aid."

65. Amutabi, *NGO Factor in Africa*, xxiii. See also contributions in Mutua, *Human Rights NGOs*; Igoe and Kelsall, *Between a Rock and a Hard Place*; and Hearn, "'NGO-isation' of Kenyan Society."

66. For discussions of the relationship between citizenship rights and human rights, among others, see Brysk and Shafir, *People Out of Place.*

67. Fassin, *Humanitarian Reason*, 3, x. Silke Roth (*Paradoxes of Aid Work*) analyzes additional dimensions related to humanitarian reason by exploring the complex experiences of aid workers who work in frameworks predetermined by neoliberal geopolitics and donor interests.

68. Stiglitz, *Globalization and Its Discontents*; Piketty, *Capital in the Twenty-first Century.*

69. These policies have been criticized for a long time, and recently it seems that the World Bank, for example, is reversing some of its devastating policy decisions. Convinced by the success of Malawi's agricultural subsidy program, which it had outlawed in the early 1990s, the World Bank has begun to provide loans for agricultural subsidy programs. Thurow and Kilman, *Enough*, 169.

70. Muehlebach, *Moral Neoliberal*, 6, 8.

71. Stockton quoted in Polman, *Crisis Caravan*, 39; Thompson, "Moral Economy of the English Crowd,"; Scott, *Moral Economy of the Peasant.*

72. Among the more well-known movies on the topic is *Heading South* (2005) by director Laurent Cantet, which tells the story of three women who pursue sexual encounters with young men in Haiti. The movie is based on short stories by Haitian Canadian novelist Dany Laferrière. *Paradise: Love* (*Paradise: Liebe*) by Ulrich Seidl explores the grey zone between romance and sex tourism and largely focuses on the agency and emotional needs of female sex tourists. Short segments about the subject are featured regularly on public television in Germany, Switzerland, Austria, and Kenya. An earlier documentary by Dennis O'Rourke, *The Good Woman of Bangkok* (1991), created controversy because the filmmaker documented his own sexual interaction with a prostitute from Thailand.

73. Williams, *Sex Tourism in Bahia*; Jacobs, *Sex, Tourism and the Postcolonial Encounter*; Schifter-Sikora, *Mongers in Heaven*; Brennan, *What's Love Got to Do with It?*; Ryan and Hall, *Sex Tourism*; Oppermann, *Sex Tourism and Prostitution.* The extent of the problem within and beyond the United States is also acknowledged by the US Sex Tourism Prohibition Improvement Act of 2002. US Congress, House Committee on the Judiciary, *Sex Tourism Prohibition Improvement.*

74. Taylor, Torpy, and Das, *Policing Global Movement*; O'Connell Davidson, *Children in the Global Sex Trade*; Seabrook, *No Hiding Place.*

75. The most comprehensive study of sex tourism and prostitution on the Kenyan coast is Kibicho, *Sex Tourism in Africa*; for an earlier study, see Kleiber and Wilke, *Aids, Sex und Tourismus*.

76. Cabezas, *Economies of Desire*; Briggs, *Reproducing Empire*; White, *Comforts of Home*.

77. Kenya National Bureau of Statistics, *Kenya Facts and Figures 2014*, "Wage Employment," 17, table 14; cf. World Travel and Tourism Council, "Travel & Tourism," 4.

78. Debord, "Theory of the Dérive."

79. While the effect of urban-to-rural remittances has received some attention, only few studies on transnational remittances exist to date. See, for example, Taylor, Wangaruro, and Papadopoulos, "It Is My Turn To Give"; Kumar, "Exploring the Nexus."

80. Jerven, *Poor Numbers*.

81. While mobile banking in Kenya has received some attention, the role of Western Union transfers from Europe and the United States has not been assessed at this point. Mbiti and Weil, *Mobile Banking*; Suri, Jack, and Stoker, "Documenting the Birth of a Financial Economy."

82. Simone, *For the City Yet to Come*, 6.

83. The result was the chapter on tourism in Berman, *Impossible Missions?* I also co-organized the Nairobi Workshop on Disability in 2007. Contributions were published in Armstrong et al., *Disability in Kenya*.

84. I thank Denis Moser from DM Tours for arranging these opportunities.

2. Land

1. An administrative reform outlined in the new 2010 constitution of Kenya renamed areas termed "districts" (in 1992) as "counties" and took back an earlier reform (2007) that had created additional districts and whereby Diani had been part of the District of Msambweni.

2. The three areas ("sublocations" under the previous administrative system) form two wards, namely, Gombato/Bongwe and Ukunda, each of which have one representative in the Kwale County Assembly.

3. The term "settlement scheme" refers to government-planned settlements, usually involving resettlement of populations.

4. A marker frequently given for the beginning of Bongwe is that it starts at Ibiza market and a mineral water plant on the west side of the road.

5. Figures according to the 2009 census. The dataset and information about the individual villages was provided by the chief's office in Ukunda.

6. City Mayors Statistics, "Largest Cities in the World."

7. Figures according to the 2009 census. See also Kenya MPYA, "Welcome to Kwale County," accessed May 2016 at http://www.kenyampya.com/index.php?county=Kwale.

8. See my comments on the use of gentrification as an analytical framework in chapter 1.

9. Atkinson and Bridge, *Gentrification*, 10.

10. Horton and Middleton, *The Swahili*, 5.

11. Ibid., 3.

12. Horton and Middleton, *The Swahili*, chapter 5, "The Trading System of the Swahili Coast," 89–114. For an exploration of the connection of the East African coast to worldwide trade, including nineteenth-century US trade, see Desai, "Oceans Connect."

13. For a historical exploration and the multiple dimensions and shifts of Swahili identity, see Mazrui and Shariff, *The Swahili*.

14. Nurse and Spear, *The Swahili*, 1–4.

15. Abungu, "Kongo Mosque Heritage Site." According to Berg, as well as other scholars, "It is possible that the Shirazi dynasties themselves came from primary Asian settlements on the southern Somali coast rather than direct from Shiraz in Iran." Berg, "Swahili Community of Mombasa," 36, 44.

16. For a discussion of sovereignty as a concept applicable to the rulers of the area during the premodern period, see Brennan, "Lowering the Sultan's Flag."

17. Ritchie, Introduction, 5.

18. For a case study on the fluidity of concepts of ethnic identification, see Parkin, "Swahili Mijikenda." Parkin acknowledges the effect of British categorization on labeling and hierarchizing ethnic groups (p. 161); see also Willis, *Mombasa*; Mazrui and Shariff, *The Swahili*, 3.

19. Willis, drawing on other scholars (such as R. F. Morton), challenges this narrative of origin in *Mombasa, the Swahili, and the Making of the Mijikenda* (pp. 19–46). He also discusses the emergence of the term "Mijikenda" in the 1930s to refer to the nine tribes in its relation to landownership status (pp. 6–7, 75, 111–113, 127, 173, 192–200). With his account, Willis reconsiders aspects of Spear, *Kaya Complex*, especially the "straightforward understanding of oral history" (p. 14). Johann Ludwig Krapf recounts that one of the chiefs of Mombasa, "Bana Hamade," identifies Shunguaya as the original homeland of the Swahili, while the "Wanika" (Nyika, the term used for the population of Mombasa's hinterland well into the twentieth century) migrated from "Rombo in Dschagga." *Reisen in Ostafrika*, 1:359. John Middleton writes, "Whatever it may have been in history, the idea of Shungwaya provides a common origin for the coastal peoples." "The Peoples," 103.

20. Several scholars suggest that Bantu settlements were already present in the Kwale area in the first half of the first millennium. Horton and Middleton, *The Swahili*, 38, 42.

21. Berg, "Swahili Community of Mombasa," 36–37.

22. Spear, *Kaya Complex*, 27. Kaya Kinondo has become an ecotourism location sustained by, among other organizations, the World Wildlife Fund and the Ford Foundation and is often identified as "the senior most Kaya for the Digo community." Kaya Kinondo Ecotourism Project, "About Us," accessed May 2016 at http://www.kaya-kinondo-kenya.com.

23. Berg, "Swahili Community of Mombasa," 46.

24. Ibid., 47.

25. Willis emphasizes that the relationship between Kilindini and Digo is one of kinship. *Mombasa*, 37.

26. Spear, *Kaya Complex*, 85, 108.

27. Ibid., 109–110. See also Krapf, *Reisen in Ostafrika*. His comments on Digo settlements on the south coast can be found mostly on pp. 226, 246–247, 280, 345 (vol. 1) and 45, 56, 90–93, 172–175 (vol. 2).

28. Spear, *Kaya Complex*, 118–119; Hinawy, *Al-Akida*, 47.

29. Anglo-German Treaty.

30. For the text of the 1895 treaty, see Robertson, *Kenya Coastal Strip*.

31. Brennan, "Lowering the Sultan's Flag," 838.

32. Ibid., 839.

33. Ibid., 838.

34. Gregory, *Foundation of British East Africa*, 148–150.

35. Cashmore, "Sheikh Mbaruk," 111.

36. Among Alamin M. Mazrui's numerous publications about the Swahili people, culture, and language, two in particular aim to combat the misrepresentation of the Digo people and advocate for them: see *Kayas of Deprivation* and *Kayas Revisited*. Ali Mazrui (1933–2014) was

one of the leading scholars in African studies. Sheikh Hammad Muhammad Kassim Mazrui was chief qadi of Kenya from 2002 until 2010.

37. See Cashmore, "Sheikh Mbaruk," 109–137; also Gregory, *Foundation of British East Africa*, 144–161.

38. Cashmore, "Sheikh Mbaruk," 114; Gregory, *Foundation of British East Africa*, 157; Gerlach, "Social Organization," 15.

39. Brantley, *Giriama and Colonial Resistance*, 18–19, 29–31, 39, 43–51; Spear, *Kaya Complex*, 143; Cashmore, "Sheikh Mbaruk," 132; Krapf, *Reisen in Ostafrika*, 1:408, 2:93; Hinawy, *Al-Akida*. According to Mazrui and Shariff, the alliance between Swahili, Omanis, and Mijikenda goes back to their shared struggle against the Portuguese. *The Swahili*, 167–168 n7.

40. Brantley, *Giriama and Colonial Resistance*, 44–45; Cashmore, "Sheikh Mbaruk," 123.

41. Glassman, *Feast and Riot*, 199–200.

42. Moyse-Bartlett, *King's African Rifles*, 102–111.

43. Parsons, *African Rank-and-File*, 15; on recruitment, see 61–65.

44. Moyse-Bartlett, *King's African Rifles*, 110.

45. Gregory, *Foundation of British East Africa*, 161.

46. Willis, *Mombasa*, 118.

47. Okoth-Ogendo, *Tenants of the Crown*, 11–12.

48. Ibid., 12.

49. Anderson, *Histories of the Hanged*, 23.

50. Ibid., 41.

51. Okoth-Ogendo, *Tenants of the Crown*, 54.

52. Ibid., 44.

53. Sorrenson, *Origins*, 210; Okoth-Ogendo, "Development and the Legal Process," 62.

54. Sorrenson argues that the reserves were originally intended to protect African land rights. *Origins*, 210. Okoth-Ogendo refutes the argument convincingly in *Tenants of the Crown*, 30–31.

55. Mambo, "Nascent Political Activities," 99.

56. Ibid., 100–102.

57. Sorrenson, *Origins*, 224.

58. Okoth-Ogendo, "Development and the Legal Process," 62. For a discussion of legislation regarding the reserves throughout the period of colonial rule, see Okoth-Ogendo, *Tenants of the Crown*, 53–78.

59. Kanyinga, *Re-Distribution from Above*, 37.

60. Cooper, *From Slaves to Squatters*, 173; see pp. 176–178 for detail regarding court cases concerning manumission and compensation.

61. The widespread assumption, held by both advocates of a free market economy and Marxists, that a mobile salaried labor force (divorced from the means of production) is a precondition for the development of capitalism is contradicted by a recent study that documents the extent to which the economic power of the United States, as it emerged especially in the nineteenth century, was based on the slaveholder society of the South. Baptist, *Half Has Never Been Told*.

62. See Catherine Boone's discussion of the persistent relevance of landownership issues in contemporary African countries in *Property and Political Order in Africa*. The studies by both Boone and Baptist (ibid.) suggest that a more complex approach to understanding capitalism and economic development more broadly is needed.

63. Cooper, *From Slaves to Squatters*, 175.

64. Ibid., 202–203.

65. Ibid., 192.
66. Republic of Kenya, *Report of the Commission*, introduction, 1–2.
67. Palmer supports "the authors of the ethnographies on the Kamba and Nyika tribes [who] do not paint the traditional scene as one of total communalism." "Shimba Hills Settlement Scheme," 87.
68. Kayamba, "Notes on the Wadigo," 90.
69. A resident of Mwaroni recounted that "one villager, for example, would ask another villager who owned more land, to use a quarter acre of his land to plant crops and vegetables. After harvesting, they would give a portion of the crop as a token of appreciation (but there was no requirement)."
70. See Sandra F. Joireman's reference to the British government anthropologist C. K. Meek in *Where There Is No Government*, 29.
71. Cynthia Gillette writes, "In Digo society, individuals gain rights over land by receiving it from other persons, by clearing vacant land or by purchasing land, but legitimate occupation and ownership is not recognized without some visible sign of cultivation." "Test of the Concept of Backwardness," 123.
72. Cooper, *From Slaves to Squatters*, 193.
73. On the Three Nations, or *Thelatha Taifa*, of Mombasa and their relationship to the Nine Nations, or *Tisa Taifa*, see Berg, "Swahili Community of Mombasa," 35–56.
74. Cooper, *From Slaves to Squatters*, 193–196, 201.
75. Ibid., 196–201.
76. Ibid., 209.
77. Parkin points out: "Even by the mid-seventies alarm was expressed by land development officers at the propensity of the Digo to sell off valuable plots at knockdown prices. This concern was still being expressed in 1988." "Swahili Mijikenda," 168.
78. Willis, *Mombasa*, 2–3.
79. Sorrenson, *Origins*, 221.
80. Cooper, *From Slaves to Squatters*, 205.
81. Kenyatta, "Kenya," 805.
82. Sorrenson, *Origins*, 221.
83. Eisemon, "Educational Marginalization of Coastal Kenya," 251.
84. Khan, "Rahimkhan Family," 7.
85. Ibid.
86. Anderson, *Histories of the Hanged*, 22.
87. Khan, "Rahimkhan Family," 7. Khan also writes that "Oberholzer's land in Diani Beach was repossessed by the government" in 1965 (p. 9).
88. The spelling of this name could not be verified.
89. A summary on the value of colonial Blue Books is given in Preston, "Colonial Blue Books."
90. Kenya Colony and Protectorate, *Blue Book for the Year 1935*, 555; *Blue Book for the Year 1938*, 558.
91. The history of hotel development on the south coast, as provided here, is for the most part based on oral history interviews with current and former managers and owners of hotels and longtime residents of the area. Most of the interviews were conducted between 2009 and 2013; some information is based on research conducted in the 1990s.
92. "Happy Valley" refers to a region near the Aberdares in Kenya that was settled in the 1920s by notoriously hedonistic colonialists.
93. See Woods, "Revealed."

94. For examples documenting the degree to which the British colonial criminal justice system was rooted in racist legal codes, see Wiener, *Empire on Trial*, 193–221. An analysis of master-servant laws by David M. Anderson ("Master and Servant") also sheds light on the legal inequality and differential regimes of punishment in colonial Kenya.

95. Shadle, "Settlers, Africans," 63.

96. Wa-Githumo, *Land and Nationalism*, 300.

97. Wiener, *Empire on Trial*, 209–210; see also Wa-Githumo, *Land and Nationalism*, 289–318.

98. Anderson, *Histories of the Hanged*, 3.

99. Denham, *Kenya*, 3.

100. Resettlement schemes affected Kwale as well, although later than in other areas of the country. In the Kwale area, a settlement scheme in Shimba Hills dates from 1952 and involved groups both from the coast (Digo, Duruma, Girima) and from upcountry (Taita, Nandi, Kamba). Hoorweg, "Experience with Land Settlement," 315–317. On the Shimba Hills settlement scheme, see Palmer, "Shimba Hills Settlement Scheme." See also Okoth-Ogendo, *Tenants of the Crown*, for discussions of the legal framework relevant to these various aspects.

101. Anderson, *Histories of the Hanged*, 22. For another case of failed expectations regarding the activities of the Land Commission, see Shilaro, "Kakamega Gold Rush."

102. Kenya Colony and Protectorate, *Blue Book for the Year 1933*, 225.

103. Ibid., 538. Luther Paul Gerlach, in 1960, listed the number of Digo who lived in the Coast Province of Kenya as 55,000; he suggested 2,000 square miles (5,180 square kilometers) as the area of the "Digo District." "Social Organisation," 6.

104. Figures according to Kenya National Bureau of Statistics, *2009 Kenya Population and Housing Census*.

105. Mambo, "Nascent Political Activities," 100–102.

106. Khan, "Rahimkhan Family," 7, and interviews I conducted with longtime residents.

107. See Mambo regarding, among others, the Digo Welfare Association, the Young Duruma Association, and the Mijikenda Union (the latter of which was more politically effective) in "Nascent Political Activities," 107–110.

108. Salim, *Swahili-speaking Peoples of Kenya's Coast*, 215; Mambo, "Nascent Political Activities," 111–112.

109. Estimates regarding the percentage of arable land vary between 30 percent and close to 50 percent. The latter figure is cited by the World Bank, "Agricultural Land (% of Land Area)."

110. Leo, *Land and Class*, 42; Wa-Githumo, *Land and Nationalism*, 414.

111. Leo, *Land and Class*, 69.

112. Ibid., 70, 73.

113. Ibid., 96, 100.

114. Leys, *Underdevelopment in Kenya*, 74.

115. Ibid., 75.

116. Leo, *Land and Class*, 111.

117. Kamau, "Seeds of Discord—Settlement Schemes," 15–18.

118. The report of the Waki Commission (officially the Commission of Inquiry on Post-Election Violence, CIPEV) identified land-related grievances as one of the root causes of the violence that erupted after the 2007 presidential elections; see especially the section "Land and Inequality." Commission of Inquiry into Post-Election Violence, *Full Kenyan Post Election Violence Report 2008*, 30–33. See also Wakhungu, Nyukuri, and Huggins, *Land Tenure and Violent Conflict*.

119. For an account from a conservative perspective, see Harbeson, *Nation-building*.

120. Wasserman, *Politics of Decolonization*, 175.

121. Maughan-Brown, *Land, Freedom and Fiction*, 23.

122. Robertson, *Kenya Coastal Strip*, 1.

123. Ibid., 9, 33–38.

124. Mambo, "Nascent Political Activities," 113–115.

125. Robertson, *Kenya Coastal Strip*, 12.

126. Okoth-Ogendo highlights the continuity of basic principles of law and governance in the rural sector in "Law and the Legal Process in Kenya" (pp. 59–83) and "The Continuity of Agrarian Law" (pp. 155–167) in *Tenants of the Crown*.

127. The issue of communal and public versus individual tenure is addressed in a number of studies mentioned here, including Kabeberi, *Ours by Right*, 6, 92–105.

128. Klaus, "Claiming Land."

129. Hoorweg, "Experience with Land Settlement," 310.

130. Maas, *Women's Social and Economic Projects*, 21; Klaus, "Claiming Land," 81–83.

131. Hoorweg, "Experience with Land Settlement," 317.

132. Hoorweg et al., "Nutrition in Agricultural Development," 162.

133. Ibid., 175; Maas, *Women's Social and Economic Projects*, 23–24.

134. Hoorweg, "Experience with Land Settlement," 318.

135. Kamau, "Seeds of Discord—Scramble for Beach Plots," 6.

136. Ibid., 7.

137. See "The Trials and Tribulations of National Consciousness," in Fanon, *Wretched of the Earth*, 97–144.

138. Clough, "Mau Mau and the Contest for Memory," 255. As Lotte Hughes has also shown, "suppression of public memory continues and paradoxically co-exists with the flowering of Mau Mau memorialisation in present-day Kenya." "'Truth Be Told,'" 186.

139. Kamau, "Seeds of Discord—How Civil Servants Schemed for Beach Plots," 9.

140. See also Peal, "Dan Trench."

141. Matiba and Smith bought the shares of Malmqvist in the mid-1970s, and from then on, they owned the company in equal parts. Smith is a European Kenyan who was born in Kenya.

142. Kamau, "Seeds of Discord—How Civil Servants Schemed for Beach Plots," 11. Thomas P. Wolf also provides figures that shed light on the extent to which in some areas, upcountry Kenyans acquired more coastal land than any other group after independence. "Contemporary Politics," 132–133.

143. The question of collaboration is contentious to this day. See Branch, *Defeating Mau Mau*; also Wamagatta, "African Collaborators."

144. Mathai, *Report of the Select Committee*, 1. Similar to Robertson's 1961 report, this document also acknowledges a sense of urgency and makes a number of reasonable recommendations.

145. Ministry of Lands, *National Land Policy*, articles 184–186, p. 38, quoted in Mghanga, *Usipoziba ufa Utajenga Ukuta*, 17.

146. See, for example, a parliamentary debate on July 3, 1970, "Eviction of Unregistered Squatters from Ukunda Farm." Republic of Kenya, *Kenya National Assembly Official Record*, 2074–2075.

147. See, for example, Kanyinga, *Re-Distribution from Above*, which focuses mostly on the situation in the Kilifi District.

148. Willis and Gona, "*Pwani C Kenya*"; Goldsmith, "Mombasa Republican Council." For an earlier discussion of the relationship between Arabs, Swahili, and Mijikenda at the moment of independence, see Salim, *Swahili-speaking Peoples*, 203–246.

149. Republic of Kenya, *Report of the Commission* [also known as the Ndungu Report], "Trust Lands as Public Land," 139–140. See Roger Southall's discussion of the extension report, including appendices. "Ndungu Report," 142–151.

150. The appendix on "Coast Province" includes a table on "Irregularly Allocated Houses—Kwale," which lists a total of one house, two plots, and two camps (p. 740). Annex 19 of volume 2, "Complaints from the Public," in the (comparably short) section on Coast Province, items no. 54 (by an individual from Ukunda) and nos. 56–58 (by the South Coast Residents Association) includes complaints voiced by residents of the Diani area but not related to Diani itself. More items are listed in the "Forestlands, National Parks, Game Reserves, Wetlands, Riparian Reserves and Protected Areas" file, especially related to Shimoni, another south coast location (pp. 160–161). Otherwise the south coast, Kwale County, or, more specifically, Diani, are absent from the report.

151. In Republic of Kenya, *Report of the Commission*, see the table "Forestlands, National Parks, Game Reserves, Wetlands, Riparian Reserves and Protected Areas" (p. 169). Even before publication of the Ndungu Report, the issue made it into a parliamentary debate in 2003.

152. Southall, "Ndungu Report," 148.

153. Republic of Kenya, *Report of the Commission*, "Settlement Schemes and Trust Land," 147,

154. Jackson, "Problems of Tourist Industry Development," 62.

155. Ibid., 62.

156. See Pollman's Tours & Safaris, "About Pollman's Tours & Safaris," accessed November 23, 2015, at http://www.pollmans.com/index.php?option=com_content&view=article&id=57 &Itemid=29.

157. See Diani Sea Resort at http://dianisearesort.de/de/ and Diani Sea Lodge at http://dian isealodge.de/all/, both accessed November 23, 2015.

158. Two Fishes was particularly popular with Germans. In 1978, it was bought by a Mr. Sommer, Gerhard Matthiessen, and two others. After the latter three investors left the hotel in 1982, Sommer continued to run it alone. After he died, it was owned by an African Kenyan company. It burned down in late 1997 or early 1998, and locals have clearly agreed that the fire was due to arson. Two Fishes was one of the first hotels that allowed mixed couples to rent rooms. Currently, a beach bar called Kim4Love is run on the plot, and while it caters predominately to African Kenyans, many mixed couples frequent the establishment. See Kim-4Love, accessed November 21, 2015, at http://www.kim4love.net.

159. See, among others, Taylor, "India's Rise in Africa," 779–798; Pedersen, "Second Wave." Presently, there is a lack of data regarding Indian economic activity in Kenya specifically.

160. Figures according to Harald Kampa, chairman of the coastal branch of the Kenyan Association of Hoteliers and Caterers (KAHC); interviews in July 2012 and October 2013.

161. For a portrait of a Swedish man who led an adventurous life in Kenya and beyond, see Berman, "Neils Larssen."

162. According to one informant, earlier the land had been owned by a Mrs. Wales, who might have acquired it from East African Estates. Other accounts stated that Juma Boy bought land from the Afrikaner Oberholzer. Kassim Mwamzandi, who served as Kwale East member of parliament during 1963–1983 and then 1988–1997 also is said to have been involved in illegal land transfers and was included in a "List of Shame" published in 2000—"Former MPs Boy Juma Boy, Kassim Mwamzandi and Gonzi Rai allegedly allocated 402 Kwale County Council plots meant for squatters to other people." Mugonyi, "Kenya: Top Officials Named in the List of Shame." Countless other reports charge various area members of parliament as being involved in illegal land transfers, including to Swiss and German investors.

163. Juma Boy died in 1983. He represented Kwale District in parliament twice and was one of Kenya's leading trade unionists. His son, Boy Juma Boy, became a member of parliament in 1983 and served three terms until he lost his seat in the 1997 elections. He has also been implicated in the 1997 election violence (as has Kassim Mwamzandi). Boy Juma Boy was back as a political force in 2012, having being elected senator for Kwale County.

164. Because lawsuits were pending, it was difficult to find villagers who were willing to volunteer information. Information about the history of DARAD was gathered in interviews with various Diani residents, including villagers, hotel managers, and Klaus Thüsing, who was the country director for the German Development Agency (DED) in Kenya from 1988 to 1993.

165. Under these names until 2010; now both part of the Deutsche Gesellschaft für Internationale Zusammenarbeit (GIZ) (Corporation for International Collaboration).

166. See the Center for International Migration and Development, accessed November 23, 2015, at http://www.cimonline.de/en. CIM is today folded into GIZ, which is the result of a merger between the DED and GTZ. I contacted GIZ and CIM to corroborate data gathered during interviews, but after an initial exchange, I received no further responses once representatives realized what kind of information I was interested in. They responded that they had no access to information involving the previous organizations ("Wir führen kein Archiv zu der Arbeit der Vorgängerorganisationen der GIZ"; "Leider liegen uns keine Informationen oder Dokumente zu dem von Ihnen geschilderten Fall vor"). Email communication, February 2015.

167. Krüger's collaboration with Meister ended around that time as well, presumably because he had not been paid properly; he left with some of his machines overnight, which caused additional scandal at the time.

168. Rodgers and Burgess, "Taking Conservative Action," 328.

169. See "LTI Hotels Company Details," accessed November 23, 2015, at http://www.lti.de/en/Home/lti-service—-comfort/Company-Details.html.

170. See, among others, Ali, "Kenya: 'Squatters' Invade"; Ndurya, "Kenya: Hotel in Threat to Raze Estate"; Nation Reporter, "Kenya: Govt Revokes"; Machuhi, "Hotel Sues Leaders"; Machuhi and Michira, "Leisure Lodge Files Court Bid"; Machuhi, "Court Order Issued."

171. Swamy, "Kenya: Patchy, Intermittent Commitment"; World Bank, *Kenya: Re-Investing*.

172. International Monetary Fund, "IMF Approves Three-Year Loan."

173. Wanjiru, *IMF Policies and Their Impact*, 17.

174. See "Diani Homes: Kenia Immobilien" at http://www.dianihomes.de/impressum.htm, and Diani Homes, "Über Uns," at http://dianihomes.volker-pullig.de/ueber-uns.html; both accessed November 23, 2015.

175. According to Krapf, locals used the small island of Kuale ("das Inselchen Kuale") to store their belongings in times of war. *Reisen in Ostafrika*, 2:175.

176. *Erbpacht* separates ownership and land use and has been outlawed in Germany since 1900.

177. According to representatives of a local competitor, the company does not operate as a licensed real estate company, but rather as a consulting business.

178. For the different types of work/residence permits, see Ministry of Interior and Coordination of National Government, "Department of Immigration Services, Issuance of Kenya Entry Permits Checklist," at http://www.immigration.go.ke/downloads/Checklist.pdf, accessed July 14, 2016.

179. Volker Pullig, a partner of Brunlehner's, is said to have lived mostly in Germany since 1997 "wegen schlechter Presse" (because of bad press) (1999 interview with Neugebauer).

180. See "Romantic Hotels Kenya," accessed November 23, 2013, at http://romantichotelskenya.com/.

181. "Prügelprozess gegen Prinz Ernst August."

182. See the case of Andreas Költz, Steinkühler, "Verbrechen im Mafia-Paradies." Both Brunlehner and Pullig (his name was crossed out in this article) play a role in this story as well.

183. For discussions of the Italian mafia presence on the coast, see Gitau, "How Italian Mafia Gained Control of Malindi"; Dabbs, "Kenyans See the Italian Mafia's Hand."

184. Wadhams, "Fleeing Justice."

185. Odhiambo, "Interest Rate Reforms"; see figure 1 on p. 297. For interest rates 1991–1995, see table 1 in Republic of Kenya, *Kenya: Economic Reforms for 1996–1998*, 61. Martin Brownbridge's analysis sheds light on the repercussions of lending and deposit strategies of Kenyan banks during the 1990s. "Financial Distress in Local Banks."

186. World Bank, *Kenya: Country Assistance Evaluation*. A draft of the document was circulated in 1998.

187. See Base Titanium, "Company Overview," accessed November 21, 2015, at http://basetitanium.com/company-profile/company-overview. Canadian and Chinese contractors were involved earlier in the mining project.

188. See Kenya Vision 2030, accessed November 28, 2015, at http://www.vision2030.go.ke.

189. Baobab Homes & Holidays Kenya, accessed November 21, 2015, at baobab-homes-holidays.com/pages/english/home-service.php?lang=NL.

190. In late 2013, the company's online platform was voted the No. 1 realtor in Kenya by one of the largest international real estate platforms, Mondinion. Worldwide they were listed as No. 9 among 8,933 real estate companies. See Mondinion, "Kenya Realtors & Real Estate Agents," accessed December 11, 2013, at http://www.mondinion.com/Real_Estate_Agents/country/Kenya/.

191. For a summary of the key changes, see Coulson Harney Advocates, "Snapshot," especially "(b) Pre-emption rights on expired grants."

192. I thank Professor Mochoge of the Department of Agricultural Resource Management at Kenyatta University for pointing out this alternate meaning of the Mombasa Republican Council's rallying cry.

193. Ndungu, "Tackling Land Related Corruption," 5.

194. For an overview, see Coulson Harney Advocates, "Snapshot."

195. Kazungu, Atieno, and Mwanbeo, "A Week Later."

196. This method, most often associated with ideas voiced by Guy Debord and other Situationists, proved to be the most appropriate and successful for immersing myself in the area and exploring Diani.

197. I use various names for my research assistants throughout this study to protect their privacy.

198. The fact that women are often not registered on title deeds is a major issue of contention in divorce cases.

199. The number of children from mixed marriages is difficult to estimate; it might be somewhere between 100 and 150. Many African Kenyan partners already have children at the time of entering a relationship with a European, and many European women are beyond childbearing age. The largest percentage of children living in mixed households are African Kenyan, including some who have been adopted. See also the discussion in chapter 3, "Charity," and table 14 (appendix).

200. Eidgenössisches Departement für auswärtige Angelegenheiten EDA, *Auslandschweizerstatistik*, 4; data for Austrians per email communication with the Austrian Embassy in Nairobi (Gerald Golatz, Botschaftsrat [VA] und Konsul, Österreichische Botschaft Nairobi), February 11, 2015.

201. Several researchers argued to debunk this image during the 1960s and 1970s. Among other examples, Gillette's study "A Test of the Concept of Backwardness" shows that Digo men and women work no more or less than other ethnic groups. See also Gerlach, "Social Organization," 245.

202. Fanon, *Wretched of the Earth*, 44; Pearce, *Land Grabbers*, 61–62.

203. Kenya Coast Planners Ltd., *Report to the Government of Kenya*.

204. Barume, *Land Rights*, 75, 79.

205. Kenda Mutongi makes similar observations in her study of attitudes toward the former British colonizer. *Worries of the Heart*, 2–3.

3. Charity

1. Neither utsi nor mweria is mentioned in the classic accounts by Luther Paul Gerlach and Cynthia Gillette. Gerlach focuses primarily on kinship relations, but he does mention the term *adui ya utsi*, which he translates as "enemy of the people." "Social Organisation," 276, 302. Gillette, who considers questions of labor among the Digo, offers a discussion of two additional forms of communal support and acknowledges (in 1978) the "disappearance of reciprocal labor exchange and village-wide labour groups." "Test of the Concept of Backwardness," 142.

2. The term "able-bodied" was used by villagers I interviewed.

3. For a description of collection efforts for a *mahanga*, see Gerlach, "Social Organisation," 174–197.

4. Gerlach provides a discussion of *uganga* in ibid., 428–443.

5. Among other customs that were described as utsi were fishing with a big net (*dzuja*) and fishing with a big box (*kuvua matole*).

6. Gerlach reports a different use of the term mweria, one tied to a division of Digo society into generation sets that "expired by the end of the 19th century." "Social Organisation," 243. Earlier anthropological accounts also mention the term in this sense.

7. Gillette, "Test of the Concept of Backwardness," 132, 74.

8. Ibid., 139–141.

9. Gerlach, "Social Organisation," 104.

10. Ngau, "Tensions in Empowerment," 523.

11. Ibid., 528–530, 533.

12. Orvis, "Bringing Institutions Back," 103–106. See Barbara P. Thomas-Slayter for the benefits of *harambee* to the Kikuyu community. "Class, Ethnicity, and the Kenyan State," 306, 309.

13. Jennifer A. Widner writes that "harambee already existed in an uninstitutionalized form when Kenyatta took power." This assessment does not capture the fact that harambee was built upon existing institutions that had essentially and effectively sustained communities. *Rise of a Party-State*, 61.

14. Mambo, "Nascent Political Activities," 97.

15. See also ibid., 108–109.

16. The Utsi Society supported the Kenyan African Union and Kenyatta. Salim, *Swahili-speaking Peoples*, 215.

17. Feierman, "Reciprocity and Assistance," 4, 21.

18. Ibhawoh, *Imperialism and Human Rights*, 23.

19. Though increasing, initiatives such as the 2011 fundraiser "Kenyans for Kenya," which was coordinated by the Kenya Red Cross in collaboration with local corporations in response

to the famine in the Turkana area, remain rare. For a summary of the fundraiser, see Kenya Red Cross, "Kenyans 4 Kenya."

20. Deutsches Zentralinstitut für soziale Fragen, "Spendenbilanz 2013," 1. Deutscher Spendenrat suggests a lower figure, approximately €4.7 billion; see Deutscher Spendenrat e.V., "Bilanz des Helfens 2014," 6, 9.

21. Ullrich, *Wohin fließen die Spenden?*, 12; Betterplace Lab, SlideShare, "Spenden in Deutschland 2015," slide 20, "Zwei Drittel der Spenden für humanitäre Hilfe," accessed May 2016 at http://www.slideshare.net/betterplacelab/spenden-in-deutschland-2015.

22. Deutsches Zentralinstitut für soziale Fragen, "Deutschland."

23. "Für die Flutopfer in Pakistan spendeten Herr und Frau Schweizer über 42 Millionen Franken." Müller, "Schweizer spenden Millionen."

24. "Die Glückskette hat innerhalb eines Monats rund 20 Millionen Franken Spenden für Ostafrika erhalten." "Schweizer spenden fleissig für Ostafrika."

25. "Spendenvolumen in der Schweiz wieder gestiegen."

26. Fundraising Verband Austria, *Spendenbericht 2013*, 1–2.

27. Ibid., 7.

28. Ibid., 3.

29. Global Impact, *2013 Assessment of US Giving*, 4. Figures are based on *Giving USA 2013* and other reports published by the Lilly School of Philanthropy.

30. See, for example, Fundraising Verband Austria, *Spendenbericht 2013*, "Warum und wie spenden die ÖsterreicherInnen," 6.

31. The United States has a comparable domestic history of "good intentions" that focuses on improving the situation of, among others, African Americans. Ryan, *Grammar of Good Intentions*.

32. See Linda Polman's critique of Dunant, whom she juxtaposes with Florence Nightingale, who argued that "voluntary efforts, which reduced the expense faced by war ministries, merely made it easier for governments to engage in wars more often and for longer." *Crisis Caravan*, 5; see also 2–7. See also John F. Hutchinson, *Champions of Charity*, who discusses the larger cast of activists who founded the organization, demonstrating that the Red Cross often functioned to support militarism.

33. Berman, "Civilizing Mission."

34. See, among others, Quataert, *Staging Philanthropy*; Prelinger, *Charity, Challenge, and Change*; Arbeiterwohlfahrt Bundesverband, *Humanitäres Handeln aus politischer Verantwortung*.

35. Heinl and Lingelbach, "Spendenfinanzierte private Entwicklungshilfe." See also Lingelbach, *Spenden und Sammeln*.

36. Wildenthal, *Language of Human Rights*, 11.

37. Rothberg, *Multidirectional Memory*; for a discussion of the new concept of the "Responsibility to Protect," see Hilpold, *Die Schutzverantwortung*.

38. Angel et al., *Community Lost*; Levitt and Whitaker, *Hurricane Katrina*; Klein, *Shock Doctrine*, 406–416.

39. For a discussion of contemporary faith-based development in Zimbabwe, see Bornstein, *Spirit of Development*. Naomi Klein, *Shock Doctrine*, highlights the centrality of disaster for the functioning of contemporary capitalism. Essays in Sarat and Lezaun, eds., *Catastrophe*, emphasize the consequences of natural and manufactured catastrophe on law and politics more broadly.

40. Fassin, *Humanitarian Reason*, 7; Muehlebach, *Moral Neoliberal*. See also the discussion in chapter 1 of this book regarding the moral economy.

41. Mortenson and Relin, *Three Cups of Tea*. See also Krakauer, who exposes Mortenson's fraudulent scheme in *Three Cups of Deceit*.

42. In 1981, the late Böhm founded Menschen für Menschen, an organization dedicated to providing humanitarian assistance to Ethiopia. See Menschen für Menschen, accessed November 1, 2015, at http://www.menschenfuermenschen.de. A German version of Bob Geldof's Band-Aid concert was organized by Herbert Grönemeyer in 1985; Band für Afrika produced a single, "Nackt im Wind," and gave a concert in July 1985. In 2011, the Bavarian soccer organization, in conjunction with the Philipp Lahm Foundation, promoted a fundraiser in support of projects in Africa. See "Tore für Afrika," accessed November 1, 2015, at http://www.philipplahm.de/fileadmin/Dateien/stiftung/pdf/Ankuendigungsschreiben_fuer_HPs.pdf.

43. Anne Orford, for example, writes that "some of the appeal of the idea of humanitarian intervention lies in the moral authority of the notion of democracy." *Reading Humanitarian Intervention*, 18.

44. For select studies on the discourse of human rights, see, among others, Heinze, "Reality and Hyper-reality of Human Rights"; for a comparative study on human rights discourses and agency, see Khor, *Human Rights Discourse*; for a study of the literary deployment of the human rights discourse, see Slaughter, *Human Rights, Inc.*; for a study of human rights discourses in West Germany, see Wildenthal, *Language of Human Rights*; see also Kaul and Kim, *Imagining Human Rights*.

45. A web-based search for relevant organizations yields, among others, the following examples: Ukunda-Hilfe, Wir helfen in Ukunda, Projekt Ukunda, Keniahilfe, Kenia Kinder Hilfe, Kenia-Hilfe Köln, Keniahilfe Schwäbische Alb, Keniahilfe Buxheim, Keniahilfe Essen, Hermann Marx Kenia Hilfe, Lebenshilfe für Afrika, Afrika-Hilfe, Hilfe für Afrika, Afrika-Hilfe-Stiftung, Hilfe für Kinder in Afrika, Wasser für Senegal, Hilfe für Namibia, Ghanahilfe, Madamfo Ghana, Asante Tansania, Tansania Hilfe Braunschweig, Kinderhilfe in Ruanda, Projekt Schwarz-Weiß, and Kinderrechte Afrika.

46. A number of academic studies and a large archive of newspaper and other media reports discuss the effect of German tourists in Thailand, Tunisia, Turkey, the Canary Islands, Spain, and other popular destinations. For a study documenting relations between Germans and locals on Mallorca, see Waldren, *Insiders and Outsiders*; for a study on the effect of retirement migration, see Breuer, "Retirement Migration."

47. For a discussion of the activities of repeat visitors in Diani during the 1990s, see "Tourism: Repeat Visitors Turned Aid Workers in Kenya," in Berman, *Impossible Missions?*, 175–212, 221–233.

48. To ensure anonymity, I have changed the names of all individuals I interviewed, along with altering other aspects of their stories.

49. Polman, "MONGOs," in *Crisis Caravan*, 48–62. Polman argues that nobody knows how many MONGOs (My Own NGO) exist (p. 53).

50. In Berman, "Contraband Charity: German Humanitarianism in Contemporary Kenya," I discuss the activities of the Müllers in the context of historical patterns of aid to Africa.

51. I also maintained email contact with Müller throughout that period, during which he shared with me the regular publications of his organization. In addition, I followed up on the information he provided me (for example, regarding the prices of items he bought and projected building costs), interviewed some of his local contacts, and corroborated information about school principals and other beneficiaries with whom Müller and his organization interact.

52. I interviewed Bäumler in 2012, 2013, and 2014; I also interviewed two local African Kenyans who knew her well and one of her Swiss friends. In addition, her efforts were mentioned often in conversations over the years.

53. Moyo, *Dead Aid*, 7; for a brief overview of the recent history of aid to Africa, see pp. 10–28.

54. Lancaster, *Aid to Africa*, 4.

55. The literature on INGO activities is substantial and controversial. Among relevant titles that focus specially on highly visible INGOs are Missoni and Alesani, *Management of International Institutions and NGOs*; Redfield, *Life in Crisis*; Horton and Roche, *Ethical Questions and International NGOs*; Rubenstein, "Distributive Commitments of International NGOs"; and Porter, Smyth, and Sweetman, *Gender Works*. For a discussion of human rights INGOs, see, among others, publications by Amanda Murdie, including "Ties That Bind."

56. Jan Verkaart founded Verkaart Groep, a company specializing in technical installation and employing about 160 employees; see Verkaart Groep, accessed November 22, 2015, at http://www.verkaart.nl/particulier.

57. See the website of the Verkaart Development Team at http://www.vdt.nl (accessed May 2016). I interviewed a representative of the organization in 2007, visited a number of the schools sponsored by the Verkaart Development Team, and interviewed individuals, including governmental officials, who interact with the organization.

58. Since 2007, the primary schools are developed through Tenda Pamoja, which emerged from the Verkaart Development Team. See Tenda Pamoja, "Stichting Tenda Pamoja Kenia," accessed November 22, 2015, at http://www.tendapamoja.nl/index.php/organisatie/anbi.

59. Verkaart Development Team, "Reizen," accessed May 2016, at http://www.vdt.nl.

60. *Watoto* is Kiswahili for "children."

61. See Eine Welt Stiftung, accessed November 22, 2015, at http://eineweltstiftung.de. Additional information about the history can be found on the website of Watoto e.V. under "Die Historie," accessed May 2016, at http://www.watoto.de/ueber-uns/#historie/.

62. Mekaela Academies, "Our Services," accessed November 1, 2015, at http://mekaela.co.ke/index.php/en/our-services.

63. See the agency's website at http://nobleda.com/ (accessed May 2016).

64. Micki Wentzel, email exchange July 18, 2014.

65. Micki Wentzel, email exchange, July 18, 2014.

66. Girls' Hope e.V., "Wir über uns," accessed November 1, 2015, at http://www.girlshope.de/.

67. Girls' Hope e.V., "Finanzen," accessed November 1, 2015, at http://www.girlshope.de/.

68. See betterplace.org at https://www.betterplace.org/de/; Bildungsspender at https://www.bildungsspender.de/; and Rolf Buscher Stiftung at http://www.rolf-buscher-stiftung.de/ (all accessed November 22, 2015). Other fundraising activities included a collaboration with a Dutch university and a group of students who collected refundable bottles; ticket sales for the Biennale in Berlin; shoes and shirts donated by the soccer club Schalke 04 that were auctioned on eBay; fundraising at the Christmas Market in Mühlheim; donations by individual organizations (Schulfreunde in Kenia, Bündnis 90/Die Grünen); and various social events organized by individuals and groups such as Rotary for Women and the Soroptimists in Gelsenkirchen. The Futura Stiftung, the Miranda Lux Foundation (based in San Francisco), and the Sternstunden Stiftung are some other key sponsors.

69. Girls' Hope e.V., "Finanzen: Jahresbericht 2013," 5, accessed November 1, 2015, at http://girlshope.de.

70. This international organization of business and professional women lobbies and volunteers to empower women and girls worldwide. For the German branch, see Soroptimist International Deutschland, accessed November 22, 2015, at http://www.soroptimist.de/home/.

71. The website that provided details on the program has been discontinued.

72. As of 2015, Global Care has supported projects in more than fifty-two countries. See the Global Care website at http://www.global-care.knorr-bremse.com/en/.

73. Bundesministerium für wirtschaftliche Zusammenarbeit und Entwicklung, "Weltwärts: Der entwicklunspolitische Freiwilligendienst," accessed November 22, 2015. http://

www.bmz.de/de/was_wir_machen/wege/bilaterale_ez/zwischenstaatliche_ez/freiwillligendi
enst/index.html.

74. Girls' Hope e.V., "Praktika im Ausland," accessed May 2016, at http://www.girlshope.de.

75. Girls' Hope e.V., "Praktikumsdokumentation" and "FAQ's," both accessed November 2015, at http://www.girlshope.web-devel.net/de/Dokumente/Praktikantendoku.pdf and http://www.girlshope.web-devel.net/de/Dokumente/FAQ2014.pdf, respectively.

76. Girls' Hope e.V., "Praktikumsvertrag," accessed November 1, 2015, at http://www.girlshope.web-devel.net/de/Dokumente/Prakvertrag2014.pdf.

77. Deputy President William Ruto announced an internship program for college graduates a few months after my conversation with Langefeld on the issue. See DPPS, "Kenya to Launch Volunteer Programme."

78. See, for example, articles on the interactions between colonizers and colonized in Berman, Mühlhahn, and Nganang, *German Colonialism Revisited.*

79. See Racine and Perron, "Unmasking the Predicament of Cultural Voyeurism," 190–201. See also Swan, "I'm Not a Tourist."

80. See First Community Church, accessed November 22, 2015, at http://fcchurch.com/mexico/. For other volunteer and intern programs, see Projects Abroad, "Volunteer and Intern in Mexico," accessed November 22, 2015, at http://www.projects-abroad.org/volunteer-destinations/volunteer-mexico/.

81. Asner, Foreword.

82. Adams and Borland, Introduction, 5.

83. Benson, Introduction, 1. Benson also provides an overview of the research on the subject (p. 2).

84. Ouma et al., *Estimating the Size of the Underground Economy,* iii.

85. Perlin, *Intern Nation,* xvii. Perlin's critique of unpaid internships focuses mostly on the situation in the United States.

86. While research on the extent of the informal economy and on the role of remittances in economies of the global south has steadily increased, I have not been able to find discussion and particularly figures detailing the economic effect of international volunteering.

87. Prevost, "Assessing Women," 765, 768, 771.

88. Wildenthal, *German Women for Empire,* 13.

89. Ibid. For the German case, see also Mamozai, *Herrenmenschen*; and Bechhaus-Gerst and Leutner, *Frauen in den deutschen Kolonien.* For a discussion of the writings of female British philanthropists, see Richardson, "Women, Philanthropy, and Imperialism."

90. See East Africa Women's League, accessed November 22, 2015, at http://eawl.org/index.html. Prevost designates the period after World War I as the "heyday of women's missionary institutions." "Assessing Women," 782.

91. Van Tol, "Women of Kenya Speak," 435, and throughout. See also Shadle, *Souls of White Folk,* 87, 94, 97, 99, 100, 104, 106.

92. Van Tol, "Women of Kenya Speak," 442.

93. The argument about money and work was also mentioned in 2012 and 2013. I interviewed chairs and members of the organization between 2009 and 2014; in addition, I observed activities of the organization during fieldwork in 2005, 2007, and 2009–2010.

94. See, for example, a 2010 video that comments on tapestries made by EAWL members in 1958 and clearly glorifies the colonial past. "East Africa Women's League—1958 Tapestries," YouTube. Posted by FarmFieldFireside, June 5, 2001, at https://www.youtube.com/watch?v=k3c36LA-WGA.

95. See van Tol, "Women of Kenya Speak." Recent scholarship has been able to sketch a more nuanced picture of the interplay between imperialist and feminist dynamics in missionary

and civilizing work. See the comprehensive overview of scholarship on these topics in Prevost, "Assessing Women."

96. Van Tol writes that "the League also deemed poor whites undesirable." "Women of Kenya Speak," 443.

97. East Africa Women's League, "South Coast Branch" and "Mombasa Branch," both accessed November 22, 2015, at http://eawl.org/South%20Coast%20Branch.html and http://eawl.org/Mombasa%20Branch.html, respectively.

98. That program was largely run by one EAWL member who set it up and used her own money to keep it running.

99. In 2010, a Dutch woman without relevant professional background mismanaged an organization in Kwale County intended to help disabled children. She ran a boarding institution even before she received government approval. Once her funding structure proved to be insufficient, the children, who had been removed from often dismal living conditions and undergone a difficult process of adjustment, had to be sent back home, often to the dismay of parents.

100. Among the studies that focus on evaluating INGO practices are Wood, Apthorpe, and Borton, *Evaluating International Humanitarian*; Steinberg, Herzberg, and Berman, *Best Practices*; Schoenhaus, *Training for Peace*; and Eade and Ligteringen, *Debating Development*.

101. See, among others, Leo, "Is Anyone Listening?" For a discussion of community participation from a Panafricanist perspective, see Adejumobi, "Popular Participation."

102. See, for example, Rotary International, *Communities in Action*," which stresses the need to involve communities at any level of project planning and execution.

103. Christoffel Blindenmission, "Es gibt eine Milliarde behinderte Menschen," accessed November 29, 2015, at https://www.cbm.de/unsere-arbeit/daten-und-fakten/Zahlen-und-Fakten-412965.html.

104. Christoffel Blindenmission emphasizes work with local partners and communities and explicitly states that it "does not support the 'charity model' of disability and of rehabilitation." *CBM Disability and Development Policy*, 6.

105. World Health Organization, Disability and Rehabilitation, various publications on "Community Based Rehabilitation (CBR)," accessed May 2016, at http://www.who.int/disabilities/publications/cbr/en/. See also Peat, *Community Based Rehabilitation*.

106. Christoffel Blindenmission, "Politische Arbeit," accessed November 1, 2015, at https://www.cbm.de/unsere-arbeit/politische-arbeit/index_396474.html; see also the United Nations webpage "We Can End Poverty," which is dedicated to the millennium development goals; accessed November 22, 2015, at http://www.un.org/millenniumgoals/.

107. For representative case studies regarding stigma, discrimination, and coping mechanisms of children with disabilities and their caregivers in coastal Kenya, see Gona, Newton, and Hartley, "Caring for Children"; and El Sharkawy, Newton, and Hartley, "Attitudes and Practices."

108. Republic of Kenya, *Persons with Disabilities Act*. In 2007, a workshop was held in Nairobi with the goal of assessing the situation of persons with disabilities in Kenya. See contributions in Armstrong et al., *Disability in Kenya*.

109. Republic of Kenya, *Persons with Disabilities Act*, Section 16, "Incentives to Employers": "A private employer who engages a person with a disability with the required skills or qualifications either as a regular employee, apprentice or learner shall be entitled to apply for a deduction from his taxable income equivalent to twenty five percent of the total amount paid as salary and wages to such employee."

110. Regarding the challenges persons with disabilities face in Kenya, see, for example, the April 2014 interview of Jeff Koinange by Winne Orwa and Karani Kinyua at KTN news,

"Jeff Koinange Live with The Cluster Foundation," accessed May 2016, at www.standardme-dia.co.ke/ktn/?videoID=2000077150&video_title=jeff-koinange-live-with-winne-orwa-and -karani-kinyua-beyond-disability.

111. I have been visiting and following the events at KDEC since 2005.

112. See CBM's web page on the Kwale District Eye Centre, accessed November 1, 2015, at https://www.cbm.de/projekte/Kwale_District_Eye_Centre-393024.php.

113. Eyes for East Africa, "Supporters" and "Contact Us," both accessed November 1, 2015, at http://www.eyesforeastafrica.org/supporters.html and http://www.eyesforeastafrica.org /contact-us.html, respectively.

114. Diani Rules, accessed November 22, 2015, at http://www.dianirules.com/.

115. Eyes for East Africa, "Statistics," accessed November 1, 2015, at http://www.eyesforeast africa.org/statistics.html.

116. Information provided per email by Catherine Jakaiti Ogeya, August 10, 2009.

117. Hoenig, "'Missionary' Redefined," 15–16; see also Eyes for East Africa, "Our Staff," ac-cessed July 10, 2016, at http://www.eyesforeastafrica.org/our-staff.html.

118. I thank Catherine Jakaiti Ogeya for the time she took to explain operations at KDEC in July 2005 and for allowing me to attend the screening in Tiwi in June 2007. I also thank Dr. Helen Roberts for providing additional information in numerous email exchanges and conversations over the years.

119. The main principles of Sightsavers are health, education, social inclusion, and commu-nity participation. An emphasis on the role of governments in the process of attaining goals in these areas is evident in an overview at Sightsavers, "Policy and Research," accessed November 1, 2015, at http://www.sightsavers.org/policy-and-research/.

120. Kwale District Eye Centre, "Brochure," 2010. Copy in the author's possession.

121. Eyes for East Africa, "More Statistics," accessed November 1, 2015, at http://www.eyes foreastafrica.org/statistics-prev-yrs.html.

122. World Bank, "Poverty Rates."

123. Media reports lamenting mismanagement in the Kenyan health-care sector are ubiquitous; see, for example, Transparency International Kenya, "Tackling Corruption Key in Improving Access," January 31, 2011, at http://www.transparency.org/news/pressre lease/20110131_quality_healthcare. For additional reports published by Transparency Interna-tional Kenya, see http://www.tikenya.org/.

124. Fassin, *Humanitarian Reason*; Muehlebach, *Moral Neoliberal*.

125. Mann, *From Empires to NGOs*.

126. See chapter 1 of this book. A positive view of foreign aid to Kenyan educational insti-tutions, one that ignores the larger effect of such aid, is provided by Colclough, "Triumph of Hope over Reason?"

127. Interviews with government officials, who chose to remain anonymous, took place in 2010, 2011, 2012, and 2013.

128. See EDUWEB, "Primary Schools in Kwale," accessed November 1, 2015, at http:// www.eduweb.co.ke/listings.php?t=primary&pr=Kwale&p_id=11&pagi=80. This database on schools in Kwale is incomplete but provides a sense for the number of schools in the county.

129. Moyo, *Dead Aid*, 49. The argument is also made at length by George B. N. Ayittey in *Af-rica in Chaos*. See also Michaela Wrong's account of the story of John Githongo (*It's Our Turn to Eat*). While Wrong's narrative is often sensationalist and conceptually flawed, Githongo's descriptions of Kenyan graft and corruption are chilling.

130. An Internet search turns up numerous articles related to corruption in Kenya's educa-tional and health-care sectors; see, for example, Voice of America, "Corruption Puts Kenya's

Educational Funding at Risk," June 19, 2011, at http://www.voanews.com/content/article—corruption-puts-kenyas-educational-funding-at-risk-124203949/158335.html.

131. See Transparency International Kenya, *Kenyan Health Sector Integrity Study Report.*

132. While the relationship between philanthropy and tax write-offs is well researched within the Western world, few studies address the issue with regard to global humanitarian aid. See, for example, Pinheiro, "Drug Donations."

133. See Bate, Hess, and Mooney, "Antimalarial Medicine Diversion."

134. Siringi, "AIDS Drugs Being Sold Illegally"; Crumplin, "EU Reimporting Drugs Meant for Africa."

135. For a comparative case of linguistic subversion during the period of colonial rule, see Nyada, "'Germans cannot master our language!'"

136. Digo practices in this regard differ from what China Scherz (*Having People, Having Heart*) has observed in rural Uganda, where material contributions from INGOs are preferred to self-sustainability projects, as the former match more closely indigenous forms of solidarity.

137. Achille Mbembe (*On the Postcolony*) provides an account of the continuities of colonial structures in postcolonial African states.

138. See essays on the situation of youth and youth culture in Njogu and Oluoch-Olunya, *Cultural Production and Social Change*; Njogu, *Culture, Performance and Identity.*

139. According to Fredrick O. Wanyama, data on successful community-based initiatives in Kenya remain scarce. "Grass-roots Organization for Sustainable Development," 56.

140. The question of communal solidarity across the country requires comparative research. Media reports about individual cases of humanitarian support extended by Kenyans to other Kenyans, especially *beyond* ethnic and family solidarity, highlight how rare these instances are in the country. The story of Joseph Kamau and his wife Lucy Muthoni, who supported five orphaned children from an ethnic group other than their own on his meager salary, is exceptional in many ways but also highlights the tremendous need that exists in Kenya. Kimani and Mwololo, "Would You Have Done What He Did?"

141. Gomm, "Harlots and Bachelors," 105. Gerlach, in his 1960 study, referred to the unwillingness of Digo to "work for others," including "other Africans." "Social Organisation," 11–12. Gillette's 1978 study ("Test of the Concept of Backwardness") is an attempt to refute the idea that the Digo are "backward" and "lazy." Oendo also emphasizes the importance of free birth to Digo. "Marriage Instability and Domestic Continuity," 47.

142. The organization was founded by Eileen Willson and later folded into the government-run District Health Stakeholders' Forum. See Berman, "Negotiating Local Knowledge."

143. Mwangi is an outspoken critic of Western humanitarianism. See Hermann, "An African's Message for America."

144. Central Intelligence Agency, "Population Below Poverty Line"; Kenya National Bureau of Statistics, "Poverty Rate by District."

145. According to Carole Adelman, "these three private financial flows from all donor nations to developing nations account for 83 percent of the industrialized world's economic dealings with poor countries. Official flows are only 17 percent." "Global Philanthropy and Remittances," 23–24.

146. Mann, *From Empires to NGOs*; Amutabi, *NGO Factor in Africa*; Buffett, "Charitable-Industrial Complex."

147. The literature on these topics is vast and controversial. For recent discussions of alternatives to the current situations, see Fee, *How to Manage an Aid Exit Strategy*; Brenton, *Africa Can Help Feed Africa*; Johnson, "Lobbying for Trade Barriers"; and Suttle, "Equality in Global Commerce."

148. Schama, *Embarrassment of Riches*, 326.

149. "*The Samaritans* is a snarky, scripted series centered around the absurdities of Aid for Aid, a dysfunctional, fictitious non governmental organization (NGO). In the Kenya field office, the cosmopolitan staff deal with the strange demands and decisions of UK headquarters and hopelessly inept local bureaucracies, all under the guise of 'Saving Africa.'" From *The Samaritans: Aid for Aid* at http://www.aidforaid.org.

4. Romance

1. In May 2013, for example, a pornography franchise led by Swiss national Christopher Clement Weissenrieder made headlines for several weeks.

2. Kibicho, *Sex Tourism in Africa*, 22. For studies on child sex tourism, see O'Connell Davidson, *Children in the Global Sex Trade*; Seabrook, *No Hiding Place*; and various contributions in Oppermann, *Sex Tourism and Prostitution*.

3. Kibicho, *Sex Tourism in Africa*, 19, 20. Kibicho draws on data by K. Ndune and the Provincial Tourism Liaison Committee.

4. Kibicho's study *Sex Tourism in Africa* is the most comprehensive and recent investigation of prostitution on the coast; it includes a comprehensive bibliography. Among the German-language studies Kibicho does not consider is Kleiber and Wilke, *Aids, Sex und Tourismus*.

5. David Jamison ("Brotherhood of Coconuts"), who has an otherwise good sense of the various social groups in Malindi, does not mention romantic relations or marriage between Kenyans and tourists. The same is true for Schoss, "Beach Tours and Safari Visions."

6. Williams, *Sex Tourism in Bahia*; Cabezas, *Economies of Desire*; Schifter-Sikora, *Mongers in Heaven*; Briggs, *Reproducing Empire*.

7. Eva Kurt, whose research dates back to the early 1980s, suggested that meaningful cross-cultural interaction between tourists and locals was "an illusion." *Tourismus in die Dritte Welt*, 70. A study conducted in the early 1980s by a Kenyan research team suggested the "on the whole, most of the residents have little interaction with tourists other than seeing them" and that the "nature of interaction between the local residents and the tourists is largely in business." Migot-Adholla, Mkangi, and Mbindyo, *Study of Tourism in Kenya*, 109.

8. Schurian-Bremecker observes that some tourists get married and have long-term relationships with Kenyans but focuses on prostitution. *Kenia in der Sicht deutscher Touristen*, 263–266, 279.

9. Oppermann, *Sex Tourism and Prostitution*, 158.

10. Brennan, *What's Love Got to Do with It?*

11. See contributions in Cole and Thomas, eds., *Love in Africa*.

12. See graph in Kibicho, *Sex Tourism in Africa*, 76. Kibicho's analysis provides significant detail on the economic factors engendering Kenya's sex tourism industry. See especially the chapter "Socio-economic Base of Sex Tourism," 121–141.

13. For an example of the kind of story that circulates in Kenya, see Oketch, "Pharmacist, 50, Finds Love."

14. For a discussion of the shift of the German interest in East Africa more broadly (with its roots in the colonial period) to Kenya in the postwar period, see chapter 1.

15. Corinne Hofmann published three additional autobiographical books, *Zurück aus Afrika* (2003), *Wiedersehen in Barsaloi* (2005), and *Afrika, meine Passion* (2011). The movie was directed by Hermine Huntgeburth.

16. The Kenya segment of the series *Der Traummann—Liebe ohne Grenzen* was aired on RTL on May 7, 2014.

17. The reality show was aired on RTL in the summer of 2013. For a critique of the show's propagation of colonial clichés, see Frank, "Kritik an 'RTL-Wild Girls.'"

18. Among others, Sparrer, *Wo die Liebe hinfällt*; Fisseler-Skandrani, *Die Maghrebländer*; Abdel Aziz, *Binationale Ehe zwischen Muslimen und Nichtmuslimen*; Basel and Frick, *Tapas zum Abendbrot*; Kern, *1001 Tausendundeine Lüge*; and Ismail, *Mein Ägypter ist anders!*

19. For instance, Catherine Oddie's *Enkop Ai: My Life with the Maasai* (1994; translated as *Enkop Ai: Mein Leben als weiße Massai*, 1996) and Francesca Marciano's *Rules of the Wild: A Novel of Africa* (1998; translated as *Himmel über Afrika*, 1999). Kuki Gallmann, who became famous for her autobiography *I Dreamed of Africa* (1991), offered German readers more stories about Kenya in translation, such as *Afrikanische Nächte* (1999), *Ich träumte von Afrika* (2000), and *Die Nacht der Löwen* (2001).

20. For select book publications, see Schmalmack, *Türkischer Honig auf Schwarzbrot*; Wasmundt, *Der Heuchler aus dem Morgenland*; Wallen-Lundy et al., *Liebesgeschichten*; and Mtawa, *Sternendiebe*.

21. 1001Geschichte.de, "Willkommen auf 1001Geschichte.de," accessed November 28, 2015, at http://www.1001geschichte.de.

22. A movie version with Sally Field as Betty Mahmoody was released in 1991.

23. Woesthoff, "Foreigners and Women," 422–442.

24. See also Hilliges, *Eine Liebe in Kenia*; Hachfeld-Tapukai, *Mit der Liebe einer Löwin*; Hachfeld-Tapukai, *Der Himmel über Maralal*; and Greshake, *Wir lieben Kenia*.

25. For a discussion of the distinctions between twenty-five "direct" and "indirect" forms of prostitution, see Harcourt and Donovan, "Many Faces," 201–206. See sections on the behavior of female tourists in Kibicho, *Sex Tourism in Africa*, especially chapter 5, "Kenya's Tourism Industry," 97–119.

26. Kibicho suggests that in the present period, female sex tourists outnumber male sex tourists; accordingly, direct prostitution is offered primarily by Kenyan women while indirect prostitution is pursued by both sexes. *Sex Tourism in Africa*, 75. For a study on female sex and romance tourists in Egypt, see Jacobs, *Sex, Tourism and the Postcolonial Encounter*.

27. Cabezas, *Economies of Desire*, 8. Kibicho states that 60 percent of respondents to a survey she conducted with female tourists "did not perceive their encounters as CSW-client transactions, nor did they view their partners as CSWs." *Sex Tourism in Africa*, 103.

28. "People equally envied, admired, and chastised them [sex workers] for their ability to navigate the social and economic changes taking place." Cabezas, *Economies of Desire*, 2; Luise White writes that "women saw prostitution as a reliable means of capital accumulation, not as a despicable fate or a temporary strategy." *Comforts of Home*, 1–2.

29. Clearly a side effect of election-related violence and unrest, a significant drop in marriages of British citizens occurred in 2008 and 2009, to only about 13 percent and 15 percent, respectively, of the overall marriages registered for those years. No table is included here on marriage among British citizens, but data are available from the author.

30. A small margin of error exists in the calculation of the data because marriage licenses do not provide applicants' nationalities. Individuals list their names, ages, places of residence, and professions. In those (very few) cases in which Europeans indicated Kenya as the place of residence, I used their names as the basis to assess nationality, which increases the error margin by a small percentage, as differences between Swiss, Austrian, and German surnames are not obvious.

31. Berman, "Tourism," 226, table 4.

32. When conducting research in 2013 at the Office of the Registrar of Marriages in Mombasa I was told that, since 2010, the office was responsible for data from the entire coast. While the number of certificates increased significantly from 2004 to 2005, I saw no further increase after 2010 (tables 3 and 4).

33. Ministry of East African Affairs, Commerce and Tourism, Department of Tourism, "International Arrivals 2009"; table available from author.

34. Berman, "Tourism," 207.

35. The average age at first marriage in Austria, for example, was 29.8 for women and 32.2 for men (2013). Statistik Austria, "Eheschließungen." Data from Germany is comparable; see Bundesinstitut für Bevölkerungsforschung, "Durchschnittliches Heiratsalter."

36. Kibicho, *Sex Tourism in Africa*, 26, 27.

37. Anja Conradi-Freundschuh of the Statistisches Bundesamt Germany wrote: "Eheschließungen von Deutschen im Ausland können auf Antrag im Eheregister bei einem deutschen Standesamt nachbeurkundet werden. In der Statistik der Eheschließungen sind alle bei einem deutschen Standesamt geschlossenen Ehen und auch die nachbeurkundeten Eheschließungen enthalten." Email to the author, August 19, 2014.

38. Kenya National Bureau of Statistics, *Kenya Facts and Figures 2014*, 67, table 57.

39. "Wage Employment in Modern Sector, 2010–2013," ibid., 17, table 14.

40. O'Rourke, "To Have and to Hold," 476–497.

41. For Germany, see Schroedter, *Binationale Ehen in Deutschland*; Klein, "Intermarriages," 325–346; Woesthoff, "Foreigners and Women."

42. In most cases, partners arranged interviews so that they would meet me alone. I realized that most people would be more open with me if their partners were not present; thus I pursued interviews with both partners only when the situations seem conducive to a relaxed conversation.

43. See Breuer, "Retirement Migration?"

44. I interviewed both partners several times between January 2010 and December 2014.

45. *Flocke* ("flake") here is Berlin dialect for "beautiful woman."

46. I interviewed both partners several times and stayed in touch with Esther after the couple broke up in early 2012.

47. I interviewed only Thomas; since his relationship to Betsy seemed volatile, I decided not to pursue an interview with her, but I met her several times throughout my stays.

48. Besser, "Tropenkoller."

49. Sartre, Preface, li–lv. See also Fabian, *Out of Our Minds.*

50. I interviewed Rita and James frequently between 2010 and 2015.

51. See Jeff Koinange's interview with human rights activists Kennedy Odede and his US-born wife Jessica Posner on July 31, 2014. Koinange, "Jeff Koinange Live."

52. Verband binationaler Familien und Partnerschaften, "Wir über uns," accessed November 1, 2015, at http://www.verband-binationaler.de/index.php?id=wir-ueber-uns. For additional figures, see "Zahlen und Fakten," accessed November 28, 2015, at http://www.verband-binationaler.de/presse/zahlen-fakten/.

53. For Austria, see Medien-Servicestelle Neue Österreicher/innen, "Fast jede vierte Ehe ist binational," accessed August 22, 2013, at http://medienservicestelle.at/migration_bewegt/2012/04/17/fast-jede-vierte-ehe-ist-binational/; for Switzerland, see statistics provided by Interessengemeinschaft Binational, accessed November 29, 2015, at http://www.ig-binational.ch.

54. Lucassen and Laarman, "Immigration, Intermarriage," 58.

55. Menz, "By Tenderness and Flattery," 101.

56. See, for example, the website of the Swiss Union of Counseling Centers for Binational and Intercultural Couples and Families, particularly "Was ist bei binationalen Paaren anders?," accessed November 29, 2015, at http://www.binational.ch/de/?Vorbemerkungen___ Was_ist_bei_binationalen_Paaren_anders%3F.

57. "Msichana wa Kihindi."

58. For a definition and discussion of the concept, see Yeates, "Global Care Chains."

59. Oendo, "Marriage Instability," 49–50.

60. Gomm, "Harlots and Bachelors," 109.

61. Oendo, "Marriage Instability," 56.

62. Ibid., 56–57.

63. Gomm, "Harlots and Bachelors," 109.

64. Oendo, "Marriage Instability," 52.

65. Mraja, "Reform Ideas," 245–278.

66. Gomm, "Harlots and Bachelors," 95–96.

67. See the broad discussion of polygamy in the Kenyan media following news in early 2010 that South African president Jacob Zuma, who had five wives at the time, had fathered a child out of wedlock.

68. See Republic of Kenya, *Marriage Act.*

69. Gubernskaya, "Changing Attitudes," 189.

70. Kollman, *Same-Sex Unions*; Boele-Woelki and Fuchs, *Legal Recognition.*

71. Bodenmann et al., "Attractors and Barriers to Divorce," 1–23.

72. Numerous studies explore the representation of the subject in literature, film, and culture, but academic research is rare. According to data provided by the German agency Statista, 64 percent of women and 62 percent of men indicated that they knew about at least one affair of their partner. See "Wieviele Seitensprünge Ihres Partners in Ihrer jetzigen Beziehung, einschließlich des aktuellen, sind Ihnen (Frauen) bekannt?" and "Wieviele Seitensprünge Ihrer Partnerin in Ihrer jetzigen Beziehung, einschließlich des aktuellen, sind Ihnen (Männer) bekannt?" both accessed November 23, 2015, at http://de.statista.com. According to a 2013 poll by the Pew Research Center, 60 percent of Germans and 80 percent of Kenyans said that "married people having an affair is morally unacceptable." Wike, "French More Accepting of Infidelity."

73. See results of a survey regarding reasons to get married at Statista, "Was sind für Sie gute Gründe zu heiraten?," accessed November 23, 2015, at http://de.statista.com/statistik /daten/studie/291340/umfrage/umfrage-in-deutschland-zu-guten-gruenden-zum-heiraten.

74. Ortner, *Making Gender*, 182–183.

75. Mkenyaujerumani, "The German Who's Been Sweeping Streets," posted August 31, 2013, at mkenyaujerumani.de/2013/08/31/the-german-whos-been-sweeping-streets-in-mom basa-since-2009.

76. For a study on the clichés of African laziness, see Gronemeyer, *Der faule Neger.*

77. Auma Obama, President Barack Obama's sister, wrote her dissertation on Kenyan and German notions of labor. Obama, "Arbeitsauffassungen in Deutschland."

78. The militant Kenyan men's organization Maendeleo ya Wanaume suggests that "nearly 80 per cent of non-Kenyan men married to Kenyan wives living at the Coast are victims of domestic violence." Mwakio, "Foreign Husbands Prone to Wife Battery." My research indicates that this statement is exaggerated, but the relentless public debates over husband and wife battery indicate that many Kenyan marriages display significant degrees of physical violence. According to recent reports, men are more often victims than previously assumed, and many of these cases are the result of women defending themselves. In 2015, Kenya passed the

Prevention of Domestic Violence Act to address the widespread issue of domestic violence through preventive and protective measures.

79. McHugh, "Three Faces of Ageism," 176, 178, 165–185.

80. Benson and O'Reilly, "Migration and the Search for a Better Way of Life," 609, 607–625. See also Wallis, "Increasingly, Retirees Dump Their Possessions."

81. The trilogy-documentary *Oma will nach Thailand, Oma bleibt in Thailand,* and *Oma lebt in Thailand* tells the story of German seniors who have emigrated to Thailand, often because of lack of retirement funds. Directed by Wolfgang Luck, 2010–2014.

82. McHugh, "Three Faces of Ageism," 166. US retirement migration to Mexico and Central America is pronounced and growing. Between 2003 and 2005, for example, visas to Panama in the categories used by seniors "more than tripled"; see Papademetriou et al., *America's Emigrants,* 43.

83. Until 2014, the following requirements were applicable: "Class K: Residence permit issued to persons who have an assured income derived from sources outside and undertakes not to accept paid employment of any kind." Class K requirements are "documentary proof of assured income"; a nonrefundable processing fee of KSh10,000; and KSh100,000 "per year or part thereof. See Ministry of Interior, "Permits and Passes," accessed November 21, 2015, at http://www.immigration.go.ke/Information.html. Since then, requirements have become stricter, but German residents reported that in practice, the new rule requiring proof of an annual income of at least $24,000 was handled in flexible ways. For the requirements, as of 2016, see Ministry of Interior and Coordination of National Government, "Department of Immigration Services, Issuance of Kenya Entry Permits Checklist," http://www.immigration.go.ke/downloads/Checklist.pdf, accessed July 14, 2016.

84. Sunil, Rojas, and Bradley, for example, identify "financial circumstances, the natural environment, a sense of community and friendship, and a better quality of life" as the main reasons given for migrating to Mexico. "United States' International Retirement Migration," 489–510.

85. Kenyans who interact with tourists tend to simplify Kiswahili terms; in this case the more familiar singular *mzungu* was used instead of the grammatically correct plural *wazungu.* Greetings, such as "Hujambo," are also modified (to "Jambo") in order to adjust to or mimic the way tourists use the language.

86. For studies of communities that accept interracial relations for economic benefit, see Briggs, *Reproducing Empire*; Cabezas, *Economies of Desire*; Coquery-Vidrovitch, "Prostitution"; White, *Comforts of Home*; and Walther, "Sex and Control."

87. Analyses of transnationalism often emphasize the innovative effect of contemporary transnational flows whereas my discussion also acknowledges how previously existing factors (e.g., the colonial period and landownership issues) shape the transnational interaction. For a discussion of theoretical models of transnationalism, especially with regard to retirement migration, see Gustafson, "Transnationalism in Retirement Migration."

Epilogue

1. Burite, "German Tourist Killed"; VOA News, "German Tourist Killed."

2. Christiaensen, De Weerdt, and Todo, "Urbanization and Poverty Reduction."

3. For an overview of areas of economic activity, see the Kwale County Government website at http://www.kwalecountygov.com.

4. Nkirote, "Work Begins on Dongo Kundu Bypass."

5. Bocha, "Shıbn Ferries Plan to Ease Transport at Likoni."

6. See, for example, Tobias Chanji, "Reformed Al Shabaab Militant is Shot Dead," *Standard Digital*, accessed May 14, 2016, at http://www.standardmedia.co.ke/article/2000201708 /reformed-al-shabaab-militant-is-shot-dead.

7. See Human Rights Watch, *Playing with Fire*, 25–65.

8. Agence France Presse, "Kenya Closes NGOs in Security Crackdown."

9. Generally, *wazee* refers to both old men and women, but in practice, the term is used primarily to refer to old men.

10. Gramsci, *Prison Notebooks*, 48–52. For a discussion of the terms "subaltern," "spontaneity," and "common sense" in the work of Gramsci, see Green and Ives, "Subalternity and Language," 3–30.

11. Mazrui, *Chembe cha Moyo*, 6–7. I thank Ali Wasi for pointing me to this poem and Ken Walibora Waliaula for providing an original translation.

12. See suggestions made for addressing global inequality by Suttle in "Equality in Global Commerce."

Bibliography

Abdel Aziz, Mohamed. *Binationale Ehe zwischen Muslimen und Nichtmuslimen: Tipps und Empfehlungen für heiratswillige Paare.* Zürich: Diwan, 2010.

Abungu, Patrick O. "Kongo Mosque Heritage Site, Kwale, South Coast." Unpublished paper, September 2011, in the author's possession.

Adams, Abigail E., and Katherine Borland. Introduction to *International Volunteer Tourism: Critical Reflections on Good Works in Central America*, edited by Katherine Borland and Abigail E. Adams, 1–6. New York: Palgrave Macmillan, 2013.

Adejumobi, Said. "Popular Participation and Africa's Development Agenda: Projecting a Citizen-Based United States of Africa." *Politikon* 36, no. 3 (Dec. 2009): 403–422. doi: 10.1080/02589341003600213.

Adelman, Carole. "Global Philanthropy and Remittances: Reinventing Foreign Aid." *Brown Journal of World Affairs* 15, no. 2 (2009): 23–33.

Agence France Presse. "Kenya Closes NGOs in Security Crackdown after al-Shabaab Attacks." *Guardian*, December 16, 2014. http://www.theguardian.com/world/2014/dec/16/kenya-ngo-crackdown-al-shabaab.

Aktionskomitee Zürcher Entwicklungshilfe im In- und Ausland. "Antworten auf die Einwände gegen die Entwicklungshilfe." *Neue Wege* 66, no. 6 (1972): 188–191.

Ali, Abdulsamad. "Kenya: 'Squatters' Invade Hotel Land." *Daily Nation*, September 3, 2008. http://allafrica.com/stories/200809040029.html.

Amutabi, Maurice Nyamanga. *The NGO Factor in Africa: The Case of Arrested Development in Kenya.* New York: Routledge, 2006.

Anderson, David. *Histories of the Hanged: The Dirty War in Kenya and the End of Empire.* New York: Norton, 2005.

———. "Master and Servant in Colonial Kenya, 1895–1939." *Journal of African History* 41, no. 3 (2000): 459–485.

Angel, Ronald J., Holly Bell, Julie Beausoleil, and Laura Lein. *Community Lost: The State, Civil Society, and Displaced Survivors of Hurricane Katrina.* New York: Cambridge University Press, 2012.

Anglo-German Treaty [Heligoland-Zanzibar Treaty]. Berlin, 1890. Translated by Adam Blauhut. German History in Documents and Images. Accessed May 2016. http://germanhistorydocs.ghi-dc.org/pdf/eng/606_Anglo-German%20Treaty_110.pdf.

Arbeiterwohlfahrt Bundesverband. *Humanitäres Handeln aus politischer Verantwortung.* Bonn: Arbeiterwohlfahrt, Bundesverband, 1987.

Armstrong, Philip, Nina Berman, Kimani Njogu, and Mbugua wa-Mungai, eds. *Disability in Kenya: The Nairobi Workshop on Disability, Culture, and Human Rights.* Special issue, *Disability Studies Quarterly* 29, no. 4 (2009). http://dsq-sds.org/issue/view/42.

Asner, Ed. Foreword to *Volunteer Vacations: Short-Term Adventures That Will Benefit You and Others*, edited by Bill McMillon, Doug Cutchins, and Anne Geissinger, xiii–xiv. Chicago: Chicago Review Press, 2009.

Atkinson, Rowland, and Gary Bridge, eds. *Gentrification in a Global Context: The New Urban Colonialism*. London: Routledge, 2005.

Avery, Natalie. "Stealing from the State (Mexico, Hungary & Kenya)." In *50 Years Is Enough: The Case against the World Bank and the International Monetary Fund*, edited by Kevin Danaher, 95–101. Boston: South End, 1994.

Ayittey, George B. N. *Africa in Chaos*. New York: St. Martin's, 1998.

Baptist, Edward E. *The Half Has Never Been Told: Slavery and the Making of American Capitalism*. New York: Basic Books, 2014.

Barkham, Richard. *Real Estate and Globalisation*. Hoboken, NJ: Wiley-Blackwell, 2012.

Barnett, Michael. *Empire of Humanity: A History of Humanitarianism*. Ithaca, NY: Cornell University Press, 2011.

Barume, Albert Kwokwo. *Land Rights of Indigenous Peoples in Africa*. Copenhagen: International Work Group for Indigenous Affairs, 2010.

Basel, Nicole, and Marike Frick. *Tapas zum Abendbrot: Wie man eine internationale Beziehung (über)lebt*. Munich: Heyne, 2012.

Bate, Roger, Kimberly Hess, and Lorraine Mooney. "Antimalarial Medicine Diversion: Stock-outs and Other Public Health Problems." *Research and Reports in Tropical Medicine* 2010, no. 1 (2010): 19–24. doi: http://dx.doi.org/10.2147/RRTM.S13242.

Bechhaus-Gerst, Marianne, and Mechthild Leutner, eds. *Frauen in den deutschen Kolonien*. Berlin: Links, 2009.

"Begegnungen in Kenia." *Der Stern* 11 (1987): 96.

Benson, Angela. Introduction to *Volunteer Tourism: Theoretical Frameworks and Practical Applications*, edited by Angela M. Benson, 1–6. New York: Routledge, 2011.

Benson, Michaela, and Karen O'Reilly. "Migration and the Search for a Better Way of Life: A Critical Exploration of Lifestyle Migration." *Sociological Review* 57, no. 4 (2009): 608–625. doi: 10.1111/j.1467-954X.2009.01864.x.

Berg, F. J. "The Swahili Community of Mombasa, 1500–1900." *Journal of African History* 9, no. 1 (1968): 35–56. doi: http://dx.doi.org/10.1017/S0021853700008343.

Berman, Nina. "The Civilizing Mission: Albert Schweitzer in Gabon." In *Impossible Missions? German Economic, Military, and Humanitarian Efforts in Africa*, 61–97. Lincoln: University of Nebraska Press, 2004.

———. "Contraband Charity: German Humanitarianism in Contemporary Kenya." In *The History and Practice of Humanitarian Intervention and Aid in Africa*, edited by Bronwen Everill and Josiah Kaplan, 67–92. Houndmills, Basingstoke: Palgrave, 2013.

———. *Impossible Missions? German Economic, Military, and Humanitarian Efforts in Africa*. Lincoln: University of Nebraska Press, 2004.

———. "Negotiating Local Knowledge: Networking Disability on the Community Level." In *Disability in Kenya: The Nairobi Workshop on Disability, Culture, and Human Rights*, edited by Philip Armstrong, Nina Berman, Mbugua wa-Mungai, and Kimani Njogu. Special issue, *Disability Studies Quarterly* 29, no. 4 (November 2009). http://dsq-sds.org/article/view/967/1176.

———. "Neils Larssen: A Life Afloat." *South Coast Resident's Association Newsletter* 37 (August 2011): 4–5; and vol. 38 (September 2011): 3–4.

———. "Tourism: Repeat Visitors Turned Aid Workers in Kenya." In Nina Berman, *Impossible Missions? German Economic, Military, and Humanitarian Efforts in Africa*, 175–212, 219–233. Lincoln: University of Nebraska Press, 2004.

Berman, Nina, Klaus Mühlhahn, and Patrice Nganang. Introduction to *German Colonialism Revisited: African, Asian, and Oceanic Experiences*. 1–28. Ann Arbor: University of Michigan Press, 2014.

———, eds. *German Colonialism Revisited: African, Asian, and Oceanic Experiences*. Ann Arbor: University of Michigan Press, 2014.

Besser, Stephan. "Tropenkoller: Zur Psychopathologie des deutschen Kolonialismus." *Sozialistische Positionen*. Accessed November 21, 2015. http://www.sopos.org /aufsaetze/469c207f2308e/1.html.

Bin Shomari, Mwalimu Mbaraka. "Vita na Hassan bin Omari." In *Kala Shairi: German East Africa in Swahili Poems*, edited by Gundrun Miehe, Katrin Bromber, Said Khamis, and Ralf Großerhode, 294–303. Cologne: Rüdiger Koope, 2002.

Bocha, Galgalo. "Shɪbn Ferries Plan to Ease Transport at Likoni." *Daily Nation*, November 5, 2014. http://www.nation.co.ke/counties/mombasa/Ferries-plan-to-ease -transport/-/1954178/2510908/-/148wtioz/-/index.html.

Bodenmann, Guy, Linda Charvoz, Thomas N. Bradbury, Anna Bertoni, Raffaella Iafrate, Christina Giuliani, Rainer Banse, and Jenny Behling. "Attractors and Barriers to Divorce: A Retrospective Study in Three European Countries." *Journal of Divorce and Remarriage* 45, no. 3/4 (2006): 1–23. doi: 10.1300/J087v45n03_01.

Boele-Woelki, Katharina, and Angelika Fuchs, eds. *Legal Recognition of Same-Sex Relationships in Europe: National, Cross-Border and European Perspectives*. Cambridge: Intersentia, 2012.

Boone, Catherine. *Property and Political Order in Africa: Land Rights and the Structure of Politics*. New York: Cambridge University Press, 2014.

Bornstein, Erica. *The Spirit of Development: Protestant NGOs, Morality, and Economics in Zimbabwe*. Stanford, CA: Stanford University Press, 2005.

Bornstein, Erica, and Peter Redfield. "An Introduction to the Anthropology of Humanitarianism." In *Forces of Compassion: Humanitarianism between Ethics and Politics*, edited by Erica Bornstein and Peter Redfield, 3–30. Santa Fe, NM: School for Advanced Research, 2010.

Branch, Daniel. *Defeating Mau Mau, Creating Kenya: Counterinsurgency, Civil War, and Decolonization*. Cambridge: Cambridge University Press, 2009.

Brantley, Cynthia. *The Giriama and Colonial Resistance in Kenya, 1800–1920*. Berkeley: University of California Press, 1981.

Brennan, Denise. *What's Love Got to Do with It? Transnational Desires and Sex Tourism in the Dominican Republic*. Durham, NC: Duke University Press, 2004.

Brennan, James. "Lowering the Sultan's Flag: Sovereignty and Decolonization in Coastal Kenya." *Comparative Studies in Society and History* 50, no. 4 (2008): 833–838. doi: http://dx.doi.org/10.1017/S0010417508000364.

Brenton, Paul. *Africa Can Help Feed Africa: Removing Barriers to Regional Trade in Food Staples*. Washington, DC: World Bank, 2012.

Breuer, Toni. "Retirement Migration or Rather Second-Home Tourism? German Senior Citizens on the Canary Islands." *Die Erde* 136, no. 3 (2005): 313–333.

Briggs, Laura. *Reproducing Empire: Race, Sex, Science, and U.S. Imperialism in Puerto Rico*. Berkeley: University of California Press, 2002.

Brownbridge, Martin. "Financial Distress in Local Banks in Kenya, Nigeria, Uganda and Zambia: Causes and Implications for Regulatory Policy." *Development Policy Review* 16, no. 2 (1998): 173–188. doi: 10.1111/1467-7679.00057.

Brown-Saracino, Japonica, ed. *The Gentrification Debates*. New York: Routledge, 2010.

Brysk, Alison, and Gershon Shafir. *People Out of Place: Globalization, Human Rights, and the Citizenship Gap*. New York: Routledge, 2004.

Buffett, Peter. "The Charitable-Industrial Complex." *New York Times*, July 26, 2013. http://www.nytimes.com/2013/07/27/opinion/the-charitable-industrial-complex.html.

Bundesinstitut für Bevölkerungsforschung. "Durchschnittliches Heiratsalter nach dem bisherigen Familienstand der Ehepartner in Deutschland, 1971 bis 2012." In *Eheschließungen*. Berlin: Bundesinstitut für Bevölkerungsforschung, 2015. http://www.bib-demografie.de/DE/ZahlenundFakten/04/Abbildungen/a_04_14_durchschnittl_heiratsalter_familienstand_d_ab1971.html.

Burite, Joseph. "German Tourist Killed in Mombasa in Second Shooting This Month." Bloomberg, July 25, 2014. http://www.bloomberg.com/news/articles/2014-07-25/german-tourist-killed-in-mombasa-in-second-shooting-this-month.

Cabezas, Amalia L. *Economies of Desire: Sex and Tourism in Cuba and the Dominican Republic*. Philadelphia: Temple University Press, 2009.

Casas-Beltrán, Diego Armando, Luis Felipe Beltrán-Morales, Aradit Castellanos, and Aurora Breceda Solís-Cámara. "Turismo residencial y migración de jubilados extranjeros en México: un estudio de caso sobre sus implicaciones ambientales y de servicios en Baja California Sur." *Estudios Fronterizos, nueva época* 14, no. 28 (2013): 51–77.

Cashmore, T. H. R. "Sheikh Mbaruk bin Rashid bin Salim el Mazrui." In *Leadership in Eastern Africa: Six Political Biographies*, edited by Norman Bennett, 109–138. Boston: Boston University Press, 1968.

Central Intelligence Agency. "Population Below Poverty Line." In *The World Factbook 2013–2014*. Washington DC: Central Intelligence Agency, 2013. https://www.cia.gov/library/publications/the-world-factbook/fields/2046.html.

Christiaensen, Luc, Joachim De Weerdt, and Yasuyuki Todo. "Urbanization and Poverty Reduction: The Role of Rural Diversification and Secondary Towns." *Agricultural Economics* 44, no. 4–5 (2013): 447–459. doi: 10.1111/agec.12028.

Christoffel-Blindenmission. *CBM Disability and Development Policy*. Bensheim: Christoffel-Blindenmission, 2007.

———. *Hilfe—100 Jahre Christoffel-Blindenmission: Ein Bilderbuch*. Bensheim: Christoffel-Blindenmission, 2007.

City Mayors Statistics. "The Largest Cities in the World by Land Area, Population and Density." January 6, 2007. http://www.citymayors.com/statistics/largest-cities-density-125.html.

Clough, Marshall S. "Mau Mau and the Contest for Memory." In *Mau Mau and Nationhood: Arms, Authority and Narration*, edited by E. S. Atieno Odhiambo and John Lonsdale, 251–267. Oxford: James Currey, 2003.

Colclough, Christopher. "A Triumph of Hope over Reason? Aid Accords and Education Policy in Kenya." *Comparative Education* 48, no. 2 (May 2012): 263–280. doi: 10.1080/03050068.2011.608902.

Cole, Jennifer, and Lynn M. Thomas, eds. *Love in Africa*. Chicago: University of Chicago Press, 2009.

Commission of Inquiry into Post Election Violence. *Full Kenyan Post Election Violence Report 2008 [Waki-Report]*. Accessed November 28, 2015. https://file.wikileaks.org/file/wakireport-2008.pdf.

Cooper, Frederick. *From Slaves to Squatters: Plantation Labor and Agriculture in Zanzibar and Coastal Kenya, 1890–1925*. New Haven, CT: Yale University Press, 1980.

Coquery-Vidrovitch, Catherine. "Prostitution: From "Free" Women to Women with AIDS." In *African Women: A Modern History*, translated by Beth Gillian Raps, 117–128. Boulder, CO: Westview, 1997.

Coulson Harney Advocates. "A Snapshot of the New Land Laws in Kenya." May 31, 2012. http://www.coulsonharney.com/News-Blog/Blog/A-snapshot-of-the-new-land -laws.

Crumplin, Geoff. "EU Reimporting Drugs Meant for Africa Is Only Part of Story." *British Medical Journal* 326, no. 7383 (February 2003): 285. doi: 10.1136/bmj.326 .7383.285.

Cultural Survival. "Ethiopia: Stop Land Grabbing and Restore Indigenous Peoples' Lands." February 15, 2012. https://www.culturalsurvival.org/take-action/ethiopia -stop-land-grabbing-and-restore-indigenous-peoples-lands/ethiopia-stop-land.

Dabbs, Brian. "Kenyans See the Italian Mafia's Hand in Worsening Drug Trade." *The Atlantic*, July 30, 2012. http://www.theatlantic.com/international/archive/2012/07 /kenyans-see-the-italian-mafias-hand-in-worsening-drug-trade/260508/.

Debord, Guy. "Theory of the Dérive." Paris, 1958. Bureau of Public Secrets. Accessed November 21, 2015. http://www.bopsecrets.org/SI/2.derive.htm.

Denham, E. B. *Kenya: Tours in the Native Reserves and Native Development in Kenya*. London: His Majesty's Stationary Office, 1926.

Desai, Gaurav. "Oceans Connect: The Indian Ocean and African Identities." *PMLA* 125, no. 3 (2010): 713–720. doi: 10.1632/pmla.2010.125.3.713.

Deutscher Spendenrat e.V. "Bilanz des Helfens 2014." Report presented at Berliner Pressekonferenz, March 5, 2014. http://www.staathilfe.de/pdf/Bilanz_des _Helfens_2014.pdf.

Deutsches Zentralinstitut für soziale Fragen. "Deutschland: Schon 91 Mio. Euro Spenden für die Hungernden in Ostafrika," August 9, 2011. http://www.dzi.de /dzi-institut/ueber-uns/presse/presse-detailansicht/?9040.

———. "Spendenbilanz 2013: Katastrophenspenden bringen Wachstum," March 5, 2014. http://www.dzi.de/dzi-institut/ueber-uns/presse/presse-detailansicht/?10933.

"Deutschland, deine Touristen." *Der Stern* 5 (1990): 74–76, 78, 82, 83.

DPPS. "Kenya to Launch Volunteer Programme for University Graduates." *Standard Digital*, August 6, 2014. http://www.standardmedia.co.ke/article/2000130710 /kenya-to-launch-volunteer-programme-for-university-graduates.

Eade, Deborah, and Ernst Ligteringen. *Debating Development: NGOs and the Future*. Oxford: Oxfam GB for Oxfam International, 2001.

Easterly, William. *The White Man's Burden: Why the West's Efforts to Aid the Rest Have Done So Much Ill and So Little Good*. New York: Penguin, 2006.

Eidgenössisches Departement für auswärtige Angelegenheiten EDA. "Auslandschweizer- statistik 2014 nach Wohnländern und Konsularkreisen." January 5, 2015. Distributed by EDA, Auslandschweizerbeziehungen. https://www.eda.admin.ch/content/ dam/eda/de/documents/publications/AuslandschweizerinnenundAuslandschweiz- er/Auslandschweizerstatistik/2014-Auslandschweizerstatistik_DE.pdf.

Eisemon, Thomas Owen. "The Educational Marginalization of Coastal Kenya." In *Kenya Coast Handbook: Culture, Resources and Development in the East African Littoral*, edited by Jan Hoorweg, Dick Foeken, and R. A. Obudho, 249–260. Hamburg: LIT, 2000.

El Sharkawy, G., C. Newton, and S. Hartley. "Attitudes and Practices of Families and Health Care Personnel toward Children with Epilepsy in Kilifi, Kenya." *Epilepsy and Behavior* 8, no. 1 (2006): 201–212.

Embassy of the Federal Republic of Germany Nairobi. "50 years of German-Kenyan Relations." Accessed November 10, 2015. http://www.nairobi.diplo.de/Vertretung /nairobi/en/000__Startseite__englisch/50__Jahre__DEU__KEN__en.html.

Erler, Brigitte. *Tödliche Hilfe: Bericht von meiner letzten Dienstreise in Sachen Entwicklungshilfe*. Freiburg: Dreisam, 1985.

Fabian, Johannes. *Out of Our Minds: Reason and Madness in the Exploration of Central Africa*. Berkeley: University of California Press, 2000.

Fanon, Frantz. *The Wretched of the Earth*, translated by Richard Philcox. New York: Grove, 2004.

Fassin, Didier. *Humanitarian Reason: A Moral History of the Present*. Translated by Rachel Gomme. Berkeley: University of California Press, 2012.

Fee, Derek. *How to Manage an Aid Exit Strategy: The Future of Development Aid*. London: Zed, 2012.

Feierman, Steven. "Reciprocity and Assistance in Precolonial Africa." In *Philanthropy in the World's Traditions*, edited by Warren F. Ilchman, Stanley N. Katz, and Edward L. Queen II, 3–24. Bloomington: Indiana University Press, 1998.

Ferguson, James. "Seeing like an Oil Company: Space, Security, and Global Capital in Neoliberal Africa." *American Anthropologist* 107, no. 3 (2005): 377–382. doi: 10.1525/ aa.2005.107.3.377.

"Ferien '86: Urlaubslust wie noch nie." *Der Stern* 52 (1985): 18, 20.

Fisseler-Skandrani, Renate. *Die Maghrebländer Marokko, Algerien, Tunesien: Informationen für binationale Paare*. Frankfurt: Brandes and Apsel, 2003.

Frank, Arno. "Kritik an 'RTL-Wild Girls': Übles Spiel mit Kolonial-Klischees." *Spiegel Online*, July 19, 2013. http://www.spiegel.de/kultur/tv/gruene-kritisieren-rtl-doku-soap-wild-girls-a-912075.html.

Freeston, Jesse. *Resistencia: The Fight for the Aguan Valley*. Film. Directed by Jesse Freeston. 2014.

Fundraising Verband Austria. *Spendenbericht 2013*. Vienna: Fundraising Verband Austria, 2014. http://www.fundraising.at/LinkClick.aspx?fileticket=cLtw4yhBQC8%3d &tabid=421&language=de-DE.

Gerlach, Luther Paul. "The Social Organisation of the Digo of Kenya." PhD diss., University of London, 1960.

Ghertner, D. Asher. "Why Gentrification Theory Fails in 'Much of the World.'" *City: Analysis of Urban Trends, Culture, Theory, Policy, Action* 19, no. 4 (2015): 552–563. doi: 10.1080/13604813.2015.1051745.

Gillette, Cynthia. "A Test of the Concept of Backwardness: A Case Study of Digo Society in Kenya." PhD diss., Cornell University, 1978.

Gitau, Paul. "How Italian Mafia Gained Control of Malindi." Standard Digital, updated July 3, 2012 http://www.standardmedia.co.ke/?articleID=2000061045&pageNo=1.

Glassman, Jonathon. *Feast and Riot: Revelry, Rebellion, and Popular Consciousness on the Swahili Coast, 1856–1888*. Portsmouth, NH: Heinemann, 1995.

Global Impact. *2013 Assessment of U.S. Giving to International Causes*. Alexandria, VA: Global Impact, 2013. http://charity.org/sites/default/files/userfiles/pdfs/Assessment%20of%20US%20Giving%20to%20International%20Causes%20FINAL.pdf.

Goldsmith, Paul. *The Mombasa Republican Council. Conflict Assessment: Threats and Opportunities for Engagement*. Nairobi: Kenya Civil Society Strengthening Programme, 2011.

Gomm, Roger. "Harlots and Bachelors: Marital Instability among the Coastal Digo of Kenya." *Man* 7, no. 1 (March 1972): 95–113. doi: 10.2307/2799858.

Gona, V. Mung'ala-Odera, C. R. Newton, and S. Hartley. "Caring for Children with Disabilities in Kilifi, Kenya: What Is the Carer's Experience?" *Child: Care, Health & Development* 37, no. 2 (March 2011): 175–183. doi: 10.1111/j.1365-2214.2010.01124.x.

Goss, John, and Bruce Lindquist. "Conceptualizing International Labor Migration: A Structuration Perspective." *International Migration Review* 29, no. 2 (Summer 1995): 317–351. doi: 10.2307/2546784.

Gramsci, Antonio. *Prison Notebooks*. Vol. 2, translated by Joseph A. Buttigieg. New York: Columbia University Press, 2011.

Green, Marcus E., and Peter Ives. "Subalternity and Language: Overcoming the Fragmentation of Common Sense." *Historical Materialism* 17, vol. 1 (2009): 3–30. doi: 10.1163/156920609X399191.

Gregory, John Walter. *The Foundation of British East Africa*. London: Horace Marshall and Son, 1901. Reprint, New York: Negro Universities Press, 1969.

Greshake, Bernard. *Wir lieben Kenia. Kenia aber liebt nur unser Geld: Ein Einblick in die Seele der Menschen und über den Umgang mit seinen Gästen*. Hamburg: Books on Demand, 2010.

Gronemeyer, Reimer, ed. *Der faule Neger: Vom weißen Kreuzzug gegen den schwarzen Müßiggang*. Reinbek bei Hamburg: Rowohlt, 1991.

Gubernskaya, Zoya. "Changing Attitudes toward Marriage and Children in Six Countries." *Sociological Perspectives* 53, no. 2 (2010): 179–200. doi: 10.1525/sop.2010.53.2.179.

Gustafson, Per. "Transnationalism in Retirement Migration: The Case of North European Retirees in Spain." *Ethnic and Racial Studies* 31, no. 3 (March 2008): 451–475. doi: 10.1080/01419870701492000.

Hachfeld-Tapukai, Christina. *Der Himmel über Maralal: Mein Leben als Frau eines Samburu-Kriegers*. Cologne: Bastei Lübbe, 2011.

———. *Mit der Liebe einer Löwin: Wie ich die Frau eines Samburu-Kriegers wurde*. Cologne: Bastei Lübbe, 2006.

Hall, Amy. "Hotspots: Some of the World's Biggest and Most Controversial Land Deals." *New Internationalist* (May 2013): 24–25.

Harbeson, John W. *Nation-Building in Kenya: The Role of Land Reform*. Evanston, IL: Northwestern University Press, 1973.

Harcourt, Christine, and Basil Donovan. "The Many Faces of Sex Work." *Sexually Transmitted Infections* 81, no. 3 (2005): 201–206. doi: 10.1136/sti.2004.012468.

Hatton, Timothy J., and Jeffrey G. Williamson. *Global Migration and the World Economy: Two Centuries of Policy and Performance*. Cambridge, MA: MIT Press, 2005.

Hearn, Julie. "The 'NGO-isation' of Kenyan Society: USAID and the Restructuring of Health Care." *Review of African Political Economy* 25, no. 75 (1998): 89–100. doi: 10.1080/03056249808704294.

Heinl, Annett, and Gabriele Lingelbach. "Spendenfinanzierte private Entwicklungshilfe in der Bundesrepublik Deutschland." In *Stifter, Spender und Mäzene: USA und*

Deutschland im historischen Vergleich, edited by Thomas Adam, Simone Lässig, and Gabriele Lingelbach, 287–312. Stuttgart: Franz Steiner, 2009.

Heisler, Martin O., and Barbara Schmitter Heisler. *From Foreign Workers to Settlers? Transnational Migration and the Emergence of New Minorities.* Beverly Hills, CA: Sage, 1986.

Heinze, Eric. "The Reality and Hyper-reality of Human Rights: Public Consciousness and the Mass Media." In *Examining Critical Perspectives on Human Rights*, edited by Robert Dickinson, Elena Katselli, Colin Murray, and Ole W. Pedersen, 193–216. Cambridge: Cambridge University Press, 2012.

Hermann, Cassandra. "'An African's Message for America.'" *New York Times*, January 5, 2015. http://www.nytimes.com/2015/01/06/opinion/an-africans-message-for -america.html?_r=1.

Hilliges, Ilona Maria. *Eine Liebe in Kenia: Auf den Schwingen des Marabu.* Berlin: List, 2002.

Hilpold, Peter, ed. *Die Schutzverantwortung (R2P): Ein Paradigmenwechsel in der Entwicklung des Internationalen Rechts?* Leiden: Nijhoff, 2013.

Hinawy, Mbarak Ali. *Al-Akida and Fort Jesus Mombasa.* Nairobi: East African Literature Bureau, 1950.

Hoenig, Stacy L. "'Missionary' Redefined: German Mission Work in 21st-Century East Africa." Honor's thesis, The Ohio State University, 2009.

Hofmann, Corinne. *Afrika, meine Passion.* Munich: A1 Verlag, 2011.

——. *Die weiße Massai.* Munich: A1 Verlag, 1998.

——. *Wiedersehen in Barsaloi.* Munich: A1 Verlag, 2005.

——. *Zurück aus Afrika.* Munich: A1 Verlag, 2003.

Hoorweg, Jan. "The Experience with Land Settlement." In *Kenya Coast Handbook: Culture, Resources and Development in the East African Littoral*, edited by Jan Hoorweg, Dick Foeken, and R. A. Obudho, 309–326. Hamburg: LIT, 2000.

Hoorweg, Jan, Dick Foeken, Wijnand Klaver, Walter Okello, and Willem Veerman. "Nutrition in Agricultural Development: Land Settlement in Coast Province, Kenya." *Ecology of Food and Nutrition* 35, no. 3 (1996): 162.

Hoorweg, Jan, Dick Foeken, and R. A. Obudho, eds. *Kenya Coast Handbook: Culture, Resources and Development in the East African Littoral.* Hamburg: LIT, 2000.

Horton, Keith, and Chris Roche, eds. *Ethical Questions and International NGOs: An Exchange between Philosophers and NGOs.* Dordrecht: Springer, 2010.

Horton, Mark, and John Middleton. *The Swahili: The Social Landscape of a Mercantile Society.* Oxford: Blackwell, 2000.

Hughes, Lotte. "'Truth Be Told': Some Problems with Historical Revisionism in Kenya." *African Studies* 70, no. 2 (August 2011): 182–201. doi: 10.1080/00020184.2011.594626.

Human Rights Watch. *Playing with Fire: Weapons Proliferation, Political Violence, and Human Rights in Kenya.* New York: Human Rights Watch, 2002.

Hutchinson, John F. *Champions of Charity: War and the Rise of the Red Cross.* Boulder, CO: Westview, 1996.

Ibhawoh, Bonny. *Imperialism and Human Rights: Colonial Discourses of Rights and Liberties in African History.* Albany: State University of New York, 2007.

Igoe, Jim, and Tim Kelsall, eds. *Between a Rock and a Hard Place: African NGOs, Donors and the State.* Durham, NC: Carolina Academic Press, 2005.

International Monetary Fund. "IMF Approves Three-Year Loan for Kenya under the ESAF." April 26, 1996. http://www.imf.org/external/np/sec/pr/1996/pr9621.htm.

Ismail, Annelies. *"Mein Ägypter ist anders!" Besondere Paare von heute.* Leipzig: Engelsdorfer, 2012.

Jackson, R. T. "Problems of Tourist Industry Development on the Kenyan Coast." *Geography* 58, no. 1 (1973): 62–65.

Jacobs, Jessica. *Sex, Tourism and the Postcolonial Encounter: Landscapes of Longing in Egypt.* Farnham: Ashgate, 2010.

Jamison, David. "The Brotherhood of Coconuts: Tourism, Ethnicity, and National Identity in Malindi, Kenya." PhD diss., University of Florida, 1993.

Jerven, Morten. *Poor Numbers: How We Are Misled by African Development Statistics and What to Do about It.* Ithaca, NY: Cornell University Press, 2013.

Johnson, Martha C. "Lobbying for Trade Barriers: A Comparison of Poultry Producers' Success in Cameroon, Senegal and Ghana." *Journal of Modern African Studies* 49, no. 4 (2011): 575–599. doi: 10.1017/S0022278X11000486.

Joireman, Sandra F. *Where There Is No Government: Enforcing Property Rights in Common Law Africa.* Oxford: Oxford University Press, 2011.

Kabeberi, Njeri. *Ours by Right, Theirs by Might: A Study on Land Clashes.* Nairobi: Kenya Human Rights Commission, Land Rights Program, 1996.

Kabou, Axelle. *Et si l'Afrique refusait le développement?* Paris: L'Harmattan, 1991.

Kamau, John. "Seeds of Discord: The Secrets of Kenya's Land Settlements—How Civil Servants Schemed for Beach Plots," November 13, 2009. *Business Daily Africa.* http://www.businessdailyafrica.com/blob/view/-/685698/data/113008/-/kk7nk3z/-/-Seeds+of+Discord.pdf.

———. "Seeds of Discord: The Secrets of Kenya's Land Settlements—Scramble for Beach Plots Deepens Squatter Crisis," November 12, 2009. *Business Daily Africa.* http://www.businessdailyafrica.com/blob/view/-/685112/data/112766/-/s7443u/-/Seeds+of+Discord.pdf.

———. "Seeds of Discord: The Secrets of Kenya's Land Settlements—Settlement Schemes: What Went Wrong?" November 9, 2009. *Business Daily Africa.* http://www.nation.co.ke/blob/view/-/683626/data/112118/-/4ckuvkz/-/seeds.pdf.

Kang'ara, Sylvia Wairimu. "When the Pendulum Swings Too Far: Structural Adjustment Programs in Kenya." *Third World Legal Studies* 15, no. 1 (1999): 109–151.

Kanyinga, Karuti. *Re-distribution from Above: The Politics of Land Rights and Squatting in Coastal Kenya.* Uppsala: Nordiska Afrikainstitutet, 2000.

Kaul, Susanne, and David Kim, eds. *Imagining Human Rights.* Boston: De Gruyter, 2015.

Kayamba, H. M. T. "Notes on the Wadigo." *Tanganyika Notes and Records* 23 (1947): 80–96.

Kazungu, Kalume, Winnie Atieno, and Mwangombe Mwambeo. "A Week Later, Villagers in Coast Sell Their Land." *Daily Nation,* September 13, 2013. http://mobile.nation.co.ke/News/A+week+later++villagers+in+Coast+sell+their+land/-/1950946/1991914/-/format/xhtml/-/1574kar/-/index.html.

Keller, Peter, and Thomas Bieger. *Real Estate and Destination Development in Tourism: Successful Strategies and Instruments.* Berlin: Erich Schmidt, 2008.

"Kenia: Wie Watamu unter die Touristen fiel." *Der Stern* 3 (1986): 22–40.

Kenya Coast Planners Ltd. *A Report to the Government of Kenya for the Development of Tourism at Diani*. Nairobi: Kenya Coast Planners, 1975.

Kenya Colony and Protectorate. *Blue Book for the Year Ended 31st December 1933*. Nairobi: Government Printer, 1934.

———. *Blue Book for the Year Ended 31st December 1935*. Nairobi: Government Printer, 1936.

———. *Blue Book for the Year Ended 31st December 1938*. Nairobi: Government Printer, 1939.

Kenya National Bureau of Statistics. *Kenya Facts and Figures 2014*. Nairobi: Kenya National Bureau of Statistics, 2014.

———. "Poverty Rate by District." In *District Poverty Data KIHBS, 2005/6*. Nairobi: Kenya Bureau of Statistics, 2006. Kenya openData, https://opendata.go.ke /Poverty/Poverty-Rate-by-District/i5bp-z9aq.

———. *The 2009 Kenya Population and Housing Census*. Nairobi: Kenya National Bureau of Statistics, 2009.

———. "Wage Employment in Modern Sector, 2010–2013." Table 14 in *Kenya Fact and Figures 2014*. Nairobi: Kenya National Bureau of Statistics, 2014.

Kenya National Commission on Human Rights. *On the Brink of the Precipice: A Human Rights Account of Kenya's Post-2007 Election Violence, Final Report*. Unpublished government document, October 15, 2008. https://file.wikileaks.org/file/full-kenya -violence-report-2008.pdf.

Kenya Red Cross. "Kenyans 4 Kenya—One Year Anniversary Review," August 28, 2012. Reliefweb. Accessed November 21, 2015. http://reliefweb.int/report/kenya /kenyans-4-kenya-one-year-anniversary-review.

Kenyatta, Johnstone. "Kenya." In *Negro: An Anthology*, edited by Nancy Cunard, 803–807. New York: Negro Universities Press, 1969. First published 1934 by Wishart.

Kern, Evelyne. *1001 Tausendundeine Lüge—Bezness, das Geschäft mit den Gefühlen europäischer Frauen und Männer*. Bayreuth: Kern, 2012.

Khan, Nabil. "Rahimkhan Family Play Pivotal Role in Ukunda-Diani Beach." *Old Africa* (December 2014–January 2015): 6–10.

Khor, Lena. *Human Rights Discourse in a Global Network*. Farnham: Ashgate, 2013.

Kibicho, Wanjohi. *Sex Tourism in Africa: Kenya's Booming Industry*. Farnham: Ashgate, 2009.

Kimani, Joyce Njeri, and Millicent Mwololo. "Would You Have Done What He Did?" *Daily Nation*, March 5, 2014. http://www.nation.co.ke/lifestyle/Living/Would-you -have-done-what-he-did/-/1218/2231346/-/bxohg1z/-/index.html.

Kincaid, Jamaica. *A Small Place*. New York: Farrar, Straus, and Giroux, 1988.

Klaus, Kathleen F. "Claiming Land: Institutions, Narratives, and Political Violence in Kenya." PhD diss., University of Wisconsin–Madison, 2015.

Kleiber, Dieter, and Martin Wilke. *Aids, Sex und Tourismus: Ergebnisse einer Befragung deutscher Urlauber und Sextouristen*. Baden-Baden: Nomos, 1995.

Klein, Naomi. *The Shock Doctrine: The Rise of Disaster Capitalism*. Toronto: Knopf, 2007.

Klein, Thomas. "Intermarriages between Germans and Foreigners." *Journal of Comparative Family Studies* 32, no. 3 (2001): 325–346.

Koinange, Jeff. "Jeff Koinange Live [Part 1]: Ordinary Kenyans Doing Their Best against All Odds." KTN News video, 19:24. August 1, 2014. http://www.standardmedia

.co.ke/ktn/index.php/video/watch/2000081555/-jeff-koinange-live-part-1-ordinary
-kenyans-doing-their-best-against-all-odds.

Kollman, Kelly. *The Same-Sex Unions Revolution in Western Democracies: International Norms and Domestic Policy Change.* Manchester: Manchester University Press, 2013.

Krakauer, Jon. *Three Cups of Deceit: How Greg Mortenson, Humanitarian Hero, Lost His Way.* New York: Anchor, 2011.

Krapf, Johann Ludwig. *Reisen in Ostafrika, ausgeführt in den Jahren 1837–1855.* 2 vols. Stuttgart: Brockhaus, 1964.

Kumar, Ronald. "Exploring the Nexus between Tourism, Remittances and Growth in Kenya." *Quality and Quantity* 48, no. 3 (2014): 1573–1588. doi: 10.1007/s11135-013 -9853-1.

Kurt, Eva. *Tourismus in die Dritte Welt: Ökonomische, sozio-kulturelle und ökologische Folgen: Das Beispiel Kenya.* Saarbrücken: Breitenbach, 1986.

Kwalanda, Miriam, with Birgit Theresa Koch. *Die Farbe meines Gesichts: Lebensreise einer kenianischen Frau.* Frankfurt am Main: Eichborn, 1999.

Lancaster, Carol. *Aid to Africa: So Much to Do, So Little Done.* Chicago: University of Chicago Press, 1999.

Lees, Loretta, Tom Slater, and Elvin Wyly, eds., *The Gentrification Reader.* London: Routledge, 2010.

Lekan, Thomas M. "'Serengeti Shall Not Die': Bernhard Grzimek, Wildlife Film, and the Making of a Tourist Landscape in East Africa." *German History* 29, no. 2 (June 2011): 224–264. doi: 10.1093/gerhis/ghr040.

Leo, Benjamin. "Is Anyone Listening? Does US Foreign Assistance Target People's Top Priorities?" CGD Working Paper 348, Center for Global Development, Washington, DC, 2013. http://www.cgdev.org/sites/default/files/anyone-listening-us -foreign-assistance-target-top-needs_final.pdf.

Leo, Christopher. *Land and Class in Kenya.* Toronto: University of Toronto Press, 1984.

Levitt, Jeremy I., and Matthew C. Whitaker, eds. *Hurricane Katrina: America's Unnatural Disaster.* Lincoln: University of Nebraska Press, 2009.

Levy, Diane K., Jennifer Comey, and Sandra Padilla. "In the Face of Gentrification: Case Studies of Local Efforts to Mitigate Displacement." *Journal of Affordable Housing & Community Development Law* 16, no. 3 (2007): 238–315.

Leys, Colin. *Underdevelopment in Kenya: The Political Economy of Neo-Colonialism, 1964–1971.* Berkeley: University of California Press, 1974.

Lingelbach, Gabriele. *Spenden und Sammeln: Der westdeutsche Spendenmarkt bis in die 1980er Jahre.* Göttingen: Wallstein, 2009.

Lucassen, Leo, and Charlotte Laarman. "Immigration, Intermarriage and the Changing Face of Europe in the Post War Period." *History of the Family* 14 (2009): 52–68.

Maas, Maria. *Women's Social and Economic Projects: Experiences from Coast Province.* Nairobi: Ministry of Planning and National Development, Food and Nutrition Planning Unit, 1991.

MacCannell, Dean. *The Tourist: A New Theory of the Leisure Class.* New York: Schocken, 1989. First published 1976 by University of California Press.

Machuhi, Eunice. "Court Order Issued to Hotel Is Withdrawn." *Business Daily Africa,* February 4, 2011. http://www.businessdailyafrica.com/Court-order-issued-to -hotel-is-withdrawn/-/539552/1101070/-/j44gmrz/-/index.html.

———. "Hotel Sues Leaders over Beach Plots." *Daily Nation*, January 10, 2011. http://www.nation.co.ke/News/Hotel%20sues%20leaders%20over%20beach%20plots%20/-/1056/1087490/-/9potphz/-/index.html.

Machuhi, Eunice, and Moses Michira. "Leisure Lodge Files Court Bid to Reclaim Sh700m Diani Plot." *Business Daily Africa*, September 22, 2011. http://www.businessdailyafrica.com/Corporate-News/Leisure-Lodge-files-court-bid-to-reclaim-Sh700m-Diani-plot/-/539550/1240458/-/1q9utj/-/index.html.

Mambo, Robert M. "Nascent Political Activities among the Mijikenda of Kenya's Coast during the Colonial Era." *Transafrican Journal of History* 16 (1987): 92–120.

Mamozai, Martha. *Herrenmenschen: Frauen im deutschen Kolonialismus*. Reinbek bei Hamburg: Rowohlt, 1982.

Mann, Gregory. *From Empires to NGOs in the West African Sahel: The Road to Nongovernmentality*. New York: Cambridge University Press, 2015.

Mathai, Mwangi. *Report of the Select Committee on the Issue of Land Ownership along the Ten-Mile Coastal Strip of Kenya*. Nairobi: Government Printer, 1978.

Maughan-Brown, David. *Land, Freedom and Fiction: History and Ideology in Kenya*. London: Zed, 1985.

Mazrui, Alamin. *Chembe cha Moyo*. Nairobi: Heinemann Kenya, 1988.

———. *Kayas of Deprivation, Kayas of Blood: Violence, Ethnicity, and the State in Coastal Kenya*. Nairobi: Kenya Human Rights Commission, 1997.

———. *Kayas Revisited: A Post-Election Balance Sheet*. Nairobi: Kenya Human Rights Commission, 1998.

Mazrui, Alamin A., and Ibrahim Noor Shariff. *The Swahili: Idiom and Identity of an African People*. Trenton: Africa World Press, 2006.

Mbembe, Achille. *On the Postcolony*. Berkeley: University of California Press, 2001.

Mbiti, Isaac, and David N. Weil, *Mobile Banking: The Impact of M-Pesa in Kenya*. Cambridge, MA: National Bureau of Economic Research, 2011.

McGuire, Virginia C. "House Hunting in . . . Bali." *New York Times*, May 8, 2013. http://www.nytimes.com/2013/05/09/greathomesanddestinations/real-estate-in-bali.html?_r=0.

McHugh, Kevin E. "Three Faces of Ageism: Society, Image and Place." *Aging and Society* 23 (2003): 165–185. doi: http://dx.doi.org/10.1017/S0144686X02001113.

Menz, Margarete. "'By Tenderness and Flattery': Construction and Reconstruction of 'Cultural Difference' in Research on Intermarriage." *Journal of Comparative Family Studies* 44, no. 1 (2013): 99–106.

Mghanga, Mwandawiro. *Usipoziba ufa Utajenga Ukuta: Land, Elections, and Conflicts in Kenya's Coast Province*. Nairobi: Heinrich Böll Stiftung, 2010.

Middleton, John. "The Peoples." In *Kenya Coast Handbook: Culture, Resources and Development in the East African Littoral*, edited by Jan Hoorweg, Dick Foeken, and R. A. Oduho, 101–114. Hamburg: LIT, 2000.

Migot-Adholla, S. E., Katama G. C. Mkangi, and Joseph Mbindyo. *Study of Tourism in Kenya: With Emphasis on the Attitudes of Residents of the Kenya Coast*. Nairobi: Institute for Development Studies, 1982.

Ministry of East African Affairs, Commerce and Tourism. "Tourism Performance Overview 2010." Nairobi: Government Printers, 2014. http://www.tourism.go.ke/ministry.nsf/pages/facts_figures (site discontinued).

Missoni, Eduardo, and Daniele Alesani. *Management of International Institutions and NGOs: Frameworks, Practices and Challenges.* Abingdon: Routledge, 2014.

Morales, Omar Lizárraga. "The US Citizens Retirement Migration to Los Cabos, Mexico: Profile and Social Effects." In "Lifestyle Migration." Special issue, *Recreation and Society in Africa, Asia & Latin America* 1, no. 1 (March 2010): 75–92.

Mortenson, Greg, and David Oliver Relin. *Three Cups of Tea: One Man's Mission to Promote Peace . . . One School at a Time.* New York: Penguin, 2006.

Mowforth, Martin, and Ian Munt. *Tourism and Sustainability: New Tourism in the Third World.* London: Routledge, 1998.

Moyo, Dambisa. *Dead Aid: Why Aid Is not Working and How There Is a Better Way for Africa.* New York: Farrar, Straus, and Giroux, 2009.

Moyse-Bartlett, H. *The King's African Rifles: A Study in the Military History of East and Central Africa, 1890–1945.* Aldershot: Gale and Polden, 1956.

Mraja, Mohamed S. "The Reform Ideas of Shaykh 'Abdallāh Ṣāliḥ al-Farsī and the Transformation of Marital Practices among Digo Muslims of Kenya." *Islamic Law and Society* 17, no. 1 (2010): 245–278. doi: 10.1163/092893809X12529150696079.

"Msichana wa Kihindi aamua kumpenda Mbukusu licha ya kukatazwa na wazaziwe." KTN News video, 3:16. July 29, 2014. http://www.standardmedia.co.ke/ktn/index .php/video/watch/2000081469/-msichana-wa-kihindi-aamua-kumpenda-mbuku su-licha-ya-kukatazwa-na-wazaziwe.

Mtawa, Nicole. *Sternendiebe: Mein Leben in Afrika.* Munich: Knaur, 2009.

Muehlebach, Andrea. *The Moral Neoliberal: Welfare and Citizenship in Italy.* Chicago: University of Chicago Press, 2012.

Mugonyi, David. "Kenya: Top Officials Named in the List of Shame." *Daily Nation,* May 10, 2000. http://allafrica.com/stories/200005100073.html.

Müller, Adrian. "Schweizer spenden Millionen." 20 Minuten, July 28, 2011. http:// www.20min.ch/news/dossier/hornvonafrika/story/Schweizer-spenden— Millionen-14721839.

Murdie, Amanda. "The Ties That Bind: A Network Analysis of Human Rights International Nongovernmental Organizations." *British Journal of Political Science* 44, no. 1 (2014): 1–27. doi: http://dx.doi.org/10.1017/S0007123412000683.

Mutongi, Kenda. *Worries of the Heart: Widows, Family and Community in Kenya.* Chicago: University of Chicago Press, 2007.

Mutua, Makau, ed. *Human Rights NGOs in East Africa: Political and Normative Tensions.* Kampala, Uganda: Fountain, 2009.

Mwakio, Philip. "Foreign Husbands Prone to Wife Battery." Standard Digital, January 25, 2013. http://www.standardmedia.co.ke/?articleID=2000075802&story _title=Foreign-husbands-prone-to-wife-battery.

Nation Reporter. "Kenya: Govt Revokes 345 Irregular Land Titles." *Daily Nation,* December 8, 2010. http://allafrica.com/stories/201012090199.html.

Ndungu, Paul. Introduction to *Report of the Commission of Inquiry into the Illegal/ Irregular Allocation of Public Land by Republic of Kenya,* 1–2. Nairobi: Government Printer, 2004.

———. "Tackling Land Related Corruption in Kenya." Unpublished manuscript, November 2006. http://siteresources.worldbank.org/RPDLPROGRAM/Resources /459596-1161903702549/S2_Ndungu.pdf.

Ndurya, Mazera. "Kenya: Hotel in Threat to Raze Estate." *Daily Nation*, January 3, 2010. http://allafrica.com/stories/201001040159.html.

Nelson, Lise, Laurie Trautman, and Peter B. Nelson. "Latino Immigrants and Rural Gentrification: Race, 'Illegality,' and Precarious Labor Regimes in the United States." *Annals of the Association of American Geographers* 105, no. 4 (2015): 841–858. doi: 10.1080/00045608.2015.1052338.

Ngau, Peter M. "Tensions in Empowerment: The Experience of the *Harambee* (Self-Help) Movement in Kenya." *Economic Development and Cultural Change* 35, no. 3 (1987): 523–538. doi: 10.1086/451602.

Njogu, Kimani, ed. *Culture, Performance and Identity: Paths of Communication in Kenya*. Nairobi: Twaweza Communications, 2008.

Njogu, Kimani, and G. Oluoch-Olunya, eds. *Cultural Production and Social Change in Kenya: Building Bridges*. Nairobi: Twaweza Communications, 2007.

Nkirote, Miriam. "Work Begins on Dongo Kundu Bypass." *Construction Business Review*, May 23, 2015. http://www.constructionkenya.com/1997/dongo-kundu-by -pass-project-on-course/.

Nurse, Derek, and Thomas Spear. *The Swahili: Reconstructing the History and Language of an African Society, 800–1500*. Philadelphia: University of Pennsylvania Press, 1985.

Nyada, German. "'The Germans cannot master our language!' German Colonial Rulers and the Beti in the Cameroonian Hinterlands." Translated by Amber Suggitt. In *German Colonialism Revisited: African, Asian, and Oceanic Experiences*, edited by Nina Berman, Klaus Mühlhahn, and Patrice Nganang, 50–70. Ann Arbor: University of Michigan Press, 2014.

Obama, Auma. "Arbeitsauffassungen in Deutschland und ihre literarische Kritik in ausgewählten Texten der deutschen Gegenwartsliteratur zwischen 1953 und 1983: Ein Beitrag zum Kulturvergleich Deutschland-Kenia." PhD diss., University of Bayreuth, 1996.

"Ob Malediven, Kuba oder Kenia." *Der Stern* 1 (1987): 20.

O'Connell Davidson, Julia. *Children in the Global Sex Trade*. Cambridge: Polity, 2005.

Odhiambo, Nicholas M. "Interest Rate Reforms, Financial Deepening and Economic Growth in Kenya: An Empirical Investigation." *Journal of Developing Areas* 43, no. 1 (2009): 295–313. doi: 10.1353/jda.0.0044.

Oendo, Ayuka W. "Marriage Instability and Domestic Continuity in Digo Society." *Cambridge Anthropology* 12, no. 2 (1987): 47–63.

Oketch, Willis. "Pharmacist, 50, Finds Love in Standard One Drop-Out Who Is 21 Years Younger." *Standard Digital*, June 20, 2014. http://www.standardmedia.co.ke /lifestyle/article/2000125461/pharmacist-50-finds-love-in-standard-one-drop-out -who-is-21-years-younger.

Okoth-Ogendo, H. W. O. "Development and the Legal Process in Kenya: An Analysis of the Role of Law in Rural Development Administration." *International Journal of the Sociology of Law* 12 (1984): 59–83.

———. *Tenants of the Crown: Evolution of Agrarian Law and Institutions in Kenya*. Nairobi: African Centre for Technology Studies, 1991.

Oppermann, Martin, ed. *Sex Tourism and Prostitution: Aspects of Leisure, Recreation and Work*. Elmsford: Cognizant Communication Corp., 1998.

Orford, Anne. *Reading Humanitarian Intervention: Human Rights and the Use of Force in International Law.* Cambridge: Cambridge University Press, 2003.

O'Rourke, Kate. "To Have and to Hold: A Postmodern Feminist Response to the Mailorder Bride Industry." *Denver Journal of International Law and Policy* 30, no. 4 (Fall 2002): 476–497.

Ortner, Sherry B. *Making Gender: The Politics and Erotics of Culture.* Boston: Beacon, 1996.

Orvis, Stephen. "Conclusion: Bringing Institutions Back into the Study of Kenya and Africa." In "Creating the Kenya Post-Colony." Special issue, *Africa Today* 53, no. 2 (Winter 2006): 95–110.

Ouma, Shem, James Njeru, Anne Kamau, Dickson Khainga, and Benson Kiriga. *Estimating the Size of the Underground Economy in Kenya.* Nairobi: Kenya Institute for Public Policy Research and Analysis, 2007.

Palmer, Gary Bradford. "The Shimba Hills Settlement Scheme: The Administration of Large-Scale Innovation in Kenya." PhD diss., University of Minnesota, 1971.

Papademetriou, Demetrios G., David Dixon, Julie Murray, and Julia Gelatt. *America's Emigrants: US Retirement Migration to Mexico and Panama.* Washington, DC: Migration Policy Institute, 2006.

Parkin, David. "Swahili Mijikenda: Facing Both Ways in Kenya." *Africa: Journal of the International African Institute* 59, no. 2 (1989): 161–175.

Parsons, Timothy H. *The African Rank-and-File: Social Implications of Colonial Military Service in the King's African Rifles, 1902–1964.* Portsmouth: Heinemann, 1999.

Peal, Neta. "Dan Trench: A Pioneer of the Kenya South Coast Tour Industry," *Coastweek,* September 6–12, 1991. http://www.coastweek.com/obit/obit-68.htm.

Pearce, Fred. *The Land Grabbers: The New Fight over Who Owns the Earth.* Boston: Beacon, 2012.

Peat, Malcolm. *Community Based Rehabilitation.* London: W. B. Saunders, 1997.

Pedersen, Jørgen Dige. "The Second Wave of Indian Investments Abroad." *Journal of Contemporary Asia* 38, no. 4 (November 2008): 613–637. doi: 10.1080/00472330802311787.

Penny, H. Glenn. *Kindred by Choice: Germans and American Indians since 1800.* Chapel Hill: University of North Carolina Press, 2013.

Perlin, Ross. *Intern Nation: How to Earn Nothing and Learn Little in the Brave New Economy.* Brooklyn, NY: Verso, 2011.

Piketty, Thomas. *Capital in the Twenty-First Century.* Translated by Arthur Goldhammer. Cambridge, MA: Harvard University Press, 2014.

Pinheiro, Christina P. "Drug Donations: What Lies Beneath." *Bulletin of the World Health Organization* 86, no. 8 (August 2008): 580–581. http://www.who.int /bulletin/volumes/86/8/07-048546/en/.

Piore, Michael J. *Birds of Passage: Migrant Labor and Industrial Societies.* New York: Cambridge University Press, 1979.

Polman, Linda. *The Crisis Caravan: What's Wrong with Humanitarian Aid?* Translated by Liz Waters. New York: Metropolitan, 2010.

Porter, Eenella, Ines Smyth, and Caroline Sweetman. *Gender Works: Oxfam Experience in Policy and Practice.* Oxford: Oxfam, 1999.

Prelinger, Catherine M. *Charity, Challenge, and Change: Religious Dimensions of the Mid-Nineteenth-Century Women's Movement in Germany.* New York: Greenwood, 1987.

Preston, Sarah. "The Colonial Blue Books: A Major Resource in the Royal Commonwealth Society Library." Cambridge University Library. Accessed November 22, 2015. http://www.lib.cam.ac.uk/deptserv/rcs/FriendsofCULibraryarticle.htm.

Prevost, Elizabeth. "Assessing Women, Gender, and Empire in Britain's Nineteenth-Century Protestant Missionary Movement." *History Compass* 7, no. 3 (2009): 765–799. doi: 10.1111/j.1478-0542.2009.00593.x.

"Prügelprozess gegen Prinz Ernst August: 'Der Joe hat uns verarscht.'" Spiegel Online, July 7, 2009. http://www.spiegel.de/panorama/justiz/pruegelprozess-gegen-prinz-ernst-august-der-joe-hat-uns-verarscht-a-634878.html.

Quataert, Jean H. *Staging Philanthropy: Patriotic Women and the National Imagination in Dynastic Germany, 1813–1916.* Ann Arbor: University of Michigan Press, 2001.

Racine, Louise, and Amélie Perron. "Unmasking the Predicament of Cultural Voyeurism: A Postcolonial Analysis of International Nursing Placements." *Nursing Inquiry* 19, no. 3 (September 2012): 190–201.

Rahmato, Dessalegn. "The Perils of Development from Above: Land Deals in Ethiopia." Special issue, *African Identities* 12, no. 1 (2014): 26–44. doi: 10.1080/14725843.2014.886431.

Redfield, Peter. *Life in Crisis: The Ethical Journey of Doctors without Borders.* Berkeley: University of California Press, 2013.

"Reise: Camping in Kenia." *Der Stern* 27 (1987): 74.

"Reiseziel Sex: Die Deutschen erobern weltweit Plätze der Lust." *Der Stern* 49 (1988): 36, 46.

Republic of Kenya. "Eviction of Unregistered Squatters from Ukunda Farm." In *Kenya National Assembly Official Report*, Vol. XX, part II (February 1970).

———. *Kenya: Economic Reforms for 1996–1998: The Policy Framework Paper.* Nairobi: Government of Kenya, 1996.

———. *The Marriage Act, 2014.* Nairobi: Government Printer, 2014.

———. *The Persons with Disabilities Act.* Nairobi: Ministry of Lands, 2003.

———. *Report of the Commission of Inquiry into the Illegal/Irregular Allocation of Public Land.* Nairobi: Government Printer, 2004.

———. *Sessional Paper No. 3 of 2009 on National Land Policy.* Nairobi: Ministry of Lands, 2009.

Richardson, Sarah. "Women, Philanthropy, and Imperialism in Early Nineteenth-Century Britain." In *Burden or Benefit? Imperial Benevolence and Its Legacies*, edited by Helen Gilbert and Chris Tiffin, 90–102. Bloomington: Indiana University Press, 2008.

Rist, Gilbert. *The History of Development: From Western Origins to Global Faith.* Translated by Patrick Camiller. London: Zed, 1997.

Ritchie, J. McL. Introduction to *The History of the Mazru'i Dynasty of Mombasa*, by Shaykh al-Amin Bin 'Ali Al Mazru'i, 1–14. Oxford: Oxford University Press, 1995.

Robertson, James W. *The Kenya Coastal Strip: Report of the Commissioner.* London: Her Majesty's Stationary Office, 1961.

Rodima-Taylor, Daivi, and Erik Bähre. "Mutual Help in an Era of Uncertainty." Special issue, *Africa* 84, no. 4 (2014): 507–613.

Rodgers, W. A., and Neil D. Burgess. "Taking Conservative Action." In *Coastal Forests of Eastern Africa*, edited by Neil D. Burgess and G. Philip Clarke, 317–334. Cambridge: IUCN, 2000.

Rono, Joseph Kipkemboi. "The Impact of the Structural Adjustment Programmes on Kenyan Society." *Journal of Social Development in Africa* 17, no. 1 (2002): 81–98.

Rotary International. *Communities in Action: A Guide to Effective Projects 605A*. Evanston, IL: Rotary International. http://www.rotary.org/ridocuments/en_pdf/605a_en.pdf.

Roth, Silke. *The Paradoxes of Aid Work: Passionate Professionals*. New York: Routledge, 2015.

Rothberg, Michael. *Multidirectional Memory: Remembering the Holocaust in the Age of Decolonization*. Stanford, CA: Stanford University Press, 2009.

Rubenstein, Jennifer C. "The Distributive Commitments of International NGOs." In *Humanitarianism in Question: Politics, Power, Ethics*, edited by Michael Barnett and Thomas G. Weiss, 215–234. Ithaca, NY: Cornell University Press, 2008.

Ruiz-Ballesteros, Esteban, and Macarena Hernández-Ramírez. "Tourism That Empowers? Commodification and Appropriation in Ecuador's Turismo Comunitario." *Critique of Anthropology* 30, vol. 2 (June 2010): 201–229.

Ryan, Chris, and C. Michael Hall. *Sex Tourism: Marginal People and Liminalities*. London: Routledge, 2001.

Ryan, Susan. *The Grammar of Good Intentions: Race and the Antebellum Culture of Benevolence*. Ithaca, NY: Cornell University Press, 2003.

Sachs, Jeffrey. "The Case for Aid." *Foreign Policy*, January 21, 2014. http://foreignpolicy.com/2014/01/21/the-case-for-aid/.

Salim, A. I. *The Swahili-Speaking Peoples of Kenya's Coast, 1895–1965*. Nairobi: East African Publishing House, 1973.

Sarat, Austin, and Javier Lezaun, eds. *Catastrophe: Law, Politics, and the Humanitarian Impulse*. Amherst: University of Massachusetts Press, 2009.

Sartre, Jean-Paul. Preface to *The Wretched of the Earth*, by Frantz Fanon, li–lv. Translated by Richard Philcox. New York: Grove, 2004.

Sassen, Saskia. *The Global City: New York, London, Tokyo*. Princeton, NJ: Princeton University Press, 1991.

Schama, Simon. *The Embarrassment of Riches: An Interpretation of Dutch Culture in the Golden Age*. New York: Knopf, 1987.

Scherz, China. *Having People, Having Heart: Charity, Sustainable Development, and Problems of Dependence in Central Uganda*. Chicago: University of Chicago Press, 2014.

Schifter-Sikora, Jacobo. *Mongers in Heaven: Sexual Tourism and HIV Risk in Costa Rica and in the United States*. Lanham, MD: University Press of America, 2007.

Schmalmack, Birgit. *Türkischer Honig auf Schwarzbrot: Bikulturelle Liebesgeschichten*. Frankfurt: Brandes and Apsel, 2007.

Schoenhaus, Robert M. *Training for Peace and Humanitarian Relief Operations: Advancing Best Practices*. Washington, DC: United States Institute of Peace, 2002.

Schoss, Johanna H. "Beach Tours and Safari Visions: Relations of Production and the Production of 'Culture' in Malindi, Kenya." PhD diss., University of Chicago, 1995.

Schroedter, Julia H. *Binationale Ehen in Deutschland*. Wiesbaden: Statistisches Bundesamt, 2006.

Schurian-Bremecker, Christiane. *Kenia in der Sicht deutscher Touristen: Eine Analyse von Denkmustern und Verhaltensweisen beim Urlaub in einem Entwicklungsland*. Münster: Lit, 1989.

"Schweizer spenden fleissig für Ostafrika," News.ch, August 11, 2011. http://www.news.ch/Schweizer+spenden+fleissig+fuer+Ostafrika/503884/detail.htm.

Scott, James C. *The Moral Economy of the Peasant: Rebellion and Subsistence in Southeast Asia*. Princeton, NJ: Princeton University Press, 1976.

———. *Seeing like a State: How Certain Schemes to Improve the Human Condition Have Failed*. New Haven, CT: Yale University Press, 1998.

Seabrook, Jeremy. *No Hiding Place: Child Sex Tourism and the Role of Extraterritorial Legislation*. London: Zed, 2000.

Shadle, Brett. "Settlers, Africans, and Inter-Personal Violence in Kenya, ca. 1900–1920s." *International Journal of African Historical Studies* 45, no. 1 (2012): 57–80.

Shadle, Brett L. *The Souls of White Folk: White Settlers in Kenya, 1900s–1920s*. Manchester: Manchester University Press, 2015.

Shilaro, Priscilla M. "The Kakamega Gold Rush and the Kenya Land Commission, 1932–34." In *A Failed Eldorado: Colonial Capitalism, Rural Industrialization, African Land Rights in Kenya, and the Kakamega Gold Rush, 1930–1952*, 13–58. Lanham, MD: University Press of America, 2008.

Simone, AbdouMaliq. *For the City Yet to Come: Changing African Life in Four Cities*. Durham, NC: Duke University Press, 2004.

Siringi, Samuel. "AIDS Drugs Being Sold Illegally on Market Stalls in Kenya." *The Lancet* 363, no. 9406 (January 31, 2004): 377. doi: http://dx.doi.org/10.1016/S0140-6736(04)15479-2.

Slaughter, Joseph R. *Human Rights, Inc.: The World Novel, Narrative Form, and International Law*. New York: Fordham University Press, 2007.

Sofield, Trevor H. B. *Empowerment for Sustainable Tourism Development*. Amsterdam: Pergamon, 2003.

Sorrenson, M. P. K. *Origins of European Settlement in Kenya*. Nairobi: Oxford University Press, 1968.

Southall, Roger. "The Ndungu Report: Land & Graft in Kenya." *Review of African Political Economy* 32, no. 103 (2005): 142–151.

Sparr, Pamela. *Mortgaging Women's Lives: Feminist Critiques of Structural Adjustment*. London: Zed, 1994.

Sparrer, Petra. *Wo die Liebe hinfällt: Geschichten von Paaren aus zwei Kulturen*. Stuttgart: Gatzanis, 2001.

Spear, Thomas T. *The Kaya Complex: A History of the Mijikenda Peoples of the Kenya Coast to 1900*. Nairobi: Kenya Literature Bureau, 1978.

"Spendenvolumen in der Schweiz wieder gestiegen: Über 1,6 Mrd." Swissfundraising, October 3, 2013. http://www.swissfundraising.org/index_de.php?TPL=26010&x26000_ID=596.

Statistik Austria. "Eheschließungen." In *Bevölkerung*. Vienna: Statistik Austria, 2015. http://www.statistik.at/web_de/statistiken/menschen_und_gesellschaft/bevoelkerung/eheschliessungen/index.html.

Stein, Howard. *Beyond the World Bank Agenda: An Institutional Approach to Development.* Chicago: University of Chicago Press, 2008.

Steinberg, Gerald M., Anne Herzberg, and Jordan Berman. *Best Practices for Human Rights and Humanitarian NGO Fact-Finding.* Leiden: Martinus Nijhoff, 2012.

Steinkühler, Karl-Heinz. "Verbrechen im Mafia-Paradies." *Focus Magazin* 41 (1995). Focus Online, October 8, 1995. http://www.focus.de/politik/deutschland/verbrechen -im-mafia-paradies_aid_156069.html.

Stiglitz, Joseph E. *Globalization and Its Discontents.* New York: Norton, 2002.

Sunil, T. S., Viviana Rojas, and Don E. Bradley. "United States' International Retirement Migration: The Reasons for Retiring to the Environs of Lake Chapala, Mexico." *Ageing and Society* 27 (2007): 489–510. doi: http://dx.doi.org/10.1017/S0144686 X07005934.

Suri, Tavneet, William Jack, and Thomas M. Stoker. "Documenting the Birth of a Financial Economy." *Proceedings of the National Academy of Sciences of the United States of America* 109, no. 26 (2012): 10257–10262. doi: 10.1073/pnas.1115843109.

Surrealist Group of France. "Murderous Humanitarianism." Translated by Samuel Beckett. In *Negro Anthology*, by Nancy Cunard, 574–575. New York: Negro University Press, 1969. First published 1934 by Wishart.

Suttle, Oisin. "Equality in Global Commerce: Towards a Political Theory of International Economic Law." *European Journal of International Law* 25, no. 4 (2015): 1043–1070. doi: 10.1093/ejil/chu072.

Swamy, Gurushri. "Kenya: Patchy, Intermittent Commitment." In *Adjustment in Africa: Lessons from Country Case Studies*, edited by Ishrat Husain and Rashid Faruqee, 193–237. Brookfield, VT: Ashgate, 1996.

Swan, Eileadh. "'I'm Not a Tourist. I'm a Volunteer': Tourism, Development and International Volunteerism in Ghana." In *African Hosts and Their Guests: Cultural Dynamics of Tourism*, edited by Walter van Beek and Annette Schmidt, 239–255. Woodbridge, Suffolk: James Currey, 2012.

Taabazuing, Joseph, Isaac Luginaah, Godwin Djietror, and Kefa M. Otiso. "Mining, Conflicts and Livelihood Struggles in a Dysfunctional Policy Environment: The Case of Wassa West District, Ghana." *African Geographical Review* 31, no. 1 (2012): 33–49.

Taylor, Georgina, Jane Wangaruro, and Irena Papadopoulos. "'It Is My Turn to Give': Migrants' Perceptions of Gift Exchange and the Maintenance of Transnational Identity." *Journal of Ethnic and Migration Studies* 38, no. 7 (2012): 1085–1100. doi: 10.1080/1369183X.2012.681450.

Taylor, Ian. "India's Rise in Africa." *International Affairs* 88, no. 4 (2012): 779–798.

Taylor, S. Caroline, Daniel Joseph Torpy, and Dilip K. Das, eds. *Policing Global Movement: Tourism, Migration, Human Trafficking, and Terrorism.* London: Taylor and Francis, 2013.

Thomas-Emeagwali, Gloria, ed. *Women Pay the Price: Structural Adjustment in Africa and the Caribbean.* Trenton: Africa World Press, 1995.

Thomas-Slayter, Barbara P. "Class, Ethnicity, and the Kenyan State: Community Mobilization in the Context of Global Politics." *International Journal of Politics, Culture, and Society* 4, no. 3 (1991): 301–321.

Thompson, E. P. "The Moral Economy of the English Crowd in the 18th Century." *Past & Present* 50 (1971): 76–136.

Thurow, Roger, and Scott Kilman. *Enough: Why the World's Poorest Starve in an Age of Plenty*. New York: PublicAffairs, 2009.

Transparency International Kenya. *The Kenyan Health Sector Integrity Study Report 2011*. Nairobi: Transparency International, 2011. http://www.tikenya.org/index.php/integrity-studies?download=152:the-kenya-health-sector-integrity-study-report.

Ullrich, Angela. *Wohin fließen die Spenden? Eine Analyse zur Verwendung von Spenden in Deutschland*. Berlin: betterplace lab, 2009.

Urry, John. *The Tourist Gaze: Leisure and Travel in Contemporary Societies*. London: Sage, 1990.

US Congress, House Committee on the Judiciary. *Sex Tourism Prohibition Improvement Act of 2002: Report*. 107th Cong., 2d sess., 2002. H. Rep. 107–525. http://www.gpo.gov/fdsys/pkg/CRPT-107hrpt525/html/CRPT-107hrpt525.htm.

Van Noorloos, Femke. "Residential Tourism Causing Land Privatization and Alienation: New Pressures on Costa Rica's Coasts." *Development* 54, no. 1 (2011): 85–90. doi: 10.1057/dev.2010.90.

Van Tol, Deanne. "The Women of Kenya Speak: Imperial Activism and Settler Society, c. 1930." *Journal of British Studies* 54, no. 2 (April 2015): 433–456. http://dx.doi.org/10.1017/jbr.2015.5.

Velásquez-Runk, Julie. "Indigenous Land and Environmental Conflicts in Panama: Neoliberal Multiculturalism, Changing Legislation, and Human Rights." *Journal of Latin American Geography* 11, no. 2 (2012): 21–47. doi: 10.1353/lag.2012.0036.

Visser, Gustav, and Gijsbert Hoogendoorn. "A Decade of Second Home Tourism Research in South Africa: Research Prospects for the Developing World?" *South African Geographical Journal* 97, no. 2 (2015): 111–122.

VOA News. "German Tourist Killed on Increasingly Violent Kenyan Coast." Voice of America, July 25, 2014. http://www.voanews.com/content/german-tourist-killed-on-kenyan-coast/1964882.html.

Wadhams, Nick. "Fleeing Justice, All the Way to Africa." *Globe and Mail*, March 17, 2007.

Wa-Githumo, Mwangi. *Land and Nationalism: The Impact of Land Expropriation and Land Grievances upon the Rise and Development of Nationalist Movements in Kenya, 1885–1939*. Washington, DC: University Press of America, 1981.

Wahab, Salah, and John J. Pigram, eds. *Tourism, Development and Growth: The Challenge of Sustainability*. London: Routledge, 1997.

Wakhungu, Judi, Elvin Nyukuri, and Chris Huggins. *Land Tenure and Violent Conflict in Kenya*. Nairobi: African Centre for Technology Studies, 2008.

Waldren, Jacqueline. *Insiders and Outsiders: Paradise and Reality in Mallorca*. Providence, RI: Berghahn, 1996.

Wallen-Lundy, Angie, Bettina Da Sylva, and Frauen des Africanlove Forums. *Liebesgeschichten—schwarz auf weiß: Frauen in binationalen Partnerschaften erzählen ihre bewegende Geschichte*. Hamburg: Books on Demand, 2009.

Wallis, David. "Increasingly, Retirees Dump Their Possessions and Hit the Road." *New York Times*, August 29, 2014. http://www.nytimes.com/2014/08/30/business/increasingly-retirees-dump-their-possessions-and-hit-the-road.html?_r=0.

Walther, Daniel J. "Sex and Control in Germany's Overseas Possessions: Venereal Disease and Indigenous Agency." In *German Colonialism Revisited: African, Asian, and Oceanic Experiences*, edited by Nina Berman, Klaus Mühlhahn, and Patrice Nganang, 71–84. Ann Arbor: University of Michigan Press, 2014.

Wamagatta, Evanson N. "African Collaborators and Their Quest for Power in Colonial Kenya: Senior Chief Waruhiu wa Kung'u's Rise from Obscurity to Prominence, 1890–1922." *International Journal of African Historical Studies* 41, no. 2 (2008): 295–314.

Wanjiru, Rose. *IMF Policies and Their Impact on Education, Health and Women's Rights in Kenya*. Nairobi: ActionAid International Kenya, 2009.

Wanyama, Frederick O. "Grass-roots Organization for Sustainable Development: The Case of Community-Based Organizations in Western Kenya." *Regional Development Studies* 7 (2001): 55–77.

Warner, Gregory. "Western Countries Issue Warnings; Kenyan Tourism Gets Pummeled." NPR, June 10, 2014. http://www.npr.org/sections/parallels/2014/06/10/320335669/western-countries-issue-warnings-kenyan-tourism-gets-pummeled.

Wasmundt, Anita. *Der Heuchler aus dem Morgenland: Eine wahre Geschichte*. Bayreuth: Kern, 2008.

Wasserman, Gary. *Politics of Decolonization: Kenya Europeans and the Land Issue, 1960–1965*. Cambridge: Cambridge University Press, 1976.

White, Luise. *The Comforts of Home: Prostitution in Colonial Nairobi*. Chicago: University of Chicago Press, 1990.

Whitworth, Sandra. *Men, Militarism, and UN Peacekeeping: A Gendered Analysis*. Boulder, CO: Lynne Rienner, 2004.

"Wickelkinder der Wildnis." *Der Stern* 2 (1990): 72–75.

Widner, Jennifer A. *The Rise of a Party-State in Kenya: From "Harambee!" to "Nyayo."* Berkeley: University of California Press, 1992.

Wiener, Martin J. *An Empire on Trial: Race, Murder, and Justice under British Rule, 1870–1935*. Cambridge: Cambridge University Press, 2009.

Wike, Richard. "French More Accepting of Infidelity than People in Other Countries." Pew Research Center, January 14, 2014. http://www.pewresearch.org/fact-tank/2014/01/14/french-more-accepting-of-infidelity-than-people-in-other-countries/.

Wildenthal, Lora. *German Women for Empire, 1884–1945*. Durham, NC: Duke University Press, 2001.

———. *The Language of Human Rights in West Germany*. Philadelphia: University of Pennsylvania Press, 2013.

Williams, Erica Lorraine. *Sex Tourism in Bahia: Ambiguous Entanglements*. Urbana: University of Illinois Press, 2013.

Willis, Justin. *Mombasa, the Swahili, and the Making of the Mijikenda*. Oxford: Clarendon, 1993.

Willis, Justin, and George Gona. "*Pwani C Kenya*: Memory, Documents and Secessionist Politics in Coastal Kenya." *African Affairs* 112, no. 446 (2013): 48–71. doi: 10.1093/afraf/ads064.

Woesthoff, Julia. "'Foreigners and Women Have the Same Problems': Binational Marriages, Women's Grassroots Organizing, and the Quest for Legal Equality in

Post-1968 Germany." *Journal of Family History* 38, no. 4 (2013): 422–442. doi: 10.1177/0363199013504368.

Wolf, Thomas P. "Contemporary Politics." In *Kenya Coast Handbook: Culture, Resources and Development in the East African Littoral*, edited by Jan Hoorweg, Dick Foeken, and R. A. Oduho, 129–156. Hamburg: LIT, 2000.

Wood, Adrian, Raymond Apthorpe, and John Borton. *Evaluating International Humanitarian Action: Reflection from Practitioners*. London: Zed, 2001.

Woods, Judith. "Revealed: The White Mischief Murderer." *Telegraph*, May 11, 2007. http://www.telegraph.co.uk/news/features/3632548/Revealed-the-White-Mischief -murderer.html.

World Bank. "Agricultural land (% of Land Area)." 2015. Distributed by the World Bank Food and Agriculture Organization. http://data.worldbank.org/indicator /AG.LND.AGRI.ZS/countries.

———. *Kenya: Country Assistance Evaluation*. Washington, DC: World Bank, 2000.

———. *Kenya: Re-Investing in Stabilization and Growth through Public Sector Adjustment*. Washington, DC: World Bank, 1992.

———. "Poverty Rates at National Poverty Lines." Table 2.7 in *World Development Indicators*. Washington, DC: World Bank Group, 2015. http://wdi.worldbank.org /table/2.7.

World Tourism Organization. "Kenya: Overnight Stays of Non-Resident Tourists in Hotels and Similar Establishments, by Country of Residence." Table 5 in *Yearbook of Tourism Statistics*. Madrid: UNWTO, 2015.

World Travel and Tourism Council. *Travel & Tourism: Economic Impact 2014 Kenya*. London: World Travel and Tourism Council, 2014.

Wrong, Michaela. *It's Our Turn to Eat: The Story of a Kenyan Whistle-Blower*. New York: HarperCollins, 2009.

Yeates, Nicola. "Global Care Chains: A Critical Introduction." Global Migration Perspectives Paper No. 44, Global Commission on International Migration, Geneva, 2005. http://www.refworld.org/docid/435f85a84.html.

Zweig, Stefanie. *Nirgendwo in Afrika*. Munich: Langen Müller, 1995.

Index

NINA BERMAN is Professor of Comparative Studies at Ohio State University. She has published widely on humanitarianism, transnationalism, German orientalism and colonialism, multiculturalism, disability in Kenya, and travel literature. Her most recent book publications are *German Literature on the Middle East: Discourses and Practices, 1000–1989* (2011) and a co-edited anthology (with Klaus Mühlhahn and Patrice Nganang), *German Colonialism Revisited: African, Asian, and Oceanic Experiences* (2014).

CPSIA information can be obtained
at www.ICGtesting.com
Printed in the USA
LVOW13s2328091017
551772LV00017B/251/P